Thurston County:

WATER, WOODS & PRAIRIES

Essays on the History of Washington's Capital County

Sandra A. Crowell & Shirley A. Stirling, Editors

Chris Colton, Copy Editor

A Project of the Thurston County Historic Commission
Under the direction of the Thurston County Commissioners

Publisher: Thurston County - Olympia, Washington - 2019

THURSTON COUNTY
WASHINGTON

ABOUT THE COVER

The three elements of Water, Woods & Prairies, can be seen in this historical postcard showing the upper falls of the Deschutes River in Tumwater Canyon. Pictured is a scene of an early wildlife park of locally captured animals, complete with elk (pictured), swans, and bears in a pit. Hazard Stevens, son of the first territorial governor of the state, Isaac I. Stevens, was a co-owner of the park.

The First People lived in villages near the base of the lower Tumwater Falls, finding sustenance in the local waters, the surrounding forests, and prairies. Known as the end of the Oregon Trail or Cowlitz Trail, in 1845, Tumwater Falls drew the first Euro-American settlers to the South Puget Sound region for its potential water power, while others claimed sites on nearby prairies. Timber from surrounding forests provided raw materials for buildings, docks, bridges, and fences. Later, the river's flow supplied the area's first source of electricity.

Although Tumwater is the oldest permanent Euro-American settlement on Puget Sound, the varied history of all of Thurston County provides a view of the past and present Northwest.

Contribution by, Dave Shipley, Past Chairman
Thurston County Historic Commission

Front Cover and Page 3:
Colored postcard of Tumwater Park from 1908, entitled, "Upper Tumwater Falls, Olympia, Washington." The elk pictured in this photo are captive, residents of an early wildlife park. The park was at the end of Olympia's horse-drawn trolley line and owners sought to attract citizens and visitors, with their picnic lunches, to the park. (Courtesy of Olympia Tumwater Foundation)

Back Cover:
The background image was provided by Karen L. Johnson. It is from an illustration of Tumwater, Washington from an early magazine, The West Shore, April 1889 issue, page 224. US Public Domain. (Courtesy of Washington State Library)
Canoe paddlers concluded their 3-week journey at the Port of Olympia, Washington in 2012 (Courtesy of ThurstonTalk.com)
Close-up of the dome on the Legislative Building in Olympia, ca. 1950. AR-28001001-ph001271 (Courtesy of Washington State Archives—Digital Archives)
Tumwater terminal of the James McIntosh Tram Road. Few photos of the era showed women, ca. 1880s or 1890s. HHM566 (Courtesy of Henderson House Museum, City of Tumwater)
Barn at the Thomas Rutledge Farm in Littlerock, built ca. 1864. It is one of the oldest barns in the State of Washington. April 2011. (Courtesy of the photographer Bill Holland)

First Edition

Copyright ©2019
Thurston County Historic Commission
Olympia, Washington
All rights reserved.

No part of this book may be used or reproduced in any manner whatsoever without written permission except in the case of brief quotations embedded in critical articles or reviews.
For information address: Thurston County Historic Commission,
2000 Lakeridge Drive SW, Bldg. 1 Olympia, WA 98502

ISBN: 978-1-7326360-0-2 Hard Cover / 978-1-7326360-1-9 Soft Cover
Library of Congress: 2018910542
Book Design by Shirley A. Stirling
Index by Judi Gibbs—Write Guru®

Printed in the United States of America
By Gorham Printing, Centralia, Washington

CONTENTS

Foreword .... Page 6
By David L. Nicandri

Chapter 1 - The Original Residents .... Page 8
By Sandra A. Crowell

Chapter 2 - Early Encounters .... Page 28
By Les Eldridge

Chapter 3 - Settlement, Steamers, and Statehood .... Page 40
By Les Eldridge

Chapter 4 - Early Days in Tumwater .... Page 52
By Don Trosper

Chapter 5 - Call of the Prairies .... Page 60
By Shanna Stevenson

Chapter 6 - A New County and a New Territory .... Page 70
By Shanna Stevenson

Chapter 7 - From Settlements to Cities .... Page 80
By Shanna Stevenson

Chapter 8 - The Three R'S .... Page 104
By Shanna Stevenson

Chapter 9 - The Battle for the Capital .... Page 112
By Gerry Alexander

Chapter 10 - Farms and Fields .... Page 120
By Shanna Stevenson

Chapter 11 - Inlets of Harvest and Home .... Page 134
By Shanna Stevenson

Chapter 12 - The Ebb and Flow of Communities .... *Page 142*
  By Shanna Stevenson

Chapter 13 - Big Trees, Big Business .... *Page 158*
By James S. Hannum, M.D.

Chapter 14 - Rails and Timber .... *Page 168*
By James S. Hannum, M.D.

Chapter 15 - It's the Water .... *Page 176*
By Karen L. Johnson

Chapter 16 - A Turbulent Age .... *Page 186*
By Jennifer Crooks

Chapter 17 - Facing the Future .... *Page 204*
By Drew Crooks

Maps - Cities and Towns / other maps of Thurston County .... *Page 222*

Meet the Authors .... *Page 226*

Photo Credits .... *Page 229*

Special Thanks .... *Page 230*

End Notes .... *Page 232*

Selected Bibliography .... *Page 250*

Index .... *Page 264*

FOREWORD
BY DAVID L NICANDRI

In the spring of 1973, at the annual Pacific Northwest History Conference, I spied Herman Deutsch sitting by himself in the hotel café having breakfast. I was less than a year out of graduate school from the University of Idaho, and I recognized Professor Deutsch from the history department at Washington State University. At that time Herman was quaintly referred to as the "Dean" of Northwest Historians, having taught in Pullman since the 1940s. Inviting myself to share his booth, he welcomed me graciously.

My intention was to engage in what today would be called networking. I had spent the previous year as a graduate student intern at the State Capital Museum researching the history of Olympia's Priest Point Park. After that I worked on local history projects for museum director Ken Hopkins with Tenino Mayor Ken Hedden and Tumwater's Jim Brown regarding the preservation of the old train station and pioneer cemetery in those respective communities. Unsure about my future prospects, such as whether to return to graduate school to pursue a doctorate in diplomatic history, I thought I might secure some counsel from Herman.

His advice was sure and pithy: "The Pacific Northwest is the best possible field for a historian because so little of it has been researched." He continued: "It doesn't matter what topic you pursue, you are sure to become the expert on it." I was intrigued by his perspective and recollected his comments while reading the essays in this anthology.

What Professor Deutsch said then is still very much true today, especially in the microcosm of Thurston County. Indeed, it might be said that our county history is more under-interpreted than most because Olympia's status as the capital city has tended to emphasize state of Washington contexts at the expense of purely local ones.

Books like this one, a compilation featuring an all-star cast of local historians, help fill that void. Each essay is amply illustrated, often with imagery that has not been previously published. Some topics may be familiar; others break new ground. How many modern residents of the county know, for example, that the Black Lake corridor was once a regional transportation route? A particularly vital story recounted by Gerry Alexander—how the hollowing out of Olympia's role as seat of state government was avoided—was a pivotal point in county history. Many stories mentioned herein briefly, or in sidebars, are worthy of a fuller treatment in a subsequent volume, and if not, by the next generation of scholars looking to make their mark.

David L. Nicandri, Former Director of the Washington State Historical Museum, Retired

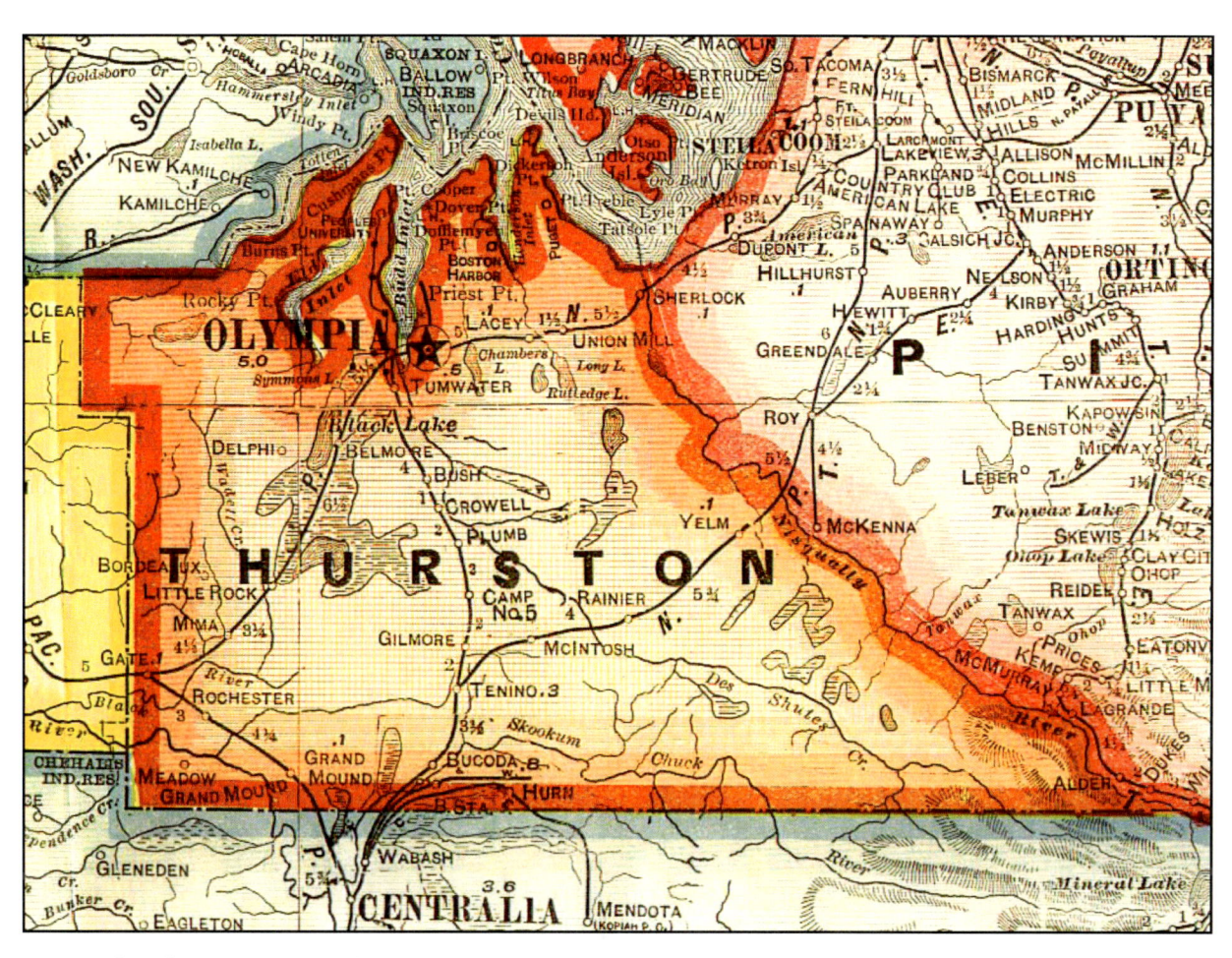

Excerpt of Washington State map, Thurston County vicinity, ca. 1909, State of Washington. Public domain. (Courtesy of USGenWeb and WAGenWeb Project Archives, as submitted by Fred Smoot)

The early people on the land now known as Thurston County thrived for eons, embracing the water, woods and prairies. The rich environment of the southern Puget Sound provided these original inhabitants with a healthy lifestyle and the freedom to roam. Long before the arrival of the Euro-Americans, they passed their specialized knowledge through the generations with oral traditions and legends. Despite the intrusion that disrupted their lives in the nineteenth century, the three tribes in this area—the Nisqually, Chehalis, and Squaxin—celebrate their cultural heritage in contemporary times.

"The Original Residents" by author Sandra Crowell views the tribes prior to Euro-American arrival and examines the effects of treaties and other events in shaping their history.

Chapter 1
THE ORIGINAL RESIDENTS
by Sandra A. Crowell

A REMARKABLE MURDER trial took place in the year 2004. The defendant, a life-long resident of the Thurston County area, could not appear on his own behalf; he died by hanging nearly 150 years previously. The death of Leschi of the Nisqually remains a symbol of social injustice; the implications of Leschi's trials—a century and a half apart—are very much alive, as are the events leading up to his demise.

In 1854, the Nisqually, Puyallup, Muckleshoot and Squaxin Island tribes met at Medicine Creek, near the Nisqually Delta, to negotiate a treaty with the new governor of the Washington Territory, Isaac Stevens.

Appointed tribal sub-chief by Stevens, Leschi and his half-brother, Quiemuth, represented the Nisqually people in the negotiations. When Leschi protested the plan to move his tribe to a reservation on the top of a rocky bluff away from the life-sustaining Nisqually River,[1] hostilities flared against Stevens's policies. Across the mountains in Yakama territory, tensions arose at the same time over the flood of non-Indians staking land claims and miners crossing Indian territory. Governor Stevens formed a voluntary militia to counter the Native unrest and offered $500 for the capture of Leschi, Quiemuth, and two others. Meanwhile, many settlers throughout Western Washington, suddenly fearful of their Indian neighbors who had been generally helpful, hurried to build block houses where they holed up for months.[2]

On October 31, 1855, A. B. Moses, a colonel in the militia, died during an ambush of his volunteer militiamen. Stevens blamed Leschi for the death and for instigating the subsequent Puget Sound

"Indian girls and canoe, Puget Sound" from Northern California, Oregon, and the Sandwich Islands, *by Charles Nordhoff, New York: Harper & Brothers, 1875. (Courtesy of Project Gutenberg, US Public Domain)*

Indian War of 1855-56. After a prolonged hunt, the proud and once-prosperous leader went on trial twice for the same crime committed during a war although no proof revealed him anywhere near the scene.[3] (The primary eyewitness, Antonio Rabbeson, also served as the chairman of the grand jury investigating the incident.) Quiemuth surrendered at the governor's office, only to be murdered. No one was ever charged in his death.

Leschi's first trial in 1856 for allegedly committing murder during a war, ended in a hung jury. Tried again for the same crime in 1857, the Indian leader was convicted and sentenced to death by hanging.

On February 19, 1858, Chief Leschi was hanged on a gallows[4] at what is presently Lakewood, near a

Generations of the Nisqually people grieved for Leschi and his unjust death, along with the unresolved murder of his half-brother Quiemuth. Tribal members re-buried Leschi in 1895. (Courtesy of Nisqually Indian Tribe)

modern-era strip mall. A pamphlet distributed after his execution read:

> Judicially murdered, February 19, 1858, owing to misunderstanding of Treaty of 1854-55. Serving his people by his death. Sacrificed to a principle. A martyr to liberty, honor and the rights of people of his native land. Erected by those he died to serve. Leschi died manfully, without fear or faltering, had his last words calmly given, but put to shame if they have any feelings, those who have persecuted him and sought his death. Editor of *"Truth Teller"* [5]

Leschi's death in 1858, the first judicial execution in Washington Territory, symbolized the clash of cultures in that era and the end to the traditional lives of the local Indian people.

In 2004, at a historical inquiry and legal review of his sentence at the Washington State Historical Museum, attorneys argued that the Nisqually man could not be convicted because a death during warfare is judicially not considered murder. People in the room, including descendants dressed in Coast Salish regalia, supporters, justices, and attorneys, not only cheered but wept when Chief Justice Gerry Alexander, along with seven other

Chief Leschi of the Nisqually (1808-1858). This undated portrait is by an unknown artist. Leschi was convicted and hung following the Puget Sound Indian War of 1855-56. He had protested the Medicine Creek Treaty placing his people on a rocky ridge away from their river and camas grounds. Leschi's exoneration is viewed as a partial reconciliation of injustices to all Indian people. (Courtesy of Wikimedia, US Public Domain)

> Friday March 29th, 1857 #147
>
> Territory of Washington } Indictment Murder
> vs
> Leschi
>
> Comes now B~~enjamin~~ F. Kendall who prosecutes in this behalf and the defendant in his own proper person comes also and files his affidavit and causes for a new trial herein (here insert) and thereupon moves the Court that a new trial be granted, which motion the Court do overrule, to which ruling defendant excepts; thereupon the defendant Leschi files his causes for arrest of judgment (here insert) and moves the Court that judgment be arrested herein which motion the Court do overrule, to which ruling of the Court defendant excepts, and files his bill of exceptions herein (insert) and the defendant saying nothing why judgment should not be pronounced against him It is considered by the Court now here, that the defendant be taken to Steilacoom in Pierce County on Wednesday the Tenth day of June in the year 1857, and there on said day between the hours of 10 o'clock in the forenoon and 4 o'clock in the afternoon, be hung by the neck until he be dead.

This hand-written document denies Leschi a third trial and proclaims his sentence: "...that the defendant be taken to Steilacoom in Pierce County on Wednesday the tenth day of June in the year 1857 and there on said day between the hours of 10^0 clock in the forenoon and 4^0 clock in the afternoon, be hung by the neck until he be dead." Territory of Washington vs. Leschi, 1856, Washington State Territorial Supreme Court, case#3. Series AR27-1-0-24 (Courtesy of Washington State Archives)

The basket was an essential utilitarian item for daily life. A beautifully made basket was also prized as an art object, elevating both the basket and basket maker. The four-pronged symbol, shown in this rare photograph of early Squaxin baskets, represented the four seasons to the Squaxin Island people. Due to the symbol's sinister connotations since the Nazi regime, and out of respect for lives lost during World War II, basket makers no longer use what is now known as the swastika in their designs. (Courtesy of Squaxin Island Tribe)

judges, pronounced Leschi cleared of the charges.

Leschi of the Nisqually was at last exonerated. In the words of John Ladenburg, the lead attorney for the defense in the legal review, "[Clearing Leschi's name] …is a rare opportunity for the people of Washington, both Indian and non-Indian, to come together to heal old wounds and create a road toward understanding and respect."[6]

The exoneration would add a new paragraph to a story, a new chapter in history books, a new panel in museum exhibits, Cynthia Iyall, a descendant of Leschi's sister, told the judges.[7]

Her words were prophetic. Leschi's exoneration created a ripple effect throughout the nation in recognition of injustices committed against all Native people, making national news, and becoming the subject of numerous books and articles. True to Iyall's words, the story was told in a 2017 Medicine Creek Treaty display featured in Washington, DC. It was part of a larger exhibit, "Nation to Nation: Treaties Between the United States and American Indian Nations" at the National Museum of the American Indian.

Bounty of Water and Woods

The original people of the land known as Thurston County lived for eons on the natural bounty of the waters, woods, and prairies. The area has long been the home of three groups of people—the Nisqually, "People of the river, people of the grass;" the Squaxin, "People of the Water;" and the Chehalis, "People of the Sands." Their names denote their territory as well as their ancient way of life.

These three groups shared a language pattern known as Salish or Salishan, along with 47 identified tribes in the Pacific Northwest from Montana through Idaho, Washington, Oregon, and British Columbia. Although the languages had similarities, the 27 or so dialects were as different as German and English; and many groups could not understand each other. Locally, the Nisqually and Squaxin people spoke Lushootseed while the dialect of the Upper Chehalis was known as Tsamosan. When Euro-Americans moved into Indian territory, they used differences in language to discern one group

Squaxin Island is the designated reservation of the Squaxin Island Tribe, as determined in the Medicine Creek Treaty of 1854. The people lived in longhouses throughout the inlets of southern Puget Sound, harvesting seafood and camas, a bulb-like plant with blue flowers found on Northwest prairies. The Squaxins were confined on the island during the Indian War, despite the lack of water and resources. (Courtesy of Squaxin Island Tribe)

from another. However, the categories were rarely simple due to intermarriage and blurred territorial lines. In many instances, bands of people from one group occupied an area simultaneously or moved into a spot vacated by a different group.[8]

Although the Salish people shared common traits, distinctions existed among the individual tribes and families. The Nisqually people relied on their river as a major food source and the grassland for harvesting camas and grazing their horses. Of the three tribes, the Nisquallies owned more horses, likely due to extensive trading with the Yakamas in Eastern Washington. Thus, their name, "People of the river, people of the grass." A prosperous, healthy tribe, they occupied at least 13 major villages on both banks of the Nisqually River, extending nearly 30 miles upstream from the Nisqually Delta. Settlements dating back 12,000 years are still being unearthed, according to Nisqually elder and archivist Joe Kalama.[9]

The oral tradition of the Nisqually people tells of their migration not from Asia but Central America to the hot and arid Great Basin, following the receding ice fields to a pass on the southern flank of the mountain they called Ta-co-bet. (Ironically, the mountain carries the name for a much shorter span of history after a British admiral named Rainier, although Mount Tacoma or Tahoma are alternatively used.) The late Cecilia Svinth Carpenter, revered Nisqually historian, wrote an account in *Where the Waters Begin: The Traditional Nisqually History of Mount Rainier:* "This group of Indian people, who would later call themselves the Squali Absch… could hardly believe their good fortune. All around them lay a land of green forests filled with a bounty of wildlife, berries, and roots. A mighty glacier-fed river that flowed westward down the mountainside held the promise that more lands lay below."[10]

The Chehalis people roamed further south and west of present-day Olympia. A Chehalis elder named Liichaat recounted, "In the old days we gathered roots and berries. We fished the Chehalis, Black, Cowlitz, Satsop, Wynoochee, Elk, Johns, Skookumchuck and Newaukum Rivers. Our people fished and hunted from the mountains, across the prairie, to Grays Harbor, and in the lower Puget Sound. In the old days, the baskets carried and stored our foods. We relied upon the baskets, the rivers, the land, the roots, the berries, the fish, and the animals. Our lives were tied together by the Creator."[11]

A very large settlement of Chehalis people lived at Grand Mound with a name meaning "long prairie" (wex'e.uws), another lived at the mouth of the Skookumchuck River near Centralia, and a third where the Black River enters the Chehalis River. This is the location of the present reservation straddling Thurston and Grays Harbor counties. Additional settlement sites can be found in the Grays Harbor and Lewis County areas.

The Squaxin, "People of the Water," originally lived along the watersheds of southern Puget Sound. They describe their territory as follows: "We are the Noo-Seh-Chatl of Henderson Inlet, Steh-chass of Budd Inlet, Squi-Aitl of Eld Inlet, Sawamish/T'Peeksin of Totten Island, Sa-heh-wamish of Hammersley Inlet, Squawksin of Case Inlet, and S'Hotle-Ma-Mish of Carr Inlet. We also belong to the surrounding watersheds."[12] In 1927 the federal government attempted to resolve land claims with Native tribes. At a hearing of the Indian Claims Commission, Squaxin John Scalopine spoke of accustomed places in the Black Hills of Capital Forest and at a village on Black Lake.[13]

In May 1792, Captain George Vancouver of the British sloop-of-war *Discovery* dispatched Peter Puget and others to explore the waters of the Sound. One of history's best descriptions of a Native village comes from Puget's journal:

> These people I should suppose were about Sixty in Numbers of all Ages and Descriptions. They lived under a kind of Shed open at the Front and Sides. The women appeared employed in Domestic Duties such as curing Clams & Fish, making baskets of various reeds, so neatly woven that they were perfectly watertight. The occupation of the men I believe consists chiefly of Fishing, constructing canoes and performing all the laborious work of the Village... (We saw) the Extravagance with which their Faces were ornamented. Streaks of Red Ochre & Black Glimmer were on some... Every person had a fashion of his own... They likewise had the Hair covered with the Down of Birds...[14]

These early people shared more similarities than differences. To enhance their lives and diets,

Geoduck harvesting. Shelton, Washington, ca. 1900s. (Courtesy of Squaxin Island Tribe)

they developed a web of trails for trade with tribes both east and west of the Cascade Mountains. The local tribes bartered such goods as salmon products, seal oil, smoked clams, and shells in exchange for luxuries like mountain sheep wool, porcupine quills, obsidian for tools and weapons, and wild meat. They traded slaves captured in warfare as well. Even before contact with European people, the tribes created a common language for trade—Chinook Jargon. Later, French and Spanish words from fur traders were absorbed into the language to benefit mutual business interests.

As their names imply, these people of the water navigated Puget Sound and its tributaries as byways for trade and interaction with other tribes. Towering forests provided them the means to build canoes of cedar trees which they chose especially for their spirit. In an intimate relationship between the mode of transportation and their way of life, all the tribes bore the name of Canoe People.

"The cedar tree is like a storybook for our people," said Charlene Krise of the Squaxin Island Tribe.[15] To the Squaxin people, cedar has always been sacred. They stripped the inside layer and softened it for baskets, clothing, rain hats, hand towels, ropes, and even diapers. Its boughs fanned out bad spirits. When hung in corners of their homes, the spirit of cedar protected the family.

The cliché "when the tide is out, the table is set" rings true; these Indians did not lack for food. They thrived on abundant seafood, wildlife, and

JOHN SLOCUM AND THE INDIAN SHAKER CHURCH

Portrait of John Slocum (1838-1897) who founded the Indian Shaker Church. (Courtesy of Squaxin Island Tribe)

John Slocum, a Squaxin who owned his own logging business, lived a life thought to be worldly in the early 1880s. He claimed to have loved gambling and horse races, eschewing religion of any kind—but nevertheless was interested in the beliefs of non-natives.

One day in 1882, he became terribly ill, and he lay on his death bed, stiff and cold. Following the custom of prayer and purification near the water, his wife Mary walked and prayed along the shores of Mud Bay. Suddenly she was overcome with a fit of shaking. At that very moment, John miraculously rose from the dead, overpowered with a bright light and a vision of Jesus calling him back to teach.

Thus began the Indian Shaker Church, which is unrelated to the American Shakers (United Society of Believers in Christ's Second Appearing).

John Slocum stressed strict morality, sobriety, and honesty in his new church. Incorporated were elements of Christianity with rituals of bell-ringing, prayer, and overtones of Catholicism.

Slocum's church caught on, and the movement spread. The Indian Shaker Church now extends from British Columbia to Northern California with small congregations.

Today Native American people practice many denominations and belief systems, of which the Shaker Church is one.

plants. The rivers teemed with salmon runs so thick, it was said, a person could almost walk across them, and shellfish cluttered the shorelines. Mud Bay, in particular, yielded clams and flounder. For tasty oysters, the Squaxin harvested the shellfish in what is now Oyster Bay, while the Chehalis journeyed to what is now Bay City near Westport. The Nisqually harvested big geoduck clams in bays. The men ventured into dark, wooded areas to hunt deer and elk. The women prepared succulent stews of wild carrots, onions, and camas simmered in cooking baskets that were heated with hot rocks.

However abundant the resources appeared, it was not by happenstance. This bounty was seen by white settlers as an endless resource, when in fact, the Native people were careful never to take more than they needed. Their prudent harvesting stemmed from astute observation, based on perfect timing of the fish runs, the moon, and changing seasons, all in balance with one another. They could smell the coming of rain.[16]

Cecelia Svinth Carpenter, the Nisqually historian, explained: "Living in the natural world, without the complexities of today, they developed a coexistence with nature which included respect and appreciation of its beneficent forces as well as fear of its demonic forces."[17]

Dan Penn, Tribal Preservation Officer, Confederated Tribes of the Chehalis Reservation, noted, "It [coexistence with nature] perpetuated abundance. They had a level of connection to the land and resources. They practiced science, based on generations of observation. This degree of knowledge and understanding meant survival for them and future generations."[18] Children gained wisdom passed on through oral tradition with secrets guarded within families for self-preservation.

The tribes enjoyed a combined diet of seafood, game, berries, plants, and roots. Of these, the blue flowering camas plants covering the prairies yielded a major source of carbohydrates. Their bulbs served as a sweetener and potato substitute.

Camas was cooked using the ancient pit baking method. The bulbs were placed in a pit four or five feet deep, lined with ferns and a fire built on top. The fire burned all night long, and by morning the roots were cooked. Sometimes the cooked bulbs were smashed and made into a loaf-like bread, dried so it could be eaten in the winter, or smoked whole and

"Yelm Jim's Fish Weir" illustrates the elaborate construction of a fish trap. General Subjects Photograph Collection, 1845-2005. AR-28001001-ph001070 (Courtesy of Washington State Archives—Digital Archives)

used in soup with fish and salmon eggs, according to "The Chehalis People" tribal history.[19] To protect the camas fields and maintain grasslands for their horses, the Indians set fire to the prairies to clear out intrusive trees. Native people used controlled burning long before European people named the practice.

As tribes return to ancient practices in the twenty-first century, the harvest of camas is experiencing a revival.[20]

"Herbal medicine was used for a variety of less severe cases of colds and fever," wrote Cecelia Carpenter in *They Walked Before: The Indians of Washington State*. "To identify, pick, and cure the various roots, berries, and plants for the Indian's medicine cabinet required an informed individual… A woman who practiced herbal medicine was always in demand."[21] Although the pioneers believed the Indians did not farm, they actually did, practicing horticulture in fields of herbs burned to ensure new growth.

A little-known practice among local tribes was unique to North America. They raised and bred dogs for their hair, using it to make blankets and clothing. Archaeologist Dr. Dale Croes noted, other than in this area, "This degree of animal husbandry can only be found in Peru."[22]

Northwest Native people cherish salmon. Besides being a major source of food and trade, salmon are spiritual beings who complete sacred journeys and give their lives to the people. In the Chehalis language, now nearly extinct, the word for salmon roughly translates to "the food" with multiple levels of meaning.[23] Native people could taste or smell a salmon and identify its species, which river it came from, and the time of year it was caught—much to the astonishment of Euro-American settlers. From late spring to early fall, the men of the tribes were occupied with fishing, while women prepared the gear and utensils. Salmon gave them life; it was the source of life.[24]

"Like other Northwest tribes, the Upper Chehalis used a combination of spears, nets, traps, and weirs to obtain their year's supply of salmon," the Chehalis history notes. "They used… seine nets, tubular nets, and dip nets. Women made the twine for nets by spinning specially prepared fibers… soaked… in lichen dye and worked with (fish) brains to keep it from getting stiff and breaking…"[25]

In contemporary times, the tribes still celebrate the "First Salmon" in the annual ceremony to honor the return of the precious fish from the ocean to the streams.

The Circle of Seasons

Daily life for the people revolved around seasons. They moved where food was readily available, following species of fish that migrated at specific times or camping near areas plentiful with berries or game. In the spring and summer months, they lived in the open. They slept under a portable shelter of mats woven of cedar and grasses, or in some cases maintained "summer homes," which were semi-permanent structures along waterways. Vacation time arrived in late summer when large parties of people met to pick berries near Mount Rainier. They celebrated a time to trade, gamble, race horses, and arrange marriages. Intermarriage between the tribes was not only common but expected; one did not usually marry within the tribe. Just as tribal lineage overlapped, territorial boundaries blurred, especially for common gathering places like berry fields.

In the rainy winters, families gathered in cedar plank longhouses to share cooking fires and shelter. Longhouses typically were built beside rivers with entrances facing east. Some housed as many as several dozen people, usually family members. Construction of longhouses without the use of modern tools required ingenuity; the builders hoisted huge logs high overhead using cedar ropes. According to Charlene Krise, Squaxin historian, "They cut the logs using natural forces of wind and fire. They skidded the logs on planks coated with salmon oil and dug a deep hole where they hoisted the log. The ropes (of cedar and sinew) made use of positive and negative forces. Then everyone gathered around to sing and bring their spirit to raise the log upright with ropes."

The area now known as Thurston County had longhouses in many locations. Squaxin John

Scalopine recalled in a 1927 Court of Claims testimony, there "were two big houses on the head of Mud Bay and three of them below the Mud Bay head on the east side of the bay," each one about seventy-two feet in length. Similar houses could be found on nearly every inlet.[26] At least seven longhouses stood[27] in a major Chehalis village near the rock pinnacle for which Grand Mound is named. The mound served as a beacon and sacred place, marking Chehalis territory. The Chehalis people also lived in winter longhouses along their waterways.

During the winter months, women and men alike created tools, utensils, and baskets. In the long dark evenings, elders passed along stories and legends. Not meant only to instill values and history, the legends schooled the next generation in knowledge critical to survival.

One character who frequently appears in legends is the Changer, or Transformer, depending on the version. In the Chehalis story, Changer was taken after his birth to the Land of the Salmon. After a long time, he escaped and set out on a very long journey to his homeland. Along the way, he changed many things and gave names to fish, animals, and birds. He created landmarks seen to this day and told the fish where to go to spawn. Eventually, Changer became the Moon and his younger brother the Sun. Because the moon has 13 cycles determining the seasons, it told the people when to gather equipment for specific runs of fish and when to gather plants or herbal remedies. Through the stories of Changer, children learned the ways of the people, how to live, and how to have good medicine.

However, no medicine could ward off the horrible decimation that struck the tribes in the 1800s. White man's diseases of scarlet fever, smallpox, and influenza ravaged entire villages, wiping out as much as 80 or 90 percent of the Indian population.

Charlene Krise of the Squaxin Island Tribe

The Medicine Creek Treaty Tree marked the spot on the Nisqually Delta where the Nisqually, Puyallup, Muckleshoot, and Squaxin, including the Steilacoom, Squawksin, S'-mamish, Steh-chass, T'Peeksin, Squi-Aitl, and Sa-heh-wamish. met with Governor Isaac Stevens to sign a treaty on December 26, 1854. This photo, ca. 1910, shows the tree which stood for over a century, then, in 2007, fell in a wind storm. (It is undetermined which tree in the photo is the Treaty Tree.) Some of the seedlings are now trees on the Thurston County Courthouse grounds. The Nisqually Indian Tribe protects other seedlings of the original tree, both in its tribal facilities and at the site of the Treaty Tree. General Subjects Photograph Collection, 1845-2005. AR-28001001-ph001474 (Courtesy of Washington State Archives—Digital Archives)

told this chilling story about her great-grandfather, William Krise. He married into another tribe a distance away and had been away from his family for a long time. After a hunting trip he stumbled into the village late at night, exhausted and unwilling to wake up his family members asleep in the longhouse. Needing shelter, he quietly crept inside and fell asleep.

When he woke up the next morning, to his horror, he discovered everyone in the lodge was dead. Stricken with grief and unable to bury them all, he set fire to the longhouse to prevent the disease from spreading further. Villages disappeared overnight, and the tribes were greatly diminished.

Times of First Contact

The original residents' first contact with Europeans came with early trappers and the Hudson's Bay Company, which built Fort Nisqually in Nisqually territory in 1833. The British-based corporation had trading posts across what is now Canada and

Group photo of scholars at Chehalis Indian Reservation, 1888. Photographer, A. P. Hadley. State Library Photograph Collection, 1851-1990. AR-07809001-ph003320 (Courtesy of Washington State Archives—Digital Archives)

the Pacific Northwest. It traded furs to provide men of the world with stylish hats of beaver fur. As businessmen, leaders of the Hudson's Bay Company diversified into agriculture to support their own trappers and trade butter and farm goods with the Russian Alaska colony.

The result was the creation of the Puget Sound Agricultural Company and the introduction of commercial farming in the Northwest. Besides a 6,000-acre farm in Lewis County, the company primarily raised livestock in Thurston County. Tolmie State Park bears the name of Hudson's Bay Chief Factor Dr. William Fraser Tolmie (1812-1886) who spent 16 years with the Hudson's Bay Company at Fort Nisqually as a physician, surgeon, botanist, fur trader and a friend of Chief Leschi. In fact, Dr. Tolmie allegedly hired a lawyer through the company to defend Chief Leschi in his trials for murder.

The Hudson's Bay Company established a peaceful, cooperative agreement with the Nisquallies, Squaxins, and Chehalis of Thurston County. Many of its employees married Native women, further cementing its bond with the tribes.

The British reign ended in 1846, and the area then became the territory of the United States, but the Hudson's Bay Company continued operations south of the new border until their rights were purchased by the American government in 1869.

When President Franklin Pierce appointed a West Point engineer named Isaac Stevens as the governor of the new Washington Territory in 1853, Stevens set out to establish the government, survey for a transcontinental railroad, and make treaties with the Native tribes to free up land for Euro-Americans. Early in December 1854, Stevens appointed a commission to draft the treaties for the tribes west of the Cascades. Michael T. Simmons served as the Indian Agent for the Puget Sound region; joining him were George Gibbs, a lawyer and surveyor, and B. F. Shaw, interpreter. In less than a month Stevens pushed through a template of the treaty format that would serve for negotiations with all tribes. The goal was to consolidate thousands of Indigenous people on a few small, sparse reservations to make way for Euro-American settlers.[28] Stevens first tackled the tribes closest to the new territorial capital in

Olympia for treaty-making: the Nisqually, Puyallup, Muckleshoot, and Squaxin, including the Steilacoom, Squawksin, S'~mamish, Steh-chass, T'Peeksin, Squi-Aitl, and Sa-heh-wamish.[29]

Stevens and his commission toyed with moving the Native people to a less desirable and barren place in Eastern Washington, perhaps to a remote part of Hood Canal, or onto tiny Squaxin Island. Instead, they settled on small reservations for each tribe. The tribes were not informed in advance of the plan for them to vacate their lands.

To manage the language barriers, Stevens's commission chose first to use a Native tongue, Lushootseed, which was re-translated into the Chinook Jargon with its limited vocabulary, despite the complexities of legal treaties. The treaties ignored individual cultures, language, and territories; the commission appointed "chiefs" without deferring to the tribes. To the tribal people, the land belonged to the Creator for everyone, not in line with the federal policy of parsing and fencing.

When Governor Stevens and his commission met with the four southern Puget Sound tribes on December 24, 1854, at Medicine Creek near the present Nisqually Delta, some 700 Native people flocked to join them. The Squaxin had been told to wear big hats to collect money since this was supposedly a business deal.[30] The Nisqually headed the largest group with half-brothers Quiemuth and Leschi as chosen leaders. Frank Shaw read the articles of the treaty—essentially an inequitable land deal where the tribes gave up their territories—to the assembled crowd. The tribes would move from their villages and ancestral lands extending from the crest of the Cascade Mountains to Puget Sound, some 2.2 million acres or over nearly 4,000 square miles. They would vacate their lands in one year and move to three reservations, each about 1,280 acres or two square miles. The Nisqually were relegated to rocky hilltops just west of the Nisqually Delta with no prairies for camas, no grazing for horses, and no rivers for their sustenance. The Puyallups received a reservation near Commencement Bay. The Squaxins were relegated to their island, four and a half miles long and a half-mile wide, which had no water. Indeed, of the entire territory, these sites were the least prized land. For their moving expenses, the government would compensate the tribes $3,250 in non-cash items, but nothing for the land they gave up.

Almost as an afterthought, Article 3 of the treaty allowed the tribes "the right of taking fish at all usual and accustomed grounds and stations… in common with the citizens of all the territory…"[31] This phrase endured the passage of time into the twentieth century and formed the basis of the 1974 Supreme Court decision known as the Boldt Decision, which recognized Northwest Indian fishing rights for treaty tribes.

A couple of months later on February 25, 1855, Governor Stevens convened a treaty session for coastal Indians ten miles upriver from Grays Harbor near the present site of Cosmopolis. The Cowlitz, Quinault, Quileute, Chinook, and Upper and

In 1905 the Native people of Thurston County were unsure of their future and that of their children. With their traditional food sources no longer available, they often lived in poverty. Pictured here is Lena Heck, Chehalis Reservation. Photographer, Edmond S. Meany. NA 1157 PH Coll 132 (Courtesy of University of Washington)

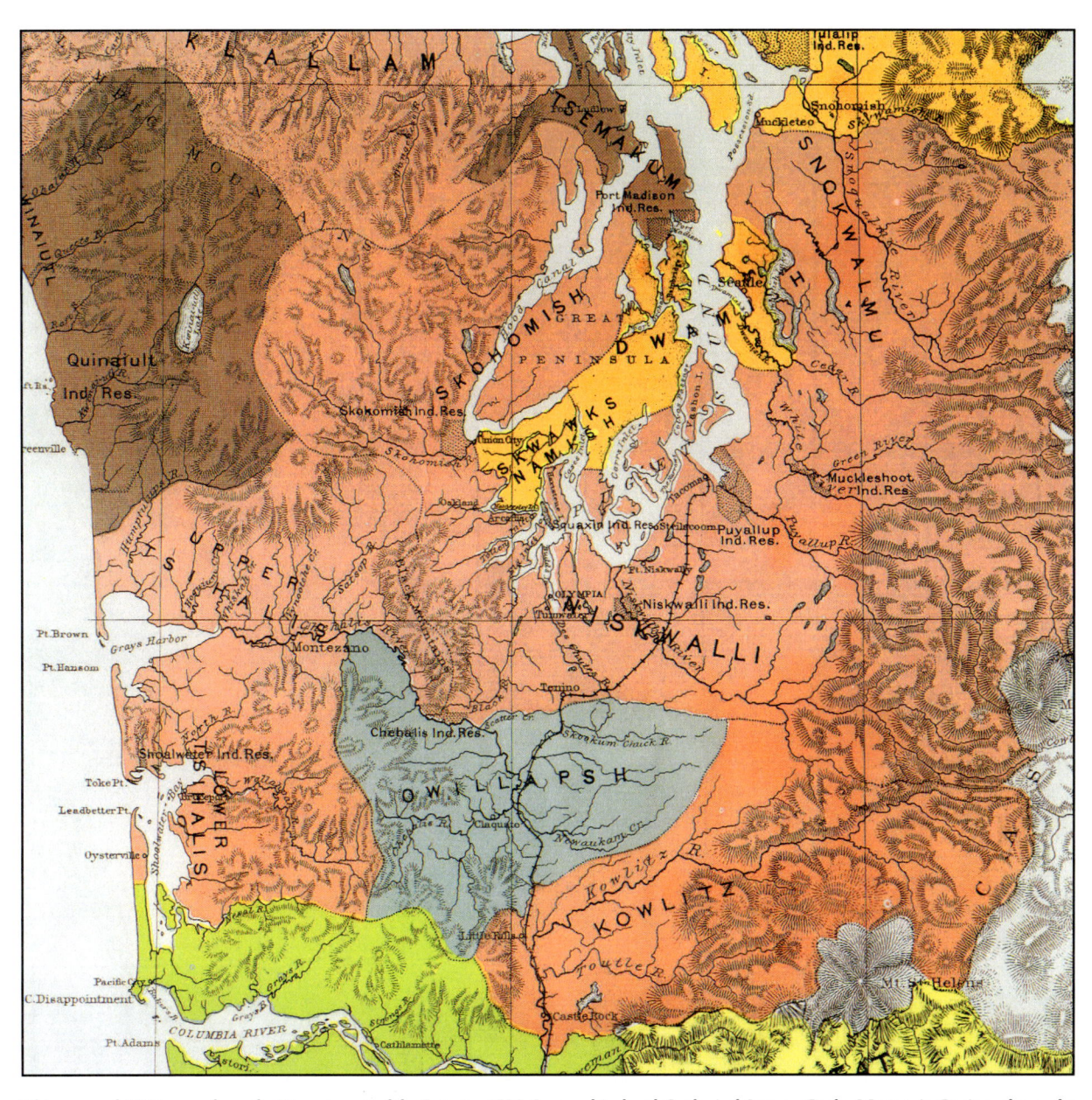

This cropped 1876 map, from the Department of the Interior / US Geographical and Geological Survey, Rocky Mountain Region, shows the Native American groups in the western part of Washington Territory. The geographic and reservation names are displayed with the official spelling used in that era, while family and tribal names are spelled phonetically as heard by the map makers. Please note in the gray area the text of "Chehalis Ind Res." and "Owillapsh" tribe with reference to the Tinneh family. The term Owillapsh is found on maps by the Department of the Interior and US Geological Survey prior to 1900. Based on work by John Wesley Powell, there is a very close connection between the extinct Owillapsh and Kwalhioqua Tribes. They were both part of the Pacific Group of the Athapascan family. The Kwalhioqua Tribe is documented as one of the Confederated Tribes of the Chehalis Reservation and its descendants are the Youckton family. The Chehalis Reservation, first established in 1860 to include the Upper and Lower Chehalis people, has consisted of a land area of approximately 4,225 acres. It goes along the Chehalis River, extending from southeastern Grays Harbor to southwestern Thurston counties. Note: Boundary lines above represent territory, not contemporary reservations. General Map Collection, 1851-2005. AR-270-B-000A28 (Courtesy of Washington State Archives–Digital Archives)

Elizabeth Jones in Shelton, Washington. Photographer unknown. (Courtesy of Squaxin Island Tribe)

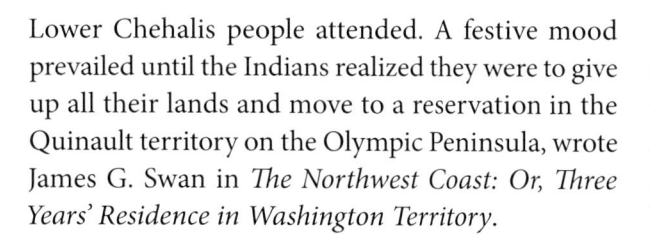

Elizabeth Jones and young relative in Shelton, Washington. Photographer Jeffers. (Courtesy of Squaxin Island Tribe)

Lower Chehalis people attended. A festive mood prevailed until the Indians realized they were to give up all their lands and move to a reservation in the Quinault territory on the Olympic Peninsula, wrote James G. Swan in *The Northwest Coast: Or, Three Years' Residence in Washington Territory*.

> We are willing to sell our land, but we do not want to go away from our homes. Our fathers, and mothers, and ancestors are buried there, and by them we wish to bury our dead and be buried ourselves. We wish, therefore, each to have a place on our own land… but we can't go to the north among other tribes. We are not friends, and if we went together we should fight, and soon we would all be killed.[32]

The session broke up when Governor Stevens tore up the paper designating a Chehalis leader as chief, and the tribes clearly did not want to move to a single reservation.[33] Thus, the Chehalis fell into a category of being a non-treaty tribe except for the clause in the Olympia Treaty of 1856 signed by the Quinault and Quileute tribes including "other fish-eating tribes." This designation posed many limitations on governing and expansion, although an executive order by President Abraham Lincoln in 1864 created the Chehalis Reservation of 4,215 acres at the confluence of the Black and Chehalis Rivers. The Executive Order of January 20, 1857, enlarged the Nisqually Reservation to 4,717 acres on both sides of the Nisqually River.

Meantime, the stirrings of unrest rippled through Washington tribes in what became known as the Puget Sound Indian War of 1855-56. "The inland tribes became indignant over… encroaching civilization… The nomadic tribes, used to moving from winter to summer camps, were becoming increasingly frustrated over… having to give up their lands and move to specific reservations. These fears drove them to thoughts of war to defend lands," wrote Cecelia Carpenter.[34]

Michael T. Simmons, the Indian Agent, rounded up the Indians considered friendly to temporary reservations where they were labeled as "non-hostiles" while their more vocal counterparts were the "hostiles." Locally, reservations were on Squaxin Island, Yelm Prairie, Grand Mound, and Cowlitz Landing. Settlers throughout the territory volunteered for militia forces, and families fled to blockhouses erected quickly for their protection, in spite of the earlier friendships with tribal people. Correspondence from that time reflected the fear generated by rumor.

Following the trials and subsequent deaths of Leschi and Quiemuth, the people of all three tribes relocated around Puget Sound, estranged from family and ancestral ties. The Squaxins rejected the small houses the government offered to them. Their families, homes, well-being, culture, and health had been torn asunder, and by not following their traditional ways, they were thrown into poverty in a white man's economy. Their ancestors' graves were even robbed of skeletons, shipped to the east coast for study.

"Our people suffered terribly," Charlene Krise said of the Squaxin Island Tribe. The Squaxins were not alone in their misery.

To survive and provide for their families, people took jobs in the timber industry, agriculture, and construction. Children were hauled off to Indian schools, forced to give up their language and traditions. Many people moved away. Those who stayed barely eked out a living. Their traditions and languages were forbidden, considered a detriment.

The Snarl of Land Ownership

In attempting to address "the Indian problem" of people roaming and "trespassing" on traditional lands, the Dawes Act of 1887 initiated a program of dividing land allotments of 40 or 80 acres to qualified Indians. Sponsors of the law believed that if Indian people became responsible for their own farms in an individualistic society, as opposed to a tribal one, they could avoid subservience and poverty.[35] The reasoning was that to assimilate the Indians into Euro-American society, they needed to become farmers and raise crops like corn and potatoes. In this case, they needed to do so on the heavily timbered land in the Northwest rain forest. Many Chehalis, Squaxin and Nisqually tribal members were allotted land, much of it on the Quinault Reservation in timber country, away from their livelihood of fishing and on land ill-suited for farming. Few chose to live there.

The Dawes Act, which remained federal policy until 1934, had the unintended effect of creating a bureaucratic nightmare due to inherited ownership, sometimes with hundreds or even thousands of owners with passing generations. Contemporary heirs could own, for example, as little as 1/11,578 of an interest in an allotment. Furthermore, the act permitted the sale of allotted Indian lands to non-Indians even on the reservations, increasing the snarl of land ownership. Local instances of this fractionated ownership include the Squaxin Island Reservation, where people other than Squaxins own much of the land, and the Chehalis Reservation, where the tribe itself owns less have half of the reservation in trust with the US Government.

The Nisqually Reservation faced a different issue in 1917 when Pierce County condemned half of the reservation land for Camp Lewis (later Fort Lewis) during World War I, uprooting cemeteries and forcing the residents of the main tribal village to relocate wherever they could in the middle of the winter. Their prized camas prairie became a bombing range for military weapons, rattling nerves and homes on the reservation for a century.

Eventually, to compensate for their loss of lands, the tribes filed claims with the Indian Claims Commission. Hearings of the claims cases through September of 1978 shows that the Chehalis were paid $745,380 or approximately 90 cents an acre; the Nisqually, $80,013; and the Squaxin, $7,661.

Native American children in a field in front of the Chehalis Indian School in Oakville, Washington, 1885. Forbidden to speak their language, the children worked in the fields and homes of non-Indians. On verso: "General view of Chehalis Reservation. Tall man in center, Charles A. Hartsuck, Supt. of farm. Other man in center, Mr. [Edwin L.] Chalcraft, Superintendent of School." Photographer A. P. Hadley. State Library Photograph Collection, 1851-1990. AR07809001-ph003325 (Courtesy of Washington State Archives–Digital Archives)

Changing Tides of Fortune

In the 1960s, still maintaining their ancestral right to fish, the Nisquallies and Puyallups refused to comply with Washington State fishery laws that denied them access to traditional fishing grounds. After several years of physical confrontations, Billy Frank Jr. along with other tribal members and Hank Adams, an activist from Olympia, led the Fish Wars of the 1960s.

The result was a federal court case titled *United States v Washington*. That proceeding resulted in the Boldt Decision of 1974 upholding Governor Stevens's treaties granting Indians the right to fish in their usual and accustomed places. Following the Boldt Decision, tribal members began to migrate back to their reservations.

About the same time, a determined petite woman who grew up on the Chehalis Reservation took on the Bureau of Indian Affairs about mismanagement of allotted land on the Quinault Reservation. Helen Sanders (Mitchell) uncovered destructive and deceptive forestry practices on Indian allotments and sued the federal government, *United States v. Mitchell I* and *II*, and the cases went before the US Supreme Court. After some 21 years of legal battles, in 1982 the Mitchell case determined for the first time that the Bureau of Indian Affairs could be held liable for its responsibility regarding Indian lands held in trust. The ruling set a precedent for *Cobell v. Salazar* in 2009, one of the largest class action lawsuits in US history. The $3.4 billion settlement awarded individual Indians compensation for mismanagement of their resources and provided for the tribal purchase of allotments.[36]

After more than a century of less than ideal living standards, the original residents of the Thurston County area experienced a turn of fortune. In 1988 Congress passed the Indian Gaming Regulatory Act,[37] which provided the legal structure for gaming on reservations and an avenue for revenue. This was nothing new to tribes who had gambled and played bone games for centuries. As a result, the Chehalis Tribe constructed the Lucky Eagle Casino in 1996, the Nisquallies expanded their small roadside casino into the modern Nisqually Red Wind Casino in 2004 and 2015, and the Squaxin built the Little Creek Casino in 1998 with a golf course in 2014. The tribes collectively employ more Thurston County residents than any entity other than state government or educational institutions.

Having substantial revenue from casinos has allowed all three tribal sovereignties to diversify into endeavors other than gaming while furthering the health, welfare, and environmental concerns of their people. The Squaxin Island Tribe became Washington's first commercial manufacturer of tobacco products when it inaugurated Skookum Creek Tobacco Company in April 2005, selling two brands of cigarettes (Complete and Premis), pouch tobacco, and a line of cigars made in the Dominican Republic called Island Blendz. Profits fund daycare for 100 children. The Nisqually Tribe established the Wa He Lut Indian School in 1974 to immerse children in tribal culture along with academics.

From 1999 to 2009 an archaeological excavation at Qwu?gwes on Eld Inlet at Mud Bay unearthed the site of a thousand-year-old Native American fishing village. This incredible dig revealed artifacts dating back 500 to 1,500 years and gave an insight into a way of life centuries before the arrival of Euro-Americans. Since then, the tribe built the new Squaxin Island Museum Library and Research Center to house and interpret the artifacts.

The Chehalis Tribe opened the Great Wolf Lodge and Water Resort in Grand Mound in 2006, expanded its hotel-casino operation near Rochester, and opened gas stations/convenience stores. The Nisqually Indian Tribe built a youth center, a new administrative building, and a correctional facility to ease crowded jails throughout the state. All the tribes own service stations and mini-marts. The Nisqually have spearheaded environmental causes for salmon preservation and habitat restoration, while all the tribes conduct valuable fisheries research and operate hatcheries. Notably, the increased educational services and opportunities for tribal members have led to a much higher number of undergraduate and graduate degrees.

Furthermore, the three tribes contribute millions of dollars in charitable giving every year from their casinos to local law enforcement, fire departments, education, and non-profit groups.

Native pride and the quality of life for Thurston County's Native people are flourishing. Perhaps the most visible effort to resurrect cherished Native culture has been the Canoe Journey. Started in 1989 as a part of the state centennial celebration, the Canoe Journey proudly revives ancient traditions of canoe-building and gift-giving while building identity and purpose for Indian youth. Paddlers in their canoes set out for neighboring reservations where they must be invited ashore by the host tribe where they camp out. The journey can last up to three weeks. At the culmination of the trip, hundreds of people enjoy meals, gifts, and ceremonies in the style of the old-time potlatches.

Ancestors who passed into the hereafter reflect these cycles of life:

Whatever the future holds, do not forget who you are!
Teach your children, your children's children, and then
Teach their children also.
Teach them the pride of a great people.
A time will come again when they will celebrate together with joy,
When that happens,
My spirit will be there with you.

Attributed to Leschi, Last Chief of the Nisquallies 1808-1858

Commissioned for the 2012 Paddle to Squaxin Canoe Journey, Joe Seymour and other Native American artists painted several murals that adorn buildings near Percival Landing, Olympia. Pictured above is a Salish welcome figure. Other images include seven canoes, representing the seven inlets of South Puget Sound whose people make up the Squaxin Island Tribe. The annual Tribal Canoe Journey has grown to become the largest gathering of Native Americans in western Washington. (Courtesy of the photographer Shirley Stirling)

The Canoe Journey, which began in 1989, revives ancient skills of canoe building for Northwest tribes. Here, in 2012, canoe paddlers concluded their 3-week journey at the Port of Olympia, Washington. Each canoe family asked permission to land and the host, Squaxin Island Tribe, granted permission. Paddlers on the journey stop along the way at reservations overnight before reaching their destination. (Courtesy of ThurstonTalk.com)

THE NATIVE "DISOBEDIENCE" OF BILLY FRANK JR.

Billy Frank Jr. fished on the Nisqually River in the same places as his father, grandfather, and ancestors. But circumstances of the times—and his own grit—led Billy Frank to become legendary far beyond the reaches of the peaceful river flowing through the Nisqually Reservation. He led many other tribal members in confronting the State of Washington. They refused to yield ancestral fishing rights granted by the Medicine Creek Treaty of 1854. They gained national attention through the Fish-Ins of the 1960s and by never giving up. Finally they witnessed the passage of the Boldt Decision of 1974 ensuring those rights.

Like the other tribes of the Northwest, the Nisqually endured the loss of their land and culture after the treaties of the 1850s. Despite Article 3, which allowed the tribes to fish in their usual and accustomed places, the State of Washington ignored the language of the treaties and enforced conservation guidelines for fishing, often arresting Native fishermen. In 1945, the first time Billy Frank Jr. was arrested for fishing on the river, he was 14. By the 1960s, he and other members of Northwest tribes experienced jail and overt violence for their courage to continue fishing. Nisqually tribal members were threatened, beaten, bloodied, and hit with stones as they continued to fish in traditional ways. Billy was arrested over 50 times.

On Thurston County waterways and the shores of Capitol Lake, the collective voice of Native Americans rose to demand social reform, joining the cry across America in the turbulent 1960s. Billy Frank was just the person to put a face on the cause. Native youth organized the first Fish-In at Frank's Landing in 1964; later that year movie star Marlon Brando was arrested on the Puyallup River. Behind the scenes, Indian activist Hank Adams from Olympia organized news coverage and documentaries while Billy Frank continued to fish and speak out—and to be hauled dripping wet off to jail for civil disobedience. Female tribal members immediately took his place on the river.

Billy Frank Jr. (Courtesy of Northwest Indian Fisheries Commission)

The arrests and strife between the fishermen of the tribe and state fish and game officials culminated in 1970 when the US Justice Department filed suit in *United States v. Washington*. Judge George Boldt presided over the US Supreme Court case and ruled that the treaties stood as the supreme law of the land, trumping state law. The tribes held the original right to half of the fish in Northwest rivers. Billy Frank and all Native fishermen won.

Billy Frank Jr. then founded the Northwest Indian Fisheries Commission and chaired it for most of the last 30 years of his life, aiding 20 tribes in sound fisheries management from its main office in Olympia. He received countless honors and awards, along with his scars from the Fish Wars. Since his death on May 12, 2014, his name has been memorialized on streets, buildings and the renamed Billy Frank Jr. Nisqually Wildlife Refuge. His birthday, March 9, is celebrated by the Nisqually and other tribal people. On November 24, 2015, President Barack Obama awarded him the Presidential Medal of Freedom, the country's highest civilian honor. Headlines read "Indigenous Hell-Raiser as National Hero."

Fish on, Billy Frank.
Your legacy follows you.

The waters of Thurston County—the inlets of Puget Sound, its rivers, and lakes—sustained the original inhabitants and fascinated early maritime explorers. For several centuries, Europeans and later Americans took to the seas to pursue new frontiers. In the context of the times, they viewed the "wilderness" as an opportunity for national expansion and a source of great curiosity. Many eagerly sought to find the famed Northwest Passage through North America and instead found the Columbia River, Grays Harbor, and Puget Sound. While oblivious to Native place names, those who journeyed by water to the Northwest Coast left English names that endure in Thurston County history.

Les Eldridge, author of Maritime Olympia and South Puget Sound *(with the late John W. Hough), shares his writing here about early expeditions by sea and the exploration of Puget Sound.*

Chapter 2
EARLY ENCOUNTERS
by Les Eldridge

THE FIRST ACCOMPLISHED sailors in what is now Thurston County, Washington, were the canoe paddlers of the First Peoples of the area, the Salish Indians and the paddlers of the fierce northern tribes that preyed upon the Salish for slaves: Haida, Tlingit, Tsimshian, Gitskan, and others. The Salish were not organized into tribes analogous to the Plains Indians but rather into groups of villages that might share the same Salish dialect.[1] Each had elders or "headmen" who, in times of crisis, would gather villages together and assume leadership. These men were highly respected throughout all the Salish villages.[2]

The "tribes" of today were formed largely at the behest of Territorial Governor Isaac Stevens and organized for his convenience in finalizing treaties and reservation boundaries. It was easier for him to deal with a few leaders who, he maintained, spoke for all.[3] It was a facade of diplomacy with little bearing on fact.

These "tribes" did have identities and shared language and traditions, just no elected governments as we know them.[4] They included the Nisqually, the Skokomish, the Squaxin, the Lower and Upper Chehalis (including the "Holloweena," although some say they were a Cowlitz band), the Cowlitz, and the Puyallup.[5] Tribes north of Point Defiance included the Duwamish, Suquamish, S'Klallam, Nooksack, Skagit, and Lummi. All traversed the length of Puget Sound for trade.[6]

Vancouver Expedition, 1774-1850

The first Europeans to visit Thurston County waters and encounter these splendid mariners were George Vancouver and Peter Puget in May 1792.

They were on an expedition with several goals: negotiating an agreement with Spain over possession of Nootka Sound on Vancouver Island (renamed later); charting the waters of the Northwest coast, and of the Pacific in general; and re-investigating the possibility of a Northwest Passage across North America. Regarding the latter, Vancouver noted his crew was amused that they had sailed on April Fool's Day, as they knew that the Hudson's Bay Company explorer Samuel Hearne had already walked from Hudson's Bay to the Arctic shore in 1771, destroying any hope of a Northwest Passage free of ice.[7]

George Vancouver commanded the expedition. He anchored near the site of the future city of Seattle with his ships HMS *Discovery* and HMS *Chatham*; dispatched the *Chatham* to chart the San Juan Islands; and sent his second lieutenant, Peter Puget, south to chart the unknown reaches of this fjord-like inlet. Puget took two of *Discovery*'s ship's boats, the launch and the cutter, sixteen men, and two other senior officers, Sailing Master (navigator) Joseph Whidbey and supernumerary naturalist, physician, and botanist Archibald Menzies. These boats could be rowed or sailed and were from 25 to 35 feet long. Menzies was aboard to gather plant specimens for the prestigious Royal Society, the finest scientific organization in England. When Vancouver's Navy Surgeon died en route, Menzies volunteered to replace him. Puget was ordered to chart the unknown inlet in five days but took seven to do so as the waters were far more extensive than Vancouver had imagined.

As they charted, they met Indians from various bands, usually friendly. Skokomish, Squaxin, Chehalis and Nisqually Indians all encountered the two boats. In Eld Inlet, Puget's men encountered two friendly Squaxin villages on either side of the inlet, near Young's Cove and Green Cove. They explored Budd Inlet; encountered the mud flats at the mouth of the Deschutes River extending one mile into the inlet; and landed to take a sun sight at 47 degrees, three minutes north.[8] They had proved that the Sound did not lead to a "Northwest Passage" through the interior of the continent. It was May 26. Being two days overdue, they headed back down the Sound to the *Discovery*'s anchorage off Blake Island, passing a fire on the beach at Ketron Island, near Steilacoom, after sunset. They assumed the fire was tended by an Indian party. Later, they learned it was Vancouver and Baker, come to find them.

Vancouver, an impatient man, had set out to find why the Puget party was two days late in returning to the ship. He commanded the longboat, and Third Lieutenant Joseph Baker was in the yawl. They camped on May 26 at Ketron and fired muskets when they saw Puget's boats at dusk in the distance. Evoking no response, Vancouver concluded they must be an Indian party. This mistake in identity led Vancouver to sail further south the next morning, so he too, landed at the southernmost point of the waters at the mouth of the Deschutes River. He would soon name "Puget's Sound." (Note that throughout Euro-American exploration, the existing names of landmarks and locales were not embraced. Instead explorers consistently renamed using terms from their own native language, giving them a sense of ownership.) Vancouver and Baker camped that night at Gull Harbor on Budd Inlet and returned to *Discovery* on May 28. Examining Puget's excellent charts, Vancouver rewarded him by naming this sound in his honor.[9]

Vancouver would never have reached Thurston County if it were not for the Spanish.[10] In 1774, Juan Perez, off Washington's coast, sighted Mount Olympus, naming it Mount Santa Rosalia.[11] The next year, Hezeta and Bodega y Quadra noted a "large river," the Columbia, as they cruised to Nootka Sound.[12] Captain James Cook stopped at Nootka next in 1778 on his third voyage of discovery.[13] That same year saw the first European settlement in what is now Washington State, Nuñez Gaona, at Neah Bay, established by Salvador Fidalgo on behalf of the Viceroy of New Spain, Don Juan Vicente de Güemes Pacheco de Padilla Horcasitas y Aguayo, Count of Revilla Gigedo. Several island and bay names in the San Juans were named from parts of the viceroy's lengthy title.

Captain George Vancouver, Royal Navy, successfully commanded the epic four-year expedition that charted Puget Sound, the straits of Juan de Fuca and Georgia, the Inside Passage, and Vancouver Island (1791-1794). He and his crew were the first Europeans to visit South Puget Sound. (Courtesy of National Portrait Gallery, Creative Commons)

The Americans and some British merchant captains also had a hand in bringing Vancouver to what we now know as Percival's Landing. British merchantman Charles William Barkley noted and named the Strait of Juan de Fuca in 1787.[14] When American trader Robert Gray told Vancouver of his 51-mile cruise up that strait in 1792, Vancouver followed with his own exploration of Puget Sound, including Thurston County. The same year Gray named the "large river" for his ship, *Columbia Rediviva*.[15]

The Hudson's Bay Company's McMillan Brigade, 1824

The waters of Thurston County were under a joint occupation treaty with the British when they were entered by a 48-man Hudson's Bay Company trek from Fort George (Astoria) to the first rapids of the Fraser River, via Eld Inlet and Dana Passage, and return, all in the year 1824. Commanded by James McMillan, the party brought the first American, William Cannon, to Thurston County, and it also brought Iroquois and Hawaiians (Kanaka) as part of the "McMillan Brigade." The Hudson's Bay Company had absorbed its major rival, the Northwest Company, and wished to establish a network of trading posts in British Canada and the Oregon Country. A joint occupation treaty had been signed by Great Britain and the United States in 1818. The border between British Canada and the US portion of the Oregon Country, later Washington Territory, would be set in 1846.

Travel from Fort George at the mouth of the Columbia to Puget Sound and beyond to British Canada was usually up the Columbia River to the Cowlitz River and through the prairies south of Budd Inlet. The Cowlitz Tribe had closed that trail to the Hudson's Bay Company over an unfortunate misunderstanding when Hudson's Bay Company men at Fort George fired on the Indians, thinking they were hostiles. Hudson's Bay Company Governor George Simpson instructed Chief Trader James McMillan to find another route and to travel to the Fraser River, looking for a site for a trading post.

In November, the party set off, crossing the mouth of the Columbia in three boats, 16 men to the boat, plus supplies. They portaged from present-day Ilwaco to Shoalwater (now Willapa) Bay, dragging or carrying the boats and using small streams and lakes en route. They rowed north to the bay mouth, portaged at Tokeland, and then sailed along the ocean shore. Each time they portaged, they unloaded and carried all their supplies, then reloaded the boats. Several men in each boat pushed the boat off the shore in the surf, using their long oars, as the others pulled the boats along with long towlines. This progress was made under what

HMS Discovery, Vancouver's flagship, was a survey sloop-of-war weighing 337 tons and 96 feet long. She carried 135 men, stores for a five-year voyage, and 10 four-pounder cannon in broadside. Owing to a recent mutiny aboard HMS Bounty, she carried a larger Marine detachment than usual. Her four ship's boats - cutter, launch, longboat and gig - under the commands of Puget, Vancouver, 2nd Lt. Joseph Baker and Sailing Master Joseph Whidbey, charted almost the entire South Puget Sound. Acrylic mural by Bill Holm of the Lincoln High School Art Department, Seattle School District. The mural was donated by the Class of 1965-1966. Photographed by Werner Lenggenhager, early 1970s. State Library Photograph Collection, 1851-1990. AR-07809001-ph003925 (Courtesy of Washington State Archives—Digital Archives)

Lieutenant (later Rear Admiral) Peter Puget, Royal Navy served as a midshipman with Vancouver in the Caribbean during the American Revolution, and then as his second lieutenant on the voyage to the Northwest coast. Above is a marker for Peter Puget placed by the Seattle Historical Society on his sarcophagus in All Saints Churchyard, Wooley, Somerset, England. Inscription: "Rear Admiral Peter Puget C. B. of his Majesty's Royal Navy who, after a long, and laborious life spent wholly in the service of his country, terminated his earthly career in the arms of his family on the 31st day of October 1822. This tablet placed by Seattle Historical Society, Seattle, Washington, USA in appreciation of Admiral Puget's Exploration of Puget Sound." Photographer Gillespie [CC BY-SA 4.0 https://creativecommons.org/licenses/by-sa/4.0] (Courtesy of Wikimedia Commons)

Born in County Donegal, Ireland, John Work came to the Hudson's Bay Company and was a clerk for McMillan's 1824 November and December expedition from Fort George to the Fraser River, exploring a new route north. The successful expedition began Work's rise in the Hudson's Bay Company ranks. He was later Chief Factor (director) of Hudson's Bay Company posts in Colville, Spokane, and on the British Columbia coast. He ultimately became the largest landholder on Vancouver Island. He was an accomplished self-taught naturalist and frequently aided David Douglas. His daughter Jane married Dr. William Tolmie, Chief Factor at Fort Nisqually. He was among the first Europeans to visit South Puget Sound, from the Black River and McLane Creek through Eld Inlet, Dana Passage, and Nisqually Reach to the Tacoma Narrows. U. S. Public Domain (Courtesy of Wikipedia)

Hudson's Bay Company clerk John Work termed in his journal as "proceeding under a weighty rain."[16]

The brigade was a rich mix of French-Canadian coureurs des bois, Hawaiians, Iroquois Indians, French, Scots, Irish, one Englishman, and one American, William Cannon, the first Yankee to be noted as traversing Puget Sound when they got that far. Three clerks kept journals for Chief Trader McMillan: Francis N. Annamour or Annance (French), Thomas McKay (Scots), and John Work (Irish).

They reached the ocean beach at the mouth of the Chehalis River, Grays Harbor, and portaged to the harbor over a narrow neck of land, then ascended the Chehalis to the confluence of the Black River. Here the journals first noted the Holloweena, people which they characterized as a "detached" part of the Upper Chehalis Nation.[17] Their principal village in the area was "a few miles off," probably a Chehalis village near Grand Mound in what is now south Thurston County. The party arranged with a Chehalis Indian to take an injured rower, Pierre Pavtin, back to Astoria. Further, in this village, they sought the well-known trapper, hunter, interpreter and guide Pierre Charles, who joined the party and was of great assistance as they proceeded to the Fraser River. The journey from Astoria to Black Lake, in what is now Thurston County, took 15 days.[18]

They sailed and rowed north, noting more Holloweenas north of the Nisqually River, and encountering Puyallups, Suquamish, Snohomish, Skagits, and Cowichans. On December 16, they reached the Fraser River, known to the Native peoples as the Cowichan River, named for the band who had fished there for millennia. They had been 28 days en route. Having found a possible site for the future Hudson's Bay Company trading post, Fort Langley, they headed south on December 21 and reached Black Lake on December 26. The party divided, McMillan, Work and eight men going overland to the Cowlitz River and then by canoe to Fort George. The rest returned in the boats by their previous route, arriving at the fort on December 30.[19]

Many lessons were learned from this voyage. The Hudson's Bay Company representatives concluded the alternative Chehalis/Black Lake route was impractical and were relieved when the Cowlitz reopened the Cowlitz trail. The Hudson's Bay Company began building excellent relationships with the Salish tribes and became a calming force as some less friendly Euro-American settlers moved into the area. John Work kindled an interest in local flora and taught himself botany and collection habits by which he was able to aid other Hudson's Bay Company-sponsored scientists, such as David Douglas, who came later. The Hudson's Bay Company soon established trading posts at Nisqually, Fort Vancouver, Fort Langley, Fort Simpson, and Victoria.[20]

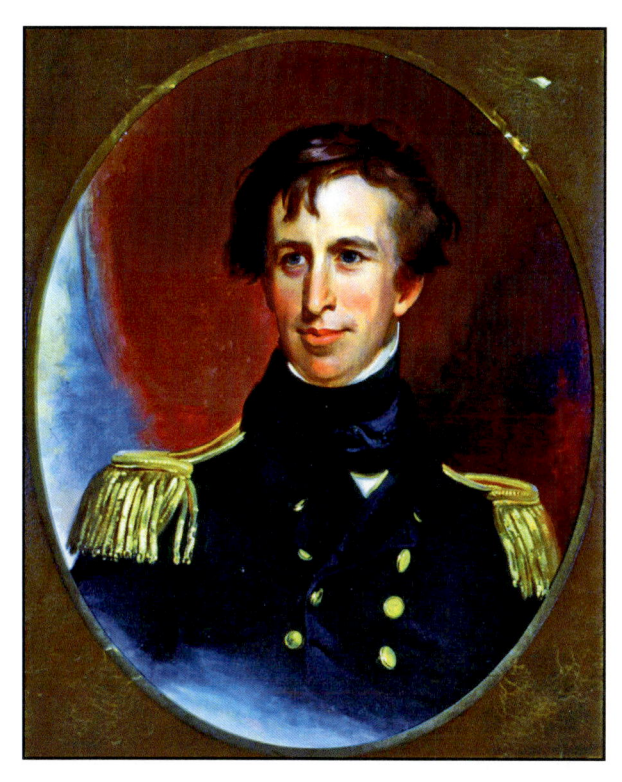

US Navy Lieutenant Charles Wilkes commanded the four-year, "around the world" US Exploring Expedition, 1838-42. Six months of the voyage were spent in Puget Sound which, at that time, was under a joint occupation treaty between Great Britain and the US. He helped ensure that what is now Washington State became US territory when the border was set in 1846. US Public Domain. (Courtesy of Wikipedia)

Charles Wilkes and the United States Exploring Expedition, 1838-1842

The third major expedition in Thurston County history was the US Exploring Expedition, commanded by Lieutenant Charles Wilkes. His six ships and 400 men circled the world, and its results were remarkable. They discovered the Antarctic land mass, charted the South Seas, and established observatories on Mauna Loa and at Nisqually. The expedition brought back enough flora, fauna, and geological specimens from its 11 scientists to require the construction of the Smithsonian Institution's first building, the "Castle." The six months in 1841 they spent in the Oregon Country went far to ensure that the area later comprising Washington State would be American, not British.[21]

Since 1818, the Pacific Northwest had been under a joint occupation treaty between the US and Great Britain. Citizens and subjects of each country could settle there, waiting for the establishment of the border between British Canada and the US. Would it be 54 degrees, 40 minutes north, near the Queen Charlotte (now Haida Gwaii) Islands? Or would it be the Columbia River at 47 degrees north? In 1846, it was drawn at the 49th parallel.

When Wilkes arrived in the Strait of Juan de Fuca and Puget Sound with two of his ships in May 1841, he did all he could to make the region "American." He placed 261 names on geographic features, using names of his crew, his scientists, American naval heroes, naval victories, and famous US Navy ships.[22]

He was guided by the accommodating Hudson's Bay Company staff. They traveled up the Sound to their trading post, Fort Nisqually, which he made his northwest headquarters.[23]

He sent land expeditions to eastern Washington, Grays Harbor, the Willamette Valley, and areas in between. His ship's boats charted Puget Sound, expanding on Vancouver's charts and finding features the British captain had missed, like Hammersley Inlet near Shelton, whose entrance is well hidden.[24]

Anchored just north of Nisqually Reach, Wilkes spent much time in the area. He discovered the Mima Prairie and speculated on the origin of the Mima Mounds. The crews from his flagship, the

This bronze marker identifies the location of the 1841 Wilkes US Exploring Expedition observatory near Fort Nisqually on land which is now part of the City of DuPont. Inscription: "Site of Wilkes Observatory Built in 1841. In this building work of United States Exploring Expedition was conducted. Marker erected by E.I. Dupont De Nemours & Co." (Courtesy of the photographer Shirley A. Stirling)

In August 1835, the steamboat Beaver left London for Fort George (later, Astoria) and the mouth of the Columbia River, arriving in March 1836, the first steamboat in the Pacific north of San Francisco. Hudson's Bay Company Governor George Simpson had lobbied for the ship to be built, citing the advantage she would give the company over Americans in the fur trade in the inlets and coves of the Northwest coast. The 187-ton side wheel paddle steamer carried 31 men including 12 "axe men" to cut the many cords of wood burned per day. She was also rigged for sail, served as a trading ship, passenger ship, and briefly chartered by the Royal Navy. After her last 18 years as a private towboat, she was wrecked in Vancouver, British Columbia, in 1888. She was a frequent visitor to Fort Nisqually and South Puget Sound, first with the Hudson's Bay Company and later as a privately owned tugboat, towing log rafts to Olympia. AR-07809001-ph005111 (Courtesy of Washington State Archives–Digital Archives)

including Colville and Grays Harbor. He also dispatched officers and crews in ship's boats to chart various portions of Puget Sound, such as Colvos Passage and the present-day Hood Canal (which Vancouver called Hood's Channel in his journal and Hood's Canal on his charts). Present-day Thurston County saw Passed Midshipmen Henry Eld and George Colvocoresses with their party travel down the Black and Chehalis rivers to Grays Harbor. Wilkes and a land party went south through the Mima Prairies with Hudson's Bay Company's Fort Vancouver and the Willamette Valley as their destination.[26]

Eld and Colvocoresses were accompanied by sloop-of-war USS *Vincennes*, and the brig USS *Porpoise* celebrated the first Independence Day in future Washington State lands near the Hudson's Bay Company Trading Post, Fort Nisqually. This was on July 5, as Independence Day fell on a Sunday, and Wilkes deferred to the Sabbath. Cannon were landed and fired a 26-gun salute, one for each state in the Union. A parade and a dinner followed, with much merriment. The British observed the high jinks and referred to "a crew of crazy Americans."[25]

Wilkes also established an observatory to measure the thickness of the earth's crust using a pendulum. It was similar to the one he built atop Mauna Loa in Hawaii, the walls of which can be seen to this day. The Wilkes Observatory Site is identified by a marker located at the south side of the mouth of Sequalitchew Creek Canyon, on a promontory overlooking Puget Sound.

Wilkes sent land expeditions in several directions,

South Sound's Eld Inlet is named for Henry Eld, a passed midshipman with the US Exploring Expedition. He commanded a party including botanist William Brackenridge and Passed Midshipman George Colvocoresses. He was later engaged to Wilkes's daughter, aided Wilkes in compiling his 15-volume journal, and died in the mid-1850s. Note: a "passed midshipman" was one who had passed the USN lieutenant's exam and had the same duties as a lieutenant but needed to wait for promotion owing to an overabundance of lieutenants. (US Public Domain)

34   Chapter 2 - Early Encounters

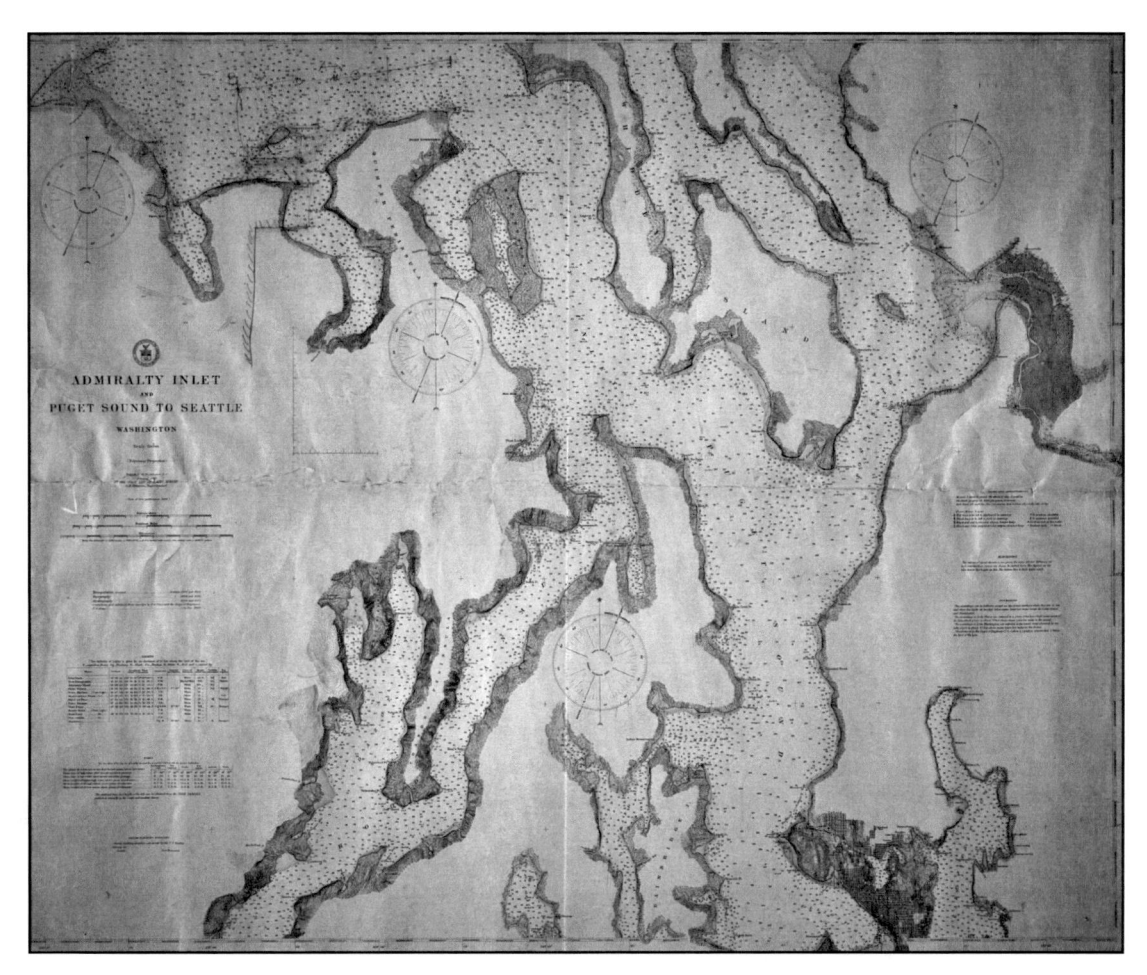

Chart of Admiralty Inlet and Puget Sound to Seattle. February 1895. By the Coast and Geographic Survey, Control General Map Collection, 1851-2005. AR-270-B-003335 (Courtesy of Washington State Archives—Digital Archives)

The ship to the left is HMS Satellite and on the right is the US Coast Survey steamer Active. The HMS Satellite was a brig-rigged steamer that cruised the waters of Puget Sound, the Strait of Juan de Fuca, and the San Juan Islands for two decades, her soundings helping to strengthen the US claim to Haro Strait as the border between British Canada and the US. Her commander, James Alden, frequently visited Olympia and Fort Steilacoom in South Puget Sound during his involvement in the Indian War of 1855-1856 and the Pig War, 1859. The US Coast Survey is the antecedent of the National Oceanographic and Atmospheric Agency (NOAA). It was a prestigious assignment for a nineteenth Century naval or army officer. Isaac Stevens, Washington's first territorial governor, was a US Coast Survey officer and later a Civil War Union Army General. (Courtesy of National Archives)

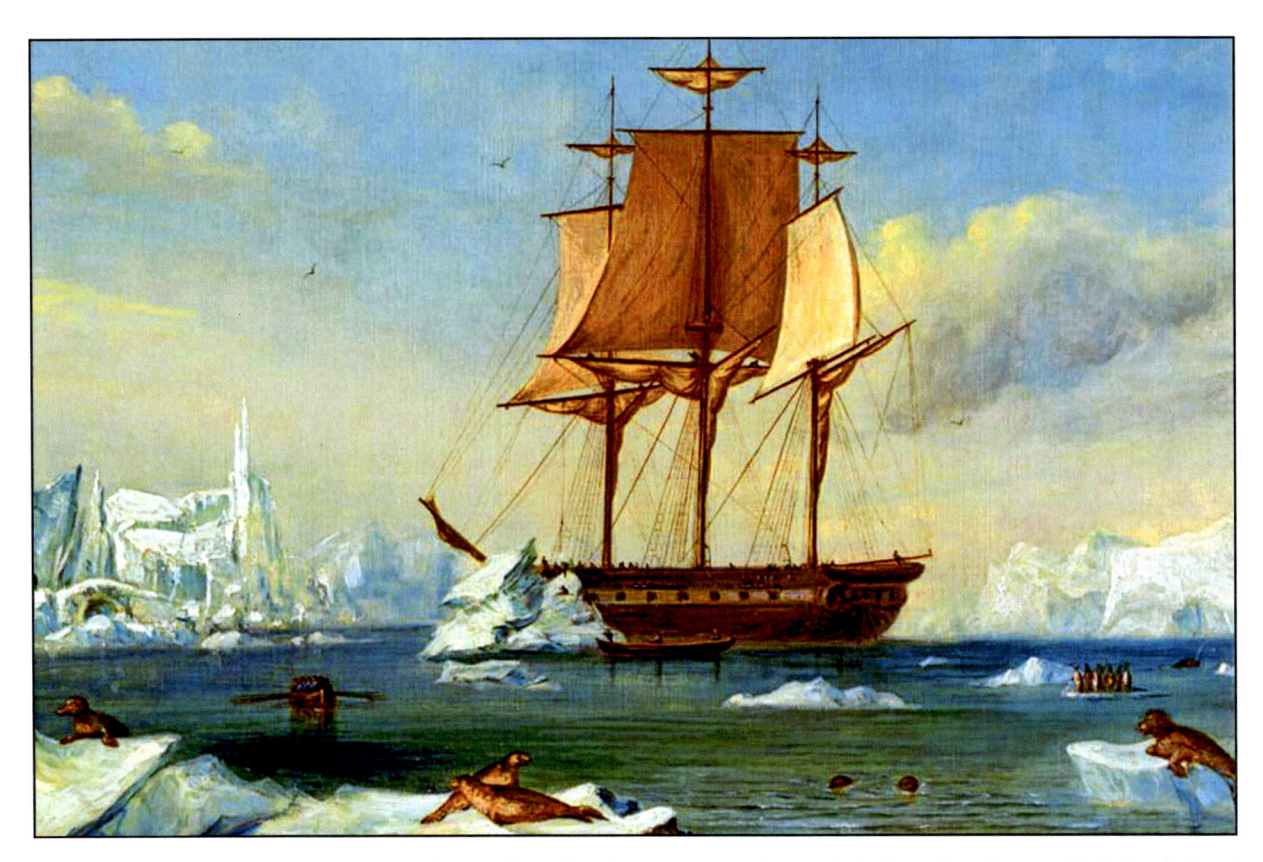

Wilkes's flagship sloop-of-war in his seven-ship squadron, the Vincennes *spent six months in Puget Sound, most of it in South Sound waters. This watercolor is attributed to Wilkes himself when he charted Antarctica. In the days before cameras, naval officers were expected to draw and paint geographic features. As the* Vincennes *entered Admiralty Inlet, she took aboard a Hudson's Bay Company pilot who guided Wilkes to his primary South Puget Sound anchorage off Sequalitchew Creek near Fort Nisqually. US Public Domain. (Courtesy of Wikipedia)*

botanist William Brackenridge. At the mouth of McLane Creek, as it enters Eld Inlet (the location also known as Mud Bay), they met a well-known woman married to a Chehalis, sometimes identified as a daughter of Chinook Chief Concomly, and referred to as "Princess Charlotte" by the Hudson's Bay Company. She was a Native American of rank and consequence. She loaned canoes to the party as they portaged from Eld Inlet to Black Lake and the Black River. She and her small Indian party then trailed the sailors to Grays Harbor, being concerned for their safety, and prevented them from being cast on a lee shore by a storm she knew was coming.

Before they left Thurston County, near the confluence of the Black and the Chehalis rivers, the explorers discovered several intricately carved Indian panels marking the site and noted the presence of a Holloweena tribal settlement.[27] In the Hudson's Bay Company journal of 1824, John Work had noted the same band. Most Native American scholars identify this group as belonging to the family of the Upper Chehalis Tribe.

As Wilkes traveled south toward the Cowlitz River route leading to Fort Vancouver in May 1841, he noted the curious mounds in the Mima Prairies near the Black River. Speculation on the origin of these six-foot-high gravel mounds swirls to this day. Wilkes and others, some reputable geologists, attributed the mounds to giant gophers. Others, equally knowledgeable, said the mounds were glacial residue left by retreating Ice Age glaciers. Thurston County government and the State Department of Public Lands have each preserved sections of this puzzling formation.[28]

Many Thurston County geographical features bear names placed by Charles Wilkes. He honored his passed midshipmen by giving their names to Eld, Totten, and Hammersley inlets. Lieutenant

Thomas Budd's inlet includes Cooper's Point named for an armorer aboard Wilkes' flagship, the USS *Vincennes*. The inlet is also connected to Dana Passage named in honor of the expedition's volcanologist, James Dwight Dana. Henderson Inlet is named for quartermaster James Henderson and Dickenson Point (later Dickerson Point) for Thomas Dickenson, carpenter's mate, in one of the crews. Wilkes was quite even-handed with names, honoring even those he despised.[29]

Wilkes's expedition legacy includes ensuring the existence of Washington Territory as a US possession, charting the Pacific, discovering the Antarctic land mass, and helping to begin

David Douglas was a Scottish plant collector and naturalist. The Linnaeus Society named the Douglas fir in his honor. US Public Domain. (Courtesy of Wikipedia)

Botanist, surgeon and physician, Archibald Menzies sailed with Vancouver as a privileged passenger to collect botanical specimens from the unexplored Pacific Northwest. Vancouver's surgeon died en route, and Menzies volunteered to replace him. In his time ashore in Oregon Country, he collected hundreds of specimens. He accompanied Puget and Whidbey from May 20 to May 27, 1792 in South Puget Sound, collecting and cataloging numerous plant specimens. US Public Domain. (Courtesy of Wikipedia)

construction of Smithsonian Institution facilities to house the thousands of specimens of flora, fauna, rocks and coral collected by his 11 "Scientifics."

Although his accomplishments were extraordinary, he also nearly brought Great Britain into the US Civil War on the side of the South through his repeated violations of neutrality, stopping British ships on the high seas or boarding them in neutral ports to search for contraband cargo, in hopes of the prize money as a result. Wilkes commanded and shaped many subordinates who later fought for the Union or the Confederacy in the Civil War. Many, if not most, passed through Thurston County.[30]

Scientist-Adventurers in Thurston County, 1792-1841

An extraordinary assembly of seagoing scientist-adventurers traversed the waters and byways of present-day Thurston County in the span of years from 1792 to 1841. These include Vancouver's naturalist/physician, Archibald Menzies (1792); Hudson's Bay Company-affiliated scholars including David Douglas (1825), John Work

Thurston County - Water, Woods & Prairies 37

waters of Thurston County.

Menzies was a Fellow of the Royal Society and a Fellow of the Linnean Society, the most prestigious scientific organization in Great Britain. When he returned to Great Britain, he met and mentored the next scientific adventurer to visit Thurston County, David Douglas.

Menzies collected plant specimens wherever his travel took him. He was known by Hawaiians as the "Man who Gathered Grass." In the Thurston County area, he was first to note salal, and his conifer discovery bears his name in Latin which is *Pseudotsuga menziesii*. The tree is now known by the name of the man Menzies mentored: David Douglas of the Hudson's Bay Company. The tree is the Douglas fir.

Some of Menzies' other discoveries while in the Northwest include sea blush (*Plectritus congesta*), Menzies' larkspur (*Delphinium*

In 1833, William Tolmie, a recent graduate in medicine from Glasgow University, arrived at Fort Vancouver and soon traveled north to Fort Nisqually collecting flora and fauna specimens. Ten years later, he was in charge of Fort Nisqually, where he stayed well into the 1850s, when he defended the cause of Chief Leschi as he was judicially murdered by the Territorial government. US Public Domain. (Courtesy of Wikipedia)

(1824), John Scouler (1825), and William Tolmie (1833); followed by the Wilkes Expedition's 11 "Scientifics" (1841) including botanist William Brackenridge, philosopher Horatio Hale, and naturalist/artist Titian Peale. In Menzies's time, the word "scientist" was not used. The term used was "natural philosopher" or "naturalist." Not until the mid-1800s did the term "scientist" come into common usage.

Archibald Menzies

The first scientist to enter what is now Thurston County was naturalist/botanist Archibald Menzies, who was also a physician. Eighteenth century scientists typically had very broad interests and expertise. Menzies accompanied Puget in his seven-day charting of South Puget Sound, including the

A linguist, philologist and naturalist from Harvard University, Horatio Hale was aboard the Peacock *when she went down on the Columbia bar. He was granted leave by Wilkes to stay in South Puget Sound after the expedition left for New York to carry out his studies of the tribal dialects and customs of the Nisqually, Squaxin, Chehalis, Cowlitz and Skokomish, among others. Hale Passage, which separates Fox Island from Wollochet Bay in South Puget Sound, bears his name. US Public Domain. (Courtesy of Wikipedia)*

menziesii), and Menzies' fiddleneck (*Amsinckia menziesii*)."[31]

The Hudson's Bay Company Affiliated Scientists

David Douglas, a Scottish plant collector and naturalist, was 26 when he journeyed for the London Horticultural Society and the Linnaeus Society on a Hudson's Bay Company ship to its Fort George post, now Astoria, in 1825. He was mentored by Menzies. After trips to The Dalles and the Willamette River, he ventured north in October with Chinook Chief Concomly's brother, Tha-mux-I, to Grays Harbor and up the Chehalis River, past the confluence with the Black River through the southern confines of South Puget Sound. In that year he noted the correct pronunciation of the plant salal; munched on wapato (arrowroot) and seashore lupine; and fished the salmon runs. His explorations took him between Puget Sound and London, crossing North America by canoe and horseback, returning to the Northwest, discovering many plants, and dying a tragic death on the Island of Hawaii in 1834.[32]

One of his Hudson's Bay Company colleagues was a young Glasgow University medical student and ship's surgeon, John Scouler, who collected many plant specimens, including a yellow-flowered lily. Scouler often accompanied Douglas on his inland ventures and also traveled as far north as the Queen Charlotte Islands, providing medical services to all tribes and settlers.[33]

William Tolmie, a 21-year-old Scottish physician and naturalist, ventured through Thurston County in 1833, on his way to Fort Nisqually, where he would remain until mid-December. As Tolmie traveled through the area, he marveled at the flora and fauna, puzzled over the mounded prairies, and admired the distant summit of Mount Rainier, which he would climb during his long stay. Tolmie returned to Fort Nisqually in 1843. As commander of the post from 1843 to 1859, he provided medical treatment for hundreds of settlers, company employees, and Indians. He was a devoted naturalist and also an excellent administrator, with a "big-picture" view of his role.

When the border between the US and British North America was established at the 49th parallel in 1846, and later when Washington Territory was created in 1853, William Tolmie saw that the Hudson's Bay Company days in the region were numbered. He decided to make the best of the situation and stay in business as long as possible. He treated Euro-American settlers and Indians alike with respect and courtesy, even though the Euro-American settlers were openly hostile to the British corporation. The company remained in what is now Washington State until 1872. The size of the Hudson's Bay Company eventual award from the US federal government upon the purchase of its holdings in 1869-1872 attested to the high regard in which the company, Tolmie, and his successor Edward Huggins were held.[34]

The "Scientifics" of the Wilkes Expedition

The four-year expedition commanded by Charles Wilkes was a US attempt to join the ranks of several other countries that had sent scientist–adventurers around the world.

Wilkes often referred to the 11 scientists on board his ships as the "Scientifics." Some of the scientists with Wilkes when he arrived in May 1841 in Puget Sound aboard USS *Vincennes* and USS *Porpoise* included Joseph Drayton, Alfred Agate, William Brackenridge, and Charles Pickering. Others joined him later when his subordinate, Captain Hudson, brought USS *Peacock* and USS *Flying Fish* to the Columbia River from their chartings in Hawaii and other Polynesian islands in July 1841.

Aboard the *Peacock*, rescued when she wrecked on a bar of the Columbia River, were James Dana (geologist), Titian Peale (naturalist/artist), William Rich (botanist), and Horatio Hale (linguist, philologist, and ethnologist). When the expedition headed back to New York, Hale stayed on in Puget Sound to complete his authoritative work on the Salish tribes.[35] Dana Passage which separates Budd and Henderson Inlets is named after Dana.

The Salish Sea includes 5,500 square miles of inland waters and estuaries including Puget Sound, the Strait of Juan de Fuca, and Strait of Georgia. The term, Salish Sea, was accepted by the US Board on Geographic Names in 2009 and pays homage to the Coast Salish peoples who lived here for thousands of years. The southern tip of the Salish Sea includes Olympia and Thurston County.

In the chapter "Settlement, Steamers, and Statehood," Les Eldridge shares the colorful saga of maritime history and the Mosquito Fleet cruising the waters of the Salish Sea.

Chapter 3
SETTLEMENT, STEAMERS, AND STATEHOOD
Maritime History of Thurston County, 1850-1922

by Les Eldridge

THE COMING OF AMERICAN settlers in the 1850s upset the delicate balance between Indian interests and those of the Hudson's Bay Company. The fierce northern tribes (Tlingits, Tsimshians, and Haida) frequently raided the Salish peoples for slaves, but their incursions were checked by a desire for summer work with the Hudson's Bay Company.

The Georgiana Incident

The Hudson's Bay Company and the Native peoples, in general, treated each other with respect. The coming of American settlers, hostile to both the Hudson's Bay Company and Indians, altered the relative peace of the region and led to the second instance of an armed US vessel in Puget Sound which was the schooner *Damariscove,* chartered to rescue the passengers of the sloop *Georgiana* from the Haida Indians in Haida Gwaii (then known as the Queen Charlotte Islands). With the discovery of gold in Haida Gwaii, the sloop left Olympia in November 1851, with 27 men aboard. She wrecked in a gale on November 18, near the Skidegate Channel in Haida Gwaii. The gold prospectors were taken captive by the Haidas for ransom.

Eventually, the Haida allowed one of the captives, Samuel D. Howe, to be escorted by a guard party to nearby Hudson's Bay Company trading post Fort Simpson to negotiate for release. Chief Trader William McNeill did not have the resources to mount a rescue.

Meanwhile, the schooner *Damariscove* commanded by Lafayette Balch, having sailed from Thurston County, pulled into Haida Gwaii, discovered the captives, and immediately fled the islands to report the capture to US officials in Olympia. Arriving on December 10 at Fort Steilacoom, a US Army post where a detachment of the US 1st Field Artillery was stationed, Captain Balch met with Captain Bennett Hill, Post Commander, and then with US Collector of Customs Simpson P. Moses in Olympia. John Work, now a Hudson's Bay Company Chief Factor, was visiting Fort Nisqually. He met with Hill, advising him to mount a strong, armed party for rescue and to offer a substantial ransom. Moses agreed, and with no US Navy ships available, chartered the *Damariscove.* On December 19, she set sail for Haida Gwaii and ransomed the captives for a reasonable amount. The Haida were paid 243 blankets, two shirts, 27 bolts of muslin, and 54 pounds of tobacco, a substantial fortune on the frontier.[1]

The US Secretary of the Treasury, Thomas Corwin, rejected Moses's bill for the $11,000 ransom. In June 1853, Moses was relieved from duty as Collector and replaced by Isaac Ebey, who was killed in 1857 while on Whidbey Island. He was beheaded by a band of Haidas who were seeking revenge for an attack by the USS *Massachusetts* at the Battle of Port Gamble in 1856, in which more than 20 Haida died.[2]

In March 1853, Washington Territory was created, and the next year, the Territorial Legislature requested $15,000 from Congress to build a depository of arms at the territorial Capital. Two of the sponsors were Representative Samuel D. Howe and Captain Lafayette Balch, who was now a member of the Territorial Council. Congress approved the request in August 1854.

USS Decatur "Beating round 'Cape Freward': Straits of Magellan, December 1854. This image is a work of a sailor or employee of the US Navy, taken or made as part of that person's official duties. US Public Domain. NH 325 (Courtesy of Wikipedia)

The Navy in the Puget Sound Indian War of 1855-56

US Navy vessels in Puget Sound, USS *Active* and USS *Decatur*, played a part in the Puget Sound Indian War of 1855-56. The *Active* was a brig-rigged steamer of the US Coast Survey, among the world's elite cartographic organizations, and was on loan to the Navy. She was commanded by Lt. James Alden, who had been aboard the Wilkes Expedition in 1841. She was useful to the Navy effort in the Sound far beyond her size and armament because the sloop-of-war USS *Decatur* was only sail-powered and dependent on wind and tide for mobility, while the *Active* could move at any time.

Territorial Governor Isaac Stevens concluded the treaty of Medicine Creek with local tribes in December 1854. The next year he went on to negotiate additional treaties with other tribes, with diminishing success. These treaties were in English, translated by non-Indian officials with limited knowledge of the various tribal dialects, and the treaty contents poorly understood by most Indians. Many tribes and bands refused to sign, but all were treated by the white settlers and the government as if they had signed and were moved to reservations inadequate to their needs, often without their consent. It was a situation that later led to resistance and violence.[3]

On May 7, 1854, an incident took place in Thurston County which foreshadowed the coming Indian War. John Butler owned a farm on the western shore of Budd Inlet at Butler's Cove. Northern tribesmen had come to work at Fort Nisqually, and Butler hired a young chief of the Tongas Tlingit tribe, Tsus-sy-uch, and some other Tlingit tribesmen, to clear his land. After completing the work, an argument ensued, and Butler ordered his foreman, Burt, to shoot the Tlingit chief; Burt followed his employer's orders. Burt and Butler were arrested, released, and indicted, but never

42   Chapter 3 - Settlement, Steamers, and Statehood

tried. The Tlingits went north with their chief's body, swearing revenge. Northern Indian raids on settlers throughout Washington increased. Both Governor Stevens and acting Governor Mason termed the act a "wanton and unprovoked murder," as did Governor James Douglas of Vancouver Island.[4]

The war itself consisted of a series of short skirmishes with relatively few deaths on the American side. Notable battles occurred in Pierce County and Seattle. The *Decatur* participated in the Seattle battles. The war ended with the capture and arrest of Chief Leschi in November 1856. Settlers returned to their farms and homes.

The Pig War and General George Pickett - 1859-61

The 1859 Pig War, although far from Thurston County, was planned, directed, and carried out from Thurston County environs. The Border Treaty of 1846 between Great Britain and the US stated that the international border would run from the 49th Parallel through the "main channel" of the San Juan Islands to the Strait of Juan de Fuca. The Hudson's Bay Company ran Bellevue Farm on San Juan Island, a region that both countries claimed. American squatters moved to the island and in 1859, the farm manager's pig rooted up potatoes in a squatter's garden, and the squatter shot the pig.

Olympia and Thurston County were immediately involved. Governor Gholson and Congressional Delegate Isaac Stevens both visited the US troops placed on the island to defend American interests. They conferred frequently with Colonel Silas Casey in nearby Fort Steilacoom, who commanded the 9th US Infantry.

Captain George Edward Pickett was dispatched to the island to try to settle the dispute.[5] He fortified the island with his company of infantry and guns from USS *Massachusetts*. The British responded with warships anchored in Griffin Bay, their guns trained on Pickett's forces. A shooting war was narrowly averted by negotiation, thus ending the Pig War.

George Edward Pickett was last in his class at West Point, decorated for valor in the Mexican War of 1848, and a US Army captain on San Juan Island when the Pig War dispute with British over possession of the San Juan Islands arose in 1859. His infantry regiment was headquartered at Fort Steilacoom and he frequently sailed there aboard US Navy vessels. US Public Domain. (Courtesy of Wikipedia)

When the Civil War began in 1861, Pickett asked his friends, Catherine and William Collins of Grand Mound and Arkadia to raise his son, Jimmie Pickett.[6] Jimmie was Pickett's son by his Haida wife, Morning Mist, who died in childbirth; the child was raised in South Sound and became an accomplished artist and journalist, later working for the *Oregonian* newspaper in Portland.[7]

The Emerging Mosquito Fleet, 1853-1922

The "Mosquito Fleet" refers to the hundreds of steamships that were Puget Sound's main means of transport from 1850 until the 1900s. They are so called because they "buzzed around" the Sound like mosquitoes.

The very first steamboat on the west coast of North America was the Hudson's Bay Company steamer *Beaver*, brig-rigged to sail around Cape Horn in 1836 with her paddle wheels struck below,

All five Virginias, *beginning in 1908, were owned by Nels Christensen. The* Virginia V *is still afloat, built in 1922, now owned by an historic foundation, and active as a charter vessel on Puget Sound. She is on the National Registry of Historic Sites and one of the last survivors of the Mosquito Fleet. The* Virginia V *is still a frequent visitor to Olympia, often during the annual Kiwanis Olympia Harbor Days tugboat races on Labor Day weekend. She is pictured here during Harbor Days, August 2007. Washington State Archive Photograph Collection. (Courtesy of Washington State Archives)*

to be assembled when she reached the Hudson's Bay Company post at Fort Vancouver. The *Beaver* sailed on Puget Sound and the Strait of Georgia until she was wrecked in 1888 in Burrard Inlet near Vancouver, British Columbia. She served as a chartered Royal Navy vessel in the 1860s and then was sold to private parties as a tugboat, often towing logs to Olympia.[8]

By 1851, Lafayette Balch, the former captain of the *Damariscove*, had built a pier at Steilacoom for lumber shipments. The year 1853 saw the side-wheeler *Fairy* on the Olympia-Seattle run, followed by the 140-foot *Eliza Anderson* in 1859, running from Olympia to Victoria. The accused murderer, John Butler, was one of her pilots. By 1861, the 143-foot Hudson's Bay Company steamer *Enterprise* was on the Sound. The *Alida* was built for the Olympia-Victoria run in 1870 but proved too fragile for the Strait of Juan de Fuca weather and ended her northern route in Port Townsend.[9]

Puget Sound became a highway, a super transportation corridor. The steamboat was the fastest, and most comfortable and dependable way to reach destinations on the Sound until the advent of the modern automobile and decent roadways. Each steamer had her own characteristics and personality. They were powered by propellers, sidewheels, or sternwheels. They raced, competed for passengers, and connived for the best routes. Often, they engaged in "rate wars," undercutting each other's prices to gain a greater passenger share.

Their skippers were salty, enterprising, hard-driving, eccentric, and often hilarious. There was "Hell-roarin' Jack" Shroll, captain of the stern-wheeler *City of Aberdeen*, who had "racing fever," and always looked for competition. He also skippered the *Vashon*, a regular Olympia visitor. Also, there were the "skilled school of whistle and dog-bark navigators." These old salts would time the interval between sounding the powerful ship's whistle and the echo bouncing back from the shore, telling them how much sea room they had. The pitch and tone of the whistle enabled them to tell if the shore was a rocky cliff, or tree-lined, or if the whistle had echoed from a farmer's barn. The farmer's dogs, each with its own distinctive bark, gave another clue to location.[10]

A notable "dog-bark navigator" was Captain Chauncey "Chance" Wyman (or Wiman), skipper of the *Verona*, the *Vashon*, the *Messenger* and the *Clara Brown*, all frequently on the Olympia-Seattle run. Another Wyman distinction was that his wife Gertrude was a licensed skipper, the first woman on the Sound to be so honored. Chance Wyman's most famous voyage aboard the propeller steamer *Verona* was his 1916 transport of 300 Industrial Workers of the World, the "Wobblies," a Centralia local of the controversial left-leaning union who came north through Thurston County and embarked at Seattle for Everett to support their organizers there. The IWW organizers in Everett were trying to organize the shingle weavers and for months had been brutally beaten by thugs hired by Everett industrialists. The Everett sheriff had armed his officers and numerous vigilantes. They met the *Verona* at the dock, defying her to disembark the Wobblies, themselves armed. A shot rang out, followed by a continuous fusillade. Many of the Wobblies rushed to the side away from the Everett gunmen. *Verona* nearly capsized, a railing gave way, Wobblies went overboard, and the firing continued. Wyman hid behind the iron safe in the wheelhouse as shots crashed through. He backed away from the dock, his ship shot through and through, with blood from the injured men trickling down the side from the scuppers. Two Everett deputies died, and 16 were wounded. The Wobblies lost five men, with 31 wounded. Also, many who had gone overboard were never found. The union faded, but most of the reforms they fought for are accepted practices today.[11]

Another notorious captain was John Vanderhoef of the *Iola*. The propeller steamer was built in Big Skookum (Hammersley) Inlet and ran from Olympia to Seattle beginning in 1885. In 1895, Vanderhoef lost his wife overboard in Colvos Passage but did not notice she was missing until he reached Seattle. She was shaking out a tablecloth and fell overboard. He retraced his route and found she had drifted near shore, kept afloat by air trapped in her voluminous skirts. She was rescued by a shoreline dweller, Thomas Redding, who had heard her cries for help.[12]

Good shipyards and marine architects were sought after. Some were in urban centers like Crawford and Reid in Tacoma, of which it was said, "they seldom built an unlovely ship." Others were in tiny boatyards on secluded inlets.

Budd Inlet was home to several yards such as Ward's Shipyard (which was on the present site of the Port of Olympia), Sloan Shipyard, and Olympia Shipbuilding Company. In 1917, World War I

The 140-foot side-wheeler Eliza Anderson *began on the Olympia, Washington to Victoria, British Columbia run in 1859 and ran for many years. US Public Domain. (From* Marine History of the Pacific Northwest, *ed. H. W. McCurdy, US Public Domain)*

Thurston County - Water, Woods & Prairies

shipbuilding spawned an effort from the Olympia Shipbuilding Company on the Carlyon Fill to build schooners for the war. Sloan Shipyard later occupied the site.[13]

Docks helped bring commerce to Thurston County. In shallow Budd Inlet, clogged with the silt from the Deschutes River, docks were greatly important. Edward Giddings built a long wharf from the foot of Main Street (now Capitol Way) in 1854. John French and B. F. Brown built Brown's Wharf a mile north of town in 1875, for lumber schooners. Early businessman and sawmill owner Sam Percival built Percival Dock in 1860; it could accommodate shallow-draft steamers. To the west of Percival was Samuel Horr's Dock. In 1887, a 4,798-foot wharf was built by the city to reach deep water.[14]

Steamer routes radiated from Olympia to either side of Harstine Island, reaching Shelton, Allyn, Arcadia, and Kamilche. The Olympia main route ran through Dana Passage and north past Key Peninsula up East Passage to Tacoma and on to Seattle. There were dozens of small village stops along the way.[15]

Fast boats were characteristic of the period just before and after statehood in 1889. Famous among passengers and race fans were the *Bailey Gatzert, Sol G. Simpson, Capital City, Fleetwood, Greyhound, Willie, Mizpah, Magnolia,* and the *Virginias*. All these boats spent some time on runs from Olympia.[16] The City of Olympia has initiated a program to name its downtown alleys after these ships, and among others, the *T. J. Potter* and the *Bailey Gatzert* have been honored.[17]

The steamship Capital City *was a frequent Olympia-run stern-wheeler and could transport 300 passengers. Pictured here at Percival's Dock on Olympia's Budd Inlet, her route often included a popular stop at Boston Harbor near the inlet's mouth. Along with the S. G. Simpson, Bailey Gatzert, Mizpah, Fleetwood, and Greyhound, she was known as a "fast boat," and races for bragging rights to the "speediest boat" were common, ca. 1900. Photographer A. D. Rogers. AR-07809001-ph000947 (Courtesy of Washington State Archives–Digital Archives)*

46   Chapter 3 - Settlement, Steamers, and Statehood

The Mosquito Fleet gradually disappeared in the 1920s and 1930s, when highways and automobiles replaced water travel. *Virginia V* is a reminder of this remarkable mode of transportation.

Wreck masters were elected county officials from 1854 until 1914, in the 11 Washington counties bordering on salt water. Their duties included determining a wreck's salvage sale compensation, arranging for towing, repairs, safeguarding property, holding auctions for perishables, safeguarding crew and passengers, appraising property value, and bonding claimants.[18] Thurston County elected its share of wreck masters, including John Chapman, A. J. Littlejohn, George Foster and S. P. Wiman.[19]

The Naval Militia was another short-lived nautical phenomenon in Washington State. From 1910 until after World War I, four 200-man divisions were formed in Western Washington, drawing members from salt-water counties including Thurston. It was the Navy equivalent of the National Guard. Reserve and retired officers taught and commanded. One division was comprised only of Native Americans in the enlisted ranks. As the US entered WWI in 1917, the members of the Naval Militia were called to regular Navy positions afloat and ashore. Apparently, the perceived need for such a state group diminished after the war, and it was disbanded in the early 1920s.[20]

Tugboats and tall ships were two other vessel categories central to territorial and state nautical life. In 1880, 75 percent of cargo entering Puget Sound was aboard sailing ships. By 1910, that percentage had fallen to 25 percent. The opening of the Panama Canal and the Great Depression hastened the end of the sail era. For Thurston County, it was never prevalent, as the uncertain

The oldest commissioned warship afloat, USS Constitution *or "Old Ironsides" was named in 1812 for its strong live oak hull that seemed impervious to attack. It visited Olympia in June 1933 for nine days as part of a national three-year, three-coast tour. This cruise was a public "thank you" to all who, from 1925-1930, helped raise over $985,000 to restore the old ship. The two photos above are from the USS* Constitution *Collection. (Courtesy of Washington State Archives)*

Thurston County - Water, Woods & Prairies 47

winds of the Upper Sound required many sailing cargo ships to pay for a towboat to make the trip south of the Tacoma Narrows. Sailing ships to Thurston County was not economical, even in the late 1880s.

Tugs, on the other hand, were essential for log raft towing and other forms of nautical assistance. Major towing companies such as Foss and Crowley Marine still thrive on the Sound. Many of the Mosquito Fleet steamers ended their days converted to towboats and continued a useful nautical life. The *Sand Man*, over one hundred years old, is now owned by an Olympia foundation. It is an iconic reminder of towing enterprises on the Olympia waterfront.[21]

Steamboats Northern Light, City of Shelton *and* Multnomah *at Percival's Dock. The 120-foot* Northern Light *was designed for the Yukon gold rush, but rarely left Puget Sound. The 143-foot* Multnomah *was built in 1885 for the Willamette River in Oregon, and purchased in 1889 by Olympia's Willey family for the Olympia-Seattle run. Photographer A. D. Rogers. Subject date 1850-1920. State Library Photograph Collection, 1851-1990. AR-07809001-ph005121 (Courtesy of Washington State Archives—Digital Archives)*

OX-HOBBLES

When local ships along the shores of South Puget Sound delivered groceries and supplies, they did not have a clock-timed schedule. Delivery time depended on tides and weather.

People who did not live on the water built "ox-hobbles"—four posts covered by a roof in a small clearing where farmers left items to be picked up and where the boats left supplies. Sometimes families left their oxen for a day or so, wearing a rope or strap on their legs to keep them from running away. The farmers also used the ox-hobbles to pick up and leave items for families living along the boats' route.

Life was regulated by the tides. Calvin Saegar towed a raft behind his small boat with a shock of hay to sell in Olympia. As charter members of the Agate Grange located along the water, Calvin and Mary Saegar caught the tide to the Grange hall for meeting and socializing. If they missed the tide going home, they spent the night at the hall dancing or playing cards. They caught the morning tide home in time to milk the cows and do chores.

Even today the Washington State ferries operate by the tides.

Contributed by Sharon Mathews
Local Lore by a long time resident

48   Chapter 3 - Settlement, Steamers, and Statehood

1922 to the Present

The Port of Olympia was formed in 1922, developing Olympia and Thurston County into a shipping and transportation hub. Shipyards were active during World War II. Following the war, a mothballed fleet of ships anchored in Budd Inlet for several years. Most were "Liberty Ships," the EC2 (Emergency Construction) class of cargo ship mass-produced for the war effort. The port remains active in shipping cargoes to serve Joint Base Lewis McChord, various logging companies, and a variety of businesses. The oyster industry vessels and recreational boats are other maritime activities much in evidence today in Thurston County waters. County government has devoted much energy and resources to maintaining and improving water quality in county tidal waters.

Over a century old, Sand Man is moored in Olympia as a living example of the city's long relationship with commerce on South Puget Sound. Completely restored, she is open to the public. (Courtesy of the photographer Shirley Stirling)

Wheel of the Sand Man, at Percival Landing Park in Olympia, Washington. April 3, 2018. (Courtesy of the photographer Shirley Stirling)

KEEPING HISTORY AFLOAT

Striking examples of exceptions to the rule of scarcity among sailing vessels in South Sound are USS *Constitution* ("Old Ironsides"), the Japanese national sail training bark *Nippon Maru*, and the replica brig-rigged *Lady Washington*, one of American fur trader Robert Gray's two ships on our coast in 1792. The *Constitution* was escorted into Olympia harbor on June 11, 1933 on one of her many stops during a three-year tour of US ports which was a public "thank you" for the funds raised to keep her from being scrapped. The ship is the symbol of the start of American dominance of the seas and is still in commission in Boston. Her visit to Thurston County brought massive crowds of visitors to go aboard, many of them school children, whose pennies helped save the ship.

Nippon Maru visited Olympia harbor in 1989, during the State Centennial Tall Ship event, and her white hull and four masts drew thousands of visitors. Her captain was pleased, when making his formal call on Governor Booth Gardner, that the governor could point to *Nippon Maru's* home port on the world globe in his office.

Lady Washington was constructed at the time of the state's centennial celebration, in large part through the efforts of one of Washington's longest serving secretaries of state, Ralph Munro, who co-chaired the State Centennial Commission. She is home-ported in Grays Harbor and has starred in television and motion picture productions. She welcomes hundreds of school children aboard each year, and is a frequent visitor to Olympia.

Lady Washington *at Percival Landing. (Courtesy of photographer Mary Eldridge)*

THE SHIP THAT SANK THE GOVERNOR

The ship that sank the governor is still afloat. The MV *Olympus*, a former yacht and sometime naval patrol vessel, was purchased at auction by the State of Washington, the sole bidder. In 1946, Governor Monrad "Mon" Wallgren had learned from his good friend, fellow US Senator and future US President Harry S Truman, that the yacht would be declared surplus property by the Navy. Harry and Mon loved to fish together.

For $104,000 the ship was refitted and put on the books as a "fisheries patrol vessel." It was, in effect, the governor's yacht. Truman was aboard many times for informal visits and fishing expeditions.

The *Seattle Post-Intelligencer* ran an exposè and Wallgren lost his re-election bid to Arthur Langlie. Langlie then ordered the yacht sold in a rigged bid won by his highest campaign contributor, creating the first scandal of his new administration.[34]

MV Olympus is pictured for sale during the Langlie Administration, ca 1949. Governor Langlie Papers. (Courtesy of Washington State Archives)

Thurston County - Water, Woods & Prairies 51

The Deschutes River meets the salt water with a beautiful section of waterfalls at the southern tip of Puget Sound—the legendary Tumwater Falls. For the local tribes, who knew it as Tum-Chuck in Chinook trade jargon, it was a prime fishing spot and along the trail to Grays Harbor. For the British-owned Hudson's Bay Company who came later, Tumwater Falls became a transfer point connecting land and water travel.

The first Euro-American settlers chose to locate near the waterfall for its potential to build a water-powered gristmill and a sawmill. Founder Michael T. Simmons proposed the name "New Market," but it didn't stick, and instead the settlers chose the Native term meaning "loud or noisy water" and adapted it to "Tumwater." Don Trosper's ancestors crossed the continent on the Oregon Trail to carve out homes, farms, and communities. Trosper writes of the first Euro-American settlement in what is now Washington State and his ancestral home—Tumwater.

Chapter 4
EARLY DAYS IN TUMWATER
by Don Trosper

YOU CAN'T TALK ABOUT the history of Thurston County without highlighting Tumwater, the first permanent American community north of the Columbia River. The story of Tumwater begins with a close-knit group of friends and family residing in Clay County, Missouri, led by Michael T. Simmons with strong support and motivation from a highly respected older gentleman, George Bush. In the very early days of the Oregon Trail, the spring of 1844, Simmons, Bush, and their families and friends made a life-changing decision to sell most of their

Artistic interpretation of how George Bush (ca. 1779-1863) might have looked. Drawing by Samuel Patrick for the Los Angeles Times book, They Had a Dream *by Samuel James Patrick and George Reasons. E 18596 R4r 1969. Los Angeles Times Syndicate.*

possessions, pack the rest onto ox-drawn covered wagons, and join a larger wagon train traveling into the wild, untamed western wilderness.[1]

What could be the reasons for taking such a risk with their families? First were the economic reasons. Farming in Missouri was a difficult way to make a living, with the up and down crop prices, droughts, insects, harsh weather conditions and widespread disease along the Mississippi, Ohio, and Missouri rivers. The stories that the pioneers heard about the rich country and mild climate in the new land of the Oregon Territory sounded very good. Second, there were patriotic reasons to make the trip. The nation was competing with the British for control of the Oregon Territory. Another important reason for the trip was pre-Civil War racism in Missouri.

Michael T. Simmons (1814-1867). WSL Manuscript No. WSL-Ms. 134 (Courtesy of Washington State Library, Washington Rural Heritage project)

Scene below the middle falls of the Deschutes River in Tumwater, Washington, no date. (Courtesy of Olympia Tumwater Foundation)

The key member of their party, George Bush, was of mixed race, or part black.[2] His wife Isabella was white, so their children were of mixed race. They saw that increasing racism in the States was leading to real danger. The idea of going far west to the new country gave them hope that perhaps they could escape some of that.

The Simmons/Bush party completed the grueling seven-month trek through the Rockies and the Blue Mountains of Oregon, finally reaching The Dalles along the Columbia River on December 7, 1844. They were exhausted, hungry, and their clothes were in rags by the time they stopped to build rafts to take them down the rapids of the river (called "the Cascades") to the new settlements on the Willamette River, the south side of the Columbia. The British Hudson's Bay Company controlled the north side at their big trading post, Fort Vancouver, which was led by the Chief Factor, John McLoughlin.

While still at The Dalles, the Simmons/Bush party sent ahead a young scout to obtain needed supplies and information about what they could find there among the early American settlers.

His report was not good. The provisional government in Oregon City had passed an ordinance that anyone of color who tried to settle there would be punished with periodic whippings. After all the hardships of their trip, they hadn't escaped racism at all. They were in a quandary about what to do.

Family of Christopher Columbus Simmons, youngest son of Michael T. and Elizabeth Simmons. HHM403 (Courtesy of Henderson House Museum, City of Tumwater)

54   Chapter 4 - Early Days in Tumwater

The old Bush homestead, Bush Prairie, near the present-day Olympia Airport. HHM443 (Courtesy of Henderson House Museum, City of Tumwater)

They decided to approach the British. With John McLoughlin's permission, they spent the first winter on the northern side and worked for the Hudson's Bay Company to earn their keep. Their good character and difficult situation made an impression on McLoughlin, so much so that, in the spring, he allowed some of the men to explore north to Puget Sound.

Simmons and other men went in canoes down the Columbia and up the Cowlitz River to Cowlitz Landing, near the present-day town of Toledo in Lewis County. From there they took the native trading path overland to the lower falls of the Deschutes River where it flowed into the salt water of the Sound. Simmons saw that the waterfalls of the Deschutes completely fulfilled his vision for a new market using the water power of the river to run industry. They traveled back south, got a letter of reference from Dr. McLoughlin to Dr. William Tolmie at Fort Nisqually on Puget Sound and brought their families, animals, and possessions on the same journey the men had taken earlier. By that time, they had to endure the miserable mud and cold, wet weather of October. Simmons' wife, Elizabeth, said that of the entire trip over the Oregon Trail, this short extension, which was soon to take on the name Cowlitz Trail, was the worst part of their journey.[3]

With the help of Fort Nisqually and the local Indians, the families survived that first hard winter of 1845 and in the spring went out to stake their

The Reverend Ebenezer Hopkins, long time pastor of the old Tumwater Methodist Church, performing a wedding. HHM676 (Courtesy of Henderson House Museum, City of Tumwater)

Watercolor and India Ink impression of the Crosby Family House located at 702 Deschutes Way, Tumwater. (Courtesy of the artist, Shirley A. Stirling)

Modern day photo of the Nathaniel Crosby Family House, adjacent to the Tumwater Historical Park. This house, built in 1860, is operated as a living history museum by the Daughters of the Pioneers of Washington. HHM456 (Courtesy of Henderson House Museum, City of Tumwater)

Interior scene of the Crosby Family House, 1950-1990. AR-07809001-ph002200 (Courtesy of Washington State Archives–Digital Archives)

claims. Simmons claimed the area around the falls and quickly began to build the first gristmill, followed soon by a crude sawmill. He eventually sold his claim and opened a general store[4] in Olympia. He also was appointed to the position of Indian Agent for the area tribes. Simmons worked in the oyster industry for a time before moving to Lewis County to live out the rest of his life on a farm. The founder of Tumwater died November 15, 1867.[5]

Bush claimed a section of prairie land to the south. His farm, located at what is today the property surrounding the Olympia Airport, became very successful, and his farm was the first sign of civilization that settlers reached coming off the Cowlitz Trail. Bush helped those bedraggled settlers with loans of seed, food, tools, and advice, telling them, "Pay me back when your crops come in." He gained so much loyalty among the early pioneers that they successfully petitioned Congress for Bush to legally obtain ownership of his farm when the new territory split away from Oregon. A man of mixed race would not have otherwise been qualified to own land.[6]

The Simmons/Bush party opened the floodgates of Euro-American settlement in

56   Chapter 4 - Early Days in Tumwater

The Olympic Auto Camp, owned by Nate and Belle Trosper, was on the Old Pacific Highway, across from where Trosper Road meets today's Capitol Boulevard. HHM960 (Courtesy of Henderson House Museum, City of Tumwater)

Thurston County, arriving overland by wagon or around the tip of South America by ship.

Such was the case of the Crosby family. Clanrick and Nathaniel Crosby were ship captains who supplied Puget Sound settlers with goods. They both fell in love with the area and brought their families from New England. Buying out Simmons's claim, they were two of Tumwater's earliest business leaders. They built the Lincoln Flour Mill, sold land to other business owners, ran a general store, and built the Crosby House residence that still stands today.[7] Nathaniel Crosby's grandson was singer Bing Crosby.

One of the area's oldest churches was built in Tumwater by the Methodists who used the little church on Tumwater Hill as the home base for the circuit-riding preachers who traveled as far south as the Black River and Oakville on their rounds to serve their flocks. One of the first Tumwater school buildings was built near that church at the turn of the century. Many one-room schoolhouses operated all around the

Tumwater's "Long Bridge" (wagon bridge) and businesses at the waterfront estuary at high tide, ca. 1890s. HM041 (Courtesy of Henderson House Museum, City of Tumwater)

Thurston County - Water, Woods & Prairies 57

Tumwater area, including one on the Bush farm.[8]

Tumwater grew and became an officially incorporated town in 1869. Tumwater's Main Street became Deschutes Parkway. Nelson Barnes was elected by the board of trustees as president, called mayor today, of the young town.

The nearby town of Olympia was founded five years after Tumwater, in 1850. Due to better access to the deeper water of South Puget Sound, it became the commercial and political center of the area. Tumwater made an unsuccessful attempt to become the county seat and remained an industrial town due to the water that powered the grist and sawmills serving the growing population of the area.

By the end of the 1800s, the water of the Deschutes River transitioned into producing hydroelectric power to provide the modern wonder of electricity to Olympia and Tumwater. The first generating plant operated at the middle falls next to the Gelbach Flour Mill.[9] The electricity generated there also powered the streetcar line from Olympia all the way to Tumwater. Soon a

The Deschutes River lower falls electric power generating plant #2 of the Olympia Light and Power Company, 1906, Tumwater. 00003 (Courtesy of Olympia Tumwater Foundation)

Interior of the Deschutes River lower falls powerhouse, Tumwater, ca. 1915. AR-07809001-ph001329 (Courtesy of Washington State Archives–Digital Archives)

The streetcar that ran from downtown Olympia to the end of the line in Tumwater at the east end of the old Custer Way Bridge, today's Boston Street Bridge. Tumwater worked to attract visitors from Olympia to travel to the end of the streetcar line. Another such effort was the maintenance of Tumwater Park at the upper falls with penned elk, a bear pit, and swans as pictured on the cover of this volume. P41.73 (Courtesy of Olympia Tumwater Foundation)

Chapter 4 - Early Days in Tumwater

larger plant was built at the lower falls utilizing a large diameter metal pipe to bring the water from the upper falls all the way to the lower falls to generate more power. The concrete platform that tourists and visitors stand upon today to gaze at the beautiful falls is all that remains of that operation.[10]

In the 1950s Tumwater experienced one more river running through town. It was a river of concrete and traffic called a freeway. Interstate 5 was going to bypass Tumwater and Olympia, but business and political interests coaxed the final route to come by the Olympia Brewery through the center of old Tumwater and on past the State Capitol. Highway 101 from the west also intersected I-5 at Tumwater, giving travelers a view of the old brewery tower and the lower falls that first attracted those early founders of the historic community.

The history of Tumwater in the 20th Century was closely tied to its largest employer, the Olympia Brewing Company, and the Schmidt family. After the brewery was sold in 1983 and closed in 2003, the town predominantly became a bedroom community for the state capital next door. Modern landmarks like the Tyee Motor Inn, Southgate Shopping Center, and the Sunset Drive-In movie theater gave way to the new city hall, national and regional retail stores, expanded schools, housing developments, and industrial areas around the Olympia Airport and Mottman Industrial Park.

The City retains and builds upon its rich heritage with the development of: Tumwater Valley; the Olympia Tumwater Foundation's Tumwater Falls Park and Schmidt House; and the Tumwater Historic District which features Tumwater Historical Park, Crosby House, and Henderson House. Many state offices are now located in Tumwater. Street improvements, landscape improvements, and planning efforts have made the community both pleasant to live in and increasingly a good place to visit.

The Interstate 5 freeway in Tumwater and Olympia was completed in 1958. HHM649 (Courtesy of Henderson House Museum, City of Tumwater)

Beginning in the mid-1800s, Euro-Americans were magnetized by the West and drawn to stake out new homes in the wilderness. The movement known as Manifest Destiny was fueled by a desire to defeat the British claim to the Northwest, a yen for adventure, and a passion to own land. Few gave thought to the idea that the land they "owned" indeed was not theirs to take but the territory of Native peoples for whom the land provided sustenance. Europeans believed their destiny lay in establishing a worldwide presence. This is the story of the first Euro-American settlers in the lands that originally belonged to the tribal people of Thurston County.

Shanna Stevenson, Thurston County historian, tells of those who made their homes on the prairies as a result of the Donation Land Act of 1850. Their settlements created the basis not only for Thurston County but the State of Washington as well.

Chapter 5
CALL OF THE PRAIRIES
by Shanna Stevenson

BY THE EIGHTEEN FIFTIES, American settlers established towns at Tumwater and Olympia and claimed land on the prairies, along rivers and trails and the shores of Puget Sound. In January 1852, the Oregon Territorial Legislature designated Thurston County, which included most of what is now Western Washington, and in March 1853, Congress created Washington Territory. By autumn of 1853, the Territory's first census counted 996 non-Native American residents in Thurston County (which included much of what we now know as Grays Harbor County and all of Mason County).[1]

Settlement on the Prairies

The 1850s-era American pioneers gravitated to the prairies as well as fertile river bottom lands where they did not have to clear forested land to begin farming and stock raising.

Prairies were attractive because even close to downtown Olympia, pioneers found the deep woods foreboding. Mary Thompson Beatty recalled that in the mid-1850s, she and her husband David "took up a homestead of 160 acres on Ayers' Hill, joining Swan's donation claim. Mr. Beatty built a cabin on one side of a stream that flowed there then . . . but it was so lonesome and the trees were so formidable that the places were abandoned."[2]

Inspired by the journals of Lewis and Clark, Thomas M. Chambers determined to relocate his family to the Pacific Northwest. In April 1845, he set out from Missouri with his wife, Letitia, and their extended family in nine wagons with a herd of cattle and horses. By the autumn of that year, they arrived in the Oregon Country, south of the Columbia River.[3]

Coming north to Puget Sound in late 1847, sons Thomas and Andrew Chambers staked out adjoining land in the southern Puget Sound area east of Tumwater on what came to be known as "Chambers Prairie," establishing some of the

David and Elizabeth Chambers Farm, painted by Edward Lange in the 1890s. WSHS C2006.0.1 (Courtesy of Washington State Historical Society)

earliest farms in the region[4] on land the Native people called Kl-ko-minn or Ilcumen.[5] After living with other family members, in 1850, David and his wife, Elizabeth Harris Chambers, located on 640 acres east of Olympia along the road leading to Fort Steilacoom, the present site of Panorama in Lacey. Elizabeth Chambers recalled moving into a log house and later a frame house on the property.

"This was the home," she said, "for which we had endured the hardships of crossing the plains and the dangers of a frontier country."[6] In 1853, several families came to Thurston County by a new route, the Naches Pass, a trail originating in Walla Walla and going through the Cascades, rather than following the Columbia River. Members of the 1853 train included James and Virinda Longmire and their family, who set up a home on the Yelm Prairie; the Biles family in Tumwater; Catherine and Andrew Frazier at South Bay; the George Himes family at Hawks Prairie; and Asher and Matilda Sargent and E. Nelson Sarjent and Rebecca Sarjent (some say Sargent) who farmed on the prairies along Scatter Creek near Grand Mound.[7]

James Longmire later described seeing his new home: "Leaving my family in camp, I crossed the Nisqually River and went to Yelm Prairie, a beautiful spot, I thought. It lay before me covered with tall, waving grass, a pretty stream bordered with shrubs and tall trees flowing through. And, the majestic mountain which the Indians almost worshiped to which they gave the name Ta-ko-bed, [Ta-Ko-Bet] as it seemed standing guard over all in its snowy coat."[8]

Former Hudson's Bay Company employees and their Native American wives chose farms when the Company withdrew from the area after the 1846 boundary agreement. John and Betsy Edgar were near Yelm;[9] Thomas and Julia Glasgow along with Thomas and Mary Linklater occupied farms at Tenalquot near Rainier.[10]

At Hawk's Prairie, originally Tyrell's Prairie, Freeman Tyrell and his wife, Rebecca Davis Prince, and her large family occupied 640 acres in the early 1850s, at a place earlier used by the Hudson's Bay Company as an outstation for farming and logging. An early name for Long Lake was likely "Tyrell's Lake."[11] The Kladys and Phillips families joined the Tyrells, and in late 1853, Tyrus and Emeline Himes bought nearby land from Henry Fowler. John W. Hawk, a widower, married Sarah Stephens and they moved to the prairie in August 1855, giving the area its current name.[12]

Newcomers, including the Hicks, Pattison, Parsons, and Conner families, gravitated toward the county lakes. Jane Pattison recalled that in 1852,

> . . .with an ox team we came to Tumwater, or Newmarket as it was called then. Crosby's mill and store was about all that there was there. We swam the oxen across the Des Chutes River and went out on what was even then called Chambers Prairie, traveling through big woods all the way.
>
> David Chambers was living on the Chambers homestead and we took up our donation claims next to his. Pattison Lake was on our place and was named from my husband.[13]

Further east, along the road from Chambers Prairie to Yelm, the McMillan, White, Eaton, and Parsons families put down roots in an area which came to be called "Freedom."[14] Residents formed their own school district in 1854 and built a stockade, Fort Eaton, during the Puget Sound Indian War of 1855-56. Nathan Eaton and Lestina Himes married in 1872 and later built a sawmill and established a photography studio.[15]

Stephen Duley and Winiford Kelly Hicks Croghan Ruddell migrated to Chambers Prairie in 1852, with their extended families. They built a log home and enclosed a stockade during the Puget Sound Indian War, on what is now Ruddell Road. Active in local politics, Ruddell served as Territorial Assessor, County Commissioner, and in the Territorial Legislature. After the death of his wife, Ruddell married Margaret Stewart White, whose husband, William, died at Chambers Prairie in the Puget Sound Indian War. The Ruddells later moved to Olympia near the home of Margaret White's daughter, Ann Elizabeth Bigelow. These extended families intermarried with other pioneers including members of the Himes, Packwood, Fleetwood, and Phillips families.

Nathan Eaton's house, 4th of July 1871. Eaton married Lestina Z. Himes in 1872. As the area grew some families found homes around Lake Saint Clair—named in the 1880s—and farms prospered along Evergreen Valley. Freedom Hall, later Spurgeon Creek Grange, now a private store, was a community gathering place where Freedom Homemaker's Club met. In 1932, area families placed a marker at the site of Fort Eaton which still stands and was restored in 2003. WSHS C1954.483.8 (Courtesy of Washington State Historical Society)

Nathan Eaton, 1843. Eaton built a fort on his land. During the "Indian Uprising," he and his brother, Charles, enlisted in the Cayuse War. In the fall of 1848, he went to California with his brother to search for gold. He returned to Thurston County in 1849, establishing a land claim on what is now know as Eaton Prairie. He lived there until 1882, when he sold his land and moved to Elma where he died a year later. 2015.0.306 (Courtesy of Washington State Historical Society)

Charcoal drawing of Charles Eaton, pioneer who settled south of Bush Prairie, Thurston County. C1948.1192.1 B/ C1948.1192.1 (Courtesy of Washington State Historical Society)

Thurston County - Water, Woods & Prairies

Ticknor family at their home in Skookumchuck Valley, ca. 1880-1890. The house, where Elizabeth Ford Ticknor and Joe Ticknor raised their family, was built ca. 1857 near the Skookumchuck River. (Courtesy of Lola Ritter Bowen Stancil)

Eliza Jane and Urban East Hicks,[16] a son of Winiford Hicks Ruddell, joined the family migration of 1853, eventually giving Hicks Lake its name. (It was previously known as Wood's Lake and Rutledge Lake.) After the death of Eliza Jane, Urban Hicks married India Ann Hartsock from a nearby family. Hicks, who had worked as a printer in Hannibal and Paris, Missouri, became a newspaper publisher and held several territorial offices.[17]

W. O. Thompson, later known as "Black Lake Thompson," came to Black Lake in 1852. After working for the Bush family and securing supplies from Fort Nisqually, he built a cabin on the lake shore. Thompson recalled, "I cut out the trail between Bush Prairie and Black Lake and made a scow to ferry people and cattle across the lake from the Olympia trail, for the convenience of settlers who were going to Miami Prairie, Gate City, and Grand Mound."[18]

W. O. Thompson, early Black Lake settler, ca. 1860-1880. Listed on verso as "Barnes album, W. O. Thompson." Photographer George A. Harnish. AR-07809001-ph004442 (Courtesy of Washington State Archives—Digital Archives)

South County Settlement

South county prairies also attracted newcomers after long westward journeys. John Rogers James said, "In the fall of 1853 a good many emigrants settled all along the prairies and the valley of Scatter Creek, from the Chehalis River to beyond Scatter Creek and to the Skookumchuck Valley east of what is now Bucoda. The prairies afforded pasturage for their stock and an opportunity to get crops of grain and vegetables growing and cows to milking."[19]

J. T. Ticknor traveled to the Skookumchuck Valley from the California Gold Rush, living on land near Sidney and Nancy Ford, in present-day Lewis County. Ticknor met a Native American who called the Skookumchuck

64   Chapter 5 - Call of the Prairies

"Niscloten" or "the place where the smoke settles." He secured 600 acres with his partner Jeremiah Mabie and built a home of split cedar. Ticknor later married Elizabeth Ford, and they raised their family on the property known as "Ticknor Prairie."[21]

Alexander and Sarah Green Yantis and their large family came to the Skookumchuck Valley in the early 1850s, establishing a sizable farm. The many Yantis daughters recalled knitting socks and mittens for area bachelors—which they sold for as much as a dollar for a pair![22] Other Skookumchuck Valley pioneers were the Northcraft, Prince, Crowder, Gibson, and Miller families. Alexander Yantis's brother Benjamin, whose wife Ann Hall died on the Oregon Trail, arrived with his family of eight children and their families at Bush Prairie in 1852, and later moved to Olympia. Both Yantis brothers served in elective Territorial offices.[23]

Families drawn to Scatter Creek included Reese and Eliza Brewer, Ignatius Colvin, Abram and Sarah Tilley, and William Martin. Arriving in 1852, the Tilleys operated a hotel and stage station along the road from Cowlitz Landing to Olympia.

A great many of the pioneers remember the Tilley Hotel on Scatter Creek five miles from Tenino on the old Stage Road from Olympia to Monticello. The old pioneers as far south as the Columbia River made this place their headquarters going to and from Olympia and Tumwater. One unidentified pioneer wrote:

> The only flour mill and saw mill was [sic] located at Tumwater, and all the old timers was [sic] compelled to go there for their flour and lumber. Most all of the farmers from Puget Sound to Columbia [River] raised their own wheat in those days and would take it to Tumwater Mill to be ground into flour and feed.[24]

Leonard D. and Lucetta Durgin, natives of New Hampshire, filed a land claim in 1853 which included a 125-foot high mound. They considered naming it "Mount Vernon" but settled on "Grand Mound," where they built a two-story home which served as a meeting place, a school and postal station for the community.[25] Durgin, a member of the first Territorial legislature, advocated at one time that the state capital be located on the Mound.[26] The land they claimed as their own was traditional Upper Chehalis Indian territory.

Alexander N. "Saunie" Yantis and Sarah Green Yantis of Thurston County, ca. 1870-1890. WSHS C1980.30X.14.19 (Courtesy of Washington State Historical Society)

The James, Goodell, and Young families set up homes near Grand Mound. Samuel and Anna Maria James, originally from Cornwall, England, came to the area in 1852 with their large family. Anna Maria, writing to her sister in Wisconsin in 1852, praised their prairie home, (writing before Washington was a separate territory from Oregon) "... the Chehalis is one of the most beautiful rivers in Oregon. Our claim stretches a mile along the banks of it, it flows through an elevated part of the country and our house though within a few rods of the river has one of the finest views in Oregon."[27]

In the fertile river bottom land along the Black River, were the Shotwells, Dodges, and brothers

Thurston County - Water, Woods & Prairies   65

Tintype of the James family at Grand Mound, 1871; seated L-R: Cornellia Saccoon James, Anna Maria James holding granddaughter Elizabeth, and Clara Minnie Hell James 2d. Standing L-R: Mary Ann Frances James, little Anna Maria James, Jon Rogers James, Richard Oregon James, Samuel James 2d, Eliza James, and William James. Boys include Arthur, Samuel David, and Thomas James. (Courtesy of David James Family Collection)

Thomas and George Washington Rutledge. After arriving in 1852, Robert and Susan Waddell claimed 320 acres near the creek of the same name.[28] Bruce Dodge came to Mima Prairie in 1853, eventually owning over 2,200 acres, including part of the James Canby Donation Claim. He married Mary Shaser; later as a widower, he married Ada Marcy, and together they reared a large family. The Dodges had extensive herds of cattle and sheep and later supplied food for the Bordeaux Logging Camp.[29] They gave their name to "Dodge Prairie," another name for Mima, called *Sat-sulth* by Native people—likely meaning the "land beyond."[30]

The James and Charlotte Smith McAllister family journeyed with the Simmons-Bush Party in 1846 and later settled at Nisqually in 1847. The family famously lived for a time in two large stumps on the property. Sarah McAllister Hartman recalled that her mother "…used the burned out roots for cupboards and closets and so we lived in them until fall."[31]

By 1852 McAllister and William P. Wells built a lumber mill at the junction of She Nah Nam and Squaquid creeks to supply lumber for the Puget Sound Agricultural Company, Fort Nisqually and local buildings.[32] James McAllister died in the Puget Sound Indian War in 1855, but the family continued to live on the claim.

McAllister's cousin, John Wesley McAllister with his wife Mary Jane Thomas McAllister, arrived at Nisqually in 1852, joining the Packwood, Shaser and Brail families. John and Mary occupied land near the springs which fed Medicine Creek.[33]

Communities were soon to blossom around the county as more pioneers arrived, and by 1880, Thurston County could boast a non-Native American population of 3,270.[34]

Charcoal drawing of Ada Dodge, wife of Robert Bruce Dodge, pioneer of Thurston County. C2016.0.176 (Courtesy of Washington State Historical Society)

James Longmire, pioneer of Thurston County. 1853 2015.0.282 (Courtesy of Washington State Historical Society)

Virinda Longmire, wife of James Longmire, pioneer of Thurston County. 1853 015.0.283 (Courtesy of Washington State Historical Society)

NANCY JIM PARSONS

Nancy Parsons (ca. 1871-1918), photo taken ca. 1910. Photo gift from Del McBride (Courtesy of Lacey Museum)
Baskets of Nancy Parsons, photos taken 2018. (Courtesy of the photographer Jack Curtright)

68   Chapter 5 - Call of the Prairies

THE BASKETRY OF NANCY PARSONS

Around the South Puget Sound region in 1871, the year Nancy Jim was born, a number of Indian women skilled in the making of traditional native basketry worked their craft.

The three basic basket types were: 1) the simple, plaited work of cedar bark strips, used for storage and carrying items; 2) the twining basket, of which the sturdy clam-gathering utility basket was the most common example; and 3) the coiled baskets fashioned of split-cedar roots. The coiled baskets were woven so tightly as to hold water. They were essential as a berry-picking container and were used in the ancient method of boiling food by dropping hot stones in liquid. They were also an aesthetic object, a symbol of personal wealth as the tightly woven surface gave an opportunity to display a great variety of stylized, abstract designs, rendered in strips of shiny bear grass or other materials, both natural and dyed, in a complicated technique called imbrication.

For a Salish girl, instruction in basketry started early in life, under the tutelage of an older female, usually the grandmother or a great-aunt. By early adolescence, those who proved proficient were encouraged to devote much of their time to gathering and preparing raw materials, as well as actual weaving.

By the time of her marriage in 1892 at Nisqually Reservation to John Parsons, Nancy already excelled in the making of coiled baskets, ranging from miniatures to the large and impressive berry baskets. Collectors were quite ready to trade for, or buy, her productions. Her superb artistry and originality of design became widely known. Among those who cherished her baskets was Catherine McLeod Mounts, the half-blood Indian wife of a prosperous Nisqually Valley farmer; the Mounts collection is now part of the Washington State Historical Society collections.

Nancy Jim Parsons' life was cut short by illness in her 46th year, and we read of her obituary in the March 19, 1918, issue of the *Morning Olympian*. By the time of her death, most of the old traditional basket-makers had passed on, materials were harder to gather with more land in private ownership, and such imported materials as raffia were replacing native roots, bark, and grasses. All of which makes her surviving work even more unique and valuable as a reminder of an ethnic tradition which had survived for many centuries among the Nisqually and allied tribes of our area.

Compiled by Delbert McBride (1920-1998) and used with permission. McBride was a noted artist and historian. He served as Curator at the Washington State Capital Museum in Olympia from 1966 to 1982.

The land north of the Columbia River was originally part of the Oregon Country, stretching as far north as Sitka, Alaska. As the wave of pioneers spread, the need for a local system of government became apparent. Thurston County came into existence before Washington was a state or even a territory. The formation of Thurston County and the man for whom it is named laid the cornerstone of Washington's capital county, as told by historian Shanna Stevenson in "A New County and a New Territory."

Chapter 6
A NEW COUNTY AND A NEW TERRITORY
by Shanna Stevenson

AS EARLY AS 1792, American and British explorers vied for control of the Oregon Country, where fur-trading companies from both countries set up posts. Although the parties engaged in diplomacy over the area after the War of 1812, no decision was made on a political division. In 1818, the US and Great Britain reached a joint occupation treaty, continued in 1827.[1] By the 1830s, the British Hudson's Bay Company managed outposts near and in present-day Thurston County and Washington State. In the 1840s, Americans streamed into Oregon's Willamette Valley and held a series of meetings to create a governmental structure.

By 1843, this loose structure became a Provisional Government in the Oregon Country, but it was little concerned with the area north of the Columbia River where few new emigrants lived.[2] Two governmental districts—Tualatin (or Tuality) and Clackamas—divided the whole area, which reached northward into what is now Canada at the 59th parallel. The boundary between the two districts bisected in what is now Thurston County.[3]

With the arrival of the Simmons-Bush Party in 1845, and other emigrants in the following years, the government of "Northern Oregon" received more attention. In 1845, the Provisional Government created a political division called the "District of Vancouver" north of the Columbia River. In December 1845, the Provisional Government carved Lewis County out of the District encompassing all of the land north of the Columbia River and west of the Cowlitz River. "Vancouver" remained the name of the eastern area until 1849, when it became Clark County.[4]

In 1846, the US and British governments reached a boundary settlement at the 49th parallel, today's border with Canada. By 1848, Oregon was officially a US Territory encompassing all of Lewis County, the predecessor of Thurston County.[5]

Americans in the future Thurston County formed political groups, often opposing the Hudson's Bay Company. In 1848, locals met at Tumwater to voice grievances against Fort Nisqually Chief Trader William Tolmie and to file a protest, maintaining that the Hudson's Bay Company's wild Spanish cattle crossed the Nisqually River, menacing the American stock and grazing on American settlers' lands.[6]

At an Olympia celebration on July 4, 1851, J. B. Chapman advocated for a separate territory from Oregon. Afterwards, a group called a convention at Cowlitz Landing (near present-day Toledo, Washington) to discuss a new territory.[7]

Daniel R. Bigelow, pioneer lawyer and politician, Olympia, Washington 1880-1905. State Library Photograph Collection, 1851-1990. AR-07809001-ph004166 (Courtesy of Washington State Archives—Digital Archives)

SAMUEL ROYAL THURSTON

Although he was never in the area, Samuel Royal Thurston influenced the history of Thurston County. A native of Maine, born in 1816, Thurston was an extraordinarily well-educated man for his time. He attended Maine Wesleyan Seminary, Dartmouth and, in 1843, graduated from Bowdoin College. After reading law, he joined the Maine bar in 1844, and the next year migrated to Iowa, where he practiced law and edited a newspaper.

Thurston arrived in Oregon in 1847, where he set up a law practice and later served in the assembly of the Oregon Provisional government. When Oregon Territory was created in 1848, voters elected Thurston as the first delegate to the US Congress. Oregon Territory encompassed what is now Oregon, Washington (including Thurston County), Idaho, and parts of Montana and Wyoming to the summit of the Rocky Mountains.

As a territorial delegate, Thurston was not allowed to vote but could lobby and present bills and speeches before Congress. Thurston advocated for the 1850 Donation Land Claim law which granted substantial land to settlers in Oregon Territory. He supported measures to extinguish Indian land claims through treaties and worked to create a Superintendent of Indian Affairs and a Surveyor General for Oregon. He helped set up mail routes and post offices with a uniform postal rate for the Territory.

Thurston backed bills for a Pacific coastal survey and provisions for lighthouses and navigational aids as well as a Customs District of Puget Sound, established in February 1851, with Olympia as a Port of Entry. He secured more than $190,000 in appropriations for Oregon and procured a pension agency for 1812 War veterans, many of whom settled in the Territory. Sometimes controversial, Thurston was an adamant foe of the Hudson's Bay Company and former Hudson's Bay Company Chief Factor John McLoughlin.

On his homeward voyage across the Isthmus of Panama, Thurston died on April 9, 1851, only a few days short of his 35th birthday. He was aboard the steamer *California* eight days out of Panama and near Acapulco where he was buried. Thurston was re-interred in Salem, Oregon, in 1853. In 1991, the Thurston County Historic Commission placed a special foot stone at his grave site, commemorating him as the eponym of Thurston County.[20]

Samuel Royal Thurston, American pioneer, lawyer, and politician. He was Oregon Territory's first territorial delegate to the 1850 United States Congress. Photography studio, Colmer, Montagu, and Charles Erskine Scott Wood. History of the Bench and Bar of Oregon. Bancpic 1905.00002–POR (Courtesy of Bancroft Library, UC Berkeley)

Twenty-six delegates, including members from Tumwater and Olympia, met at the Cowlitz Convention in August 1851, to propose a new county be formed and produce a Memorial to Congress for a separate Territory.[8] The Memorial was a 1,500-word document, over five handwritten legal pages long, listing the problems facing settlers north of the Columbia River and proposing 12 counties. On December 1, 1851, Olympians signed a petition to the Oregon Territorial Legislature to create a new county out of Lewis County, with the county seat at Olympia.[9]

The Oregon legislature acted quickly on the petition. The House created a new entity, "Simmons County," on December 17, 1851, to honor pioneers Michael T. and Elizabeth Simmons. The Oregon Council considered the bill on January 12, 1852, but Asa Lawrence, a Maine native, made a motion to change the name to "Thurston." The bill passed as amended, officially creating Thurston County, to honor Samuel Thurston who had died the previous year. With the first precincts at Olympia and Steilacoom, the first Board of County Commissioners (called County Judges), A. A. Denny, S. S. Ford, and David Shelton, met July 5, 1852, in Olympia.[10]

On July 4, 1852, townspeople gathered in Olympia to hear yet another plea for a separate territory from Oregon, this time from attorney Daniel R. Bigelow.[11] Agitation increased with Olympia's newspaper as a forum for the rhetoric. Many wanted the Territory to be called "Columbia."[12]

Acting on a petition to establish a permanent location, the Oregon Territorial Legislature named Olympia as the county seat of Thurston County on December 22, 1852.[13] Over its long history, only

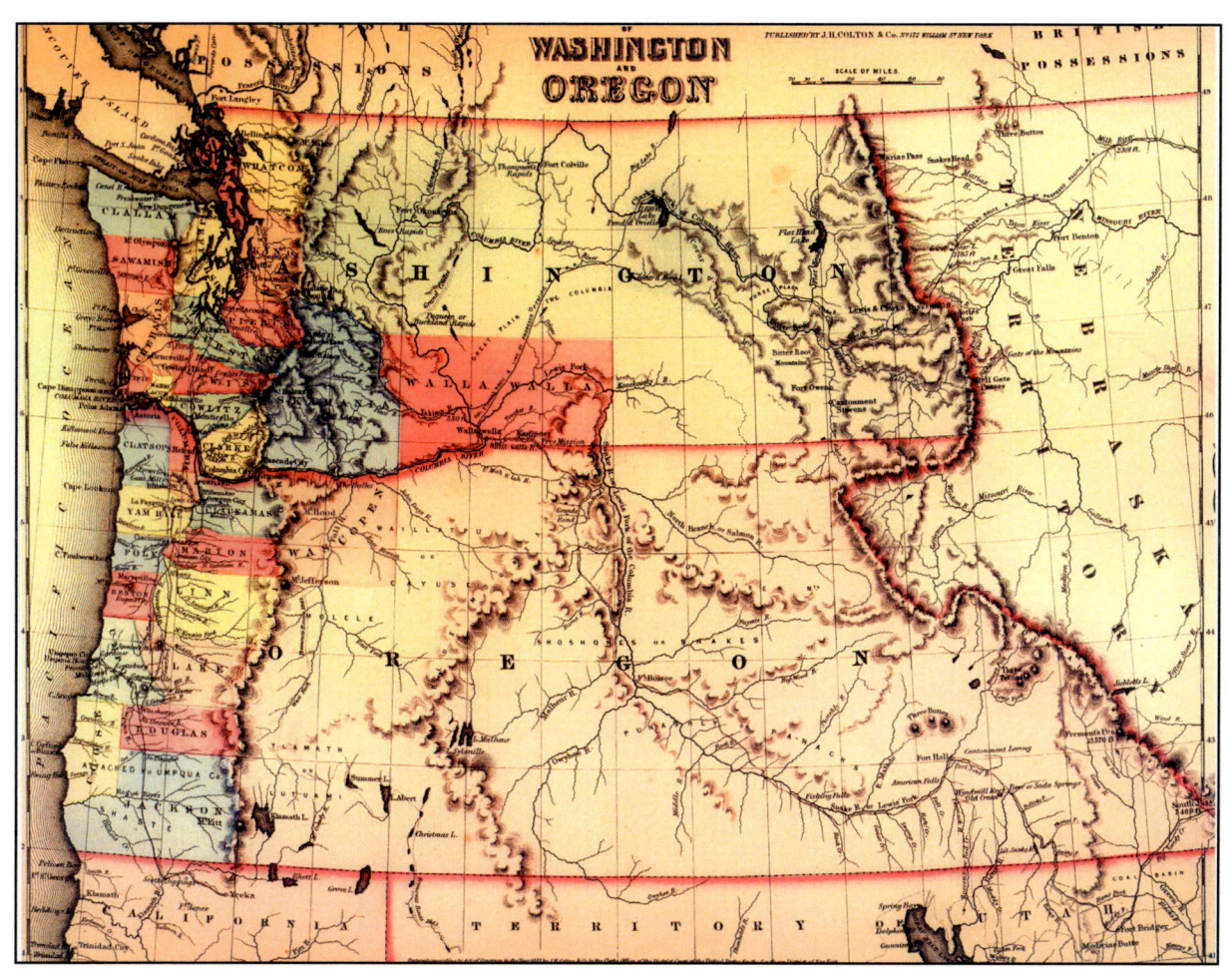

1853 map of the Oregon and Washington Territories with counties, mountain ranges, and other features marked. General Map Collection, 1851-2005. AR-270-B-000A49 (Courtesy of Washington State Archives–Digital Archives)

Thurston County - Water, Woods & Prairies

1927 dedication ceremony of a sign at the site of the November 1852 Monticello Convention and the historic black walnut tree planted circa 1852 in honor of the petition to divide Oregon Territory along the Columbia River. The sign said, "74 Years Ago on This Spot 44 Pioneers Petitioned Congress for Division of Oregon Territory and Organization of Washington Territory. Proper Recognition is to be Made... Daughters of the American Revolution." The site was on the H. D. Huntington farm in historic Monticello, between Marine View Drive and railroad tracks at 100 Tenant Way, near present-day Longview, Washington. This site was listed on the National Register of Historic Places in 1976 and on a local historic register in 2003. The 1927 sign was washed away by a flood and replaced in 2006 (though with different wording) by the Mary Richardson Walker Chapter, Daughters of the American Revolution. The historic tree survived the 1867 flood that destroyed Monticello, the 1962 Columbus Day storm, and damage by vandals who cut off large limbs. State Library Photograph Collection, 1851-1990. AR-07809001-ph005230 (Courtesy of Washington State Archives—Digital Archives)

Tumwater and West Olympia challenged the city's title in 1861, but Olympia prevailed.[14]

Following another petition, Oregon Congressional Delegate Joseph Lane introduced a congressional bill in December 1852,[15] for a new territory; the bill passed March 2, 1853, with the name changed to "Washington" from the earlier "Columbia."[16]

After the creation of Washington, new Territorial Governor Isaac Stevens arrived in Olympia in November 1853.[17] Stevens returned to the East and came back to Olympia with his wife Margaret and their children the next year.[18] Stevens likely had heard of Olympia in Washington, DC, and wanted the services of a newspaper printing plant to assist in setting up the first government for Washington. He established a temporary Territorial Capital at Olympia in 1853, made permanent in 1855. Olympia has been the capital city of Washington through the entire Territorial and State period, although tested at various times by Vancouver, Tacoma, and Ellensburg.[19]

Chapter 6 - A New County and a New Territory

Thurston County Courthouse 1889-1892. The first Thurston County Superior Court, after statehood in 1889, met in this building. Located at the northwest corner of Sixth Avenue (now Legion Way) and Franklin Street, it had served as the County Territorial Courthouse beginning in the 1870s. The building, originally a school, was remodeled in the mid-1870s with the second floor serving as a courtroom until 1892, when the county finished building a new facility. This building later housed the Daily Olympian *newspaper but was razed in the early twentieth century. In the 1920s a concrete building was erected at the site which became Selden's Home Furnishings. Susan Parish Photograph Collection, 1889-1990. (Courtesy of Washington State Archives)*

Thurston County Courthouse, ca. 1897. The first Thurston County Courthouse, built in 1892, is an outstanding example of the Richardsonian Romanesque style, popular at the time for public buildings. Thurston County occupied the building just east of Sylvester Park until it was sold to the state in 1901 for a state capitol building. The state added an east wing. Gutted by fire in 1928, the clock tower was removed, and the building was further damaged in the 1949 earthquake. Renovated in the early 1980s, the "Old Capitol" now houses the Superintendent of Public Instruction. General Subjects Photograph Collection, 1845-2005 AR-28001001-ph000530 (Courtesy of Washington State Archives–Digital Archives)

Thurston County - Water, Woods & Prairies

1851 Petition to Form Thurston County

1851 Petition to the Oregon Territorial Assembly to form Thurston County. Page 1 of 2. (Courtesy of Oregon State Archives)

Page 1 narrative:
669 To the Honorable the General Assembly of the Territory of Oregon in Session.

The undersigned Citizens of Lewis County in the Territory of Oregon would most respectfully pray your honorable body to organize a county out of a portion of Lewis County including Budd's Inlet on Puget's Sound according to the boundaries as proposed and agreed upon in convention at the Cowlitz on the 29th of August A.D. 1851. And would also pray your honorable body to establish the seat of Justice of said County at Olympia. We would also most earnestly remonstrate against any petition or petitions that may be presented to your body praying for any portion of said boundaries being changed. And we in duty bound will ever pray.

Olympia
Dec. 1st 1851

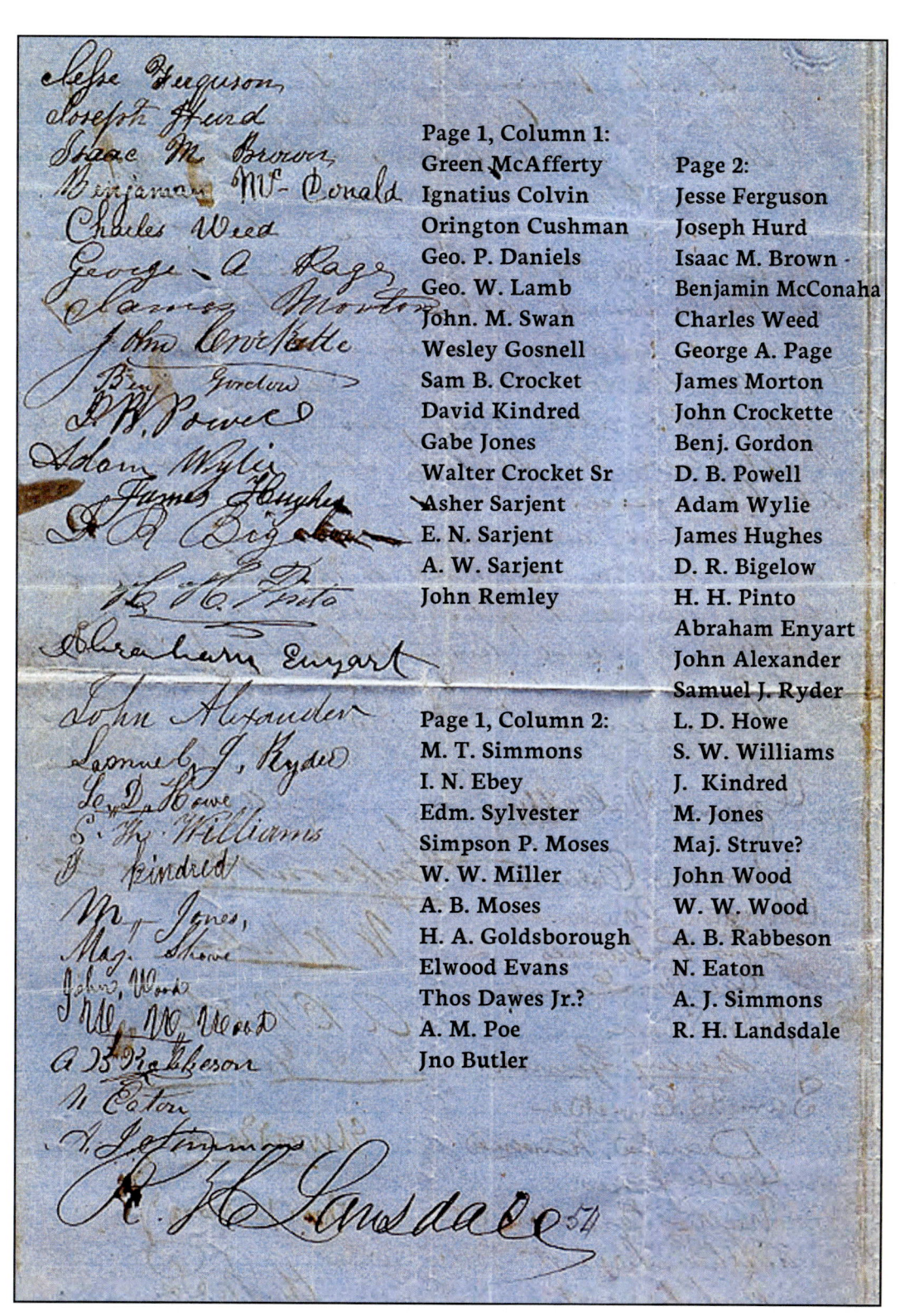

Page 1, Column 1:
Green McAfferty
Ignatius Colvin
Orington Cushman
Geo. P. Daniels
Geo. W. Lamb
John. M. Swan
Wesley Gosnell
Sam B. Crocket
David Kindred
Gabe Jones
Walter Crocket Sr
Asher Sarjent
E. N. Sarjent
A. W. Sarjent
John Remley

Page 1, Column 2:
M. T. Simmons
I. N. Ebey
Edm. Sylvester
Simpson P. Moses
W. W. Miller
A. B. Moses
H. A. Goldsborough
Elwood Evans
Thos Dawes Jr.?
A. M. Poe
Jno Butler

Page 2:
Jesse Ferguson
Joseph Hurd
Isaac M. Brown
Benjamin McConaha
Charles Weed
George A. Page
James Morton
John Crockette
Benj. Gordon
D. B. Powell
Adam Wylie
James Hughes
D. R. Bigelow
H. H. Pinto
Abraham Enyart
John Alexander
Samuel J. Ryder
L. D. Howe
S. W. Williams
J. Kindred
M. Jones
Maj. Struve?
John Wood
W. W. Wood
A. B. Rabbeson
N. Eaton
A. J. Simmons
R. H. Landsdale

1851 Petition to the Oregon Territorial Assembly to form Thurston County. Page 2 of 2. (Courtesy of Oregon State Archives)

Thurston County - Water, Woods & Prairies

Thurston County Courthouse 1902-1930. After the sale of the 1892 building to the State of Washington, Thurston County operated temporarily from the McKenny Block at 4th Avenue and Capitol Way. This courthouse was completed in 1902, at 4th Avenue and Washington Street. Featuring rusticated Tenino sandstone, it served as the Courthouse until 1930 and was razed in 1934. State Library Photograph Collection, 1851-1990. AR-07809001-ph001441 (Courtesy of Washington State Archives—Digital Archives)

Thurston County Courthouse, ca. 1930. The 1930 Thurston County Courthouse, built in an Art Moderne style, stands at 11th Avenue and Capitol Way. The building boasts Alaskan marble on the interior and a Tenino sandstone exterior. Vacant for several years, it was renovated in 1991 for offices. Photographer Merle Junk. Susan Parish Photograph Collection, 1889-1990. AR-25501080-ph001039 (Courtesy of Washington State Archives—Digital Archives)

MARJ PIERSON YUNG

Marj Pierson Yung (1935-2016) grew up in Eastern Oregon and became a nurse, attending Good Samaritan Hospital School of Nursing in Portland, Oregon. She and her husband, Vance, moved to Olympia in the late 1960s. She was soon active in local organizations and issues in Thurston County, including serving as a County Planning Commissioner and member of other advisory groups.

Active in the League of Women Voters, Yung worked on planning, parks, and shoreline management issues. She was elected as the first woman Thurston County Commissioner in 1974. In that same year she graduated from The Evergreen State College. As an Evergreen student, she worked with a team on an environmental assessment and proposed plan for the establishment of the county's Burfoot Park.

As a County Commissioner, Yung worked to modernize county government including hiring the first county administrator, merging road districts, and creating professional level services. She advocated for inter-jurisdictional coordination and helped establish 911 services as well as comprehensive planning and zoning for the county.

Yung also was an artist, author and poet. Remembered as quick-witted and warm, she paved the way for other women to serve as commissioners for the county.

"Marj Yung For County Commissioner Democrat" brochure cover when she ran for the office of Thurston County Commissioner. (Courtesy of a private collection)

Thurston County - Water, Woods & Prairies

Prior to the formation of Washington Territory in 1853, Olympia earned early recognition with the first post office in 1850 and the first Port of Entry for goods and services on 1851. Along with Tumwater (discussed in Chapter 4), it was prominent in the county. In the chapter "From Settlements to Cities," Shanna Stevenson writes of the noteworthy citizens who developed the capital city, along with the histories of other incorporated cities, Lacey, Tenino, Yelm, Bucoda, and Rainier. Each incorporated town started with a unique spirit that defines it in contemporary times.

Chapter 7
FROM SETTLEMENTS TO CITIES
by Shanna Stevenson

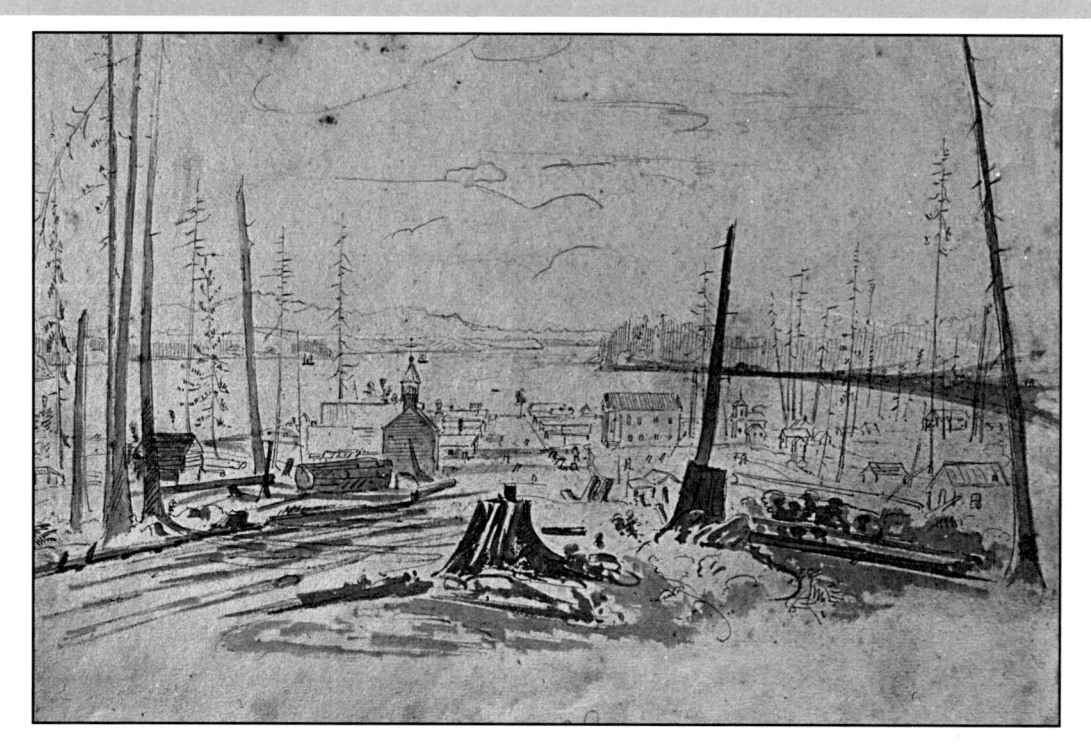

Olympia, Washington Territory, in 1857 by James M. Alden. One of the earliest views of Olympia looking north toward the waterfront. WSHS 1932.93.17 (Washington State Historical Society)

BANDS FROM THE COASTAL

Salish Indian people were the original inhabitants of the Olympia area. Ethnologist T. T. Waterman recorded a village site in what is now downtown Olympia, named "frequented by black bears" or "black-bear place." Euro-Americans anglicized the term to Schict-woot or Cheet-woot, meaning "place of the bear." A later Indian name, after Euro-American settlement, was "splicing two things together," anglicized to Steh-chass.[1] According to early accounts, Native people continued to live in several locations around Olympia after Euro-American settlement, including just west of what is now 4th Avenue and Columbia Street, continuing their traditions including the harvesting of shellfish.[2]

City of Olympia

In 1845, Edmund Sylvester, a Maine native, and Levi Lathrop Smith, originally from New York, migrated to the area. Sylvester chose land on the edge of Chambers Prairie, as described in Chapter 4, but Smith settled near Olympia's waterfront.[3] Smith was a delegate to the 1848 Oregon Provisional Legislature but died in August. He drowned after falling out of a canoe, apparently due to a seizure. Sylvester inherited Smith's land claim.[4]

Sylvester, lured to the California gold rush in 1849, returned to Olympia in January 1850, and officially platted the town. Olympia was named after the Olympic Mountains that form the background to the north.[5] John Swan, an 1849 newcomer, gave his name

THE BIGELOW FAMILY

In 1851, Daniel Richardson Bigelow, a Harvard-educated attorney, originally from New York, traveled over the Oregon Trail to Portland and came north to Olympia on the steamer *Exact*. He filed a land claim and set up a law practice. An advocate for a separate territory from Oregon in 1852, he was a member of the first Washington Territorial Legislature in 1854, and held a number of other elective offices for the county and territory. Also in 1854, Bigelow married fellow 1851 Oregon Trail veteran Ann Elizabeth White. She is remembered as one of the county's first teachers, having taught at the Packwood farm on the Nisqually River in 1853.

The Bigelows lived in a cabin on their land before they built a Gothic Revival house overlooking East Bay in Olympia, completed by 1860, which still stands. Founders of the Methodist Episcopal Church in Olympia, Daniel and Ann Elizabeth Bigelow reared a large family while actively promoting public education, rights for non-whites, woman suffrage, and temperance. They hosted noted suffragist Susan B. Anthony at their house in 1871.[6] Daniel died in 1905, and Ann in 1926. A non-profit organization acquired the house in 1993, and Bigelow descendants continued to live there until 2005. The house is now operated as a museum by the Olympia Historical Society and Bigelow House Museum.

Daniel and Ann Elizabeth White Bigelow at their wedding in 1854. (Courtesy of Olympia Historical Society and Bigelow House Museum)

Bigelow House in Olympia, ca. 1866. BH1866 (Courtesy of Olympia Historical Society and Bigelow House Museum)

to the east side of Olympia, "Swantown," before bridges connected it with downtown Olympia. West Olympia bore the name "Marshville" for Edwin Marsh. Easterners who came to the new town included lawyers Elwood Evans, Quincy Brooks, and Daniel Richardson Bigelow.

By order of Postmaster Michael T. Simmons, the US Postal Service established a post office named "Nesqually" on January 8, 1850. Interestingly, the Nesqually and Vancouver post offices were established the same day, and a mail route started between them. They were the first two post offices in what is now Washington State. On August 28, 1850, Simmons renamed the post office "Olympia."[7] Pioneer Phoebe Judson wrote of the vital role of the mail that often traveled for months to connect settlers with the East: "I can never forget how eagerly we grasped these messengers which comforted our hungry, lonely hearts informing us of the welfare of dear ones in the faraway homeland."[8]

The designation of Olympia as the first Port of Entry on Puget Sound gave the young settlement significant recognition. In 1851, Samuel Thurston, the county's eponym and Oregon Territorial Delegate to Congress, succeeded in establishing the title. Simpson Moses, who came with his wife Lizzie, and William Winlock Miller assumed federal customs duties in Olympia.[9] This designation, along with the post office, conferred official roots in Olympia. Additionally, the first newspaper north of the Columbia, appropriately named *The Columbian*, started printing in Olympia in September 1852.

In 1848, Catholic missionaries, the Oblates of Mary Immaculate, arrived in Olympia to minister to Indians. Led by Father Pascal Ricard, they first called their mission, just north of present-day Olympia, "Saint Joseph's of New Market." Father Ricard and three other priests cleared the forest, planted a large garden, and later built a chapel, a school for Indian boys, and a residence. During their 12-year stay on the site, the priests baptized Indians and helped build the new town of Olympia.[10]

After the mission officially closed in 1860, the land changed hands for several years until a group of Olympia citizens promoted the idea of a park.[11] The City of Olympia purchased the property in 1905, and it remains a favorite spot in the city—recalling its early history in the name of Priest Point Park.

Bettman Store between 4th and 5th on Main (now Capitol Way). Louis Bettman is on the left. WSHS C1982.18.30.12 (Courtesy of Washington State Historical Society)

"Chalet, Priest Point Park, Olympia, Wash." Postcard. (Courtesy of a private collection)

Thurston County - Water, Woods & Prairies

"Pine Tree" Washington Hotel in Olympia, 1858. The hotel was located on Main Street, later renamed Capitol Way. Pattison Collection 1996-011 (Courtesy of the Lacey Museum)

Michael T. Simmons and Charles Smith had a store at the corner of what is now Thurston Street and Capitol Way, but the Barnes Store, owned by George and Mary Ann Barnes, brought more general merchandise to patrons at their emporium on Thurston Street on the waterfront. Parker Colter & Co., A. J. Moses, L. Bettman, Goldman & Rosenblatt, and Louisson & Company owned other mercantile stores.[12]

Louis, Moses, and Sig Bettman opened their store in Olympia in 1853. Louis Bettman met and married Amalia Koblentzer in San Francisco in 1860. She described her first years in Olympia: The people in town then were like one big family. Every once in a while we would get together for an all-night dance. Everybody danced with everybody else. There were no cliques—nobody put on style, and everything was free and easy. My intimate friends among the pioneer women were Mrs. George [Georgiana] Blankenship, Mrs. [Kate] Rosenthal, Mrs. Chas. [Mary] Burmeister, Mrs. George [Mary Ann] Barnes and Mrs. Captain [Elizabeth] Doane.[13]

William and Sarah Cock built the Pacific House Hotel. Rebecca Howard, an African American woman, later owned and operated the establishment with the help of her husband Alexander. A crowd of settlers greeted the first Territorial Governor Isaac Stevens on November 26, 1853, at the "Pine

Olympia in the 1870s. 4th and Main which is now 4th and Capitol Way. WSHS C2013.18.85 (Courtesy of Washington State Historical Society)

84   Chapter 7 - From Settlements to Cities

PACIFIC RESTAURANT REBECCA HOWARD

PACIFIC RESTAURANT!

(FORMERLY PACIFIC HOUSE.)

OLYMPIA, - - - - - - - W.T.

THE undersigned having leased, for a number of years, the above well-known and deservedly popular house, wishes to inform the former patrons of the Restaurant, and the traveling community in general, that having

THOROUGHLY RENOVATED

the above establishment, and furnished the same with entirely new furniture from basement to garret, she is now prepared to entertain guests in greater comfort and in a more accommodating manner than can be done by any other house in the place.

The house will be kept on the restaurant principle,

MEALS AT ALL HOURS, DAY OR NIGHT!

A limited number can be accommodated with lodgings, good, clean beds, and well ventilated rooms.

Give her a call and assure yourselves of the truth of the above,

REBECCA HOWARD.

Olympia, May 16th, 1860. 26-m6.

Advertisement for Pacific Restaurant by Rebecca Howard from Pioneer and Democrat, *May 18, 1860, pg. 2. (Courtesy of Washington State Library)*

African American Rebecca Howard, an outstanding hotelier and cook, was one of Olympia's earliest businesswomen. Rebecca Groundage was born in 1827 in Philadelphia. She married Alexander Howard, a cooper, in New Bedford, Massachusetts, in 1843. By 1859, the Howards had moved to Olympia and opened a hotel and restaurant at Pacific House on Main Street (now Capitol Way). The Pacific House was recalled as the leading hotel on Puget Sound under "the ministration of Rebecca Howard, whose wit and humor...made the Pacific an oasis in the then desert of travel." Rebecca Howard died in 1881, and her husband in 1890.[14]

SISTERS OF PROVIDENCE IN OLYMPIA

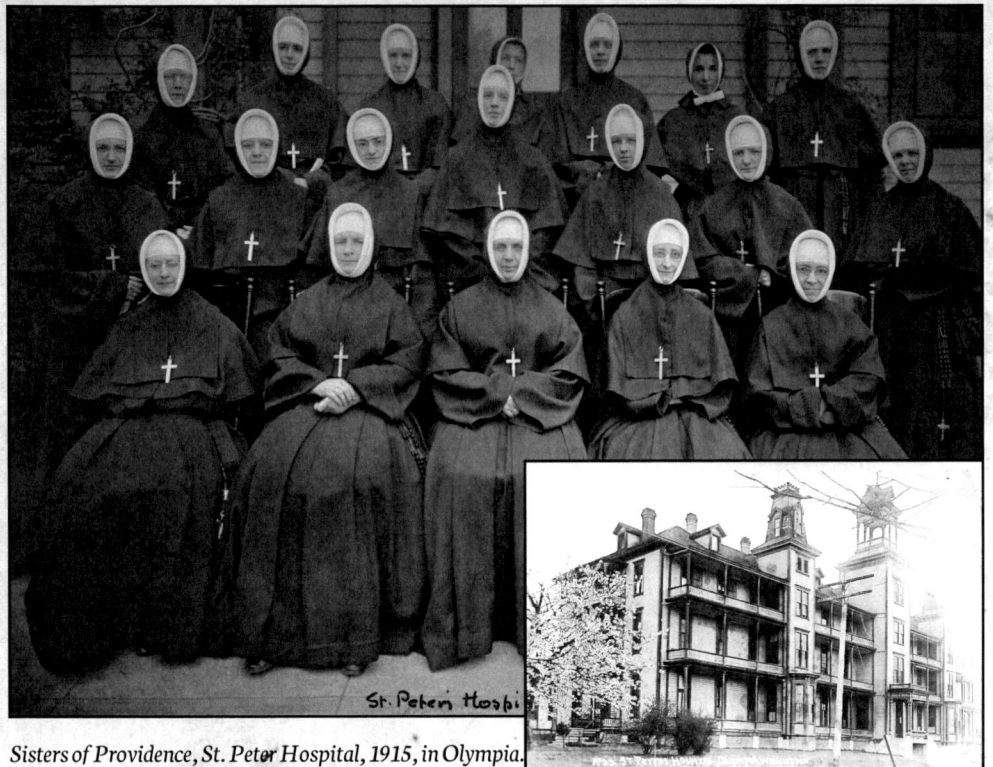

Sisters of Providence, St. Peter Hospital, 1915, in Olympia. 1915. 72.B5.1 (Courtesy of Providence Archives, Seattle)

St. Peter Hospital, postcard, undated. (Courtesy of a private collection)

The Daughters of Charity, Servants of the Poor, now known as Sisters of Providence, were organized in 1843 in French Canada. By 1881, they established a boarding school at Olympia known as Providence Saint Amable, later Providence Academy and then Saint Michael's School, which continues in Olympia.

To serve the many injured loggers and others, A. H. Chambers and other Olympians agreed to provide land if the sisters would construct a hospital. Built under the direction of Mother Joseph of the Sacred Heart, noted architect of the Northwest mission, St. Peter Hospital opened in 1887 on the present State Capitol Campus. The sisters went on "begging tours" to fund their work, but they also sold "billets" for prepaid medical care at area logging camps. So commodious was the hospital that legislators lodged there during sessions at the nearby wooden Capitol. St. Peter Hospital moved to West Olympia in the 1920s and to its present location in the early 1970s. Providence St. Peter Hospital, a regional medical center, is one of the largest employers in the area with several clinics around Thurston County.[15]

The inauguration of Governor Elisha Ferry at the old wooden Territorial Capitol building. Banner reads "E. P. Ferry, First in the hearts of the People." Inauguration of Governor Ferry Photographs, 1889. Photographer A. D. Rogers, 1889. AR-28001005-ph000001 (Courtesy of Washington State Archives–Digital Archives)

Tree" Washington Hotel on Main Street, which also hosted early legislators. Phoebe Goodell Judson wrote that Stevens surprised the residents, arriving in Olympia before he was expected: "However, they did not lose any time in apologies. On learning that this diminutive man in the rough garb was really the governor, they welcomed him with the usual demonstration, firing a salute and unfurling the stars and stripes to the breeze."[16]

Samuel and Lurana Percival sailed to Olympia in 1853 on the *Sarah Warren*. Percival took over the Kendall Company store, which he later owned, operated a sawmill, and built a steamboat dock. Lurana Percival recalled some of the American settlers in 1853, "At Tumwater were the Simmons, Crosby, Barnes, and Kindred families and Mr. and Mrs. R. M. Walker, also several families on the prairies beside the Chambers and Hays."[17] She recalled that in downtown "all along the beach were Indian huts, and the whole beach was lined with canoes."[18]

Several families established homes on the west side of Budd Inlet, including Benjamin and Mary Olney Brown; Washington and Charlotte Emily Olney French; and John French. Georgiana Blankenship noted, "Mr. Brown's next business venture was to build the historic wharf on the Westside in partnership with John French. At this wharf were unloaded all the freight that came to Olympia from San Francisco for years, until Capt. Percival built the dock which is in use at the present time [1914]. Here steamers loaded wood, which Mr. Brown had cut and hauled by the hundreds of cords from the timber in the immediate vicinity of the wharf."[19] Oscar Brown recalled that among the visitors to his parents' home was Ulysses S. Grant, then stationed at Fort Vancouver.[20]

After its official incorporation in 1859, Olympia extended new streets and services to the wooden Capitol.[21] By 1855, a wooden causeway connected the main peninsula of Olympia to Swantown, and by 1869, a bridge spanned Budd Inlet to Marshville, finally linking the downtown peninsula with the hillsides to the east and west.[22]

The city slowly developed as forests gave way to homes, churches, schools, and businesses. The area around Sylvester Park, designated in 1850 as the town square, became the hub of Olympia.

Olympia Grows Up

By 1889, when statehood was imminent, Olympians built a streetcar line, a water system, wooden sidewalks, and installed gas street lights. By 1910, the city had upgraded streets to macadam and brick and installed concrete sidewalks.[23]

In the winter of 1890, the first two horse-drawn streetcars were on Main Street (now Capitol Way)

Downtown street scene in Olympia, Washington with streetcar, ca. 1914, postcard. No 7. (Courtesy of a private collection)

Downtown street scene in Olympia, ca. 1930-1940, postcard. Photographer Ellis. Ellis1615 (Courtesy of a private collection)

between 4th and 13th Streets. Eventually electrified, streetcar service extended to both the east and west sides of the city, serving new residential areas.[24] Lumber processing became an important industry as loggers brought timber to the waterfront where mills transformed the logs into dimensional lumber. New prosperity spread through the city.

In 1889, statehood was granted by a presidential proclamation and, in 1890, confirmed by a vote. Olympia became the capital of the new State of Washington. The government offices remained in the 1850s-era wooden Capitol building south of the city. An effort in 1893 to build a more permanent structure failed because of difficult economic times and, as a result, many downtown buildings housed state offices.[25]

In 1901, the state acquired the 1890s-era Richardsonian Romanesque Thurston County Courthouse for the Capitol building and added an east wing to accommodate the legislative chambers.[26] Until 1928, state government in the downtown area created economic and civic vitality; downtown wooden storefronts were rebuilt into the more modern brick, stucco and concrete business blocks.

In 1894, the city began dredging and filling to expand the city's land mass and create a deepwater port. Efforts in the 1890s were near 4th Street and west side areas, but the most extensive dredging took place in 1910-1911. It was known as the "Carlyon Fill" after its organizer and promoter, P. H. Carlyon, who was also a mayor and state legislator. The fill added some 29 blocks of land when dredges moved two million cubic yards of mud from Budd Inlet

On Friday, April 13, 1949, a 6.7 scale earthquake struck the city, killing two people and damaging many downtown buildings, particularly those constructed of unreinforced masonry. In the aftermath of the earthquake and before the era of an historic preservation ethic, many of the city's landmarks were razed or modernized, altering the appearance of downtown. 2014.0.26 (Courtesy of Washington State Historical Society)

Olympia celebrated its 100th anniversary in 1950 with celebrations including a parade shown here near 5th Avenue and Capitol Way. The postcard is labeled "Olympia Centennial" and "Best," showing a truck themed "Bathing Beauties." (Courtesy of a private collection)

and deposited the spoil near the original downtown peninsula. Fill land provided industrial sites for the prospering mill industry north of downtown. Dredged land on West 4th Avenue supplanted earlier wooden causeways and docks. Downtown Olympia was finally joined to historical Swantown.[27]

Early Twentieth Century Olympia

With the completion of the Carlyon Fill in 1911, the northern peninsula of downtown was ready for re-development. Before the fill project, the area was the Tenderloin district where run-down mid-nineteenth century buildings housed gambling and prostitution activities until reformers from women's groups and politicians had them removed in the 1910s.[28] The Olympia Canning Company, along with lumber processing, and other resource-based industries rose on the new fill, served by a railroad spur.[29]

With the advent of the automobile era in the early twentieth century, Olympia became a hub of two major roadways—the Pacific and Olympic state highways. In 1921, a concrete 4th Avenue Bridge in Olympia connected the city with the west side for automobile traffic. (Extensively damaged in the 2001 Nisqually Earthquake, the bridge was replaced in 2004.)[30]

The 1920s saw ongoing prosperous times in the city. Olympia Veneer, started in 1922, and Washington Veneer, begun in 1925, were large, cooperatively-owned plywood mills. From the 1920s until their closure in the mid-1960s, the veneer mills fueled the city's economy with payrolls reaching over 1,000 people at the height of production.[31]

In 1922, voters created the Port of Olympia, a county-wide public port district to serve lumber processors, which, by that time, were producing 500 million board feet of lumber annually. As the northern neighbor of downtown, the port has changed focus with changing economies—from shipping of dimensional lumber to primarily logging shipments and, in recent years, to the redevelopment of waterfront property.[32]

After winning a nation-wide competition in 1911, Eastern architects Walter Wilder and Harry

White designed a group plan for a permanent Capitol which came to life at the site of the Territorial structure. The first building of the group, the Temple of Justice, rose in 1913, and by 1927, the legislature left the Old Capitol downtown to meet in the majestic new Legislative Building. Other offices relocated to the building in 1928.[33] In commemoration of the new State Capitol Campus, Main Street became Capitol Way in 1924, and all of the east-west thoroughfares were named avenues and those running north-south, streets.

Like the rest of the country, Olympia involved itself in World War II. Spotters perched atop the Legislative Building cupola looking for enemy aircraft which were reported to the nerve center at the Armory, east of downtown. P-38 aircraft from a training center at the Olympia Airport buzzed the city. Servicemen's families poured into the city as the population of nearby Fort Lewis increased. The city constructed a USO Club on the east side to accommodate the soldiers stationed nearby.[34]

By the late 1940s, the Wilder and White Plan for the campus reached completion along with the reflecting pool for the Capitol. Capitol Lake, begun in 1948 and completed in 1951, alleviated the unsightly mud flats at low tide adjacent to downtown by damming the Deschutes River. The lake eliminated the tidal flat shantytown known as "Little Hollywood" where houseboats were moored in unsanitary conditions.[35]

In the late 1950s, Interstate 5 sliced across the south part of the city. The route was created in part to change the traffic bottleneck at 4th Avenue and Capitol Way in downtown where all north-south and east-west traffic intersected.[36]

In 1978, a sizable westside Olympia mall opened, challenging the downtown commercial core when anchor department stores moved to the malls.[37] The city changed rapidly in the 1960s and 1970s with an increase in over 5,000 in population during the decade.[38] State government was growing while the lumber processing industries had almost disappeared from the fill area. Olympia created a new performing arts center in 1985 by rebuilding the historic Liberty Theater as a regional venue, The Washington Center for the Performing Arts.[39] Civic pride led to Olympia's designation as an All-America City in 1987.

After changing from a commission to a council form of government in 1982, the city added new amenities including a revitalized waterfront on East Bay, a boardwalk on the city's northwest edge, a Farmer's Market, and a new community center. Heritage Park, an initiative from the 1980s, enhanced the shores of Capitol Lake in the 1990s.[40]

The City of Olympia moved into its new City Hall in 2011, and on the site of former veneer mills, the Hands On Children's Museum opened in 2012 on East Bay. In the twenty-first century, Olympia anticipated new neighborhoods, parks, and downtown buildings including new landmark buildings on the State Capitol Campus.

City of Lacey[41]

Lacey's history extends to the ancestors of the present-day Nisqually Indian Tribe who were the first residents of the area including a band that lived at Chambers Prairie or "*Kl-ko-minn*" in the Native language."[42] They used the surrounding plains to gather camas and other seasonable foodstuffs, plentiful in the district.[43]

Multicultural employees from the Hudson's Bay Company settled on nearby Tyrell's Prairie and

Crowd gathered at the Lacey train depot. Undated. (Courtesy of Lacey Museum)

"Camp Jolly" at Offut Lake in Lacey, July 27, 1910. C2016.0.197 (Courtesy of Washington State Historical Society)

established Fort Nisqually in the 1830s.[44] Other early newcomers to the area were the Wood, Chambers, Hawk, Ruddell, and Himes families.[45]

An early area name recalls Isaac and Catherine Wood who, in 1852, established a land claim encompassing 320 acres around Hicks Lake, calling their farm "Wood Lawn," and the family dubbed the larger area "Woodland."[46] By 1890, J. M. Adams Acre Tracts became the town's first urban plat,[47] and *The Morning Olympian*, May 22, 1891, noted, "An exceedingly handsome railroad station has been erected by the Northern Pacific Company, which would do credit to a city."

The change from Woodland to Lacey took place over several years. Residents petitioned for a post office with the name Woodland, but their application was denied because there was another Woodland in Washington. The post office name Lacey became official in June of 1891.[48] The name Lacey is somewhat of a mystery, but it may be associated with local Justice of the Peace O. C. Lacey who was also a local realtor and lawyer.[49] By 1902, the train depot name was

Woodland Driving Park in Lacey was a horse racing track built in 1891, specifically for harness racing. In the background on the right is the Woodland Clubhouse, later renamed as Woodland Hotel. From the book Olympia published by Recorder Press, not dated. (Courtesy of a private collection)

Union Mills shingle workers in Lacey, ca. 1925. Bowker Collection. (Courtesy of Lacey Museum)

changed to Lacey and by 1908 the school's name was also changed to Lacey. By 1924, the voting precinct finally became known as Lacey instead of Woodland.[50]

Isaac Ellis, a local logger who owned 82 acres near the railway, opened Woodland Driving Park, a harness racing facility, in 1891. The track boasted barns and a clubhouse, later a hotel, in what is now the Clearbrook area. George Huggins purchased the track in 1907, used for various activities as late as the 1930s. The hotel remained in operation, but was razed in 1939.[51] The Order of Saint Benedict bought 571 acres in Lacey and by 1895 completed a new wood administration building for an abbey and school called Saint Martin's. A letter described the area in 1895: "The station is called Woodland, but the post office Lacey. The town has a freight depot, a candy store, a board[ing] house, three residences, and a large race track."[52]

In the late 1890s, Union Mills opened near Long Lake, employing many local residents including a number of Japanese-Americans. The mill burned in 1909 but the company rebuilt in 1910 as one of the first electric sawmills in the Northwest, producing dimensional lumber and other wood products. The firm first logged around Pattison Lake and floated logs through a canal connected to Long Lake. Later company timber sources were at Hogum Bay, South Bay, and in the south county. Trains dumped logs into Long Lake for storage before milling. After a fire at its timber source in Bucoda, the mill closed in 1925 and was dismantled.[53]

In 1915, reflecting the new popularity of the automobile, the Pacific Highway came through Lacey.

Dick's Place on Pattison Lake. Gwin Hicks Collection. (Courtesy of Lacey Museum)

92   Chapter 7 - From Settlements to Cities

View of the wooden Saint Martin's buildings, postcard. (Courtesy of a private collection)

Amenities such as the Foy Store,[54] complete with a gas station and post office, served the driving clientele. That same year, Mountain View Golf Course took over one of the pioneer Chambers family farmhouses, and by the early 1960s, the site was developed into a retirement community, Panorama City.[55]

During the 1920s and 1930s, automobiles brought visitors to the many lakes in Lacey where resorts had slides, docks, and bandstands at Lake Saint Clair, Hicks (Rutledge) Lake, Long Lake, Pattison Lake, and Southwick Lake.[56]

Community-minded women formed the Lacey Women's Club during the 1920s, which continues today.[57]

In 1913, Saint Martin's Abbey began replacing the first wooden college buildings, and by 1925, the majestic brick "Old Main" rose on the college hill.[58]

New developments at Tanglewilde and Thompson Place signaled changes for Lacey when the route of Interstate 5 through the city created new business opportunities in the late 1950s and early 1960s. Bob Blume developed the South Sound Shopping Center, which opened in 1966.[59] December 5, 1966 marked the incorporation of Lacey. The new Capital Pavilion at Saint Martin's (now Marcus Pavilion) also opened in the 1960s.[60] Lacey built a new City Hall in 1979, and the city opened a museum in the former City Hall and Fire Headquarters, originally the Russell House, in 1981.[61]

Into the new century Lacey has changed with new parks, a senior center, a transit center, and expanded suburban shopping. Saint Martin's University has added several new buildings, and South Puget Sound Community College opened a Lacey campus in 2016. Boasting a population of over 45,000 residents, many associated with nearby Joint Base Lewis-McChord, the City of Lacey celebrated its 50th anniversary of incorporation in 2016.

City of Tenino

Tenino was home to Coastal Salish Indian people who ranged widely on seasonal rounds to gather food. The name "Tenino" apparently is derived from

Labor Day parade in Tenino. Ivy Gilmore Wilson as Miss Liberty, ca. 1910. WSHS 1995.115.1.13 (Courtesy of Washington State Historical Society)

its location as a "meeting place," or "fork in the trail" for these people although other derivations are mentioned in some sources. The site was part of an overland trail used by American Indians and later by the Hudson's Bay Company as early as 1824.[62]

In 1852, Stephen and Deborah Hodgdon claimed land in Tenino, and others soon joined them, attracted to the area by open prairie farmland. By the 1860s, Hodgdon built a station on the stage route, and Tenino was known as "Hodgdon's Station."[63] The post office "Coal Bank" was less than a mile northeast of the current town in 1860.[64]

The Northern Pacific built a depot with the official name of "Tenino," permanently replacing the earlier names of Hodgdon's Station and Coal Bank. A hotel and store soon followed, and in 1873, Stephen Hodgdon and the Lake Superior and Puget Sound Land Company filed a plat for the town. By the following year, trains were regularly running through Tenino from the Columbia River to Tacoma.[65]

Quarries and lumber and shingle mills boosted Tenino's population and prosperity. In 1890, some businesses followed the relocated Northern Pacific depot near what is now 6th Avenue but eventually moved back to the Sussex Street area. By 1891, with a population of 335, the town boasted a school, hotels, four saloons, new business district, and newspaper. An economic downturn in the mid-1890s, termed the Panic of 1893, dampened Tenino's growth which returned by the turn of the twentieth century.[74]

In 1906, a devastating fire destroyed the entire south side of Sussex Street. Rebuilding began almost immediately. With the Tenino Stone Company quarry barely two blocks away, the town became a showplace for sandstone construction.

Tenino incorporated in 1906, perhaps to levy the $500 license fee on the six saloons operating at the time. The city suffered another fire in 1917, but by the 1920s, new businesses arose to serve increasing automobile traffic along Pacific Highway running through the heart of downtown.[75]

When Interstate 5 opened in the late 1950s,

"Street Scene Tenino, Wash." Photographer Ellis. Postcard. (Courtesy of a private collection)

TENINO RAILROAD HISTORY

by James S. Hannum, M.D.

Geography is the reason why Tenino has the richest railroad history of any community in Thurston County. The Northern Pacific Railroad built the first major rail line in Washington Territory, choosing to enter Tenino from the south in October 1872. The lay of the land near Tenino influenced that choice greatly. Relatively level grades could be achieved south and northeast of that place, whereas a path to the north, from Tenino toward Tumwater and Olympia, would have required trains to ascend a steep hill, so the Northern Pacific resumed track-laying in the spring of 1873, adopting a path through Rainier and Yelm, to tidewater at Tacoma.

With the completion of the Olympia & Tenino Railroad in 1878, a narrow-gauge line established the connection to Tumwater and West Olympia, as it was able to handle the heavy grade north of town. By 1890, it was rebuilt to standard-gauge as the Port Townsend Southern Railroad. Also, by that time, the local logging economy was in full swing. Blumauer Lumber Company, Mentzer Brothers, and the Harm & Brown Lumber Company all had their own logging railroads. The Jonas Spar & Lumber Company was another local employer. Part of the Blumauer railroad was used initially for mining coal at the Black Bear Mine, south of Tenino.

Spurs from the Northern Pacific and the Port Townsend Southern served the various stone quarries in

Billy Huston and Sol Blumauer with Chinese section gang, ca. 1883. Art Dwelley Collection. (Courtesy of Washington State Historical Society)

Tenino. In 1915, the Hercules Sandstone Company, in conjunction with the Skookum Railway & Logging Company, reopened much of the then-abandoned Blumauer Lumber Company railroad to remove stone from a quarry in the Bald Hills.

After beginning work at Tenino in 1912, the Northern Pacific finished the Point Defiance Line, a new, double-track mainline opened officially on December 15, 1914. The Northern Pacific built a new stone station on the line, west of downtown. Years later, that station was moved to its present location and is now the Tenino Depot Museum.[66]

Tenino was home to a considerable population of Chinese workers during railroad construction. However, when white workers demonstrated at a coal mine near Tenino in 1874, the Chinese were forced out and replaced with Caucasian workers.[67]

TENINO SANDSTONE

In 1888, two quarrymen from the Midwest, S. W. Fenton and George N. Van Tine, came to work on a hotel in Portland, Oregon. The work fell through and Fenton and Van Tine came to Olympia where they saw a building under construction using sandstone trim. They found the source of the stone near Tenino and selected a site for a quarry near the railroad track south of town. Competitors sought to claim other quarry land, but Fenton and Van Tine won out at this site. Joined by experienced Scots quarryman, W. M. McArthur, they started the quarry in 1888 and made their first shipment of stone in 1889. They built a saw house that year and installed a gang saw, later utilizing channelers and building a cutting plant.

Meanwhile another quarry, the Eureka Quarry, opened west of town in 1890, and McArthur joined with H. P. Scheel, a Tacoma stonecutter, to establish the Hercules Quarry in 1891, also west of Tenino on a hillside above Scatter Creek.[68]

The Tenino Stone Company was idled in 1892, due to a widespread financial downturn, but re-constituted with new financing from Dr. Donald G. Russell who joined Fenton and re-capitalized the firm installing new equipment.[69]

Tenino sandstone is a fine grained, dark color stone which contains mostly quartz with

Tenino Sandstone Quarry cutting area, ca. 1909. Asahel Curtis Photo. WSHS 1943.42.14652 (Courtesy of Washington State Historical Society)

some mica. The stone was used in many buildings all over the Northwest from Vancouver, British Columbia, to California. The market for the stone began to decline about 1910, when concrete came into widespread use. By 1913, the Tenino Stone Company closed except for minor cutting and production of "holystones" used in polishing ship decks.[70] By 1926, all its operations had ceased. The Hercules Company quarries supplied rubble stone for jetties but closed in the late 1930s. The Tenino Stone Company quarry eventually filled with water and is now the town swimming pool. Other quarries outside of town have re-opened on a limited basis and supply a small amount of stone for building use, including some newer buildings in Tenino.[71]

TENINO WOODEN MONEY

The southern part of the county suffered economic reverses during the Depression years, but Tenino made the most of it when it issued its world-famous "wooden money." After a money shortage and failure of the Citizen's Bank of Tenino in 1931, the Tenino Chamber of Commerce issued paper scrip to bank depositors in exchange for an assignment to the Chamber of up to 25 percent of the depositor's bank account balance. Depositors could later redeem that scrip for cash when the economy improved. The group used "slicewood" (veneer) for the scrip, and it became famous—particularly popular with collectors. Although only $40 of the $10,308 in scrip were redeemed, eight issues were printed from 1931 to 1933. The South Thurston County Historical Society has since re-issued commemorative versions of the money over the years.[72]

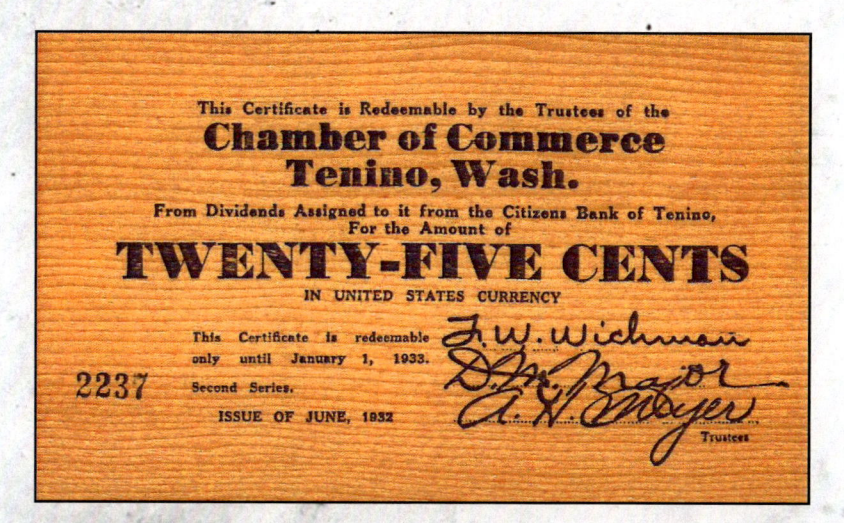

Tenino wooden money (see above) and Olympia wooden money (see below). Olympians issued wooden money in the 1930s when "Old Ironsides," the USS Constitution, visited in 1933. The Olympia Chamber of Commerce issued $2,900 worth of the "oyster money."[73] (Courtesy of a private collection)

Thurston County - Water, Woods & Prairies   97

it bypassed Tenino by ten miles to the west, and many of the Pacific Highway services closed.

In more recent years, the town has experienced residential growth as a bedroom community. After 1910, the city had decreased in population until the 1980s, reaching approximately 1,725 in the twenty-first century, only about 600 more residents than its early high point the century before.

Early hotel in Yelm, Washington in 1912, taken from the middle of an unpaved street. WSHS 2003.71.6 (Courtesy of Washington State Historical Society)

City of Yelm

The name "Yelm" reflects close ties to the Native people who knew the area as "schelm" or "chem", so named for the visible heat waves or mirages often seen there.[76] By the early 1850s, Hudson's Bay Company men and their Native American wives settled in the Yelm area.[77]

Street Scene - Yelm, Washington. 1970. Photographer Ellis. WSHS 1990.82.6812 (Courtesy of Washington State Historical Society)

The Longmire family arrived in 1853, and other Euro-American settlers including the Rice, Mosman, McKenzie, and Coates families joined them on the prairies. Sawmills operating in Yelm in the 1890s were the Shore and O'Dell Mill on the river, later joined by operators Pettit, Castle Brothers, and Jim Case. A decade later, several more mills also located in Yelm, including the Harstad Lumber Company which sold out to Gruber and Docherty.[78]

One author recalls the rage of the early 1900s in Yelm, "The first decade of the new century might be called the 'bicycle decade.' This means of travel was so prevalent that a good toll trail was kept up between Yelm and Olympia."[79]

Though the railroad tracks to Yelm were built in 1873, the Northern Pacific Railroad Depot in Yelm was not established until 1912. Its presence re-created the townscape. Major fires ravaged Yelm in 1908, 1913, and 1924. "The entire business district of Yelm burned to the ground Saturday night, May 24 with an estimated loss of $125,000," one paper reported.[82] The last fire prompted the Yelm Women's Civic Club to advocate for incorporation to provide for better water and fire service. They succeeded, and Yelm incorporated that same year.[83] However, two more fires, one in 1932 and another in 1941, burned the Yelm grade school, gym, and high school.[84]

During the years of the Yelm Irrigation District (1911-1954), described in Chapter 10, the community celebrated the resulting productivity with the annual Berry Pickers' Ball: "Although the ball was named for berries, workers would've been working the green bean fields also. After long days to earn a living, buy school clothes budget, or just for spending money, everyone looked forward to the big night." Organizers even put cornmeal on the street to help the dancers![85]

YELM'S FAMOUS WOMAN MOUNTAINEER

Fay Fuller dressed in mountaineering attire. WSHS 2009.0.473 (Courtesy of Washington State Historical Society)

Fay Fuller, famed as the first Euro-American woman to summit Mount Rainier, came with her family from her 1869 birthplace in New Jersey to Tacoma in the early 1880s and later accepted a teaching position in Yelm.

In 1890, Fuller ascended the mountain to Paradise with the Philemon Beecher Van Trump party. She then joined a Seattle group that headed for the summit. "Fay blackened her face with charcoal and wore goggles. . . Her climbing outfit was heavy flannel underwear, a thick blue flannel bloomer suit, woolen hose, heavy calfskin boy's shoes with caulks, and a small straw hat."[80] Fuller and her party reached Columbia Crest on August 10.

Fay Fuller later wrote a newspaper column about mountaineering, kept up her interest in the sport, and helped form several climbing clubs. She summited Mount Rainier again in 1897. Following a writing career, she left the Northwest at the turn of the century and later married Fritz von Briesen, an attorney. She passed away in California in 1958.[81]

J. Z. Knight established Ramtha's School of Enlightenment on an 80-acre campus near the town in 1988, attracting both visitors and potential residents from across the nation and abroad. The extension of sewer service to Yelm in the late 1990s enabled growth, and, coupled with an influx of population from Joint Base Lewis-McChord, the community now boasts a population of nearly 7,000 residents.

Early Bucoda, ca. 1912-1913. (Courtesy of Lewis County Historical Museum)

Bank of Bucoda, ca. 1890. Paul Davies Collection. P6051 (Courtesy of Lewis County Historical Museum)

Town of Bucoda

Ohioan Aaron Webster was the first Euro-American settler in what is now Bucoda. He first secured 160 acres in 1856 and then also purchased the same amount of land in the area that Native people called Seatco, from the Coastal Salish word "Tsi-at-co," meaning "devil" or "ghost place." A year later, Webster started a water-powered sawmill on the Skookumchuck River, one of ten industries listed in Thurston County by 1860.[86]

After Webster married neighbor Sarah Yantis in 1861, they sold their farm to Oliver Shead, who later acquired the water-powered sawmill from then owners, J. D. Bolander and William McElroy. The Northern Pacific railroad came through the area in 1872, and entrepreneurs opened a sash and door factory, mined coal, and promoted other businesses.

Three locals, William Buckley, Samuel Coulter, and J. B. David, decided on a new name, using the first two letters of their last names to coin the word Bucoda, which went on the new town train station.

Despite the loss of the prison, the town prospered in the 1890s, boasting a population of 945 in the 1890 census. Jerome Garland and Francis Rotch bought the Seatco Manufacturing Company.[90] Scorched by fires, the Seatco Company closed and was followed by the Bucoda Lumber Company. In 1898, fire again swept

Bucoda Skookum Brand card from Bucoda Shingle Company. (Courtesy of a private collection)

100   Chapter 7 - From Settlements to Cities

SEATCO PRISON

Seatco Prison in Bucoda, ca. 1885. The prison was at the (later named) address of 720 SW Factory Street in Bucoda. State Library Photograph Collection, 1851-1990. AR-07809001-ph003446 (Courtesy of Washington State Archives—Digital Archives)

Bucoda, once called Seatco, became the site of the first penitentiary in Washington Territory. Businessman Oliver Shead, Pierce County Sheriff Jeremiah K. Smith, and Thurston County Sheriff William Billings proposed the establishment of a prison that would use the labor of prisoners in nearby industries. The Territorial Legislature accepted their proposal and passed a bill in 1874 which transferred all individuals convicted of felonies from local jails throughout the territory into this prison run by private contractors. It was a 40-foot by 100-foot wooden structure owned by Superintendent Oliver Shead, was named Seatco Prison, and opened in mid-1878. By 1880, it held as many as 47 prisoners.[87] The prisoners, including some women, worked under contract for 70 cents per day in local mines, sawmills, brickyards, and cooperages.[88]

The Seatco prison developed a reputation for brutality and the Legislature abandoned the contract system after nine years and after having confined over 500 inmates. In 1887, Seatco was closed and 93 inmates were transferred to the newly established Washington Territorial Penitentiary, located in Walla Walla. The Seatco Prison building was destroyed by fire in 1912 and the site was hidden beneath a loading dock of the Mutual Lumber Company until it was exposed in the mid-1950s. In 1974, Neil B. Corcoran, Bucoda Mayor and local historian, located the prison site, now listed on the National Register.[89] Many stories remain of the horrors inside its doors.

through the community, destroying businesses.

In 1902, local lumbermen opened Mutual Lumber Company, which endured until mid-century, bringing prosperity to Bucoda. Like so many others, the mill suffered a fire, which occurred in 1912. The mill temporarily relocated to Tenino and, by 1919, a rebuilt Mutual Lumber Company opened in Bucoda, with modern equipment. Over the next several years new timber sources supplied the mill, making Bucoda "The Little Town with the Million Dollar Payroll." Company worker housing, some of which still stands, went up in the 1920s. Mutual Lumber Company closed from 1930 to 1933, reopened, and then closed in 1944, but briefly manufactured bridge components during World War II before closing again in 1946. A planing mill held on until the mid-1950s.[91] The last vestige of the Mutual mill, the water tower, toppled in 1982.

Several historical markers dot the town, which is especially proud of its Volunteer Park opened in 1959. The rejuvenated Odd Fellows Hall was a highlight of Bucoda's centennial of incorporation in 2010.[92]

City of Rainier

In 1890, Albert and Maria Gehrke, German immigrants, claimed 170 acres, including much of the present-day City of Rainier. Named for its view of Mount Rainier, the town was platted in 1891 by a New York concern, in hopes of establishing a development. Street names, however, such as "Binghampton," recall that New York connection. Several lumber mills—Pettit and White, Lindstrom and Hanford, Bob White, Fir Tree, Deschutes, and Gruber and Docherty—brought prosperity in the 1910s and 1920s, but Rainier suffered large fires in 1915 and during the 1920s. The city, incorporated in 1947, touts its "small town atmosphere" with striking views of Mount Rainier.[93]

In 1896, together with his brothers and neighbors, Gehrke built a one-room school, but by 1902, the school moved to a new structure. The Zion Evangelical Lutheran Church, organized in 1893, purchased the building where many of the town's German community worshiped.

The new school conducted early church services in German, and the building served as a community center. When the school burned in 1915, classes returned to the church building until a new school was built. Maintained by the Gehrke family for many years, it is now owned by the City of Rainier.[94]

City of Rainier from the Bob White mill, July 1, 1909. Photographer Asahel Curtis. WSHS 1943.42.15120 (Courtesy of Washington State Historical Society)

Chapter 7 - From Settlements to Cities

City of Rainier welcome sign with an image of the iconic mountain. (Courtesy of the photographer Cami Petersen)

Rainier School & Zion Evangelical Church, built in 1896 by brothers Albert, Theodore, and Paul Gehrke. It was originally used as a second school as well as a church. In 2007, it became the first of Rainier's historic structures listed on the Washington State Heritage Register. (Courtesy of the photographer Cami Petersen)

As pioneer communities looked toward their future, they established schools for their children. Education is a significant force in stabilizing settlements and provides a focus for building the skills needed for society to prosper. "The 3 R's" by Shanna Stevenson looks back at the first Thurston County schools.

Chapter 8
THE THREE R's
Public Education in Thurston County
by Shanna Stevenson

"THE PIONEERS TURNED their attention to schools soon after they had a roof over their cabin," wrote one early settler. The first school in Thurston County was established in 1848, at what later became Priest Point Park, by the Oblates of Mary Immaculate. They were French Catholic missionaries whose goal was to educate Indian boys. After Thurston County was created in 1852, the territory established a system of public schools. In fact, Olympia, the territorial capital, likely had the first public schoolhouse in Washington. It was built in 1852 and was soon followed by a series of rural public schools throughout the county.[1]

The surprisingly large number and wide geographic distribution of early schools reflected the settlement patterns of the county and the overriding concern of parents to educate their children. Parents established a school at Bush Prairie near Tumwater by 1852. Soon others were at Ruddell's farm near Lacey, in the Packwood home at Nisqually, and at the Freedom School on Yelm Prairie – all started in the early 1850s.[2] Ann Elizabeth White recalled her days at the Packwood home:

> My school was on the Nisqually flats. I taught the three R's with no frills. The schoolroom was one of the bedrooms in the Packwood house, and my pupils were the Packwood, McAllister, and Shaser children. Every Monday morning I rode to my school on horseback, turned the horse loose and it would run home. On Fridays, my brother came for me.[3]

Watercolor sketch of the Indian Boys' School at Priest Point painted from memory of the Saint Joseph Olympia mission by Helen Parker McMicken (1856-1942), who lived with her family near the Oblate-run mission as a young girl. McMicken Family Papers, Special Collection Divisions, Negative #UW 39132 (Courtesy of University of Washington Libraries)

Thurston County - Water, Woods & Prairies

Tumwater School, ca. 1905, postcard. HHM146 (Courtesy of Henderson House Museum, City of Tumwater)

Thurston County residents pursued education even in adversity—school was conducted during the Puget Sound Indian War in the Fort Henness stockade near Grand Mound in 1855.[4] Some of the earliest public schools were organized as subscription schools paid for by the parents of schoolchildren. In these "rate bill schools," the teacher was employed by the county, which in turn collected a rate per pupil per day from parents.[5]

Initially, school was often conducted in homes, churches, and even granaries until permanent structures could be built. As with early schools across the territory, the earliest Thurston County schoolhouses were of log construction or a simple frame construction with relatively large windows. They were usually built with volunteer labor and often located on donated property. However, by the l860s, frame schools had replaced most of the log structures because of the availability of milled dimensional lumber.

As early as 1854, a county superintendent managed the schools, but locals retained control of their often one-school districts[6]—choosing their own teachers, building their own schools and raising money for operations. Under the direction of early County Superintendent Daniel R. Bigelow, Olympia hosted territory-wide educational and teacher conferences aimed at upgrading education and teachers' training. With the capital at Olympia, Thurston County schools and educators had access to the most current and progressive educational practices and ideas of the time.[7]

The first statistical report of territorial education in 1872 reported that Thurston County had 17 school houses and 500 children enrolled. Only Clark (27 schools and 641 students) and Walla Walla (37 schools and 1,035 students) counties had larger educational programs than Thurston County, although school was usually only in session a few months a year throughout the Territory.[8]

By the 1880s, the population in the rural parts of the County was growing dramatically, with the increase in logging, lumbering, and other industries. By 1880, 1,217 children lived in the County, and

Bush Prairie School, Thurston County. State Library Photograph Collection, 1851-1990. AR-07809001-ph004718 (Courtesy of Washington State Archives—Digital Archives)

Teacher Diana Spoon with her students at Bush Prairie School, 1910, Thurston County. State Library Photograph Collection, 1851-1990. AR-07809001-ph004720 (Courtesy of Washington State Archives—Digital Archives)

Thurston County - Water, Woods & Prairies   107

825 enrolled in school.[9] New mill towns, fed by the leaping growth of the lumber industry, sprang up as others followed railroad branch lines. The first Maytown school met in 1876, at what was likely the original Gunstone home. By 1892, the community paid its teachers $40.00 per month[10] in a new building.

Schools grew apace, and by 1890, the County had 45 school districts with 31 female and seven male teachers.[11] By 1912-1913, there were 64 districts and 4,283 students. Female teachers averaged $73.11 a month in salary.[12]

One Yelm resident recalled, "It wasn't just the teaching. They were expected to do much more… and they did. They'd be in charge of clubs, special activities, coach, health nurse, chauffeur, substitute parent on occasion, counselor and whatever someone felt was a teacher's responsibility."[13]

Many students attended only until eighth grade and took the County examination for graduation at that level. In the 1880s, Olympia had one of the earliest high schools, and by the 1926-27 school year, of the 7,196 Thurston County students, 1,439 were in high schools. Of a total of 45 schools, 17 of them were still one-room facilities.[14] Early teachers often boarded with families, but nine districts built teacher's cottages during the 1920s and 1930s. Eventually, nearly 80 school districts were organized in the county.

Increasingly after 1920, new rural schools served consolidated districts. Of necessity, these schools were larger, with more classrooms and sometimes gymnasiums. In the 1930s, some of the schools were enlarged or upgraded through the efforts of a New Deal federal program, the Works Progress Administration.

With the effects of the Depression and the depletion of first growth timber in the 1940s, many smaller rural districts closed as timber-related jobs in rural areas fell away. Children transferred to larger buildings in small towns such as Rainier, Rochester, and Yelm. One-room schools

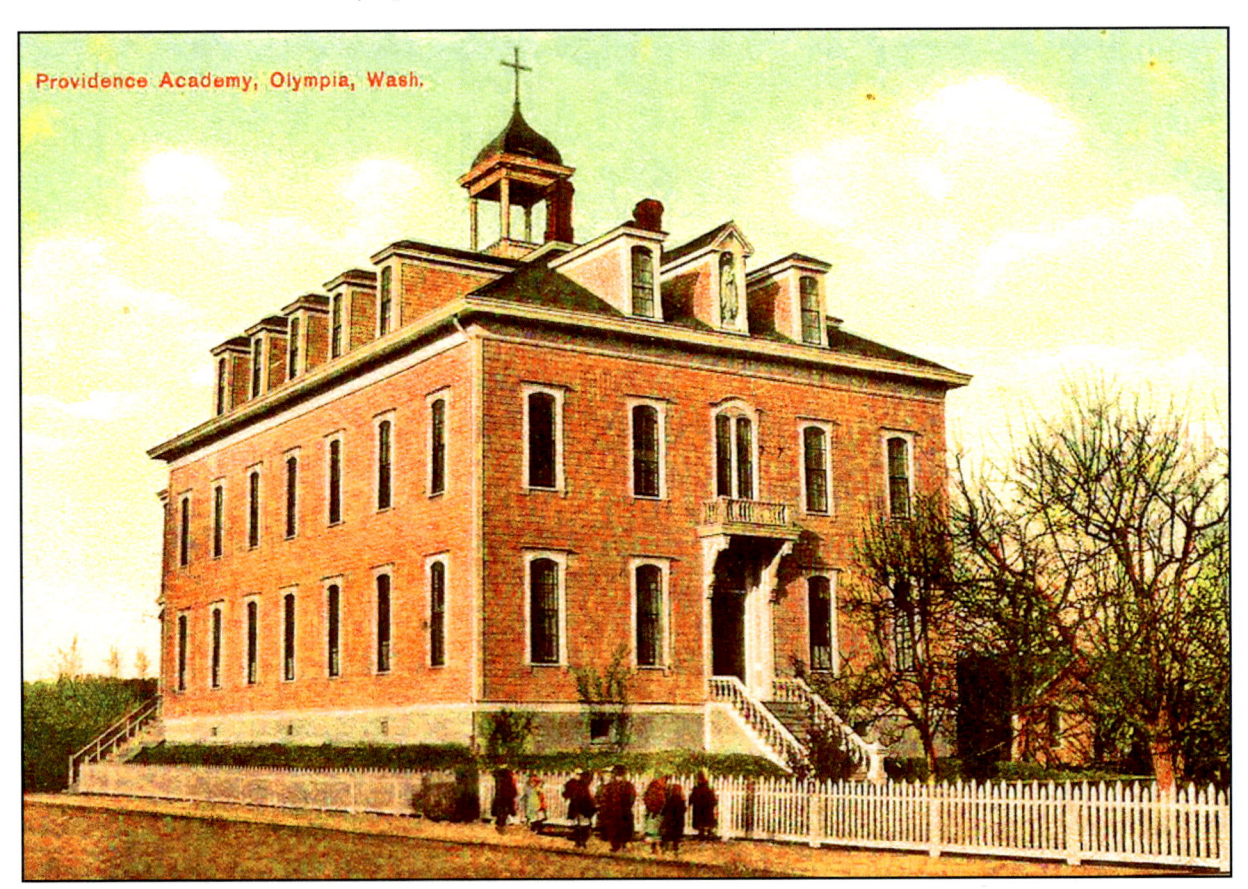

Providence Academy, run by the Catholic Sisters of Providence, Olympia, Washington, 1880, postcard. (Courtesy of a private collection)

Chapter 8 - The Three R's

Students in front of the old Central School at Union Street and Washington, Olympia, Washington, ca. 1882. Professor Follensby, Principal, center front. Minnie Freeman, teacher, afterward married Judge Reavis. Photographer A. D. Rogers. Library Photograph Collection, 1851-1990. AR-07809001-ph000929 (Courtesy of Washington State Archives—Digital Archives)

progressively disappeared during the 1940s as districts consolidated; by the 1960s, only eight remained in operation.

Rural schools, in general, were threatened with closure after 1960, as large regional school systems replaced the individual rural community schools. No longer needed for educational purposes, these smaller schools were often abandoned, torn down, or remodeled for residences.

Others, however, were sold to community groups and continue to function as important civic structures. Examples of this include the South Bay School which is now the South Bay Grange, as well as the Delphi School, a one-room school house, which is well preserved and now owned by the Delphi Community Association. The (second) Washington School, "Old Washington," was converted into the Olympic School District office and later Avanti High School. In the twenty-first century, the county has more than 60 schools in nine districts as well as several private schools.

Three-story wooden building with "Public School" over the front door. Photographer Robert Esterly, Tumwater, Washington. State Library Photograph Collection, 1851-1990. AR-07809001-ph004747 (Courtesy of Washington State Archives—Digital Archives)

Thurston County - Water, Woods & Prairies

School buses labeled "School District No. 320 Olympia Wash." They are parked at the three-story William Winlock Miller High School, built in 1907, later known as Olympia High School. State Library Photograph Collection, 1851-1990. AR-07809001-ph004730 (Courtesy of Washington State Archives—Digital Archives)

Grades five and six at Garfield School, 1919, Olympia, Washington. Photographer G. F. Cooke. State Library Photograph Collection, 1851-1990. AR-07809001-ph004716 (Courtesy of Washington State Archives—Digital Archives)

110   Chapter 8 - The Three R's

PAMELA HALE

Pamela Case Hale, Olympia, Washington. Photographer E. R. Rogers, Olympia, Washington. WSHS C1961.1185.11.1 (Courtesy of Washington State Historical Society)

An 1852 graduate of Mt. Holyoke College (South Hadley, Massachusetts),[15] Pamela Tower Case came to Olympia in 1871 after being widowed, and immediately opened a private school.[16] She married widower Calvin Hale the next year. Pamela taught at the Union Academy and became principal of Olympia Schools in 1880.[17]

Appointed to the Territorial Board of Education in 1881,[18] she was elected as Thurston County Superintendent in 1882—the first woman elected to public office in the county.[19] She also worked with the State Teachers' Association. Hale was a founder of the Woman's Club of Olympia,[20] a founder and first President of the Olympia Ladies Relief Society in 1888,[21] and active in the cause of women's suffrage.[22]

Hale subscribed $1,000 toward building the Hotel Olympia in 1889, and she was an owner of the Olympia Gas Works.[23] An entrepreneur, she built a block of apartments and stores in downtown Olympia[24] and even conducted lay services for the Unitarian Church.

She was the mother of one son with her first husband and an adopted son with Calvin Hale. She died in California in 1915.[25]

Olympia has always been the capital of Washington, dating back to territorial days. But the title hasn't gone unchallenged. In his essay "The Battle for the Capital," retired Supreme Court Chief Justice Gerry Alexander shares the struggles Olympia faced to remain the capital city.

Chapter 9
THE BATTLE FOR THE CAPITAL
Olympia's Legal Battles to Retain the Capital

by Gerry L. Alexander

OLYMPIA HAS EXISTED for over a century and a half. It is significant that during all of that time, save for three years, Olympia has been Washington's capital city. But the crown that Olympia has worn since 1853 has not always rested easily; there have been numerous attempts to move the seat of government to other Washington cities. Although many of these efforts cannot be described as serious, several were legitimate threats to Olympia's claim to the capital. Two of these attempts are the primary subject of this essay. Both incidents were litigated and ended up being resolved by a judicial decision favorable to Olympia. The first of these decisions was handed down in December 1861, by the Supreme Court of the Territory of Washington.[1] The other was issued almost 100 years later by the Supreme Court of the State of Washington.[2]

The older of the two cases is appropriately titled the *Seat of Government* case and reported in Volume One of the Washington Territorial Reports. When the first territorial governor, Isaac Stevens, initially arrived in Olympia on a drizzly day in November of 1853 bearing his appointment from President Franklin Pierce, he designated Olympia as the provisional capital of the territory and the place where the territory's first legislative assembly would meet.[3] Governor Stevens's decisions made good sense because Olympia was the most populous city within the new territory, containing somewhere between 200 and 300 of the approximately 4,000 non-native Americans then living in the territory. Olympia was also centrally located in the western portion of Washington and was the closest port on Puget Sound to the territory's older settlement at Vancouver, Washington Territory.

Stevens, who by all accounts was an energetic person, immediately began asserting his gubernatorial prerogatives from his headquarters in Olympia. He quickly divided the territory into legislative and judicial districts and called for an election of a territorial legislative assembly that would meet in Olympia in February 1854.[4]

Importantly, Congress had given this about-to-be constituted legislative assembly the power

Delegates of the second constitutional convention at the Territorial Capitol building, Olympia. Also pictured are support personnel, some wives, pages, and local grade school students. The delegates met July 4 through August 22, 1889, and a vote of the people ratified the constitution on October 1, 1889. Inauguration of Governor Ferry Photographs, 1889. AR-28001005-ph000003 (Courtesy of Washington State Archives—Digital Archives)

Thurston County - Water, Woods & Prairies

to select a permanent seat of the territorial government.

The elected legislature did assemble in Olympia that year and immediately began doing what legislatures do—passing statutes. Although the legislature did not enact a statute relating to the location of the capital in the 1854 session, Olympians undoubtedly took heart when the 1855 session of the assembly adopted a statute establishing the seat of government in Olympia on ten acres of land that had been deeded to the territory by prominent Olympian, Edmund Sylvester.[5] The legislative assembly of 1858 provided more good news to Olympia's citizens when it passed a bill establishing a commission "to superintend the erection of the capitol building at Olympia, the seat of government of the Washington Territory." The legislators even appropriated the then princely sum of $20,000 for the building of the capitol on the Sylvester land grant.[6]

The erection of a territorial capitol building did not, however, deter efforts by legislators from other areas of the territory to move the capital out of Olympia. In 1860, lawmakers from Vancouver, working with legislators from Jefferson County who wanted the penitentiary in Port Townsend and others from Seattle who coveted the territorial university for their city, managed to get a bill through the legislative assembly making Vancouver the capital. Inexplicably, another statute relating to the location of the capital was passed in that same legislative session. It provided that the voters of the territory were to decide at the next annual election what their choice was for the seat of government. That bill did not, however, say what effect, if any, the vote would have. Additionally, it did not refer to the act purporting to move the territorial capital to Vancouver. Significantly, both statutes lacked an enacting clause and an indication of the date of passage.[7]

The upshot of all of this was that the issue of the validity of the statute moving the capital to Vancouver was squarely presented to the Supreme Court of Washington Territory in the December term of 1861, only the 30th case heard by that court since its 1854 organization. The Supreme Court of the Territory of Washington initially had three judges, all of whom were appointed by and served

A woman standing in front of a Territorial Capitol replica, May 5, 1960. Photographer Merle Junk. Susan Parish Photograph Collection, 1889-1990. AR-25501080-ph000887 (Courtesy of Washington State Archives–Digital Archives)

at the pleasure of the President of the United States. These judges also served as the trial judges for this immense territory. Consequently, each was obliged to preside over trials that took place in one of the three judicial districts within the jurisdiction.[8] Only in December of each year did these judges assemble in Olympia to hear appeals from decisions they had made as trial judges during the preceding months of that year. A glaring defect in this process was that, in many of the cases that came before them in the territory's Supreme Court, one of the judges would be called upon to render a decision on the propriety of his own earlier ruling as a trial judge. This problem was not remedied until 1884, when a fourth judge was added to the territorial judiciary, thereby relieving the judges of an obligation to sit in review of their own decisions.[9]

The manner in which the Seat of Government case reached the court was somewhat unusual in that it had not been before any of the judges in their capacity as trial judges. Instead, the evidence was presented directly to the Supreme Court of the Territory of Washington in a pleading titled a "plea of abatement of a writ of error." In essence, this was a challenge to the territorial Supreme Court's jurisdiction to hear any of the cases that it had docketed for the December 1861 term of court in Olympia on the stated grounds that Olympia was not then the seat of government of the territory.

After considering the matter and observing that the territory's legislature assembled in "an unorganized quorum awaiting the action of the Supreme Court" and that "the controversy had been passed in review before the court and occupied more than three entire days of discussion," the court rendered its decision. In a well-crafted opinion, a two-member majority of the court discussed the flaws in the statute that purported to move the capital to Vancouver and struck it down. In an obvious effort to not appear arbitrary and unmindful of the prerogatives of the legislative branch of the territorial government, it prefaced its conclusion by saying that "a conflict of opinion between the legislature and judicial branch is always to be regretted." It went on to observe, however, that if an act is unconstitutional or wanting in the "requisite elements," the court is "bound to declare it void and of no binding effect."[10]

The court's majority indicated in its opinion that it was not unmindful of the Organic Act that Congress passed to establish the Washington Territory, an act that allowed the legislative assembly of the territory to create the seat of government. Nevertheless, it quickly added that the act of moving the capital to Vancouver had to be struck down because it had no enacting clause, the words "be it enacted," and was minus the date of passage. In reaching this decision, the majority judges relied to some extent on the fact that the other act passed by that same legislature, which put the question of the location of the seat of government to a vote of the people, had to be read hand-in-hand with the Vancouver act. After doing so, the judges said both could not survive. That being the case, they added a decision consonant with the will of the people was preferred. In that regard, they noted that the election had already taken place and that Olympia had won out over Vancouver, 1,239 to 639 votes. Seattle, which was then smaller than Olympia, received a paltry 23 votes. For good measure, perhaps wanting to appear somewhat deferential to the national government, the majority pointed out that a lot of public money, $30,000 to be exact, had been appropriated by Congress to build a capitol building in Olympia and $20,000 was already expended.

In a final rhetorical flourish, the majority judges made a statement, as courts sometimes do when they strike down an act of the legislature for a technical failing. They said, "If we have erred in

1928-era family photo of the construction of the Capitol building in Olympia, Washington. (Courtesy of Sharon Mathews)

Various detail shots of the legislative building in Olympia, Washington including a construction shot, ca. 1926. (Courtesy of Washington State Archives—Digital Archives)

116   Chapter 9 - The Battle for the Capital

refusing to give binding force and effect to this act, consolation remains that it is in the power of Congress, the territorial legislature, or the Supreme Court of the United States to correct the error and the disappointed are not without remedy."[11]

Associate Justice Ethelbert Oliphant, an appointee of President Abraham Lincoln, wrote the majority opinion. He was joined by the Chief Justice, C. C. Hewitt, another Lincoln appointee. Judge Hewitt was the great-grandfather of Judge Hewitt A. Henry on the Thurston-Mason County Court. Justice James Wyche, also a Lincoln appointee, filed a lengthy dissent in which he chided the majority for its adherence to form over substance and urged the court carry out the intention of the legislature to move the capital to Vancouver.[12]

In sum, Olympia's position as the home of the territorial capital was upheld by the slimmest of margins, thanks to the fortuity of a missing enacting clause and the absence of a date of enactment. In his book, *Rogues, Buffoons & Statesmen*, the noted Olympia historian, Gordon Newell, speculated that the flaws in the statute (no date and no enacting clause) might have been intentional, committed by a legislative clerk acting at the urging of Olympia boosters.[13] Although we will never know if it did happen that way, the unknown person deserves Olympia's gratitude.

After the smoke settled from that legal contretemps, Olympia hung on to the capital throughout the rest of Washington's days as a federal territory. Undoubtedly the residents of Olympia took additional solace from the fact that shortly after Washington was admitted to the union as the 42nd state, the citizens of the new state voted on the location of the capital and selected Olympia. Furthermore, the state Constitution, enacted as a condition of achieving statehood, made it very difficult to change the seat of government. It required the legislature to submit the issue to the people and approval of two-thirds of all qualified electors.[14]

Nevertheless, it did not take the legislature of the new state very long to try moving the capital out of Olympia. Indeed, in 1905, it passed a statute making Tacoma the capital. Although the act was

Governor Arthur B. Langlie's son Jimmie eating an apple on his bicycle in front of the legislative building and the World War I Winged Victory monument, ca. 1940. Progress Commission Photographs, 1937-1945. AR-09701002-ph000083 (Courtesy of Washington State Archives—Digital Archives)

subject to a constitutional challenge, the voters had not approved a change of the seat of government, and so the issue did not have to be resolved in court. That was because Washington's then Governor, Albert Mead, vetoed the bill moving the capital and did so in a somewhat sharp veto message. The Governor's action was great for Olympia, but it may have hurt Mead politically, the Governor being defeated in the 1908 Republican primary by an elderly veteran of the Civil War, Samuel Cosgrove.[16]

Happily for Olympia, things remained quiet on the seat of government stage for the next several decades. However, in the 1950s Olympia faced the most significant challenge to its position as Washington's capital. Unlike those described above, the effort to move the capital did not occur in the legislative branch. What happened can best be described as a gradual erosion of Olympia's position as the capital city, as 13 agencies within the executive branch of government simply chose to abstain from

Thurston County - Water, Woods & Prairies

having a local presence, favoring instead to be located in Seattle. Although some of these organizations, like the State Boards of Pharmacy and Accounting, were small, others like the Departments of Game, Fisheries, and Health were sizable. This de facto relocation of a substantial portion of Washington's government did not go unnoticed by Olympia's business leaders, and it led four of them—Gerry Lemon, James Frederick "Fritz" Mottman, George Eklund, and George Draham—to consult with an attorney and ultimately commence an action in Thurston County Superior Court.[17] The lawsuit, initiated in January 1954, named as respondents the then Governor of the State of Washington, Arthur B. Langlie, as well as the directors and members of the various departments, boards and commissions of the agencies that had moved to Seattle.

The petitioners claimed in their suit that the respondents were not complying with the state Constitution as well as the act of the United States Congress that enabled Washington to become a state. Thus, they sought an order compelling respondents to "return to and maintain at the capital city of Olympia, the principal offices of, together with books and records of, the respective state agencies which they constitute…"

The lead attorney for the Olympia business men was legendary Thurston County attorney, Smith Troy. Troy, a native Olympian and the son of pioneer Olympia lawyer, Preston Troy, had served as Thurston County Prosecuting Attorney in the 1930s, and as Washington State Attorney General in the 1940s and early 1950s.[18] Not coincidentally, Smith Troy was the brother-in-law of Gerry Lemon, one of the petitioners. Troy had the able assistance of John Spiller, an attorney from Seattle who once served as an Assistant Attorney General under Smith Troy.

The state officers and agencies were represented by Assistant Attorney General Ralph Davis, who years later served as President of Puget Sound Power and Light Company.[19] The Thurston County Superior Court Judge assigned to hear the case was Charles T. Wright, a veteran trial judge who had succeeded his father, D. F. Wright, on the Superior Court.[20] After a hearing at the Thurston County Courthouse that lasted less than a full day, Judge Wright acceded to the petitioner's request and granted a writ mandating the return of the agencies to Olympia. Not surprisingly, the respondents appealed that decision to the Washington Supreme Court. The Supreme Court heard the appeal not long afterward at the Temple of Justice, in a building in Olympia that had been its home since 1913.

The State's principal argument for overturning the decision was that the seat of government provision in Washington's Constitution, Article 14, required only the offices of executive departments that existed at the time of the adoption of the state constitution to be in Olympia. Those entities, it pointed out, are enumerated elsewhere in that document. Its secondary argument was that the four Olympia businessmen had no standing to maintain their suit.

In a decision authored by Justice Charles Donworth, a Seattle native, a bare majority of the nine-member court rejected the State's arguments. They determined that the petitioners, as taxpayers, had standing to maintain the suit and that the intention of the framers of the constitution and the citizens of the Washington Territory who voted to adopt it was that all executive offices of the State's government be maintained in Olympia at the seat of state government.

Justice Mathew Hill, who also hailed from Seattle, wrote a dissent that was joined by three of his colleagues. The result, though, was that the Olympia businessmen prevailed by the slim margin of one vote, and, thus, the 13 agencies were required to move back to Olympia. Significantly, the Thurston County Superior Court was vested with authority to maintain continuing jurisdiction over compliance by the agencies with the Supreme Court's ruling. After that, under Judge Wright's supervision, the agencies began moving back to Olympia and upon doing so filed certificates of compliance with the Superior Court.[21]

The dispute was not, however, entirely resolved by the certificate filing. The petitioners challenged the Game Department's compliance with the Supreme Court's mandate, contending that the Department had not established a bona fide headquarters in Olympia. Consequently, they asked Judge Wright to hold the Game Department's Director and the members of the Game Commission in contempt of court.

Judge Wright held a hearing on their motion and found the Game Commission's Director and the Commission members in contempt. He concluded that the establishment of a tiny office in Olympia amounted to a "sham, a fraud upon the court, and a calculated attempt to circumvent the lawful order of this court as affirmed by the Supreme Court of the State…" Despite this strong language, Judge Wright allowed a purge of the contempt charge finding if they moved the full office back to Olympia within four months. They complied, thus ending the lawsuit and the move out of Olympia.

It is unclear what credit Smith Troy and John Spiller ever received for their accomplishment. The same may be said of the four businessmen named in the lawsuit. From a purely Olympian perspective, these persons could be viewed as heroes because the outcome of the suit undoubtedly contributed to the economic well-being of the Olympia area.

More significantly, though, they made sure that the intention of Washington's founders, as embodied in the State's Constitution, was upheld.

Although it seems unlikely that the future will see similar efforts to move the capital out of the Olympia area, that is not a certainty. Undoubtedly some would prefer to see the capital located elsewhere. Whether such an effort would be successful will depend on the resolve of citizens to ensure, as did their forebears, that the provisions in the Washington State Constitution relating to the location of the capital are not altered or subverted.

The Legislative Building and Capitol Lake from 4th Street bridge, Olympia, Washington, February 1955. Photographic slide. Port of Olympia, Commissioners Photograph Collection. SW-684A01022-ph000069 (Courtesy of Washington State Archives—Digital Archives)

The Indians grazed their horses and harvested camas roots and other crops on the local prairies. Then the British entrepreneurs of the Hudson's Bay Company developed extensive farms to support their own fur traders and extend trade to the Russian settlements in Alaska. Many Euro-Americans who settled in the region were farmers, intending to till the soil.

Shanna Stevenson writes in "Farms and Fields" about agriculture as an occupation which started with the Native peoples and continues today in Thurston County. Long-time resident Sharon Mathews tells about the role of the Grange in rural life.

Chapter 10
FARMS AND FIELDS
Agriculture in Thurston County

by Shanna Stevenson

NATIVE PEOPLE USED the open prairies of the county to supply a variety of foods and their horses fed on the abundant foraging grasses. They also managed the prairies, burning every fall for grasses and every three years for berries.[1]

In the 1840s, the Puget Sound Agricultural Company, a subsidiary of the Hudson's Bay Company, conducted the first large-scale farming in the area. Operating near the Nisqually River, the Company provided wool, hides, tallow (rendered animal fat), and agricultural products for export and their trading posts.[2] The Company also operated outstations in what are now Pierce, Thurston, and Lewis Counties that raised livestock and crops.[3]

Notable Pioneer Farms

Part of the American migration to Puget Sound in 1845, George and Isabella Bush with their family played a vital role in the beginnings of Washington Territory. The son of Quaker parents in Philadelphia, George Bush was a mixed-race man who traveled widely before making his way west in 1844 with his wife and children. In Missouri, he had married a white woman named Isabella James, and together they raised six sons.

1845 view of Fort Nisqually, a center of farming. Fort Nisqually on Puget's Sound, watercolour over pencil on cream paper, Tacoma, Washington, by Henry James Warre (1819-1898). #ROM2018_16530_12. (Courtesy of Royal Ontario Museum, Toronto)

DRAWING SETTLERS TO THE OREGON COUNTRY
The Donation Land Claim Act of 1850

While the Donation Land Claim Act of 1850 drew many people to the area, it may have encouraged a family to stay. Above is an excerpt from a Donation Land Claim in Thurston County, signed in 1853, by former Hudson's Bay Company employee and naturalized citizen, John Edgar. He was married to Native American Elizabeth "Betsy" Yelm and he lists their four children, Jane, John, William, and Mary. (Courtesy of Washington State Library)

The federal *Donation Land Claim Act of 1850* **specifically applied to the Oregon Territory, which at the time included present-day Thurston County. Under this law which lured settlers with the promise of free land, a married couple coming to the territory before 1850 could claim up to 640 free acres of land, with half in the wife's name. Single men could claim 320 acres. For those arriving after 1850 and before 1855, settlers could claim half that amount, but the joint-ownership provision remained the same. The act required claimants to live on the land and cultivate it for four consecutive years. US citizens or those who declared their intent to become citizens could secure land, as could American mixed-race Indians. In Thurston County, 232 claims were filed. Settlers also gained lands under several other federal provisions including the 1854 extension of the Preemption Act of 1841, the Homestead Act of 1862, the Timber Culture Act of 1873, and school lands and railroad land grants.**[4]

Even after escaping the black exclusion laws of the Oregon Provisional Government by moving north of the Columbia River, the Bush family still faced prejudice. While white settlers were entitled to free land under the provisions of the Donation Land Claim Act, it took an act of the US Congress to grant George and Isabella Bush their land because of his color. Fifty-five members of the newly formed Washington Territorial Legislature petitioned Congress in 1854 to grant George and Isabella Bush their 640-acre land claim, which Congress finally did, in 1855.

Because the family was famous for its generosity, the Bush farm was often a stopping-off place for those struggling to reach Puget Sound over the last miles of the trail. Historian Clinton Snowden said of Bush, "He provided the settlers with food for their first winter and with seed for the first sowing. If they had no money, he still supplied them with what they needed, asking only that each should pay him when he could, and taking no security."[5] The well-provisioned family continued supplying the new settlers. John Rogers James recalled that their family got a small mill for grinding grain from the Bushes and later bought some sheep from them.[6]

The Bush farm was an agricultural showplace. Isabella Bush established gardens with berry bushes and fruit trees, and started turkeys and chickens from eggs obtained from Fort Nisqually. She tended a fine flock of sheep for wool, and it was said that her watermelons were the envy of other Thurston County gardeners.

The Bush sons, William Owen, Joseph Tolbert (sometimes spelled Talbot), Rial Bailey, Henry Sanford, January Jackson, and Lewis Nesqually, were all farmers on the large Bush farm which eventually encompassed over 700 acres near the Deschutes River. It was William Owen Bush, however, who became one of Washington's most famous farmers. After a trip to the California Gold Rush in 1850, he lived, for several years, in Grand Mound Prairie south of Tumwater with his wife Mandana Smith Kimsey Bush. After his parents died, Bush, with his family, moved back to their farm.

The Thurston County Fair began in 1871, but was called Mutual Aid Fair. It was designed to aid farmers in their agricultural work and encourage immigration to the area by means of the proud display of agricultural achievement. William O. Bush took great interest in the promotion of

The Bush family and neighbors preparing for the 1893 World's Fair. (Courtesy of Gale Johnson Photography)

Thurston County - Water, Woods & Prairies

agriculture and in 1872, with his wife and brothers, organized the Western Washington Industrial Association to advance agricultural exhibits.

At the end of the 1875 Thurston County Fair, William O. Bush packed up his crates of produce and took them to exhibit at the Centennial International Exhibition of 1876 in Philadelphia, the first official World's Fair in the United States. There the Bush family won international acclaim for the wheat and oats that they grew on their farm with the first premium for Best Wheat and Highest Yield of Wheat. His exhibit went to the Smithsonian Institution. The gold medal and the accompanying diploma that he won in Philadelphia were exhibited at the 1877 Thurston County Fair.

In the 1891 Thurston County Fair, fair records show that he won six categories in the grain division alone, first place with cabbage, Hubbard squash, corn, and 89 varieties of potatoes.

Bush garnered more medals for produce at the World's Fairs in 1893 (Chicago), 1901 (Buffalo), and 1904 (St. Louis).

Not only was Bush a prosperous farmer, he also served in the first Washington State Legislature in 1889 as a Thurston County representative. In 1890, he lobbied to create a college for the study of the "Science of Agriculture," which became Washington State College, later Washington State University.[7]

On their farm at Grand Mound, the James family grew a variety of crops (including wheat) and cultivated orchards from stock tracing back to their native Cornwall, England. By the 1850s, the sheep they procured from Isabella Bush were flourishing: "Often we would take a fat mutton to Olympia to market, and the Government officials would declare it was the best mutton they had ever tasted. The prairie bunch grass was very nutritious and certainly did produce good beef and mutton."[8]

In what was to become downtown Olympia, Levi Smith grew a variety of vegetables and raised livestock in a two-acre enclosure. At Priest Point, the Catholic missionaries eventually cleared over eight acres and planted a variety of vegetables.[9] *The Columbian* reported in 1852, "Persons who are sceptical [sic] about the richness of the soil immediately upon the Sound, would have all their doubts removed upon visiting the garden at the Mission of St. Josephs under charge of Rev. Pierre Ricand [sic] where they would find every species of vegetables growing in the most luxurient [sic] profusion and mammoth size."[10]

At Nisqually, one McAllister family member

The Chambers family successfully sowed and harvested crops on their prairie land. Andrew Chambers noted, "We raised plenty of wheat, potatoes, peas, and other vegetables." He went on to boast that their beef cattle could fatten even in February and that one beef could yield 60 pounds of tallow, a valuable commodity. This property is now part of Indian Summer Golf & Country Club. Postcard. (Courtesy of a private collection)

Barn at the Thomas Rutledge Farm in Littlerock, built ca. 1864. It is one of the oldest barns in the State of Washington. April 2011. (Courtesy of the photographer Bill Holland)

commented, "After coming to the valley, we were quite prosperous, so fertile was the soil that we raised a third crop of wheat without plowing the land. Vegetables grew to wondrous size, potatoes from eight to ten pounds were not uncommon. Everything that we put in the ground grew. We soon had an orchard, the trees grew from the seed, but they bore fine fruit."[11]

Meadow hay spread in abundance along the Black River where the Rutledges harvested and sold it as a cash crop to livery stables and other concerns in Olympia for about $10 per load.[12] John Swan in Olympia and Leonard Durgin at Grand Mound both had tree nurseries which supplied area homesteads. John Rogers James noted, "Mr. Gangloff and Mr. Durgin started a nursery of apple, pear, and plum trees near the mound."[13]

Mary Thompson Beatty recounted how precious the first fruits of the trees were to the settlers:

> I remember the first apples ever grown in Thurston County. They were grown on a tree planted by Mr. Axtel [Axtell] on Grand Mound prairie. Mrs. Axtel [Axtell] told the boys that if they did not touch the fruit when it was ripe she would make them a pie. They obeyed and when that pie was made, so precious were the apples they went in, peel and all. No wasting good fruit by taking off even the thinnest peeling.[14]

Thurston County's Centennial Farms

First recognized by the Washington Department of Agriculture in 1989 at the 100th anniversary of Washington Statehood, Thurston County has four Centennial Farms, each of which by 2014 had remained in the same family for over 125 years—the Rutledge Farm at Littlerock, the Colvin Ranch near Tenino, the Spirlock-Nelson Farm on Rocky Prairie, and the Hilpert Farm in the Skookumchuck Valley.

Thomas Rutledge traveled over the Oregon Trail with his parents to Tumwater in 1852 and settled at Littlerock, then known as Black River. In 1854, he and neighbor John Shotwell slashed the first road between Littlerock and Tumwater. In 1856, Rutledge married Louisa Shotwell who bore nine children before her death in 1877. Rutledge later married Luella Miles, and they became the parents of two more children. The farm is on the "Black Lake Portage" used by Indians and early explorers as a water and land route from Puget Sound to Grays Harbor. One of the finest barns in the county—an 1864 Maryland style structure built with huge pegged beams—is on the property. The Rutledge farmland along the Black River has 139 acres of the original land grant and the home built in 1861 (with an 1893 addition). The town of Littlerock is the namesake of the rock that rests in front of the Rutledge house.[15] The farm is listed on the Thurston County Register of Historic Places.

Ignatius Colvin, a native of Boone County, Missouri, came west as a driver of a US Government commissary wagon destined for Fort Vancouver and later established a large ranch on Scatter Creek. After his marriage to Emma Peck Rector in 1866, the Colvins acquired almost 3,000 acres, raising cattle and other livestock on the original mounded prairie. Settlers burned the fields every third year varying among Rochester, Tenino, and Yelm, following the practice of the Native Americans to keep more trees and large bushes from encroaching on the grasslands. Still owned by the Colvin family and encompassing 240 acres of the original land as well as the 1877 farmhouse and historic barn, the ranch is listed on the National Register of Historic Places.[16] The farm is protected through a US Department of Agriculture easement that ensures it will always be used for farming.[17]

William Plumb, who gave his name to the area along Old Highway 99, was the first owner of the Spirlock-Nelson Farm. Plumb's adopted daughter, Cordelia Ricker, married James Dillard Spirlock, a farmer on Rocky Prairie which is located between Tumwater and Tenino. The Spirlocks' daughters, Orpha and Della Pearl, married two brothers, Andrew and Gustave Nelson, respectively. The Spirlock-Nelson farm, covering over 900 acres along the Deschutes River including the 140 acres of the original Spirlock land, has remained in the Nelson family.[18] The fifth generation of the family continues to farm, focusing on sustainable methods to raise beef, hay, wine grapes, and grain.[19]

David A. Hilpert, a native of Germany, arrived in Washington in 1856 and filed a land claim on the Skookumchuck River in 1858. After David traveled to the Midwest to marry Magdalena Gephart, the couple added more land in Thurston County, clearing it for farming, livestock, and orchards while building a large farmstead. Hilpert descendants still own 80 acres of the original farm.[20]

Hop fields near Olympia, ca. 1889. Hops were a bonanza crop in the late 1800s in Western Washington and Thurston County. Hop-picking was a way to garner cash at a time when it was hard to come by. Native Americans often picked with their non-Native counterparts in the autumn. Pickers gathered the crop into boxes which were hauled by wagon to a kiln where hops were dried over fires and baled for shipment. Native people made a circuit from Puyallup to Tenino, and into Oakville. Disaster struck in the early 1890s when a lice epidemic ruined crops, collapsing the hops market. WSHS C1958.2.65.6 (Courtesy of Washington State Historical Society)

Late Nineteenth Century

From the early American settlement period until the turn of the twentieth century, Thurston County grew rapidly as the timber industry flourished. Sawmill towns created important markets for farm products, enabling farmers to specialize in their products.[21]

After railroads came to Thurston County in 1873, small towns and trading centers such as Littlerock, Rochester, and Grand Mound grew up along the Northern Pacific tracks. Many immigrants worked in the forest industries and created small farms on logged-off land where they grew berries, raised cattle, operated small dairies, and managed chicken farms.

In the early 1900s, farmers engaged in diversified farming producing a variety of grains and vegetables. Other farmers grew berries and other fruits and engaged in dairying.[22] At the turn of the twentieth century, 665 farms in the county totaled 128,822 acres with the average size of 194 acres per farm.[23]

Cutover Farms

In 1900, a significant number of farms were "stump" or "cutover" operations. Loggers cleared first growth timber creating thousands of acres of stump land in the county. The timber workers, often of Scandinavian descent, not only worked in the forests but often established small farms with the support of wives and family.

They slowly cleared the land much as Indian people had done; often using a massive tool called a "Swede hoe" which was similar to a pickaxe or mattock. They also built fires capped with clay to create an oven in which they burned stumps. Other settlers used dynamite to dislodge the stumps.

Sometimes encompassing only 20 acres, the farms "provided some of life's necessities including milk, meat, eggs, vegetables, but very little cash."[24] If farms grew to 30-40 acres, farmers could pasture more cows and calves to produce butter, cream, and milk. Almost all farmers raised chickens and sold eggs.

After World War II, these small farms languished due to mechanization and rising costs. Family members, often a vital workforce, moved away, unwilling to continue subsistence farming.[25]

Residents bartered eggs for groceries before the 1920s and 1930s, when larger poultry and egg

Jonas and Maria Lovisa Erickson farmstead, ca. 1910, in Independence Valley near Rochester. The Ericksons operated a typical Scandinavian-style farm before World War II. They produced oats, peas, wheat, vetch, hay, and potatoes. They also raised a few cows, pigs, and chickens. Grain was cut with horse-drawn binders and threshed by steam powered threshing machines, which often traveled from farm to farm with neighbor crews. Not until 1940 was the first combine used for grain harvest. Individual farms slaughtered their calves and hogs, often fattened on peas, and sent them to market via the railroad.27 Listed on the National Register of Historic Places. (Courtesy of Dick Erickson)

Affectionately dubbed as the "Yelm Ditch," the Yelm Irrigation System is pictured here while under construction with local residents both observing and working on the project. (Courtesy of Yelm Prairie Historical Society)

farms came into vogue. Trucks from nearby towns brought feed to the poultry farmers and picked up eggs. Dairymen joined cooperatives in the 1920s where farmers bought shares in the creamery at $10.00 per cow milked, and they shipped cans of milk to a central processor.[26]

Farming Organizations

The Grange was the largest farm organization, instrumental in the development of rural society. A fraternal, non-partisan organization, it gave men and women equal leadership roles and brought communities together in a spirit of cooperation.

Nationally 4-H began in 1902, as a club for rural children to develop their skills. By 1912, Washington had its first club. After becoming part of the Cooperative Extension Service, the clubs grew rapidly as part of the home front efforts in World War I. Several clubs were active in South Bay and other farming areas of the county, and 4-H continues into the twenty-first century.[28]

Yelm Irrigation District

As a source of great pride and innovation at the start of the 1900s, the Yelm Irrigation Company flumes and pipes sent water from the Nisqually River to irrigate thousands of acres in the Yelm area. L. N. Rice and Company of Seattle engineered the project, and residents built the infrastructure themselves with lumber from the Salsich Lumber Company in nearby McKenna. In 1917, Thurston County Commissioners approved the creation of the Yelm Irrigation District, which could issue bonds and collect levies. The irrigation system encompassed approximately 6,000 acres with Nisqually River water transported 11.2 miles through the Yelm Ditch before flowing through deep wooden flumes. Residents constructed the gravity flumes, posts, caps, and stringers from cedar trees on the right-of-way. The project, completed in 1916, required the moving of 250,000 cubic yards of dirt.

Realtors offered adjacent land at $50 per acre with a low down payment and interest. Soon crops of raspberries, blackcaps, strawberries, and Blue Lake string beans sprouted along the waterways to be sold to local canneries. Berries were a Yelm community symbol at annual picnics and events like the "Berry Pickers' Ball."

The irrigation system started to fail in 1930 when the flumes began to leak, and water delivery became sporadic. Although repairs were made, further difficulties coincided with the years of the Great Depression. The canal system limped along before closing in 1950. In 1954 the irrigation system ended in bankruptcy.[29]

Brown Farm

In 1872, George Shannon, a Northern Pacific Railway Company employee, acquired about 1,100 acres at Nisqually, including the original Shaser Donation Land Claim. He diked the land and cultivated hops, hay, pastureland, and grain on 150 acres.

Alson L. Brown, a Seattle attorney, and his wife Emma purchased the Shannon land and additional acreage in 1904 including 850 acres on the McAllister Creek hillside and 1,500 acres on the delta. Brown built a four-mile, U-shaped, earthen dike bordered by the Nisqually River, McAllister Creek, and Puget Sound. One-way gates let fresh water pass through the delta into the Sound. Initially, workers built the dike with a horse and scoop, but in 1910,

About 14 men standing in a row with individual work horses and teams of horses, in front of a barn on the A. L. Brown Farm on the Nisqually Delta, Thurston County, Washington. WSHS 1943.42.28172 (Courtesy of Washington State Historical Society)

Brown brought a dredge to reinforce the dike and fill in the remaining sloughs. After three years, the once-saline soil became viable for farming.

Brown set about building an extensive model of agricultural enterprise that included not only farming and stock raising but also marketing and processing. The farm supported a large crew of men who lived in company housing and even shopped at a general store on the premises. The farm enterprises included a 300-cow dairy, a creamery, a flock of 24,000 chickens, and the slaughtering of 4,000 hogs each year.

Despite its scale, Brown's Farm was short-lived. Financial reversals during World War I caused the farm to go into bankruptcy. After an auction in 1924, new owners P. B. Truax, C. D. Clinton, and Robert Olden continued to operate the farm with a newly raised dike. In 1932, they built the large Jamesway barns which are still known as the "Twin Barns." When the US Fish and Wildlife Service purchased the property in 1974, they razed the other buildings and, in 2009, removed the dikes. In 2015, the wildlife preserve was renamed in honor of Nisqually leader Billy Frank, Jr.[30] as the Billy Frank Jr. Nisqually National Wildlife Refuge, an official wildlife refuge of the US Fish and Wildlife Service.

Cloverfields

Hazard Stevens, son of the first Territorial Governor, Isaac Stevens, arrived in the Washington Territory in 1854 at age 13. He accompanied his father in meetings with the Indians and participated in the Puget Sound Indian War of 1855-56. He later served in the Civil War, attaining the rank of brevetted General and receiving the Medal of Honor for his gallantry. After the war, General Stevens returned to the Northwest and in 1914, developed a model dairy farm called "Cloverfields" on a large tract of land in south Olympia. As the president of the Olympia Light and Power Company, Stevens promoted the use of electricity with an electrified barn and milking machines. His herd of 73 Holstein cows, an unknown breed locally, meant he had to provide assurances that the milk was as good as that from the more familiar Jerseys. Holsteins grazed on the lush clover on the property, and angora goats kept the lawns closely cropped. Stevens also planted an extensive orchard of fruit trees.

After his death in 1918, the farm passed to Stevens's sister, Kate Stevens Bates, who, with her

Thurston County - Water, Woods & Prairies

Farm in Nisqually Valley. Progress Commission Photographs, 1937-1945. Photographer Bert W. Huntoon. AR-09701002-ph000067 (Courtesy of Washington State Archives—Digital Archives)

husband, ran the farm until it was divided into housing parcels in the 1930s-1940s. Olympia High School stands on the dairy portion of the property.[31]

Maple Lane School

In 1913, the legislature authorized a separate State School for Girls near Grand Mound, 15 miles away from Greenhill School in Chehalis, the site of the boys' institution. The State School for Girls, later renamed Maple Lane, offered not only traditional education but also a course in farming and animal husbandry on a farm of over 200 acres. The girls milked cows, kept bees, and harvested crops from squash to berries. They raised and slaughtered livestock and canned produce. This work coupled with a succession of psychological and behavioral theories sought to affect changes in the troubled girls. After farming ceased, the girls transferred to another institution when Maple Lane converted into a juvenile institution for boys in 1978. It closed permanently in 2011.[32]

Cannery Ranch

The National Canning Company began operations in 1912 in Olympia on newly dredged fill land in the city's north end. The operation packed fish, fruits, and rhubarb, later processing a wide variety of berries, other fruits, and vegetables.

West Coast Grocery bought the operation and by 1916, renamed it to Olympia Canning Company. As many as 1,500 workers, mostly women, worked during the height of the canning season from May through February. One resident estimates that nearly everyone in Olympia worked there at one time or another.

Early on, the cannery sent most of its production to England. Under its slogan, "Canners of Northwest Fruits," the firm later packed for several labels and shipped to premium grocers throughout the US and Europe. Produce came from Eastern Washington, the company's ranch near Gull Harbor, and local farms at Yelm and Rochester. Fruit also arrived via boat from Vashon, Fox, and Harstine Islands. The cannery sold bulk vinegar, frozen berries, and at one time canned 95 percent of the Washington pear crop, some 12,000-16,000 tons per year. Cannery employee Henry Skog developed machinery to peel pear halves, which revolutionized the cannery business.

Chapter 10 - Farms and Fields

Schilter Family Farm in the Nisqually Valley near Olympia, Washington. (Courtesy of the photographer Rob Kirkwood)

The cannery owned Sunnybay Plantation at Gull Harbor which grew fruit from 1919 into the 1940s. Pie cherries, Italian prunes, strawberries, raspberries, and loganberries flourished on the 300-acre farm along with experimental black, pink, and white strawberries. Workers hauled the fruit daily to the cannery via truck and steamboat. At the peak of the season, 200 women worked on-site. Other cannery ranch workers, many of whom were farmers of German and Russian descent from Eastern Washington, formed the Gull Harbor Community.

By the 1940s, the ranch, whose lands were depleted by berry growing, raised turkeys, specializing in white and bronze varieties. Later, the ranch grazed Black Angus cattle.[33]

Mid-Twentieth Century Farming

In the 1930s Yelm boasted several dairy farms as well as truck gardens while Rochester in the southern part of the county was known as the "Berry Capital." By 1935, Thurston County had 2,000 dairy farms and 200 poultry farms, but agriculture reached a high point in 1940 with 2,876 farms. During the post-World War II period, many farmers left for industrial or government employment. Nevertheless, the county was considered the blueberry center of the state in 1950 with specialty crops of rhubarb, flowers, bulbs, lavender, and filberts as well as the developing Christmas tree industry.

By the mid-1950s, farm size declined because of part-time farmers, costs for cut-over lands, and subdivisions of large homesteads. Although many farms became woodland or pasture, county farmers led the state in three crops: lavender, mushrooms, and strawberry plant stock.[34] As the population grew, Thurston County preserved 900 acres of prime farmland in the Nisqually Valley in 1995 through Purchase of Development Rights. As required by the Washington State Growth Management Act, the county zoned about 12,000 acres with a Long Term Agricultural designation.[35] Thurston County's farmland has decreased by 75 percent since 1950, although 1,288 farms currently produce about $118 million in crops. Eggs, poultry, nurseries, flora-culture, greenhouses, and sod dominate production.[36] Thurston County has several active farmers' markets—Olympia, West Olympia, Tumwater, Lacey, and Tenino—offering opportunities for farm-to-market agriculture.

Community-supported agriculture and agritourism also flourish in the county. In 2014, Thurston County established a special project to link many of the agritourism sites in the county, dubbed "The Bountiful Byway." The project was designed to highlight the 68,000 acres of farmland in the county as well as other attractions.[37]

*Thurston Bountiful Byway logo by artist **Nikki McClure**. (Courtesy of Experience Olympia & Beyond)*

Thurston County - Water, Woods & Prairies

THE GRANGE IN THURSTON COUNTY

by Sharon Mathews

The Grange Movement began in 1867 to promote agriculture and serve the needs of farmers. Patrons of Husbandry, or Grange as it is more commonly known, started in Thurston County before statehood. The first Grange was Olympia #10, organized by Oregon State Master Daniel Clark, on January 27, 1874. Twenty members signed including D. R. Bigelow, Mrs. A. E. Bigelow, and S. T. Ruddle [sic].

In 1889 farmers organized Washington State Grange two months before statehood because the Grange had many concerns regarding the upcoming statehood, especially the proposed constitution—including too much government and too many offices as well as salaries and provisions for secret sessions of the legislature. By 1908, granges had been established near Tumwater at Chambers Prairie and in north Thurston County in Valentine at Gull Harbor. Also by that time, Pleasant Glade near Lacey joined Brighton Park. Further, in 1908, 30 charter members created the Pomona or coordinating grange in Olympia. The movement grew rapidly and by 1939 granges dotted the county with granges at Brighton Park, Chambers Prairie, Deschutes, Spurgeon Creek, South Bay, Prosperity, McLane, Skookumchuck, Michigan Hill, Rochester, South Union, Black Lake, Nisqually, Littlerock, and Violet Prairie. Several halls are still used by local granges while others have been repurposed.[38]

The Grange has been a leader in voting rights. The organization started the open primary in which voters could vote for anyone on the primary ballot regardless of party, crossing party lines from one office to another.

Again in 2004, the Grange led the fight against declaring a party and having only one choice. Washington voters now

Brighton Park Grange First and Second Degree Team Members, ca. 1941. (Courtesy of a private collection)

Chapter 10 - Farms and Fields

have the right to vote for the person no matter if the candidate is a member of any party or none at all. Republicans and Democrats stood side by side to fight this initiative all the way to the US Supreme Court where the Grange won by a seven to two decision.

Women have always been equal members in the Grange, voting and holding office since the Grange was first organized in 1867, which was 53 years before the Nineteenth Amendment. Women of the Grange were very active in the suffrage fight in Washington in 1909-1910.

Farmers often had difficulty obtaining insurance. One of the first Grange projects was the formation of the Washington Fire Relief Association which later changed its name to Grange Insurance Association.

Rural Free Delivery began in a Grange discussion with a woman who proposed a resolution that worked its way to the Pomona, State, and National Granges. In 1887 the Grange went on record nationally favoring the establishment of a US parcel post system for small packages. The victory came in 1912.

Early Grange Halls became the center of community life and education as places to gather and discuss local, state, and national issues and together form helping hands in most areas of life. Grangers were urged to consult together, play together, and work together. Lecturers presented programs on the most modern farming methods and homemaking. The Granges included social life and a little fun. Dances were often the meeting place for young couples.

Many Grange Halls were once small local schools, purchased when the schools consolidated. From the beginning children were important and the Juvenile Grange, now the Junior Grange, was formed for children from five to fourteen when they could join the Subordinate Grange. They learned parliamentary procedure, leadership skills, and social skills.

Governor Daniel J. Evans, seated, signs a proclamation for Grange Week in Washington State, ca. 1967. State Governor's Negative Collection, 1949-1975, State Patrol Photographer, #3153, AR2-9-10-19670327 (Courtesy of Washington State Archives—Digital Archives)

The inlet waters of Thurston County contain a wealth of seafood. Aquaculture, the harvest of a variety of shellfish, played a major role in our economy. Oysters, a delicacy once shipped from Olympia by the ton, are still a delicious choice for the seafood connoisseur. Shanna Stevenson looks at the inlets of South Puget Sound, their harvest, homes, and hopes.

Chapter 11
INLETS OF HARVEST AND HOME

by Shanna Stevenson

Aquaculture[1] as practiced near Olympia, Washington, ca. 1925. Six men are harvesting oysters. Pedrose Collection. 2015.15.2.10 (Courtesy of Washington State Historical Society)

THE INLETS OF PUGET

Sound have the optimal conditions for shellfish in terms of the salinity of the water, amount of diatoms, current flow, and water temperature.

American Indian people gathered shellfish in the county's inlets long before Euro-American settlers began to commercially harvest oysters and clams; after American settlement, Indian people, especially women, continued to sell shellfish.[2] The Olympia oyster, *Ostrea lurida*, a small oyster known for its delicate taste, flourished in these waters. Native people called them "kloch kloch." Entrepreneurs shipped oysters from the Northwest coast to San Francisco as early as the 1850s. During the territorial period, individuals were allowed the use of 20 acres of land for oysters.[3] Established in 1878, Olympia Oyster Company was the earliest organized oyster grower in the county. J. A. Gale, A. J. Smith, and David Helser began harvesting oysters on Oyster Bay or Totten Inlet in 1878. As early as the 1880s, native Olympia oysters were over harvested, and the Olympia Oyster Company re-seeded the lands at Oyster Bay.[4]

Prior to statehood, the title to tidelands rested with the federal government, and several laws governed the shellfish industry after 1889. The 1895 Bush Act allowed cultivators to obtain shellfish grounds at a low cost, provided that the land was used for oyster culture. The state

J. J. (John Joseph) Brenner Oyster Company staff with harvesting rakes on September 19, 1910 in Thurston County, Washington. Photographer Asahel Curtis. 1943.42.19966 (Courtesy of Washington State Historical Society)

retained the right to cancel the land ownership.[5] The Callow Act revoked the cancellation privilege, but other laws regulated cultivation of shellfish and ownership of tidelands.[6]

Later, anyone could own tidelands, whether or not the land had already been cultivated. The Olympia Oyster Company, Simmons Oyster Company, and J. J. Brenner Oyster Company cultivated and harvested oysters on both Totten and Eld Inlets.[7]

By the 1890s, oyster growing firms adopted the French method of diking and filling oyster lands to maintain a constant water depth over the shellfish. In this system, they placed a layer of soil on the mud flats and then built dikes, first made of wood, later concrete, to surround the grounds.[8]

According to one account, in 1909, growers managed 100 acres of oyster land on Mud Bay (Totten Inlet); 420 acres on Oyster Bay (Eld Inlet); and 340 acres on Henderson Inlet. In 1908, operators shipped 810,726 pounds of opened oysters and 1,602,745 pounds of oysters in the shell from Olympia.[9]

Families, often Japanese, lived in "culling houses" on the bays and harvested and sorted the oysters which were then transferred by small boats to opening houses on the Olympia waterfront. Later the opening houses moved to the bays.[10] Sulfite poisoning from pulp mills on Oakland Bay and adverse weather conditions decimated the oysters during the 1920s. By some accounts, the Japanese oyster drill (a boring worm) caused part of the decline. After the pulp mills ceased operation, oysters returned to Eld and Totten Inlets although the non-native Pacific oyster accounted for most of the production.[11]

Tribal and private growers continue to grow Olympia oysters, Pacific oysters, European flat oysters, manila clams, and on county inlets. After 1974 and 1994 court decisions, tribes and private growers reached an agreement in 2007, to work together to manage shellfish resources.[12]

Boston Harbor

Dofflemyer Point was known as "house-pits" by Native American people who called the point east of the cove "Sandhill crane's house." The 1841 US Exploring Expedition named the promontory "Brown's Point" for James B. Brown, a carpenter's mate on one of the ships. [13]

Isaac and Susan Allen Dofflemyer came by ox team from Bonaparte, Iowa, to Portland, Oregon, in 1850, and located at the point in 1851 or 1852.[14] Many early area residents lived primarily on subsistence lots and at the point itself, the Robinson family owned a shrimp processing plant.

In 1904, Seattle pioneer newspaperman and lawyer P. P. Carroll announced plans for a seaport at Dofflemyer Point called "Harriman City," renaming the bay "Port Olympic." Carroll advertised but did not deliver on long wharfs and wide boulevards in a town with sawmills, brick and tile factories, and an electric railway from downtown Olympia to the new metropolis.[15]

In 1907, another promoter, C. D. Hillman, who had fostered boom towns throughout the Northwest, promoted a new town, Boston Harbor. He sponsored steamboat excursions from Seattle, Tacoma, and Olympia and sold lots (sometimes more than once) in his large plat of Boston Harbor. Hillman, who built a hotel and planked sidewalks, eventually was convicted of federal mail fraud for his many ventures.[16]

Edrie Shaw recalled Hillman's work: "First, several million board feet of old Douglas Fir, growing down to the very shore, had to be cleared. When this was done, the hills were almost barren… Big two story houses were built, wood and cement sidewalks, piling driven in three or four places, a reservoir, water tank, pipe lines, a well and a spring, hotel, butcher shop and a shingle mill."[17]

In 1928, Norpia Stock Company of Olympia Investors touted "Olympia Homes," a housing development at Boston Harbor, but it too came to naught.[18] Still later in 1935, Governor Clarence Martin proposed a federal rural rehabilitation project for Boston Harbor to create an industrial community. That too failed to materialize.[19] By the 1920s, the area had a small water system, and during the early 1990s, a new sewer system spurred new growth in the area.[20]

Dofflemyer Point Lighthouse at Boston Harbor was one of the first automated in the state and is on the National Register of Historic Places. 2015. (Courtesy of the photographer Cami Petersen)

Dofflemyer Point Lighthouse at Boston Harbor

By 1887, a pole light guided ships at the point managed by Cyrus Dofflemyer.[21] Early on, a supply boat brought supplies for the lighthouse once a year including coal oil for the lantern, rope, wicks, lanterns and other supplies. The light was one of the last pole lamps on Puget Sound until it was rebuilt in the 1930s. The light was automated at that time but had a manually operated fog horn which was also automated in 1976.[22]

Original Gamma Poncin Estate Greenhouses, Johnson Point. A heating plant is at the far left. From the collection of Patricia Rambo McBride. (Courtesy of Carole Rambo Holt)

Johnson Point

Called "Squa-tsucks" by Native people and later "Point Moody" for a Wilkes Expedition member, by the 1850s the site was known as "Johnson Point" for a local doctor, J. R. Johnson. Another name, "Kanaka Jack's," recalled Kanaka Jack, a Hawaiian, and his Squaxin wife Kiki who operated a wood yard at the point for passing steamboats to take on wood and water.[23]

In 1906, as locals took up summer homes, Gamma Poncin, a Seattle businessman, and his wife Eliza purchased over 200 acres of primeval woodland and developed a large estate on Johnson Point.[24] The Poncins built a large home, an elaborate barn, greenhouses, peacock and deer enclosures, and added other exotics. Most interesting to onlookers was an enclosed concrete art gallery lit by a skylight in the European manner.[25]

After Poncin's death in 1922, the estate fell into some disrepair until it was purchased in 1927 by Henry and Irene Stumer, who opened a spa called "Beacon Beach Resort" with a number of cottages and tent houses near the former Poncin house. The Stumers later lost the property back to the Poncin family. In 1935, A. E. Schuyler of Chicago acquired the land which was, in the 1940s, subdivided, forming a community corporation to provide water to new buyers.[26] Several of the Poncin structures remain, mostly remodeled, in a community of waterfront homes. Like Boston Harbor, there was a navigation light on the point, replaced by a lighthouse on pilings offshore in the 1930s.[27]

Hunter Point

Called Djie'kc1L, a Native American name related to "foot,"[28] the point was later named "Cushman Point," for Elizabeth Cushman who purchased over 150 acres of land there for about $200 in 1865. Married in 1873, Alfred and Sara Emma Daniels Hunter came to Bush Prairie in the late 1870s. In 1877, they purchased the Cushman property, keeping 80 acres and selling the remainder of the land to locals which became known as "Hunter Point."

George Hunter logged the point, and it became a convenient "wood-up" and watering spot for steam boats that docked at a wharf. The Hunter family built a large house which had a small store also used by Indian people from Squaxin and Hope Islands.[29] Georgia Hunter Schmidt recalled, "The upstairs was all a dance hall and we used to give dances, regular old country dances. People would come in boats from miles around to dance till the wee hours of the morning."[30]

The Hunter family planted a large fruit orchard and, after closing the store around the turn of the century, used the house as a small hostelry, Old Homestead Inn, during the late teens and in the 1920s added cabins on the beach. The resort was later owned by Georgia Hunter and her husband Fritz Schmidt until 1940. A private community of homes now occupies the original Hunter property.[31]

HOW TO REACH
Old Homestead Inn
(Hunters Point)

By Automobile—
Take Olympic Highway west from Olympia toward Shelton, right-hand turn at Schneiders Prairie, 7.6 miles. Follow the swallows (yellow arrows).

By Boat from Tacoma—
Take steamer S. G. Simpson, Municipal dock, at 1 p. m. Tuesday, Thursday, Saturday.

By Boat from Olympia—
Take launch Leota, City dock, Tuesday, Thursday or Saturday at 3 o'clock.

By Private Boat—
Use Government Chart No. 6460. Hunters Point is shown on chart as Cushman Point, eight miles from Olympia.

RATES
Weekly Vacation Rates................$15.00
Chicken Course Dinner................. 1.25
Plate Dinner 1.00
Camping Privilege, per day............ .50

For other information and week-end rates, address:

OLD HOMESTEAD INN
Olympia, Washington. (Gen. Del.)
Special delivery address: Rignall, Washington.

OLD HOMESTEAD INN
HUNTERS POINT
Direction Mr. and Mrs. F. A. Schmidt

Where the Simplicity of the Farmhouse Extends Its Restful Welcome

Brochure for the former Old Homestead Inn owned by Mr. and Mrs. F. A. Schmidt, located at Hunter Point, Rignall, Washington. Their byline was, "Where the simplicity of the farmhouse extends its restful welcome." They featured a vacation rate of $15 per week. (Courtesy of Velma Rogers)

The Hunter family. Undated. (Courtesy of Velma Rogers)

Lake Lawrence

Although by some accounts, the lake was the site of a Hudson's Bay outpost, the lake was named for Lindley and Sam Lawrence who began logging on the lake in 1892.[32] Lindley Lawrence built a small lumber mill and much of the sawdust and slabs from the enterprise have been evident in the lake over the years. Frank and Jennie Conine Edwards purchased the land after 1900 and by the early 1920s, started renting boats and built the pavilion and nearby concession stand. J. B. Martin, a bridge builder for the Northern Pacific Railroad, designed the pavilion using logs from the property. From 1908-1910 the level of the lake was raised to accommodate the Olympia Light and Power generator at the Deschutes Falls in Tumwater. The generating plant was abandoned in 1932-1933. The pavilion hosted regular dances where mothers could leave their babies in individual compartments while they danced away. The pavilion fell into disuse in the late 1920s but was later repaired as a signature element of the community which grew up around the lake starting in 1974. [31]

Boat house, tent houses, home, gallery, and guest house at the Gamma Poncin Estate, Johnson Point. From the collection of Patricia Rambo McBride. (Courtesy of Carole Rambo Holt)

Barn at the Gamma Poncin Estate, Johnson Point, undated. From the collection of Patricia Rambo McBride. (Courtesy of Carole Rambo Holt)

Oystergirls, ca. 1930s. Photographer Vibert Jeffers. Susan Parish Photograph Collection, 1889-1990. D413 (Courtesy of Washington State Archives)Entiaesimus suludam prio egerte, mandamquo consi trum ex nem.

Two barges are preparing oyster beds on Puget Sound, near Olympia, Thurston County, working on covering the oyster flats with gravel, ca. 1925. A scooping bucket extends from a long arm attached to a wooden apparatus on the barge on the left. The bucket hovers over the barge on the right. Typed on accompanying piece of paper: An artificial bed is prepared by covering the flats with gravel within the separating and protecting dikes. Pedrose Collection 2015.15.2.9 (Courtesy of Washington State Historical Society)

Some Thurston county towns were once on the map but no longer exist. Others have settled into the countryside as small communities, or even prospered into the twenty-first century. Shanna Stevenson writes of their intriguing history.

Chapter 12
THE EBB AND FLOW OF COMMUNITIES
by Shanna Stevenson

THE GRAND MOUND WAS once an island in a prehistoric lake, which is why it has different soil than the surface of the surrounding prairie. The 125-foot tree-covered mound is an ancestral site for the Chehalis Tribe and was also a landmark to the earliest explorers who traveled in the Northwest. James Douglas of the Hudson's Bay Company first wrote about the Mound in 1840 and may have been the first non-Native to climb the formation.[1] The name Grand Mound was suggested by its first owner, Leonard Durgin, who built a home on top of it. As a member of the Washington Territorial Legislature, Durgin suggested Grand Mound as the site of the Territorial Capital. Religious, political, and educational gatherings made the community prominent in early Territorial history. Stagecoach service was established in 1854.

During the Puget Sound Indian War of 1855-1856, many of the homesteaders worried about possible attacks and banded together to build Fort Henness, a stockade at Grand Mound Prairie. Beginning in October 1855, the 100-by-130-foot fort housed 224 people. The men were organized

Grand Mound, named for the 125-foot-high tree-covered mound on the right. Undated. (Courtesy of Gene Weaver)

into Company F of the First Regiment of Washington Territorial Volunteers, led by Captain Benjamin Lee Henness.

Fred and George Stocking, grandsons of Samuel James who traveled the Oregon Trail, established the town of Grand Mound in 1890. Fred Stocking represented Grand Mound in the 1899 State Legislature session.

In 1914, the Washington State School for Girls (also known as the State Training School for Girls) opened at Grand Mound on 200 acres. The school was renamed Maple Lane School in 1954 and closed in 2011. The site today is operated by the Washington Department of Health and Human Services. The campus administration building is listed on the National Register of Historic Places.

In March 2008, the Great Wolf Lodge, majority-owned by the Confederated Tribes of the Chehalis Reservation, opened in Grand Mound with 398 guest suites and an indoor waterpark. Several historical markers exist in the Grand Mound area. A historical marker at a strip mall on 198th Avenue commemorates a successful attempt by the women of south Thurston County to vote in Washington Territorial elections of 1870. Just south of Grand Mound, on Old Highway 99, is an Oregon Trail marker, established in 1916 by the Daughters and Sons of the American Revolution. It is one in a series of markers from Vancouver, Washington north to Tumwater, marking the route of the 1844 Oregon Trail travelers through what was formerly part of the Oregon Territory. A monument across from Grand Mound Cemetery marks the former location of Fort Henness, a stockade built and occupied during the Puget Sound Indian Wars of 1855-1856.

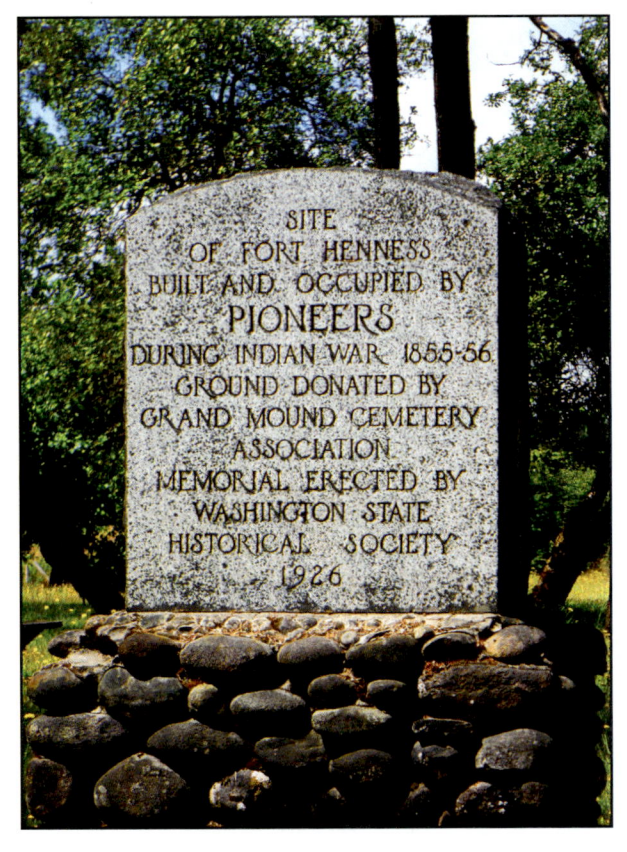

Historical marker at Fort Henness: "Site of Fort Henness built and occupied by pioneers during Indian War 1855-56. Ground donated by Grand Mound Cemetery Association. Memorial erected by Washington State Historical Society 1926." (Courtesy of the photographer Chris Colton)

Posted information at the site of Fort Henness: "Fort Henness 1855-1856..." A floor plan of the fort is drawn along with the names of the "Washington Territory Residents" residing within. (Courtesy of the photographer Chris Colton)

144   Chapter 12 - The Ebb and Flow of Communities

WOMEN VOTE AT GRAND MOUND AND BLACK RIVER

Charlotte Emily Olney French, undated. (Courtesy of the Saeger family)

Mary Olney Brown, undated. C2006.0.3 (Courtesy of Washington State Historical Society)

At a June 1870 election, held at Goodell's Point[3] school near Grand Mound, several women tested the post-Civil War constitutional amendments empowering citizens to vote. Mary Olney Brown from Olympia and her sister Charlotte Emily Olney French conspired along with other women in the area, planning a picnic dinner at the schoolhouse where the June 6, 1870 election was to be held. Charlotte Emily Olney French, like her sister, was well versed in the arguments for women's right to vote and spoke at the gathering. After the picnic, the women, seven in all, handed in their ballots which were accepted. Not to be outdone, the women at nearby Black River (near Littlerock) also awaited their turn. They had stationed a man on a "fleet horse" at the Grand Mound precinct to report if the women there were allowed to vote. The man arrived at the polling place, waved his hat and yelled "They're voting! They're voting!" The Black River women immediately cast their ballots, eight in all. These women did not succeed in changing women's rights in the 1870s but made a strong point. Although they voted for a time in the 1880s, most women in Washington permanently gained voting rights in 1910. The 1870 voting site was marked by the Thurston County Historic Commission in 2004.[4]

Street Scene in Rochester with Hotel Rochester, undated. 1917.95.40 (Courtesy of Washington State Historical Society)

The Hunter-ONeil-Boyd Company General Merchandise Store in Rochester, 1910. Two horse-drawn delivery vehicles stand on either side of the store and several people stand in front. WSHS 2008.137.5 (Courtesy of Washington State Historical Society)

Rochester

Native American people called the Rochester Prairie "Ich-tals."[7] Encouraged by the construction of the Northern Pacific Railroad, T. M. and Mary Rhoads of Centralia Land Company, along with Julia C. Fleming, filed the Rochester plat in 1890. Fleming, who lived in Centralia, owned acreage next to the new rail lines and platted out 75 blocks, naming the town after her home town of Rochester, Indiana.[8]

The town included saloons, a hotel, stores, post office, and livery stable in the 1890s. Its center moved twice during various periods: from a half mile southwest and a half mile east of the present location. After the first growth timber had been harvested in the area, dairies, poultry, and strawberry farms flourished. Two barreling plants in Rochester and Grand Mound processed strawberries during the 1920s and 1930s.[9]

The Confederated Tribes of the Chehalis Reservation is located nearby. Despite a Depression era decline, Rochester continues as an educational hub for this part of the county with a consolidated grade school and high school.

MARGARET ANNE CARTER COGWELL
BUSINESS WOMAN AND FARMER

Margaret Anne Carter Cogwell, 1878-1978. Photographer David James. (Courtesy of the James Collection)

Centenarian Margaret Ann Carter Cogwell (1878-1978) was an African American woman born on June 15, 1878, in Carterville, Texas. Her parents were ex-slaves, and she was educated in Texas where she later taught school. In 1898, she moved to Kansas where five of her eight children were born.

The family migrated to Seattle in 1910, where she became an astute businesswoman. She owned and operated a grocery store, ran a rooming house, and owned a restaurant. Her husband, James Edward Cogwell, worked for the Seattle Engineering Department.

The family moved to Rochester in 1919, where their daughter Ruby Carol Cogwell[10] was born. They farmed for a living, raising strawberries, cucumbers, hogs, turkeys, and dairy cows. They marketed turkeys at her son's Seattle store.

In Rochester, the Cogwells originated the annual "Turkey Shoot" festival. People came from great distances to participate in games and compete for prizes. Mrs. Cogwell also operated a food concession at the Southwest Washington Fair and held membership in the Rochester Grange. After she retired from farming in the mid-1950s, Mrs. Cogwell returned to Seattle to make her home.

Gate City, 1910. In the background is a stagecoach and in the foreground automobiles. Jensen Collection. P4401 (Courtesy of Lewis County Museum)

Littlerock United Methodist Church, 2018. (Courtesy of the photographer Chris Colton)

Gate

The Gate prairie was known to Native Americans as "Gel-lop-it-ith."[11] Founded in 1881, Gate City (later Gate) was considered a gateway to the Grays Harbor country and came to life as the Northern Pacific extended its line to Grays Harbor in 1890. Sam Woodruff who platted the town touted, "Prices of lots are only $40 to $150, one-fifth cash, one-fifth quarterly, without interest… Now is the time to buy. Gate is in it to stay. Here is a safe investment and a chance to get in on the ground floor."[12]

In 1891, the railroad created a junction to Centralia, connecting with the Portland line.[13] The Northern Pacific secured the gravel for ballast nearby on the Mima Prairie and operated its own quarry and sawmill west of Gate.[14] North of Gate in the Black Hills, loggers harvested timber both before and after the turn of the twentieth century. The town served as a business center for the Chehalis Indian Reservation, two miles southeast, and nearby several track-side businesses welcomed the loggers. Gate City Lumber Company had a saw, planing, and shingle mill. Ferndale Lumber shipped its product from Gate.[15] Gate City's boom collapsed in the Panic of 1893, and fires destroyed much of the town in 1902 and 1918. Gate suffered further decline with the depletion of timber and closure of a major sawmill in 1913.[16] The Gate School still stands and is listed on the National Register of Historic Places.[17]

Littlerock

First called "Black River," Littlerock is on the traditional migration route of Indian people from Grays Harbor along the Black River and to the Puget Sound.

By 1879, the Thomas Rutledge house was the home of both the Little Rock Post Office and the famous stone in front of the house, at the road's edge, gave the town its name. Some residents, however, renamed the town "Viora" in 1890, using the first letters of the names of certain residents, but this revision proved to be temporary and lasted only a little over a year. Until 1895, the town name was officially Little Rock, but the Postmaster removed the space between the two words. Still, both Little Rock and Littlerock place names were used by people into the early 20th century. Since then, Littlerock has been the accepted name.

The Tacoma, Olympia & Grays Harbor Railroad chugged through the town in 1890. Stores and homes sprang up to greet it. Once the site of Methodist denomination camp meetings, the town still boasts its 1885-era church building. The church remained on the campground site until 1905 when the congregation decided it belonged in the center of Littlerock's population. Two lots were purchased, but the building could not be moved across Beaver Creek in one piece. As a result, it was carefully dismantled and rebuilt where it stands today.[6]

148   Chapter 12 - The Ebb and Flow of Communities

Downtown Littlerock

Top photo
William Rutledge (son of Thomas & Louisa Rutledge) poses in his new Cadillac on Broadway Street, ca. 1910, in downtown Littlerock. Earl Cummins stands in the doorway of the saloon, Oxford Bar. Bert Vincent and Cecil Rutledge pose on the right. The barber shop is the small part of the building on the left. River Street is on the right of the building.

Middle photo
Clarence Rutledge in the middle, Bob Rutledge on the left horse, Mark Rutledge on the right horse, Morris standing on the porch next to Mrs. Rich who is in front of the window. Clarence, Bob, Mark, and Morris are the sons of William and Zella Rutledge. The photo was taken in front of the Littlerock Hotel.

Bottom left photo
Undated photo of Dooley's Store.

Bottom right photo
In front of Davis & Sons Store, ca. July 1, 1894. On ground, L to R: Lou Cottick, Walter Shotwell, the rest unknown. On porch: Si (Plunker) Vincent, Bernard Shotwell, J. K. Vincent, Grover Vincent, unknown, Mr. Davis, Jesse Cleveland, unknown.

(All photos on this page are courtesy of the Rutledge family)

Thurston County - Water, Woods & Prairies

Methodist Denomination Camp meeting, 1894, Littlerock, Washington. (Courtesy of the Rutledge family)

150   Chapter 12 - The Ebb and Flow of Communities

Independence

Most of the early Euro-American settlers at Independence were of Swedish and Finnish descent who sought work in the lumber industry. Many of these immigrants were Swede-Finns, Swedish-speaking Finns from the parts of Finland that were controlled by Sweden until the nineteenth century. Helsing Junction, between Independence and Rochester, gained its name from Helsinki, Finland. Over the years the Helsing area had a church, store, and Swedish Lutheran church as well as several bridges across the Chehalis River.[18]

Independence Ladies Aid at the Erickson Home, 1920s. The group held fund-raisers for the local church including a strawberry shortcake festival. (Courtesy of Dick Erickson)

On July 4, 1906, railroad tracks from Centralia and Hoquiam met here, and railroad workers renamed the town "Independence." The community boasted a section house, depot, Finnish Lutheran Church, post office, meeting hall, and mercantile.[19] In 1908, the Union Pacific and Milwaukee Railroads came through Independence to Centralia.[20] Six years later, the Ninemire-Morgan Mill brought in new workers and their families.[21] Other small businesses also served both the Wilson Brothers and the Bloomingdale Lumber and Logging operations at Independence. Today the area still boasts several farms and commemorates its Scandinavian heritage annually during Swede Days held in Rochester.

Gathering in front of Swedish Lutheran Church in Independence, Washington, ca. 1913-1914. (Courtesy of Debbie Santelli)

Thurston County - Water, Woods & Prairies

Tono

Although coal was discovered on the Skookumchuck River in the 1850s, mining began in earnest in the valley in 1877. In 1907, the Washington Union Coal Company, a subsidiary of the Union Pacific Railroad, opened a new field three miles from Bucoda and named it "Tono," likely a version of "Ton of Coal."

The town grew to a population of 700 with

View of Tono, just over the hill from Bucoda, undated. It was once a successful coal mining community with a school, saloon, and store. P4847 (Courtesy of Lewis County Museum)

300 mine workers, producing 1,400 tons of coal a day making it one of the largest operations of its kind in the west. Residents lived in company houses and enjoyed a baseball field, clubhouse, and two schools. Nearby coal towns of Mendota and Kopiah in Lewis County, neither of which exist in modern times, experienced a similar heyday. By 1931, however, production dropped, and in 1932, the Washington Union Coal Company leased the mine. By 1944, most of the houses were gone, and eventually, an airstrip was built on the town site. The mine continued both as a strip mine and underground operation until 1960.[22] Later owned by Pacific Power and Light and then by Transalta, the coal fields were closed in 2006.[23]

Vail and Woodard Bay

Weyerhaeuser Timber Company founded Vail in the 1920s with the purchase of 300,000 acres of forest land and moved a camp wholesale from Cherry Valley near Carnation. Named for a nearby rancher,[24] Vail served as the focal point for six shifting logging camps shuttling raw logs to the railhead for transfer to Woodard Bay. The logs were then towed by water to Weyerhaeuser mills at Everett. In its heyday, Vail had a general store, gas station, post office, barber shop, railroad roundhouse, and machine shop. Although more than 1,300 worked at the Vail site, company housing accommodated only 800 workers.[25]

When Weyerhaeuser began logging at Vail in 1924, the company acquired Woodard Bay as a transshipment point, which was completed in 1928.[26] Storage and maneuvering space, favorable tides, and a direct line of travel from the timberlands made the bay an attractive location. Logs came 26 miles by rail from Vail to Woodard Bay where boomsmen sorted, graded, and scaled them before the 99-mile trip north by water to the Weyerhaeuser Everett mill. Vail logs provided two-thirds of the

Vail locomotive and crew, 1938. Baldwin 2-6-6-2T Locomotive no. 111 (2nd) With 4 Wheel Caboose no. 4. Weyerhaeuser Timber Company. Photographer Darius Kinsey. John T. Labbe Collection of Logging & Railroad Photos, 1892-2010. AR255-114-0-1_L-0733 (Courtesy of Washington State Archives -Digital Archives)

raw material for the mill, and at one time, Woodard Bay handled as much as a million board feet of logs per day.[27] After shipping over one billion board feet of logs, the Woodard Bay dump permanently shut down in 1984 with the closure of mills in Everett. The state purchased the site in 1987 and maintains it as a Natural Resources Conservation Area.[28]

Bordeaux

In the early twentieth century, Bordeaux was a hard-working community in the Black Hills of Thurston County, but now it is a ghost town.

Mumby Shingle and Lumber Company, which harvested Black Hills timber with innovative methods of logging and manufacturing, headquartered its operations in Bordeaux south of Littlerock. The town was named for Canadian brothers Thomas and Joseph Bordeaux, natives of Ontario, who formed the Bordeaux Brothers Logging Company in 1885, after working in Mason County. By 1887, they turned to the Black Hills of Thurston County where the rugged topography precluded the use of the traditional ox and horse teams. The brothers introduced a new era of steam-powered railroad logging to harvest timber. They built 90 miles of railroad and spurs in the Black Hills and operated at a peak production of 600,000 board feet of lumber per day. As the harvest of timber progressed, the firm employed other methods of logging—high line, locomotive crane, caterpillar tractors, trucks, and modern steam and gas equipment. In 1902, the Bordeaux Brothers created a subsidiary lumber and shingle company to manufacture shingles and also, in 1908, started a hemlock mill. The plant had one of the first drying kilns for dimensional lumber in Western Washington. The Mumby plant at Bordeaux also processed the mammoth fir trees of the Black Hills for sailing ship spars, some measuring 120 feet long. At its height, the operation employed over 400 men in logging and saw-milling.

The company town of Bordeaux once had a hotel, post office, store, school, and company housing. The large Thomas and Margaret Bordeaux home which overlooked the mill and town site still remains. After logging over three and a half billion feet of logs, the operation closed in the Black Hills in 1941 and abandoned the town where few remnants of the bustling enterprise remain.[29]

Mumby Lumber and Shingle Company, Bordeaux, Washington. Photographic collage includes the shingle mill, dry kiln, dry shed, office, planing mill, box factory, sawmill, and round house. C1948.18X.18 (Courtesy of Washington State Historical Society)

Thurston County - Water, Woods & Prairies

The crew of Mason County Logging Company working at Bordeaux, no date. UW11937 (Courtesy of University of Washington Libraries, Special Collections)

Maytown School, undated. (Courtesy of Lila Sjodin)

Maytown

Platted in 1910 by Joseph and Sarah Gunstone Shelley, Maytown grew when Taylor Lumber and Shingle Company opened a mill there the following year. Isom (Isaam) J. Noe likely named the town after his former home, Maytown, Kentucky. Another story gives credit to Joseph Shelley who, after platting the town, is quoted to have said, "Well, it may become a town, or it may not, so I'll call it Maytown."

The mill was later purchased by George Simpson who shut it down but retained the logging and railroad operations. For a time the mill operated as a worker co-op. Simpson re-opened the mill in 1925, but a major fire in July of that year destroyed it. Tragically, two nearby worker houses were dynamited to stop the fire and other housing burned down, displacing 40 residents. The *Morning Olympian* reported that the $60,000 loss to the mill destroyed ten homes.[30] The town was not rebuilt after the fire, but at one time the community had a train station, school, and church.[31]

Summit Lake

Summit Lake was known early on as Crooked Lake and Prays Lake. Prays (sometimes spelled Preys) Lake was adopted circa 1860 in honor of an early settler in the area, James B. Pray. The name Summit Lake began to be used around 1900 after the Henry McCleary Timber Company started logging in the area. Later, Simpson Timber also logged there. An inn along the shores burned in 1925 before becoming the site of a private camp and since 1944, the location of Boy Scout Camp Thunderbird. Summit Lake also had a school, now the Summit Lake Community Club, and a resort owned by the Warner family. "Pioneer Rock" or "Calder Rock"—a large granite boulder—was a landmark on the trail from Grays Harbor to Puget Sound. In 1990, the Thurston County Historic Commission and the Department of Transportation relocated the boulder, which has an inscription by the Wood Family, from near State Route 8 to the scout camp to protect it from vandalism.[32]

Church at South Union (above) and the church's pulpit (right). Undated. The building was used by both the Presbyterian and Methodist congregations and each denomination planted a tree in front. The building was located north of Maytown, near the South Union Grange. It burned down in the 1940s. (Courtesy of the Rutledge family)

Logging camp at Sine near Summit Lake. C1945.191.5 (Courtesy of Washington State Historical Society)

THURSTON COUNTY LAND USE

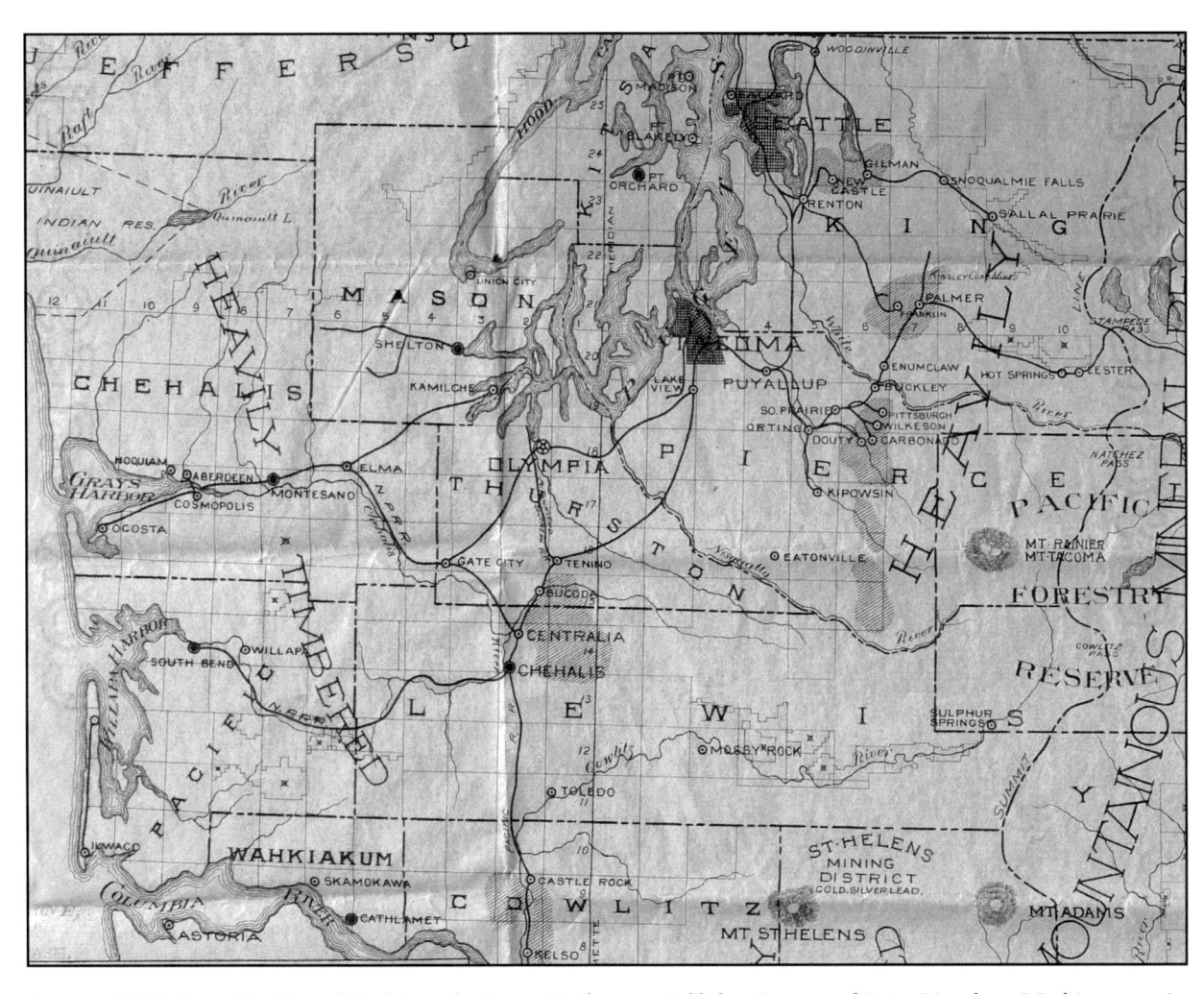

Excerpt of 1896 Map of the State of Washington by George H. Plummer, Publisher, Secretary of State. Map shows Washington, noting general categories of land use. Legend indicates townships, county lines and seats, railroads, and developed coal fields. Notes: Compiled by Washington State Immigration Association. "J. B. Hawthorne, Real Estate, Tacoma - Wash." Includes government surveys up to May 30, 1896. General Map Collection, 1851-2005 (Courtesy of Washington State Archives, Digital Archives)

THURSTON COUNTY RAILROADS

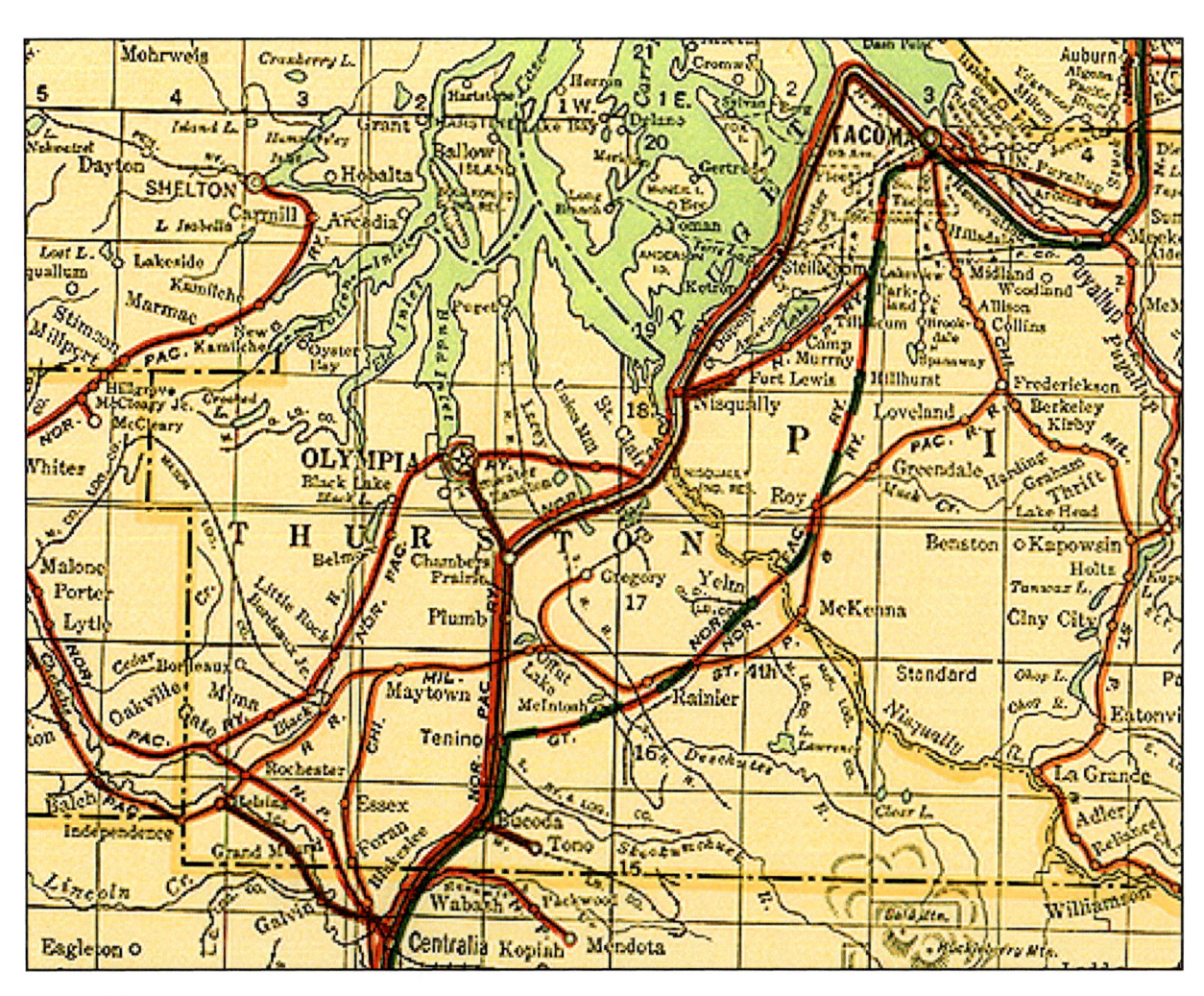

Excerpt of the 1928 Railroad Map. State of Washington State Department of Public Works. This map shows the common carrier railroads. General Map Collection, 1851-2005, AR-270-B-003144 (Courtesy of Washington State Archives, Digital Archives)

The woods of Thurston County inspired awe with their ponderous size. The first peoples used the huge trees reverently while the settlers cleared them to raise their crops. In a nation hungry for wood, entrepreneurs flocked in to harvest the impressive forests for the construction boom that began in the 1880s. Logging camps and mill towns popped up, and some disappeared almost as quickly.

Author James S. Hannum, M. D., who has written extensively about logging and logging railroads in the Northwest, shares Thurston County's logging history.

Chapter 13

BIG TREES, BIG BUSINESS

A History of Logging and Mills in Thurston County

by James S. Hannum, M.D.

PEOPLE WHO MOVED TO Thurston County in recent times see almost no evidence of the role that the timber industry played in local history. Gone are the big logging companies. Huge sawmills, once prominent on the Olympia waterfront, have disappeared; the places where they stood now serve other purposes.

Thurston County's logging and sawmill history was influenced greatly by three factors: the proximity of markets for finished lumber, available modes of transportation, and advances in the technology of logging and lumber production.

In the mid-nineteenth century, when immigrants of European origin settled in the area that would become Thurston County, local logging consisted of the cutting of trees needed by Native Americans for boats, housing, and firewood. Even after immigration was well under way, the overall population was still so low that there just wasn't much demand for lumber. Railroads had not yet arrived in the county, and although

Team of oxen hauling logs along a skid road, probably Pacific Northwest, no date. Negative # UW 1683 (Courtesy of the University of Washington Libraries, Special Collections)

Thurston County - Water, Woods & Prairies 159

1910-1912 view of the Black Lake Mill Company complex on the east shore of Black Lake. The image is from a drawing by Edward Lange who probably stood on the west shore to create this work. Lange lived in Olympia from 1889 until his death in 1912. He traveled Washington, making his living by drawing farms, businesses, and entire communities. (Courtesy of Henderson House Museum, City of Tumwater)

Tumwater terminal of the James McIntosh Tram Road, Budd Inlet in the background. A tram road consisted of wooden rails placed over 4x4 or 4x6 ties like railroad tracks. Note the flanged wheel on the middle right with a man standing above it. Few photos of the era showed women, ca. 1880s or 1890s. HHM566 (Courtesy of Henderson House Museum, City of Tumwater)

160   Chapter 13 - Big Trees Big Business

products could be shipped by sea, the population of places like San Francisco also remained relatively small. All these factors would change greatly during the last half of the nineteenth century.

As the population at the southern end of Puget Sound gradually increased, it became possible to operate both a sawmill and a gristmill profitably at the falls of the Deschutes River, in what is now Tumwater. Before 1869, the settlement there was called New Market. The mills used water power from a dam located at the site of the present spillway. Most logs came to the sawmill via the river, and the output of each mill was primarily for local consumption.

By the mid-1880s, logging was becoming a major part of the Thurston County economy. Still, no large sawmills operated in the county. That was primarily because the only railway reaching saltwater was the Olympia & Chehalis Valley Railroad. It was a narrow-gauge line, which required that any lumber, were it milled in Olympia or Tumwater, would need to be reloaded onto standard-gauge cars at Tenino. Consequently, the Olympia & Chehalis Valley Railroad was used primarily to bring logs to Budd Inlet, whence they were moved elsewhere. In addition, the long coastline of Thurston County meant that timber cut near Puget Sound could easily be towed to larger northern mills. The June 12, 1885, edition of the *Washington Standard* listed two charts: The first was of the 11 logging companies putting timber into Thurston County waterways, the number of men employed, and the mill which received the logs. The second was of just those companies that used a railroad to dump logs into Puget Sound, with the waterway, railroad, and dump location.[1]

Some of these loggers used a railroad to dump logs into Puget Sound, but by 1880, most used the

Waterway Listing for Thurston County Logging Companies - 1885

Logging Company	Waterway	Men Employed	Receiving Mill
Ike Ellis	Budd Inlet	50	Tacoma Mill Co.
Bartwell	Oyster Bay	12	Port Gamble Mill
William Callow	Oyster Bay	12	Port Gamble Mill
Alex McLoud	Mud Bay	10	Unspecified
Smith & Byrd	Mud Bay	8	Tacoma Mill Co.
Knap & Smith	Henderson Bay	10	Port Gamble Mill
Carpenter	Henderson Bay	7	Unspecified
David Barnard	Henderson Bay	20	Port Gamble Mill
William O. Bush	Budd Inlet	15	Tacoma Mill Co.
Ben Turner	Budd Inlet	30	Port Blakeley Mill
James McIntosh	Budd Inlet	30	Tacoma Mill Co.

Railroad Listing for Thurston County Logging Companies - 1885

Logging Company	Waterway	Railroad	Dump Location
Ike Ellis	Budd Inlet	Olympia & Mount Rainier	Northeast Olympia
William O. Bush	Budd Inlet	Olympia & Chehalis Valley	West Olympia
Ben Turner	Budd Inlet	Black Lake & Sherman Valley	West Olympia
James McIntosh	Budd Inlet	McIntosh Tram Road	Tumwater

Logging crew and donkey engine, Camp 2, Independence Logging Company. The introduction of the wood-burning steam donkey revolutionized logging by allowing cut logs to be removed from a landing or logging site; usually used by larger timber companies., ca. 1924. Negative # UW 1539 (Courtesy of University of Washington Libraries, Special Collections)

Logging companies often used railroad cars for multiple purposes, perhaps as bunk houses, transportation to the woods, or even an office. Pictured here is such a car and Mutual Lumber Company's Climax locomotive No. 5., Bucoda. Photographer Clark Kinsey, ca. 1930. Negative # C. Kinsey 2157 (Courtesy of University of Washington Libraries, Special Collections)

162   Chapter 13 - Big Trees Big Business

skid road to move a log from the place where it was felled. At the end of the skid road, a log might be deposited in Puget Sound, in a river like the Deschutes, or placed on a rail car. A skid road was made from logs laid cross-ways along the path of the road; the skids were lubricated with grease; logs were dragged over the skids by oxen. Later, horses were used for motive power. Dan Varner, an early Thurston County logger, used a skid road east of downtown Olympia in the mid-1870s. John Forbes, representing the Port Blakely Mill Company, constructed skid roads at Gallagher Cove in the early 1880s.

As logging by rail became better established, the use of skid roads diminished. Some loggers adopted a type of primitive railroad called a tram road. This was made with wooden rails laid length-wise on standard railroad ties. Oxen or horses were usually used to drag cars equipped with concave wheels along the rails. The Tacoma Mill Company's operation, overseen by James McIntosh, was one such tram road. It ran between Tumwater and Hewitt Lake. Before long, loggers began to use track made with standard steel rails. Spurs were built right up to an area of active logging and timber loaded directly onto the rail cars. As logging in a particular area progressed, the location of spurs changed frequently.

Eventually, it became more profitable to transport finished lumber, rather than logs, and

Sawmills in Thurston County - 1891[2]

Location	Mill
Bucoda	Seatco Manufacturing Company
Coinmo	Nisqually Mill Company
Olympia	Allen & Harkness
..	F. R. Brown
..	F. A. Collins
..	B. F. Corliss
..	Alex McLeod
..	A. M. Pierce
..	H. M. Pierce
..	Springer, White & Company
..	West Side Mill Company
Puget City	Puget City Mill Company
Tenino	Cuyler, Highlands & Nagle
..	Mentzer Brothers
..	Sarver & Vanderslice
..	Sawyer & Case
..	Tenino Lumber Company
..	Tenino Shingle Company
Tumwater	J. P. Allison & Company
..	Olympia Shingle Mill Company
..	T. Z. Slater
..	Tumwater Lumber Company
..	Tumwater Shingle Company
..	White, Marsh & Company

local sawmills began to appear. The 1891 edition of the *Rand McNally & Company's Lumberman's Directory* listed the Thurston County mills with their locations as seen in the chart on page 163.

Over the next two decades, some of these mills closed as tributary timber was exhausted. At the same time, new mills opened. The March 1909 edition of *The Coast* magazine published the names of the various mills operating in Thurston County, as listed on the following page.

The amount of lumber and shingles milled in Thurston County probably peaked between 1900 and the 1930s. During those years, most of the mills relied on logging railroads as their source of logs. One exception was the Tumwater Lumber Company (formerly the Lea Lumber Company) which received logs transported on the Deschutes River by a subsidiary business, the Deschutes River Boom Company. The Mason County Logging Company, at Bordeaux, had a large mill supported by its own extensive railroad, the Black Hills & Northwestern Railway. Nonetheless, it still made some use of the tried and true skid road. The Mutual Lumber Company at Bucoda also had its own railroad and used it to supply logs long after most of the other big mills had closed. However, it too went out of business in 1944. The Weyerhaeuser Timber Company had the last large-scale logging operation in Thurston County. It began in 1928, when Weyerhaeuser built the Skookumchuck Railroad from South Bay to Vail. Reorganized in 1936 as the Chehalis Western Railroad, it transported logs to South Bay until 1984. Weyerhaeuser never had a mill in Thurston County, choosing instead to tow its logs to Everett.

Many logging companies began truck logging in the 1930s, and logging by rail was essentially over by the mid-1940s. Trucks could efficiently access small tracts of timber and areas of hilly terrain that had previously been bypassed. As the last remaining stands of old-growth timber were felled, a new concept took root in Thurston County's logging industry: sustained yield forestry. Beginning with 33,000 acres in 1930, the Mason County Logging Company at Bordeaux sold logged-off land to the State of Washington. The price paid by the state was less than the yearly taxes on those properties. Eventually, as many as 60,000 acres in Thurston and Grays Harbor counties became part of this program. The initially sold acreage became the basis for the Black Hills Tree Farm within the Capitol State

Post-1912 view east from Tumwater Hill, along 1st Street in Tumwater. The Deschutes River is behind the Tumwater Lumber Company buildings. Most logs came to this mill via the river. (Courtesy of Kurt and Kit Anderson)

Shingle Mills in Thurston County - March 1909[3]

Location	Name of Mill
Olympia	H. G. Richardson
..	Olympia Cedar Company
..	Abqua Lumber Company
..	Frank Guslander
..	Thomas Russel
Sherlock	Card & Son
Little Rock [sic]	Viora Shingle Company
..	Deming Shingle Company
Bordeaux	Mumby Shingle Company
Tumwater	Lea Lumber Company

Lumber Mills in Thurston County - March 1909[4]

Location	Name of Mill
Bordeaux	Mumby Lumber Company *
Bucoda	Raymer Lumber Company
..	Steinhart Lumber Company
..	Mutual Lumber Company *
Centralia Post Office	Hannaford Lumber Company
Gate	Gate City Lumber Company *
Lacey	Union Lumber Company *
Little Rock [sic]	Salmon Creek Lumber Company *
..	Little Rock Lumber Company *
Olympia	Capital City Lumber Company
..	Olympia Door Company
..	Olympia Lumber Company
Rainier	Bob White Lumber Company *
..	Laramie Brothers
..	H. A. Burnham
Sherlock	Molberg & Company
..	Robinson & Swift
Tenino	Blumauer Lumber Company *
..	Mentzer Brothers *
..	Harm & Brown Lumber Company *
..	Jonas Spar & Lumber Company
Tumwater	Crowell Lumber Company
Yelm	Mossman Brothers

Used their own logging railroad

Forest and underwent extensive reforestation by the Civilian Conservation Corps during the Great Depression. Now, this area provides a balanced blend of recreation and preserved natural habitat, as well as ensuring a continuing source of forest products.

While the logging industry and the mills associated with it were a huge part of the Thurston County economy for many years, that phase of history ended long ago. Little remains of the mills that facilitated settlement of large areas of Thurston County. The clear-cutting of timberland is no longer practiced and the overall appearance of the county improves each year.

Locomotives, log trains, bunkhouses and other buildings at Weyerhaeuser Timber Company's Vail headquarters. Photographer Clark Kinsey, no date. Negative #C Kinsey 4930 (Courtesy of University of Washington Libraries, Special Collections)

View southwest toward Vail with a panorama of Weyerhaeuser Company houses and railroad tracks. The company town of Vail, in the Bald Hills south of Rainier, sprang up in 1927 with more than 50 homes and quarters for over 1,000 employees. Six outlying camps supplied logs to Vail by rail, where they were sorted and then forwarded to a log dump at South Bay on Puget Sound. From there, logs were rafted to mills in Everett, Washington. Nearly all the houses were moved away, and little remains of this once-thriving community. Photographer Clark Kinsey, no date. Negative #C. Kinsey 4859 (Courtesy of University of Washington Libraries, Special Collections)

166   Chapter 13 - Big Trees Big Business

THE COMMUNITY OF VAIL

by Don Trosper

The following essay is based on the 71st episode of the KACS/KACW local history series for southwest Washington, "Talking Over Old Times."

Vail was a company town in southern Thurston County in the Bald Hills south of Rainier. It was one of the many logging communities that sprang up in the early days and for a time was quite large. It was founded by the Weyerhaeuser Timber Company in the late 1920s with 13 large locomotives working in and out of the railhead. Vail once had more than 50 homes that housed 800 of its 1,300 employees quartered there. Vail was a logging rail center near the Deschutes River serving six different logging camps in the surrounding hills. Logging trains were formed to take logs to the South Bay log dump on Puget Sound where crews made up the logs into rafts for towing to the mills in Everett. Later the rail emphasis turned to trucks. At its high point, Vail had a general store, gas station, post office, barber shop, railroad roundhouse, and machine shop. The single men were put up in bunkhouses and fed in a combined general store and cookhouse. Their overseer was a tough, no-nonsense woods boss, R. A. McDonald. He was a rough, strong leader of men. He even offered to surrender his job to any man who could whip him in a fair fight. McDonald lived in a large, two-story house at the Vail entrance for 16 years. Overseers that followed McDonald included John Wahl, H. L Reichel, Carl Weiks, and Charlie Pike.

George Weyerhaeuser and his brother Phil both worked in the woods at Vail for a time, spending summer vacations from college to learn the timber business first-hand.

In the early days of Vail, the houses had wood-burning ranges and heaters. Families peeled the bark from stumps for fuel. Only a few families had plumbing and water; most carried water and used outhouses. One woman in Vail told of her husband who sat on their back porch shooting rats which inundated the camp by the hundreds. One afternoon he shot 66 of them. The women shopped mainly in the general store but occasionally banded together for shopping trips to Tacoma and Olympia. One Christmas Eve a group of merrymakers, led by a Scotsman named "Bagpipe Bill" McDonald, serenaded from house to house and ended up at Mrs. Oman's house for lutefisk. It was so meaningful that it became an annual event.

The rail line to South Bay, which once was used by 13 large locomotives, is now part of the Chehalis Western public hiking trail. Vail is gone from the map; the residents have moved to Rainier, Tenino, Bucoda, and other areas. The Vail logging camps are now history.

The challenge of hauling virgin timber to the many lumber mills in the area was met with logging railroads crisscrossing the hills and valleys of southwest Washington. While very few remnants of logging railroads from a century ago can be seen in Thurston County, sometimes today's forests will yield a memory of a straight and defined grade from those bygone days. James S. Hannum, M. D. tells of the logging railroads.

Chapter 14
RAILS AND TIMBER
by James S. Hannum, M.D.

THE RAILROAD OPERATING history of Thurston County began in October of 1872 when the first Northern Pacific Railroad train arrived in Tenino from the south.[1] Construction of the Northern Pacific had begun at Kalama, and late in 1873, the rails reached the railroad's terminal at Tacoma. Olympia and several other communities, including Boston Harbor, had been bypassed! Feeling deprived of the prosperity expected from the arrival of a railroad, numerous Thurston County residents banded together to build their own railway, which was originally called the Olympia & Tenino Railroad.[2] It was narrow-gauge and had its northern terminal in West Olympia. Commencing operation in 1878, it carried passengers to and from connections with the Northern Pacific Railroad at Tenino. The largest part of its freight business related to the timber industry, with several logging branches providing a source of timber for mills in Tumwater, Olympia, and Tacoma. Reorganization of the railroad in 1881 changed the name of the line to the Olympia & Chehalis Valley Railroad.[3] The Port Townsend Southern Railroad acquired this carrier in 1890 and converted it to standard-gauge.[4]

Meanwhile, logging by rail was replacing traditional methods used for timbering. Previously, skid roads were the only way to get logs to a waterway or mill. That form of transport was inefficient at distances of more than one or two miles. With a railroad, almost all interior timber stands in the county could be harvested, regardless of location. Many techniques of railroad logging, pioneered in Michigan, Wisconsin, and Minnesota, were adopted in Washington during the late nineteenth century when several logging companies from those states moved here after the Midwest timber was exhausted. The best known of these,

Benjamin Docherty in the cab of Gruber-Docherty #1, a Shay locomotive, the most popular logging locomotive used in hilly country where traction was necessary for grades up to 8 percent. Logging railroads were introduced in the woods of western Washington in the 1880s. No date. (Courtesy of the Leonard Docherty Collection)

Weyerhaeuser Timber Company, formed in 1900 and eventually built the Chehalis Western Railroad in 1936.[5]

In the 1880s, logging companies began to develop a network of rails throughout Thurston County. Loggers, in general, were a rough and tumble group, and those who experimented with the use of a railroad were especially crusty. The first logging railroad to terminate in Olympia was constructed from the west side of Budd Inlet by George Foster. Working for Charles Hanson of the Tacoma Mill Company, Foster operated a two-mile line in 1883.⁶ In 1885, using business practices that could certainly be considered devious, Benjamin Buckman (B. B.) Turner took control of the railway. Turner extended it to Black Lake, calling it the Black Lake & Sherman Valley Railroad.

B. B. Turner utilized a leveraging scheme to attain control of the railroad and nearby timberland, by mortgaging his enterprise heavily to the Port Blakely Mill Company. When the price of logs fell, Turner became insolvent. He lost the railroad and his lands, with his personal life falling into disarray. This was evidenced by a court case filed by his wife, Oretta J. Turner. By 1889, she found him impossible to live with and filed for divorce. The court case went forward:

> On the 5th day of July 1889, at the County of Thurston, W. T., the said defendant [B. B. Turner] did violently abuse plaintiff, and did then and there call and apply to her a very great many indecent, vile, and vulgar names and epithets; That the defendant has been guilty of habitual intemperance for several years past and that he has very many interests in the name of other parties for the purpose of preventing his creditors getting any portion thereof.⁷

B. B. Turner denied all of these allegations. The presiding judge ruled in favor of the husband, and Oretta resumed her role in the Turner household for many years.

Ike Ellis, who possessed a more even temperament, organized another early Olympia logging line. The Olympia & Mt. Rainier Railroad was initially a tram road powered by oxen.⁸ It was formed late in 1884 and terminated at a log dump located near the address on Plum Street occupied in modern times by the Yashiro Japanese Garden. By 1885, the Olympia & Mt. Rainier had acquired a locomotive.

In contrast to the 1870s, 1890 was a time when several common carrier railroads sought to serve

View south from Independence Road, ca. 2004, immediately west of Helsing Junction. This is the same trestle seen in the image below. (Courtesy of James S. Hannum, M.D)

View north toward Helsing Junction from Michigan Hill Road. The Union Pacific and Milwaukee Railroads met at Helsing Junction and jointly used the trestle on the left. Track in the foreground leads to the Ninemire & Morgan Sawmill, which is behind the photographer. No date. (Courtesy of Gene Weaver)

170   Chapter 14 - Rails and Timber

Bordeaux mill with a view of railroad boxcar loading area, looking west toward Mason County Logging Company store and hotel. The lumber mills and community of Bordeaux were located southwest of Littlerock in Thurston County. Photographer Clark Kinsey, ca 1919. Negative # C. Kinsey 198 (Courtesy of University of Washington Libraries, Special Collections)

Thurston County and its smaller communities. In addition to the major investment made by the Port Townsend Southern when it upgraded the Olympia & Chehalis Valley Railroad, the Northern Pacific Railroad and the Portland & Puget Sound Railroad (sponsored by the Union Pacific Railroad) both planned new routes through the county.[9] The Union Pacific, however, ran into financial difficulties during the economic Panic of 1893 and never laid any rail on its graded right-of-way. It did manage to excavate the tunnel that, to this day, carries rail traffic under Capitol Boulevard. Also, portions of its right-of-way were operated later by the Milwaukee Road south of the I-5 exit at Maytown. North of the exit, I-5 itself occupies much of the land surveyed for the former Portland & Puget Sound Railroad. The Union Pacific did eventually manage to enter Olympia in 1916.

The Northern Pacific Railroad made good on its plan to provide increased rail service to Thurston County, beginning operation of its Tacoma, Olympia & Grays Harbor Railroad in 1891.[10] The most northerly part of that right-of-way is abandoned now, between Nisqually (in Pierce County) and the former Saint Clair Station (near Lake Saint Clair). It passed Sherlock Station, immediately south of the Nisqually River. The track of the Tacoma, Olympia & Grays Harbor Railroad between Mottman Industrial Park and Gate has also been abandoned.

A major upgrade to the capacity of the Northern Pacific was completed in 1914 when its Point Defiance Line opened. This new, double track mainline was built north from Tenino and along Puget Sound in Pierce County. Immediately north of Tenino, it obliterated much of the old Port Townsend Southern right-of-way, that railroad having been absorbed previously into the Northern Pacific system. Shortly before that time, an agreement among the Northern Pacific Railroad, Great Northern Railway, The Milwaukee Road, and the Spokane, Portland & Seattle Railway allowed all of these railroads to use the Point Defiance Line.

The Chicago, Milwaukee, Saint Paul & Pacific Railroad, known as The Milwaukee Road, was a relatively late arrival in Thurston County.[11] Its mainline from McKenna to Helsing Junction (in southwest Thurston County) was completed in June 1910. In 1913, it built an additional line south to Centralia and Chehalis. That right-of-way originated at a point near the Maytown interchange of I-5 and utilized much of the grade that the Portland & Puget Sound Railroad failed to complete.

In 1909 the Union Pacific Railroad constructed a branch line from Wabash to Tono. Another

Thurston County - Water, Woods & Prairies

branch, from Centralia to Aberdeen, was put into operation in 1910. At Helsing Junction, Milwaukee Road trains were able to use Union Pacific rails to get to Aberdeen. Track from East Olympia to downtown Olympia was developed by a consortium called the Olympia Terminal Railway Company. It became part of the Union Pacific system on December 31, 1915.

After a hydroelectric dam was erected at the mouth of the Deschutes River, electricity became available for the development of a streetcar system in Olympia and Tumwater. Cars of the Olympia Light & Power Company started running in 1891.[12] The line was extended to Tumwater in 1892, where a side branch eventually provided commercial transportation for the older Olympia brewery. Service to West Olympia, which the Westside Railway Company had operated briefly in the early 1890s, was restored by Olympia Light & Power in 1911. Puget Sound Power & Light became the operator of the streetcar system in 1924.[13] The Olympia Transit Company bought the

Engine #1 of the Olympia & Chehalis Valley Railroad prepares to depart Tenino's first Northern Pacific passenger station with The Tenino Rocket, ca. 1885. The mainline track is behind the station, on the right. Negative #UW 23984 (Courtesy of University of Washington Libraries, Special Collections)

Homemade locomotive of George S. Allen & Son Logging Co., north of Littlerock along the Black River, ca. 1902. For perspective, note the man on the back of the engine. Likely, the parts were on hand to build their own locomotive. ID C1948.1210.8 (Courtesy of Washington State Historical Society)

172   Chapter 14 - Rails and Timber

Crew with Weyerhaeuser Timber Company's 2-6-6-2 Baldwin locomotive no. 120. Weyerhaeuser operated the Chehalis Western Railroad, hauling logs from as far south as Lewis County to Woodard Bay. Much of the northern portion of the railroad has been converted to a hiking and biking trail. Photographer Clark Kinsey, ca. 1938. C. Kinsey 4926 (Courtesy of University of Washington Libraries, Special Collections)

system in 1933 and quit running streetcars, opting for buses.

In the early part of the twentieth century, a rich network of common-carrier railroads had been developed in Thurston County. This allowed logging companies, large and small, to proliferate with guaranteed access to nationwide markets. Changes continued to be made in the technology used in logging. Narrow-gauge railroads, commonly used in the Midwest in the 1880s and 1890s, were almost unheard of in Western Washington in the 1900s. Using standard-gauge allowed logging companies to have a seamless interchange of traffic with the common carriers. More powerful, gear-driven locomotives were developed. These were especially useful in the hilly terrain found in some parts of Thurston County.

The railroad used by Allen & Son, immediately north of Littlerock, is an example of the small logging operations that were developed throughout the county. Constructed in 1902, it used a locally fabricated engine to propel its logging cars. The Gruber-Docherty Lumber Company was located at Rainier from 1917 to 1924, and near Yelm between 1925 and 1935.[14] It had two geared locomotives, a Shay and a Heisler.

There were also several large logging railroads in Thurston County. The Black Hills & Northwestern Railway was a subsidiary of the Mason County Logging Company. The headquarters was located southwest of Littlerock, at Bordeaux, a community which no longer exists. Originating from the Northern Pacific line between Littlerock and Gate, a spur was opened to Bordeaux in 1899. The Black Hills & Northwestern extended west into Grays Harbor County. The Mason County Logging Company began using trucks to haul logs in 1938; it closed in 1941, after exhausting its timber supply.

The Thurston County Railway was the official name for the Mud Bay Logging Company's railroad.[15] Unofficially, it was frequently called the Thurston County Central. Operating from 1911 until 1941, it used a log dump near the north end of O'Leary Street, on Eld Inlet's Mud Bay. The Mud Bay Logging Company timberland was primarily on the north side of the Black Hills, while the Mason County Logging Company worked mostly on the south and west sides. In 1930, these two companies

The Mud Bay Logging Company operated its own railway, calling it the Thurston County Central Railroad. Here, the crew of a 55-ton Heisler locomotive (constructed in 1924) poses with a gravel train in an area that had already been logged. Although an exact location is not specified, the photograph was likely obtained in the Black Hills, southwest of Olympia. This image, ca. 1928, shows Percy Bison (brakeman, standing on the track), George McIvor (engineer, forward in the cab), and Lloyd Banker (fireman, behind in the cab) resting near a hill cleared by loggers. Item W-28008005-ph000004 (Courtesy of Washington State Archives—Digital Archives)

Log cars at Mud Bay log dump, Mud Bay Logging Company. Photographer Clark Kinsey, no date. Negative # C. Kinsey 2078 (Courtesy of University of Washington Libraries, Special Collections)

signed an agreement whereby the Mason County Logging Company was allowed to use the other company's log dump at Mud Bay. During its last years of operation, the dump was used mostly for transportation of Mason County Logging Company timber. The Mud Bay dump closed in 1941.

Weyerhaeuser's logging line was called the Skookumchuck Railroad when it opened in 1926.[16] Vail was the headquarters. The line was reorganized in 1936 as the Chehalis Western Railroad. With a log dump at South Bay, and numerous branches that reached south, even as far as Lewis County, it was Thurston County's all-time largest logging railroad. It also had the lengthiest operating lifespan, closing down its log dump in 1984. The last rails were removed from its right-of-way in 1991.

In 2018, the once extensive rail network in Thurston County is a tiny fraction of its former size. Several factors caused this. Primarily, the efficiency of car and truck travel made the railroad's fixed routes and schedules obsolete. Trucks also replaced trains in transporting logs. The Staggers Rail Act of 1980 made it easier to abandon unprofitable segments of track.[17] The Point Defiance Line, now operated by Burlington Northern Santa Fe Railway, still functions as a high-density, long distance carrier. Nonetheless, imprints of the past remain. In Tenino, a small segment of rail can still be seen on the original Northern Pacific mainline.

Thurston County Railway Engine #4 at the Mud Bay log dump. (Courtesy of the Albert Farrow Collection)

Damage to Union Pacific freight house on Fourth Avenue in Olympia when a runaway train crashed into the building March 13, 1959. (Courtesy of the Roger Easton Collection)

"It's the Water" became the the Olympia Brewing Company's slogan in 1902, and appeared on almost every piece of company stationery and advertisement after that. (Courtesy of the Olympia Tumwater Foundation)

"It's the Water!" *This familiar phrase instantly brings Olympia and its iconic beer to mind. Karen L. Johnson, Archives Curator at the Olympia Tumwater Foundation, tells the story of the Olympia Brewery in Tumwater, Washington. Her chapter portrays the role of Tumwater's Olympia Brewing Company in Thurston County history and the family who started it.*

Chapter 15
IT'S THE WATER
The History of the Olympia Brewing Company
by Karen L. Johnson

IN THE EARLY 1900s, A. J. Zillman ran a very successful German bakery in downtown Olympia. A perfectionist, Zillman used only the finest ingredients in his baked goods and had fresh yeast express-shipped from Portland every week. But one November, a storm washed out a railroad bridge north of Portland, and Zillman's shipment of yeast was delayed. Desperate to fulfill his many orders, he rushed to the Olympia Brewing Company in Tumwater. There he pleaded with owner Leopold Schmidt to sell him some brewer's yeast. Leopold emphatically refused: Zillman could not *buy* yeast from the brewery, but he could *take* as much as he needed at no charge.[1]

This simple interaction illustrates the Olympia Brewing Company's importance to Thurston County, as well as the community spirit of the brewery's owners.

The Olympia Brewing Company is the most iconic business in county history, even though the brewery buildings are now empty shells. While Tumwater's springs no longer supply the copper brew kettles with that pure artesian water, "It's the Water" is still one of the most recognizable slogans in the brewing industry.

What led to a nationally known brewery and a remarkable legacy for the citizens of Thurston

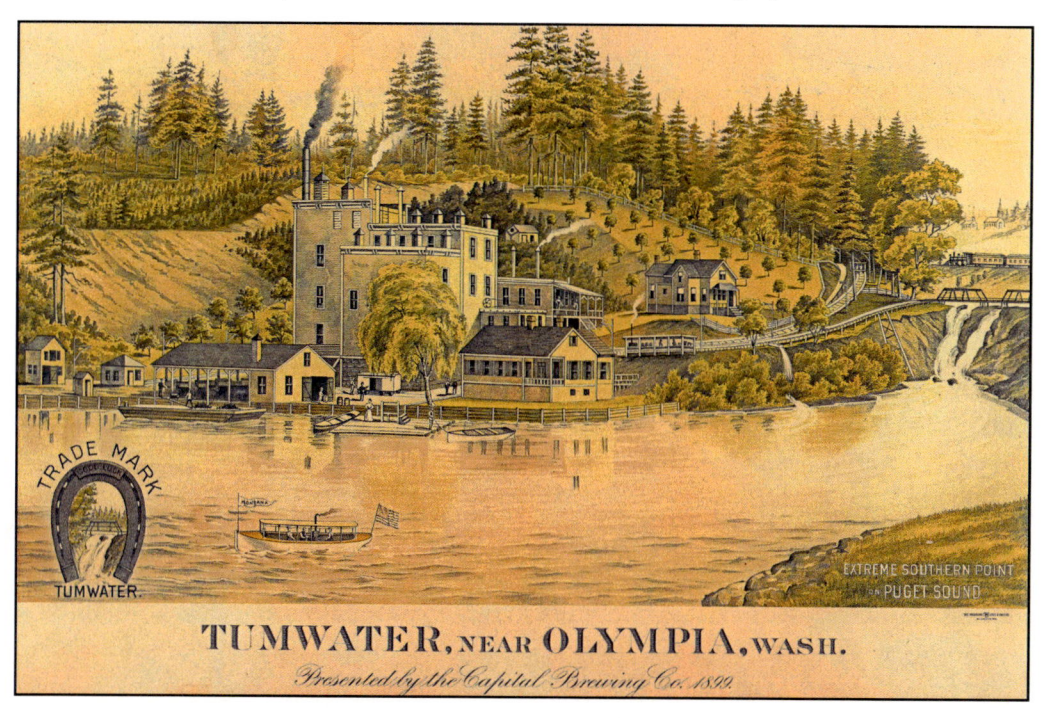

Local artist Edward Lange drew this portrait of the Capital Brewing Company's plant in 1899. Details include: the brewery's horseshoe trademark; the Montana, *a small motor launch owned by the Schmidt family; the electric trolley line which ran from Olympia to Tumwater Falls; the Hillside Inn, a residence located on the steep hill behind the brewery; and the old Methodist church, barely visible in the far right background. (Courtesy of Yale University's Beinecke Rare Book and Manuscript Library)*

Thurston County - Water, Woods & Prairies

County? To explore the rise-and-fall history of our famous local beer, one must begin with a young German boy who yearned to go to sea.

Coming to America

Born in 1846 in Germany, Leopold F. Schmidt was the son of a mining engineer but was not interested in that field. He was, however, interested in sailing, so at age 14 he enrolled at the seamen's school in Hamburg. Upon graduation, he sailed to ports in Europe, South America, and the United States. After a stint on the Great Lakes, Leopold decided to remain in America and, in 1866, made his way to Missouri where he spent a few years learning carpentry until he heard of the gold strikes in Montana.

In 1871, Leopold set off for Montana Territory, traveling by steamboat to Fort Benton. From there, he walked another 150 miles to Helena where he found carpentry work around the mines. In 1875 he was asked by a friend to temporarily manage a brewery in Deer Lodge. A lack of brewery experience did not stop Leopold from tackling the new job—the beginning of a brewing dynasty which would last more than a century.

Brewing Beer, There and Here

The brewery business appealed to Leopold so much that he started his own brewery in Butte and then traveled to Germany to learn the science of brewing. Returning to America with a brewery education and an educated bride, Johanna Steiner, Leopold eventually turned his Centennial Brewing Company into Montana's largest brewery.

In August 1895, Leopold visited the Pacific coast "on a trip for rest and

Leopold Schmidt and his eldest son and successor Peter ably ran the Olympia Brewing Company and other family enterprises for six decades. The elder Schmidt lived by two business mottoes: "Always seek to associate with those from whom you can learn" and "Quality first—quantity next." Blessed with intelligence, common sense, integrity, generosity, and a stick-to-it attitude, both men won the respect of their business colleagues and employees. Photo taken ca. 1900. 107.1.171 (Courtesy of Olympia Tumwater Foundation)

pleasure."[2] However, he managed to sneak in a little work. At that time, he was a member of the Montana legislature, which was considering building a new capitol. While in Olympia, Leopold studied the foundation of Washington's new capitol building, then under construction (due to a poor economy, the building never got past the foundation stage). Family lore suggests that while getting a haircut from a German barber, Leopold heard of some artesian springs in nearby Tumwater. Upon viewing the area, he was much taken with "the natural beauty of the place and was particularly pleased with the location and sightliness of what was known as the Biles place, at the foot of the falls."[3] Leopold also tasted the artesian spring water and instantly realized that this was an ideal water for brewing.

Leopold found his love for saltwater rekindled and also realized that his growing family needed more advantages than were available in Montana. Although the exact timing of Leopold's decision to move his family to the Northwest is a bit hazy, two dates stand out. On September 17, 1895, Leopold paid Mrs. Fannie Biles $4,550 for five acres of land comprising the old Biles and Carter tannery site.[4] And on November 9, 1895, Leopold sent a sample of Tumwater's artesian water to Chicago for testing.[5] The scientific assays confirmed Leopold's initial feeling: this water was perfect for making beer.

After moving his family to the Northwest, Leopold spent the winter of 1895-96 planning for the erection of a small brewery at the foot of the falls and engaged his brother Louis to supervise the actual construction. In the summer of 1896, Leopold wrote to a friend: "I am sure to make beer cheaper than anybody else here on the Pacific Coast The water is the best and the site ideal."[6] The new plant was christened the Capital Brewing Company and held its first stockholders' meeting on October 1, 1896.[7] Future company marketing always quoted that October 1st date as the day Olympia Beer first hit the market. However, in a letter dated October 10, 1896, Leopold wrote, "I succeeded in placing the first beer in the market on Saturday Oct 3."[8]

Early Growth

Northwest breweries of that time were making admittedly poor beer. Sales had declined since the financial Panic of 1893, and Eastern breweries shipped better beer into the region. Leopold took advantage of this market opening by brewing a good quality beer which did not carry the extra freight charges of "imported" beer. He felt sure that a higher quality product could command a higher price and a substantial market share—and he was right.

Leopold also felt that the brewery should be a family business, and so all five sons went to work in the plant. At age eighteen, his eldest son Peter became chief engineer and, after attending brewers' school in Milwaukee, was promoted to brewmaster—at only nineteen, the youngest graduate brewmaster in any American brewery.

By 1902, the Capital Brewery was due for some changes. The slogan "It's the Water" was adopted

In 1902, Leopold Schmidt changed the name of his brewery from Capital Brewing to Olympia Brewing. This transitional receipt bearing both names was used for several years while Schmidt fought the federal government for the right to trademark the name "Olympia." Although the company stationery varied over the years, this example was one of the few that did not feature the brewery's well-known horseshoe symbol. (Courtesy of Olympia Tumwater Foundation)

and quickly became a byword in the industry. Also, Leopold and his stockholders changed the business's name to Olympia Brewing Company, partly to have a unique name (as several other Capital Breweries existed across the country) and partly because the brand "Olympia Beer" was so well-recognized.

Between 1902 and 1909, the Schmidts added four breweries to their empire of beer: Bellingham and Port Townsend, Washington; Salem, Oregon; and San Francisco, California. In 1905-06, the Tumwater brewery was updated by erecting a six-story brick brewhouse, destined to become a landmark that still stands.

The End of an Era

A company history summed up the next decade: "The Olympia Brewing Company and the other associated breweries had a capacity of 350,000 barrels of beer a year. The 18-year-old company was on top of the world—but it was a troubled world and trouble came home to Tumwater.

In 1902, newly hired employee Frank M. Kenney thought Olympia Beer should have a catchy slogan. He argued with Leopold Schmidt for two days before Schmidt capitulated and accepted Kenney's tagline "It's the Water." This sketch is from the August 1951 issue of It's the Water News. *(Courtesy of Olympia Tumwater Foundation)*

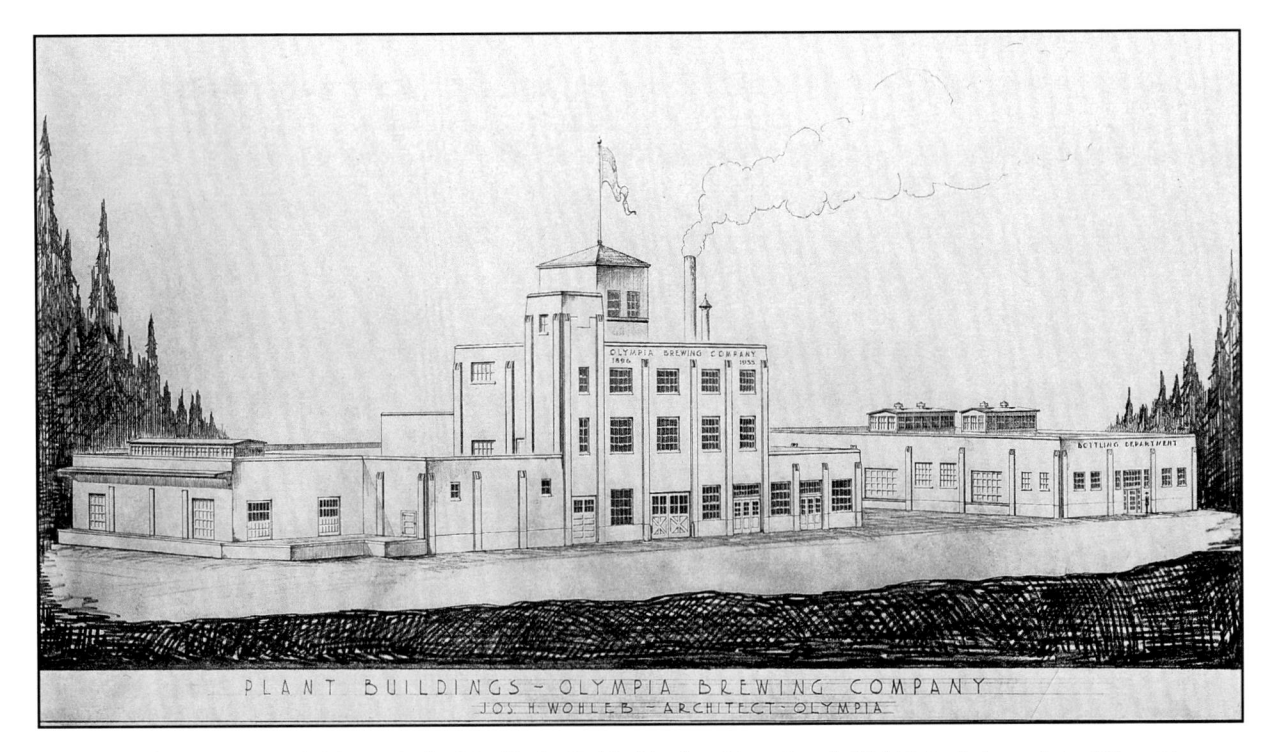

When Prohibition was repealed in 1933, the Schmidt family hired local architect Joseph Wohleb to design a state-of-the-art brewery. Although much enlarged and modernized over the ensuing years, the original building still stands above the Deschutes River. 00045 (Courtesy of Olympia Tumwater Foundation)

Olympia Beer made a national splash when syndicated cartoonist Walt Kelly sketched an Olympia beer crate into his famous Pogo comic strip in 1952. According to Kelly's son Pete, his father never accepted payment for tributes like these—he just chose people and products he liked and inked them into cartoon history. Original cartoon from the archives of the Olympia Tumwater Foundation. (Copyright Okefenokee Glee & Perloo, Inc. Used by permission)

Leopold Schmidt died in Bellingham [in 1914]. His son, Peter G. Schmidt, who had been handling most activities of the business since his father's semi-retirement in 1912, was elected president. The states of Washington, Oregon, and Idaho voted in Prohibition with one year grace granted for companies to close up. January 1, 1916, thus marked the apparent end of all the breweries with which the Schmidt family was so intimately identified."

The family, now headed by Peter, turned their attention and their brewery to making fruit juices. Although somewhat successful, that business did not last much past the end of World War I. More successful was the family's involvement in managing hotels in several Northwest cities. The Schmidts also diversified into a transportation company (which became part of Greyhound Bus Lines many years after the Schmidts had sold their interests), oyster farming, banking, and gasification plants.

Regardless of their other ventures, the Schmidts cherished hopes of someday returning to making beer. So they kept the corporate name and slogan alive during those dark, dry years. And in late 1933, their hopes were justified when the federal government finally repealed Prohibition.

A New Era Begins

The old brewery proved too antiquated to be of use post-Prohibition so Peter quickly constructed a modern brewery on land overlooking the upper falls of the Deschutes. By January 14, 1934,

This caricature of Leopold Schmidt appeared in the book Men Behind the Seattle Spirit—Argus Cartoons. *Edited by H. A. Chadwick. Seattle, Washington: Chadwick, 1906, page 156. (Courtesy of Olympia Tumwater Foundation)*

Thurston County - Water, Woods & Prairies

THE SCHMIDT FAMILY

Peter G. Schmidt Sr. family, pictured ca. 1916. From left: young Clara ("Nootchie"), Clara, Margaret ("Gradie"), Peter, and Marie ("Sis"). P41.47 (Courtesy of Olympia Tumwater Foundation)

The Schmidt family loved to support and improve the community in which they lived. Brewery founder Leopold Schmidt was known for his generosities to down-on-their-luck individuals. Peter and Clara Schmidt gave away thousands of pounds of produce from their WWII victory garden, and Clara was instrumental in bringing arts and culture to Thurston County. In 1950, Peter and his family established the Olympia Tumwater Foundation, largely as a non-profit vehicle to handle the installation and donation of the Tivoli Fountain on the State Capitol Campus. Today, the Foundation continues this community-minded philosophy by promoting education through its college scholarship program, operating Tumwater Falls Park at no charge to the public, and maintaining an archive of Olympia Brewery and Schmidt family documents at the Schmidt House.

Peter G. Schmidt became engaged to Clara Muench in the spring of 1908. That summer, Clara visited Tumwater, and Peter (a "born mechanic") decided he would take her for a spin in his motorboat, *Montana*. Decades later, their son, Peter Jr., related the following tale: "My father got into the boat and tried to start the engine. Well, many of you know how cranky the old engines were—they had to be choked and then they would flood and wouldn't start. Imagine this old engine in 1908. My father proceeded to take the engine apart while my mother sat there. And she sat there, and she sat there, and she sat there, and he had pieces and parts all over the boat and was cursing. And I don't think they ever did go on that trip." Despite the long wait and the cursing, the marriage came off in 1909 and lasted nearly fifty years.

From "State Capitol Comment" in the *State Capitol Record*, September 26, 1914:

> The late Leopold Schmidt, head of the Olympia Brewing Company of Tumwater, cherished high ideals. Yesterday an employee told a characteristic story of the well-loved employer. "One day Mr. Schmidt visited Seattle and was talking there to the local representative of the brewery. We will call him 'Doc.' Shortly before a restricted district had been established in Seattle and Doc with considerable pride boasted to Mr. Schmidt that he had secured three new customers who would buy a great deal of beer. Naturally Mr. Schmidt pressed for details and learned they were madams in the new district. Said he: 'Doc, you are a married man and have a little girl. Do you think you would care to go to those places Monday morning to collect? We do not care to have our sign or to sell our goods any place where any person is ashamed or should be ashamed to be seen in daylight.' And Mr. Schmidt never varied from that rule."

Olympia Beer was once again on the market. Production for that year reached 75,000 barrels, and over a hundred Thurston County residents found employment at the new plant. During the 1930s and '40s, the innovative "Stubby" bottle and stainless steel kegs were introduced and soon became industry standards. Although shipping restrictions were imposed during World War II, the brewery bounced back after the war was over and soon expanded its sales areas. By 1956, a million barrels of Oly Beer went to market.

In the 1950s, Peter stepped down as company president and served instead as chairman of the board of directors. A third generation of Schmidts gained prominence as Peter's nephew, Adolph Schmidt, Jr., became president, and Adolph's brothers, Trueman and Robert, rose to upper management positions.

"Uncle Peter," as he was affectionately known to all brewery employees, passed away in 1957. His nephews continued running the brewery, modernizing and expanding to better serve their customers without sacrificing quality.

In November 1964, this beauty shot of the brewery graced the cover of the It's the Water News *employee newsletter. Many county residents remember the immaculate green lawns on the steep slopes around the brewery. (Courtesy of Olympia Tumwater Foundation)*

One of America's Exceptional Breweries

For decades, the Olympia plant was the most recognizable landmark on the highway between Seattle and Portland. Huge letters on the side of the brewery proclaimed "Visitors Welcome"—and they were. The hospitality room at the brewery offered guided tours and samples of cold Olympia beer. In 1962, the tour service welcomed its one millionth visitor: a California family passing through to the Seattle World's Fair.[13]

In 1964, production passed the two-million barrel mark. Two years later, annual sales hit over $100 million.[14] By this time, the brewery was one of the largest employers in the county with over 700 workers. Land on the east side of the Deschutes was purchased for the installation of a huge warehouse facility. Up to nine brewmasters oversaw the production of the now nationally-recognized brand that appeared in movies and TV shows.

In all this time, the company never forgot Leopold's founding premise of "quality first, quantity next." As a brewery publication told shareholders, "the naturally-perfect brewing water from our artesian springs remains our single most important asset, the unique factor upon which your Company's continuing success is built."[15]

Management's main worry was how to spend so much income. Projects included still more brewery expansions, lavish employee banquets, acquisition of Hamm's and Lone Star breweries, and publicly accessible ventures like Tumwater Falls Park and the Tumwater Valley Golf Course. The Olympia Brewing Company was indeed flying high.

All Good Things...

By the mid-1970s, however, the national brewery climate had changed. Mid-sized, regional breweries struggled to keep up with the increasing market saturation achieved by industry giants such as Anheuser-Busch, Miller, and Coors. Large

At the foot of the Deschutes River falls, the iconic 1906 brewhouse stands deserted. At the top of the hill, the 1904 Schmidt House peeks through the trees. In the background, the later era brewery buildings and sign loom over the older structures. As of this writing, the 1906 brewhouse is in the process of restoration by the City of Tumwater. Photo ca. 1975. (Courtesy of Paul Knight)

breweries gobbled up little firms. So it went in Tumwater: the Pabst Brewing Company decided to buy out Oly, regardless of whether Oly wanted to sell. With increasing pressure from Pabst to join forces or die fighting, Olympia management finally recommended to stockholders that a merger with Pabst was inevitable.[16] In 1983, the deal was consummated, marking, as *The Olympian* wrote, "a quiet end to a company which, although proud and generous, couldn't keep up its sales in an increasingly competitive market." After nearly ninety years, the Schmidt family no longer controlled Oly Beer.

After the initial shock, the community mood gradually swung upward, hoping that Pabst would manage to put Olympia Brewing back near the top of the list of going concerns. But in 1985, Pabst itself was swallowed up by the S & P Company. Over the next two decades, a bewildering series of continually morphing conglomerates purchased our local brewery. By 2002, the talk was not so much of nationalization but globalization. In the final move that year, then-owner Miller Brewing merged with South African Breweries to become SABMiller, a company which saw no need for a medium-sized brewery in the Northwest. And so, in June 2003, the aging tanks were drained, the clanking of the bottle line went silent, the five o'clock steam whistle blew for the final time, and the employee parking lot emptied.

The Olympia Brewing Company died.

After the Schmidt family sold the brewery in 1983, a succession of owners kept the beer flowing for another twenty years. But on June 12, 2003, Thurston County residents listened with sadness and resignation as the brewery's steam whistle blew for the last time. Although Olympia beer is still brewed in California, it's not the water any longer. (Courtesy of the photographer Riley McLaughlin)

"A Turbulent Age" examines Thurston County through World War I, labor unrest, growth, and the Roaring Twenties. Jennifer Crooks, a lifelong resident of Thurston County and one of its newest historians, tells of the challenging times as Thurston County moved into the twentieth century.

Chapter 16
A TURBULENT AGE
Into the Twentieth Century: Change and Conflict (1889 - 1929)
by Jennifer Crooks

THE DECADES between statehood and the Great Depression formed an era of profound change and development in Thurston County. As the county experienced exponential growth in population and industry, the modern face of the county began to form. As a consequence of this growth, there were serious social and environmental costs. In response, many community members dedicated themselves through political and social action to improving and reforming society and alleviating the problems that modernization had both brought and aggravated.

Setting the Scene: Transformations After Statehood

This time also marked the end of the pioneer era with the deaths of many old-timers. Interest in the preservation of historical memory led to

Olympia's Chinatown developed in the late nineteenth century and continued well into the twentieth century. Despite many hurdles created by widespread discrimination, the Chinese immigrants became an important part of the local economy with their labor, laundries, and gardens. The Toone Ah and Nettie Chiang James family of Olympia are pictured here, ca. 1900. C1948.64.76 (Courtesy of Washington State Historical Society)

Thurston County - Water, Woods & Prairies

Artist Edward Lange lived in Olympia from 1889 to his death in 1912. Traveling around the state, he was hired to draw farms, businesses, and entire communities. This birdseye (or panoramic) view of Olympia with the accompanying vignettes portrays the flourishing Capital City of 1903. Control #75696658 (Courtesy of Library of Congress)

the publication of various reminiscences and the foundation of the Thurston County Pioneer and Historical Association in 1910 by surviving pioneers. However, attempts at historic preservation of buildings proved mostly unsuccessful. Many historically important structures were demolished in the name of progress such as the Territorial/first State Capitol building in 1911 and the Governor Stevens House in 1929.

Society

The population of Washington State grew dramatically in the decades after statehood. Thurston County was no exception. According to the US Federal Census, the population of Thurston County stood at 9,675 in 1890, 9,927 in 1900 and 17,581 in 1910. Much of this growth centered in the countryside where industries such as logging, mining, and farming thrived. The area's cities grew as well with Olympia increasing from 4,698 people in 1890 to 6,996 in 1910.[1]

Most of this population growth resulted from immigration from within the United States and internationally, enabled by the creation of extensive transcontinental railway networks from the 1880s onward. Many of these newcomers came from Scandinavia, the Balkans, and Italy, attracted by prospects of employment. Immigrants from China and Japan were also numerous. Legally barred from citizenship and land ownership or rental by the Alien Land Law of 1921 and with increasing restrictions on immigration to America, Asian immigrants encountered heavy prejudice. Still, a Chinatown developed in Olympia, noted for its laundries and other businesses. Other Chinese people in search of work found employment as gardeners and servants. Japanese immigrants were particularly prominent for their work with oysters and lumber. For example, Union Mills near Lacey recruited a number of Japanese workers.

188   Chapter 16 - A Turbulent Age

In 1911, Fred Wiseman, known as the "Birdman," piloted his bi-wing plane over Olympia. His three short flights promoted the Carlyon Fill area that had just been created by dredging and filling. This image of the "Birdman" piloting his plane was taken by noted photographer Asahel Curtis. Wiseman later became an executive in the oil industry. Negative # A. Curtis 20901 (Courtesy of University of Washington Library, Special Collections)

Olympia Knitting Mill employees pose in this ca. 1915 photograph. Notice the piles of garments lying on the tables or stored in boxes. Records indicate that the workers here served as the finishing crew for the clothing. C1951.250.27 (Courtesy of Washington State Historical Society)

Economy

This growth was also punctuated by cycles of economic prosperity and recession. The Panic of 1893 caused particular hardship in Thurston County. Many lost homes and jobs. The entire Olympia City Council resigned over debts incurred by street improvements, and the county government began a search for a location to establish a poor farm.[2] The Thurston County Courthouse was sold to the State for use as a Capitol building. This structure, now known as the Old State Capitol, still stands in downtown Olympia as the Superintendent of Public Instruction headquarters. Eventually, in the 1910s and 1920s, the center of state political activities shifted to the current State Capitol Campus with the implementation of architects Walter Wilder and Harry White's plan for a group of buildings, including the Temple of Justice and Legislative Building.

Changes to the landscape of the county also marked the era. One of the most dramatic projects was the physical expansion of Olympia's downtown, known as the Carlyon Fill. Although earlier and later fills modified the shoreline, the 1909-1911 Carlyon Fill was the most extensive. Adding many blocks to downtown, it eliminated much of Olympia's mudflats and created the deepwater port that the town had always wanted. The fill area was promoted in 1911 by special flights by early aviator Fred Wiseman (nicknamed "the Birdman"). The event was widely attended by people from across Southwest Washington although the program lost money because most visitors congregated outside of the ticket-only area closest to the makeshift airfield. Movie footage of Wiseman's three flights was taken, but unfortunately, it has been lost. Various industries, including the Olympia Cannery, built facilities on the fill. However, the long-term stability

Police operations in early 20th century Thurston County did not ignore new technology. In this ca. 1912 photograph, Olympia's first motorcycle police officer Fred Koepkey stands next to his Yale 7P motorcycle. Behind the man and machine is the local Masonic Temple, a structure built in 1911 on 8th Avenue and Main Street (now Capitol Way). C2013.18.50 (Courtesy of Washington State Historical Society)

of the infill has been an issue in the twenty-first century. Highly susceptible to earthquake damage, the area suffered more damage than the rest of the county in the earthquakes of 1949, 1965, and 2001. The land created by the fill, now heavily polluted by industrial activity, is also likely to be flooded by rising sea levels.

Agriculture stood as another pillar of the Thurston County economy. The earliest pioneers were farmers, and most of the county remained agricultural during the period. A few scientific "modern" farms dotted the county in the early twentieth century, such as Hazard Stevens's Cloverfields in what is now South Olympia and the Alson Brown farm on the Nisqually Delta. Most farms were simple family operations providing sustenance but not profit. They produced a wide variety of crops and dairy farm products, selling much of their produce to the urban market.

Civic boosterism infused all of the towns in Thurston County during this era, as the communities sought to attract people and businesses to the area. In Olympia, boosterism inspired women in the Civic Club to organize annual clean-up days in the 1910s that promoted trash pickup and lawn cutting. Boosterism also supported the creation of public places that brought communities together. Olympia's Priest Point Park was established in 1905 as a natural haven for town-dwellers. For the first few years of the park's existence, volunteers organized work parties that developed the recreational area. Priest Point Park, typically reached by boat in the era before cars, quickly became a favorite site for gatherings, picnics, and swimming. Parties and dances were often held at a Swiss chalet that Leopold Schmidt of the Olympia Brewing Company donated to the park.

Community pride was frequently expressed in elaborate commemorations of holidays such as American Independence Day. The 1910 multi-day celebration of Independence Day in Olympia, including harness horse races and a big parade, proved especially popular as noted in a *Morning Olympian* newspaper article published on Tuesday, July 5, 1910:

> One of the features of the day was the crowd. It was one of the largest ever seen in Olympia. The forces of Saturday were augmented yesterday by people from all surrounding towns. The roads into the city were lined with vehicles of every kind and the trains and boats carried capacity crowds all day yesterday. When the steamer *Greyhound* left last night for Tacoma more than 100 people were compelled to take the 8:25 o'clock train or remain in the city until this morning.[3]

Industrial Workers of the World (IWW) political sticker, 1915. In the early twentieth century the Industrial Workers of the World (often called "Wobblies") struggled in America for "one big union" that would fight for better working conditions and the end of capitalism. Intense opposition by employers and government to their activities sometimes resulted in violence. 2010.0.52 (Courtesy of Washington State Historical Society)

Dreamers helped shape the development of Thurston County. One dreamer, John Chaplin, attempted several times at the turn of the twentieth century to establish colleges in the county. His first try was the Olympic University intended for Cooper Point near Olympia. Instead, this institution enjoyed a shaky existence for a year (1894-1895) in the old Collegiate Institute buildings located in Olympia near East Bay Drive; then it closed without moving to Cooper Point. Later a second attempt by Chaplin sought to create People's University on Cooper Point. For four years (1902-1906) the university existed in Olympia's Collegiate Institute buildings before closing; it too did not make it to Cooper Point. Nevertheless, both colleges' educational ideas affected students, teachers, and the Olympia community. Interestingly, The Evergreen State College was constructed later in the twentieth century on Cooper Point where John Chaplin dreamed of building his school.[4]

In 1895 Catholic Benedictine monks opened Saint Martin's College in Woodland (now Lacey). It proved much more successful than John Chaplin's Olympic University or People's University. In recent years, Saint Martin's changed its name from College to University and remains a major educational force in the area.

Issues of the Era

Besides agriculture, the regional economy centered on extractive industries such as timber and mining. These businesses were not intended to be sustainable in the long term. When an area was logged over, the camp of workers moved on, creating a highly mobile labor force. This mobility could also affect communities that built up around lumber mills. In one case, the small unincorporated community of Zanaton formed around the Smith-Miller Mill on Chambers Prairie in the late 1910s/early 1920s. It quickly dispersed after the mill closed.

The pollution caused by these industries became a significant problem. Olympia dumped its garbage, raw sewage, and industrial waste directly into Puget Sound. Due to this pollution, fishermen faced periodic fish die-offs and by the late 1800s oysters in Budd Inlet became inedible. Although there were some regional lawsuits and complaints, it would take until the later half of the 20th century for more serious action to limit pollution.

Such an unstable economy left many people periodically unemployed and underemployed. More prosperous residents were worried about the behavior of the migrant laborers, many of whom were deemed

The lumber industry in Thurston County, including logging and milling, was difficult and dangerous. Feeding the workers well was a necessity. The dining room of Allen & Son Mill Company laborers in Littlerock is seen in this ca. 1900 photo. C1948.1210.1 (Courtesy of Washington State Historical Society)

192   Chapter 16 - A Turbulent Age

SAINT MARTIN'S UNIVERSITY

by Genevieve C. Chan

Founded by the Catholic Benedictine monks of Saint Martin's Abbey, Saint Martin's College in Lacey opened its doors in 1895 for only one student who traveled by canoe some 25 miles to attend. The college offered a mix of preparatory through commercial college classes at what was then an all-boys institution.

In the 1930s, the monks eliminated the preparatory programs and developed the high school and college. The four-year baccalaureate program was accredited and, in 1940, graduated its first students. After World War II, the G.I. Bill brought hundreds of veterans to campus, and programs in accounting, business and engineering were added. Saint Martin's became coeducational in 1965 and, in 1972, began offering extension programs at what later became Joint Base Lewis-McChord.

When Saint Martin's High School closed in 1974, more lay employees were hired to support increasing numbers of college students. The 1980s brought the addition of graduate courses and the creation of the Institute for Pacific Rim Studies, now known as the Office of International Programs and Development. In 2005, the College officially became Saint Martin's University, a more accurate reflection of the institution's nature and mission.

Saint Martin's has evolved into a co-educational university that offers 25 majors and seven graduate programs spanning the liberal arts, business, education, nursing and engineering fields with 1,550 undergraduate and graduate students at its main campus and extensions. Since the turn of the twenty-first century, Saint Martin's has added several significant buildings to its Lacey campus. In 2001, Saint Martin's opened the O'Grady Library, designed by world-renowned architect Michael Graves. In 2013, Father Richard Cebula, O.S.B. Hall, home of The Hal and Inge Marcus School of Engineering, opened with a Platinum LEED certification score that makes it among the most environmentally progressive buildings in the world.

Through decades of change and growth, the core values of faith, reason, service, and community remain central to life at Saint Martin's University.

Genevieve C. Chan is Vice President of the Office of Marketing and Communications, Saint Martin's University, www.stmartin.edu

Old Main, the oldest building of Saint Martin's University in Lacey. (Courtesy of Saint Martin's University)

Many home front organizations formed in Thurston County during World War I. This photo shows the Yelm Home Guard in 1917. Home Guard units, usually consisting of men too old to serve in the military, were established around the nation to defend against foreign and internal threats. These units remained mostly inactive during the war period but demonstrated the tensions of that time. (Courtesy of Yelm Prairie Historical Society)

to be "tramps" (homeless). A shantytown on Water Street in Olympia, nicknamed "Little Hollywood" in later years, earned a rough reputation for crime but included legitimate businesses such as blacksmith shops and other small businesses as well as poor, elderly people with no other place to go. Others congregated in places like "Hobo Point" (Warren Point, which was taken out partially by the construction of Capital Lake and the East Fourth Avenue Bridge). Although the shacks at Hobo Point were burned down by police, they soon were rebuilt since chronic poverty did not disappear.

One governmental response to the issue of poverty was the county poor farm. Located in various places around the county after 1892, it closed around 1933 at the height of the Great Depression. Residents of the farm tended to be elderly men and women in fragile health. Only a small number could be accommodated, and conditions were widely considered miserable. Reverend Lois Prater remembered visiting the poor house in her teens with a choir from the Olympia Church of God in the mid-1920s: "I remember going out there and singing for them. I used to feel so sorry...they didn't have any soft chairs. They just had hard chairs for the people to sit on...it was no comfort, nothing for these old people. It was just really pathetic..."[6]

Reform

The labor movement has a long history in Thurston County. Unionism, however, was often not welcomed by the establishment. Indeed labor radicalism in the form of the Industrial Workers of the World (IWW, often known as the "Wobblies") caused much panic in early twentieth century South Puget Sound. However, although the IWW became the face of the labor movement for many people, the organization was not representative of most union activity. The major issues for labor included higher wages and better working conditions.

The main labor unions in Olympia during the period organized under the Olympia Trades Council, founded in 1902,[7] consisting of local union representatives. The organization united existing unions and created new ones, offering financial support for striking unions and arbitration for trade disputes. Major unions included the Barbers' Union, Beer Bottlers' Union, Beer Drivers' and Helpers'

Union, Brewery Workers, Retail Clerks' Union Local 309, Shingle Weavers' Union, Bricklayers' and Masons' Union, and Federal Union.[8] Another prominent early union was the Printers' Local No. 142, founded in May 1890, which organized printers, pressmen, and mailers.[9]

This era was fraught with tension between workers and employers. The conflict led to the growth of the Industrial Workers of the World, an extreme group that preached "one big union," the overthrow of capitalism and world revolution, in addition to demands for better pay, shorter hours and safer working conditions that more moderate unions sought as well. Working conditions in logging camps and mills were particularly deadly and unsanitary, and accidents claimed the lives and health of workers every week. The actions of Wobblies created a backlash that also affected moderate unions, particularly as the IWW was seen as unpatriotic and as supporters of Russia's Bolshevik Revolution during World War I and the following Red Scare. Union agitation eventually helped improve working conditions and pay in many industries. During World War I, in response to the IWW, the government itself set up a union, the Loyal Legion of Loggers and Lumbermen (4L). Membership was mandatory, and it helped improve conditions in logging camps and mills.

In April 1912, Olympia newspapers sounded an alarm that the police had reported three IWW "scouts" had visited the town. The police feared an IWW strike at the Bordeaux camps and "agitation" at Union Mills.[10] The IWW did not claim the men seen in Olympia were scouts.[11] Later that month, Thurston County Attorney John M. Wilson received a phone call from Littlerock saying that the town was expecting an IWW contingent from Seattle to "storm" the community and nearby logging camps in the near future. Wilson, however, warned the residents of Littlerock against reacting unless the "invaders"

Some of the Olympia industries are shown in this center section of a three-part panorama of 1909 Olympia. Resulting pollution affected air, land and water. Even today current development in the Capital City often encounters the toxic residue of past industrial activity. Fortunately, many people and groups have worked in recent decades to clean up the mess. 1943.42.15114.2 (Courtesy of Washington State Historical Society)

The assassination of President William McKinley in 1901 shocked the nation. On September 19, 1901, people from around Thurston County gathered for a memorial in Olympia. After church services, lodges and clubs marched through town. A total of 660 public school children, as well as 88 students from the Catholic Providence Academy, joined in the long funeral procession. Here the children are at Main Street (Capitol Way) and 7th Street (Avenue). After the parade, the town gathered for speeches by Governor John Rodgers and other state officials. State Library Photograph Collection, 1851-1990. AR-07809001-ph000914 (Courtesy of Washington State Archives—Digital Archives)

broke laws or started "trouble." County Sheriff George Gaston refused requests to send deputies or appoint local lawmen for the town, dismissing the threat as a rumor. Fears of "invasion" fizzled as no noticeable activity occurred in the area at the time.[12]

Many people, not only unions such as the IWW, wanted to create a better society. Reforms filled the "Progressive Era" (approximately 1890-1920), including public health improvements, educational reforms, and government reorganization. Almost no aspect of life was left untouched by some attempt at reform and improvement. Women participated actively in the reform movement, winning the right to vote in 1910 in Washington State, nearly a decade before the passing of the nineteenth amendment, although voting rights were kept from most Asian immigrants and Native Americans.

Though medical advances marked the era, public health remained a major problem. Infant and maternal mortality rates were high, and epidemics of serious illnesses such as smallpox, typhoid, influenza, measles, and polio hit with frightening regularity. Logging camps, with their poor sanitation standards and overcrowding, were particularly hard hit by epidemics. When a deadly typhoid epidemic struck Camps No. 4 and 7 of the Simpson Logging Company in the Black Hills in August 1913, over a dozen loggers ended up in St. Peter's Hospital, and several others died.[13] Such events were far from rare.

While the cost of medical care was often an issue in an era without disability benefits and health insurance except through a few fraternal societies, some healthcare providers were noted for their

Fred and Iva (Ivy) Whitney Day relax on the porch of their cabin at Bordeaux in the Black Hills, Thurston County, ca. 1910. Note that the rustic building is propped up on logs and surrounded by wooden debris. The couple's economic world is clearly based on the logging and milling of timber. C1943.1006.25 (Courtesy of Washington State Historical Society)

generosity. For example, Doctor Henry S. Strickland of Olympia, who practiced for fifteen years in the Capital City, was widely admired by the poor for not asking compensation of bills when he knew that they could not afford to pay.[14] More organized efforts to meet local health needs included a free Red Cross children's health clinic that opened July 24, 1922, at the Red Cross headquarters on Franklin Street. Hospitals and drug stores volunteered to sell services at cost, funded by public donations.[15]

As part of these Progressive reforms, the Olympia Police and Fire Department expanded and professionalized. This sort of improvement also occurred in other parts of the county. In Olympia, the police force helped "boost" the town in 1910, promoting the sale of buttons that read "Olympia's different." Chief of Police Alex Wright purchased buttons for himself and the police station's beloved mascot, "Lucky" the dog.[16] But one way Olympia was not especially "different" or "lucky" was in matters of crime and social problems.

Still, one significant reform was the closing of Olympia's Tenderloin, or restricted district, in 1910. Found in many American communities of the era, this type of district held gambling, sleazy saloons, prostitution, and some narcotic use overlooked by law enforcement. The Tenderloin, located north of Fourth Avenue in the run-down former business heart of the city, was a place full of despair and violence. But the restricted district did contribute something to Olympia…and that was corruption. For example, Chief of Police Edmund Rogers was forced to resign in December 1909 after allegations that he did not enforce the law against opium smoking in the restricted district.[17] Reformers pushed periodically for the abolishment of the district, and they finally succeeded in 1910. However, as to be expected, that was not the end of crime or corruption—or prostitution—in Olympia or Thurston County.

With government welfare severely limited, private and religious charities sometimes attempted to coordinate their activities in the county. In December 1912, the Associated Charities formed, with the Reverend D. A. Thompson as temporary chairman. It united the efforts of organizations such as the Helping Hand, Ladies' Relief Society, Humane Society, Mercy (Animal Rights), Department of the Woman's Christian Temperance Union (WCTU), Trades Council, Red Cross, Young Men's Christian Association (YMCA), public schools, and the Ministerial Association.[18] The Associated Charities lasted into the 1920s.[19]

One solution to alleviate poverty was city government and private charity sponsored labor projects. In late 1911 a precursor to the Associated Charities, calling itself the "society for the aiding of unfortunates out of employment and prevention of tramps," formed to distribute food and clothes to the unemployed. The organization printed meal tickets and distributed them to homes around the city to give to any "tramp" begging at their door. The tickets could be redeemed in exchange for labor at the woodpile. It was an attempt to alleviate suffering, instill the value of hard work and to rid the Olympia area of so-called "undesirables."[20]

The city woodpile remained an institution of sorts, taken over by the Associated Charities. Wood was hauled from Priest Point Park, logged for decades to pay for the park, to the city jail where prisoners also chopped firewood as a punishment to pay fines. In January 1916, heavy rain damaged the bridge to Priest Point Park, cutting off the wood supply. In the meantime, the Associated Charities and Chief of Police A. S. Caton arranged to employ the men shoveling snow from downtown streets in exchange for a meal ticket.[21]

The Tipping Point: The Great War

World War I had a direct impact on Thurston County. Many county residents participated enthusiastically in all major war activities, from enlisting in the armed forces to home front programs such as the Red Cross and Liberty Loans. The Thurston County Council of Defense, a local division of the Council of National Defense and the Washington State Council of Defense, coordinated war activities in the area with the Woman's Work Committee of over 300 "Minute Women" to implement the programs.

The drinking fountain in Olympia's Sylvester Park is a memorial to Emma Page, a blind woman who led an active life, fighting strongly for animal rights and abstinence from alcohol. Vandalized in 1997, the fountain was repaired and re-dedicated in 2000. (Courtesy of the photographer Jennifer Crooks)

Local branches of the county council formed in many communities. Minute Women groups existed in even the smallest of districts. Although the "Home Guard" would prove unnecessary, draft-exempt men, usually middle-aged, formed Home Guard units to protect against perceived threats of invasion and internal disorder.

Although most Thurston County people supported the war and numerous young men served in the military (about 20 would die), the area was very hostile to any form of dissent. South Bay schoolteacher Charles R. Carr paid a high price for wartime dissent. A Christian pacifist and socialist, he lost his teaching license for making anti-war statements even though he apologized. The time of World War I has been noted by many historians for its restrictions on free speech.[22]

Thurston County was hit hard by the deadly 1918 Influenza Pandemic. While the flu is not usually a life-threatening disease to healthy adults, this strain killed 20 percent of its victims rather than the usual two percent, especially the young and healthy. The flu particularly afflicted logging camps and public gatherings were banned.[23] The exact death toll locally was difficult to calculate. Worldwide it killed 30 to 50 million people, including over 600,000 Americans.

Aftermath: The Search for "Normalcy"

The sudden termination of the war economy sparked economic and civil instability across the country. The year 1919 saw the largest number of strikes in American history, and Thurston County was no exception. In Olympia, the pile drivers constructing the new Fourth Street (now Fourth Avenue) bridge struck for three weeks. Although initially the Union Bridge Company of Portland claimed that work would continue unhampered by the strike,[24] construction was halted within days.[25] The strikers failed to achieve their demands.[26]

In response to pressure from the state and county organizations like the Loyal League of Washington, Cassandra Messegee, County Superintendent of Education, and her office designed a new curriculum. They decided to "outline and adopt a course of patriotic instruction to be followed in the public schools of Thurston County…." because "of the necessity for loyalty teaching in the schools and educational responsibility for symptoms of disloyal sentiment as exhibited in IWW and other propaganda opposed to the American system of government."[27] This sentiment conflated all social and economic protest into a straw-man villain (the IWW) and ignored the fact that the United States Constitution guarantees free speech

Being so close, Thurston County played an intimate role in the Lewis County events known as the "Centralia Tragedy" or the "Centralia Massacre." The tragic conflict on November 11, 1919, left four World War I veterans dead, a Wobblie brutally murdered by vigilantes, and 11 on trial in a case that left controversy and scars for decades. Officials in Thurston County received word from a man whom they believed was an IWW agent that Ole Hanson and "John Doe" Davis, wanted for their role in the Centralia events, were in the Bordeaux logging camps. Dozens of officers, mostly from Lewis County, but including a large number from Thurston County, searched the area; meeting no resistance, they arrested seven men believed to be radicals. Officers also searched boarding houses in Olympia for radicals who might be hiding. Logger Peter Doyle suffered minor injuries when two nervous Centralia officers opened fire when he shut his door on them.[28] While police labeled Bordeaux as a long-time hotbed of IWW activity,[29] the entire search had been useless. Ole Hanson was later arrested, but "John Doe" Davis was never found or arrested.

Further crackdowns on radicals occurred as the state and nation entered the grips of the Red Scare. In 1919, the state passed a criminal syndicalism act banning radical organizations, such as the IWW, that advocated for the takeover of industry and government by direct action such as general strikes and sabotage.[30] In the words of the *Morning Olympian*, the Thurston County prosecutor's office initiated a "cleanup program." The first men in the county arrested, viewed as a test case of the act, were Elias Matson and Frank

The Woodmen of the World, a fraternal society that provided life insurance as well as social benefits, march in a parade through downtown Olympia, ca. 1910. Their parade entry is pictured here in front of the Chong Lee Laundry, showing the importance of Chinese-owned businesses during the era. A sign on the side of the wagon says, "W.O.W. Can Protect You." State Library Photograph Collection, 1851-1990, AR-07809001-ph000950 (Courtesy of Washington State Archives—Digital Archives)

Hastings.[31] The prosecution's case rested on proving that the IWW was a menace to American society, seditious, and anti-government. The men were declared guilty, and they later lost an appeal to the State Supreme Court.[32]

In 1923, the IWW and sympathizers organized a national strike to force the release of all IWW political prisoners in state prisons and the United States penitentiary in Leavenworth, Kansas. Olympia citizens grew nervous as hundreds of strikers passed through the city in cars and buses en route to Tacoma, Seattle and other cities to the north. A number of men walked off the job at Olympia's mills as well. Area logging camps were left without enough workers and ran shorter shifts. Olympia Chief of Police J. E. Kuntz and Thurston County Sheriff Charles Jackson assured the public that they expected no trouble and that the men would be coming back once the strike ended.[33]

But they were overly optimistic. The Mason County Logging Company at Bordeaux and the Simpson Logging Company in Shelton stated that a large number of workers had gone on strike, some camps might have to close, and others were short staffed. An unverified report stated that Mud Bay Logging Company had its whole force out. It was estimated that 25 to 50 percent of the workers in the camps left, but some camps had even more men on strike. Men struck all around Western Washington. Still, the strike was short-lived and did not disrupt the industry as much as feared.[34]

The IWW and radical labor conflict cut deep divisions into society. There was no easy solution to economic inequalities and social injustice. Situations tended to be complicated with ambiguities. Perhaps this is best seen in an assault with a deadly weapon case that rocked Thurston County in November 1919.

In a case eagerly followed by area newspapers, Alex Sugoff was charged with an assault with a deadly weapon at the Mud Bay Logging Company Camp on November 3. Charges were dropped at a December 7 Olympia trial that reflected personal animosities created by ethnic and union tensions. Sugoff (Russian and in the pro-government Loyal Legion of Loggers and Lumbermen) had shot E. L. Bean (likely native-born and IWW).[35] Looking at it now, perhaps it is questionable that Judge John Wilson, who was noted to be biased against radicals when he presided over the Centralia trials, offered a fair judgment after viewing the contradictory evidence.

The labor movement was severely hobbled in the 1920s although unions did not disappear. For example, the United Mine Workers in Tono were a strong force. In 1927 the Ladies' First Aid held a celebration of the United Mine Workers of America's eight-hour day (achieved in 1898).[36] Unions had achieved many of their goals, but much work remained.

In a politically charged climate, justice often proved elusive. One reaction during this period was intense nativism and isolationism as many radicals were perceived to be foreigners. A revived Ku Klux Klan (KKK), with its hostility to African Americans, Jews, and Catholics, flourished in the early 1920s. In 1924, the Olympia chapter of the KKK received its official charter from the Atlanta headquarters and celebrated by burning a hundred by fifty-foot cross made out of old car tires on a hill above the Deschutes waterway while shooting off parachute bombs with American flags.[37] Although the group maintained a small profile in newspapers, eastside residents remember other meetings of robed people setting fires.[38] As many historians have noted, the "second Klan" collapsed in a few years as a result of national scandals.[39]

The Roaring Twenties

One of the more controversial progressive reforms was the Prohibition Movement, which sought to ban the manufacture, sale, and consumption of alcoholic beverages. Temperance activists disagreed about what to do about alcohol; some encouraged personal abstinence while others favored total prohibition of all alcohol manufacture, sale, and ownership. Prohibition gradually became the more prominent political movement.

Thurston County claimed a long history of temperance activism. The frontier was known for its alcoholism and heavy drinking. Reformers had banned sales of alcohol to Native Americans, but alcoholism knew no ethnicity as the years went on. Although he later turned against Prohibition, John Miller Murphy, editor of the *Washington Standard* in Olympia, was secretary of the Territorial Temperance Alliance in 1879.[40] Women formed a large number of the temperance activists, arguing that Prohibition would protect women and children from drunken men and improve society. Emma Page and her sister Mary were prominent regional Prohibition activists for the WCTU in the early twentieth century. A drinking fountain in Sylvester Park is a memorial to Emma Page, reflecting both the blind woman's lifelong passion for animal rights (as it includes a dog fountain) and for abstinence from alcohol.

The prohibition against alcohol went through various phases. In the November 1912 election, the city of Olympia voted 1,637 to 1,071 against Prohibition. But saloons were on borrowed time, as evidenced by the narrow vote. The more urban first, second, and third wards voted heavily wet; the increasingly rural fourth and fifth wards wet by narrow margins; and the sixth ward dry by only

This photo shows a young woman standing on the edge of a pond at Sylvester Park around 1910. (Note the decorative rocks and ater fountain feature.) Olympia founder Edmund Sylvester donated space for a public square when the town was initially platted. The area was first used to graze livestock but in 1893 the square was landscaped and renamed Sylvester Park to complement the new Thurston County Courthouse across the street. The building soon became the State Capitol building. This park was an important community gathering place. Presidents Teddy Roosevelt and William Taft spoke at the park during their visits to Olympia. Photographer, Robert G. Esterly. State Library Photograph Collection, 1851-1990. AR-07809001-ph000912 (Courtesy of Washington State Archives—Digital Archives)

ten votes.[41] In 1914, Washington State Initiative Number Three, which banned the manufacture and sale (but not consumption) of alcohol statewide, went to vote. The vote revealed a deep urban-rural split over Prohibition, including in Thurston County. Rural districts tended to vote dry, while Olympia voted wet. In total, the county voted 3,070 for Prohibition and 3,347 against.[42] The initiative, however, did pass in the statewide vote. In 1918 the state went "bone dry" with the approval of State Referendum Ten, banning the ownership of alcohol. In this election, Thurston County voted 1,720 for the referendum and 834 against.[43] The vote total was unusually low due to the disruption of the 1918 influenza pandemic.

Nationally, Prohibition began with the enactment of the Eighteenth Amendment and the subsequent Volstead Act. This law banned the sale and manufacture of most types of alcohol, though its passage left many loopholes. The implementation of Prohibition was troubled from the start. Bureau of Revenue employees (who enforced the law) were few in number, underpaid and too often corrupt, easily bribed.[44]

Though the Prohibition era may be remembered nostalgically by county residents, Thurston County reflected the national problems as well. Soft drink parlors replaced saloons, selling liquor illegally. The Bald Hills area, now part of Yelm, was considered a center of moonshine production. Resident Al Davidson remembered decades later that "my Dad was a bootlegger in 1924. I left home at 14 as I didn't like it, even though most in the Bald Hills and Smith Prairie were doing the same."[45]

Perhaps nothing characterizes the 1920s like the popularity of automobiles, which radically altered the way of life and physical makeup of Thurston County. Gas stations, motels and auto parks sprang up as cars became increasingly affordable. People pushed for "good roads," meaning well maintained paved roads to replace the old dirt and gravel roads. Olympia became a hub for the Pacific and Olympic State Highways. A concrete Fourth Avenue bridge, replacing an earlier wooden structure, provided easy access for vehicles to cross from downtown Olympia to the westside.

This transportation revolution decreased the need for the "mosquito fleet" of steamships that carried passengers and cargo on a regular schedule around Puget Sound. Bus transportation was introduced in the late 1910s. Although public transportation did not increase enough to meet the needs of travelers, electric streetcars continued in Olympia until the Great Depression.

The Gathering Storm

After recovering from a postwar recession, the economy of Thurston County superficially boomed in the 1920s. Sawmills, including several cooperatively-owned plywood mills, prospered in Olympia. Timber companies exported raw logs. In 1922, they towed 10 million board feet of lumber out of the harbor each month. That year countywide voters approved the creation of the Port of Olympia. Olympia's main exports were lumber products, sand, and gravel intended for the post-war building boom.[46]

For most people, however, things were not going well economically. Small

The pride of automobile ownership can be seen in this 1920s image of a man with his vehicle near Olympia. Automobiles had a major impact on American transportation in the twentieth century, creating ongoing effects on society, economics, and the natural environment. (Courtesy of a private collection)

Christopher Columbus Simmons and his wife Asenath Kennedy Simmons celebrated their 60th wedding anniversary in 1924 at Mud Bay with their many relatives and descendants. Married in 1864, Christopher was the son of Tumwater founder Michael T. Simmons and his wife Elizabeth. Photographer McKnight. State Library Photograph Collection, 1851-1990. AR-07809001-ph004420 (Courtesy of Washington State Archives—Digital Archives)

businesses flourished, but national and regional chain stores began to get a significant corner on the market. Many historians argue that the Depression started in rural America as overproduction drove down farm prices. Numerous farmers saw their standard of living decline in a decade of dramatic improvement for others. Some families tried to eke out a living as stump farmers, buying land cleared by commercial logging companies. Though this meant that the land was relatively cheap to purchase, it was often a difficult mode of making a living, as farmers had to take out the stumps themselves. Growing crops such as oats, peas, wheat, vetch hay, and especially potatoes, the farmers put much work into taming the land. For example, farmers in the Independence Valley recollected that the stumps needed blasting powder, horse stump pullers and "a whole lot of grubbing to get out."[47]

There was also a more abstract problem with Thurston County during the decade. The spirit of reform seemed to weaken, and concern to help the disadvantaged appeared to decline. Although not exclusive to the era or unique, one example of this growing callousness was the "Hard Times Frolic" held by the Olympia Golf and Country Club at Butler Cove on September 17, 1926. Around seventy couples, including high school students, from Thurston County, Shelton, and Tacoma dressed for the event in "rags and tags," farm dresses, and as "gypsies" (Roma) as a joke.[48]

Conclusion

Overall, the era from 1889 to 1929 was one of rapid change and transformation in Thurston County and the nation as the area moved from the frontier into modern times. Marked by deep social divisions as well as efforts to reform, the dark clouds of the Great Depression and a Second World War were gathering on the horizon.

As Thurston County matures, historian and author Drew Crooks looks at its past struggles and triumphs through the Great Depression, World War II, and cultural changes in "Facing the Future." This chapter examines the transitions brought by increasing population and expanding state government, as well as the growth of arts, education, and voluntarism. Contributors write of Thurston County colleges and Olympia's vibrant music scene.

Chapter 17
FACING THE FUTURE
Thurston County Since 1930
by Drew Crooks

THE NEW YORK STOCK Exchange crash in late October 1929 marked the beginning of the Great Depression, a time of severe economic difficulties that afflicted people around the world, including the United States, for over a decade.

Surviving the Lean Years

Not everyone in America suffered equally, but numerous banks closed, many businesses shrank in size or failed, millions lost their jobs, and families fell into poverty. It took a while for the Depression to reach Washington State and Thurston County. By the end of 1930, however, economic difficulties hit the region hard. People with steady employment did fine, and a few even prospered. But for most, it was tough to survive the lean years of the Great Depression.

Crash

In Thurston County, several banks closed. For example, the Citizens Bank of Tenino went out of business in December 1931, and Olympia National Bank shut its doors the following month. These closures seriously affected communities as families and organizations saw their savings disappear. One personal response was recorded in Yelm: in Bob Wolf's baby book his mother wrote, "The banks have crashed. We've lost everything that we had in the banks. ... we'll never get that back."[1]

The Great Depression proved to be a time of hardship for many businesses in Thurston County besides banks. They were often forced to cut back expenses. Sometimes they even ceased operations for a time or permanently. One significant example of this was Mutual Lumber Company, which played a vital role in the economy of Bucoda. This sawmill and logging venture closed from November 1930 to August 1933, causing much hardship in the local community. In the Yelm area, weak economic conditions and mosaic plant disease combined to devastate the once flourishing berry industry.

Though existing before the Great Depression, Olympia's shanty town Little Hollywood increased in size and population during the lean years of the 1930s. It was situated along the Deschutes River estuary parallel to Water Street. The residents, some criminal but most just poor, lived a difficult life. The local government in 1941-1942 systematically tore down the houses of Little Hollywood. This harsh operation concluded with a celebratory bonfire. (Courtesy of Washington State Archives—Digital Archives)

Thurston County - Water, Woods & Prairies

Difficult times often motivate people to take desperate measures. In February 1933, during the depths of the Great Depression, unemployed people went on a March of the Hungry to Olympia's State Capitol in search of government relief. Both this demonstration (seen in the photograph) and a follow-up march the next month proved unsuccessful in producing political action at the State level to increase assistance for the poor. Susan Parish Photograph Collection, 1889-1990. (Courtesy of Washington State Archives - Digital Archives)

Tough times ensued for people suffering from unemployment and underemployment. Other individuals saw their salaries reduced. For example, grade school teachers in the two Tenino districts saw their wages cut 15 to 30 percent in April 1932. Olympia police officers later that year went to 12-hour work shifts with a salary reduction of 10 percent. These economic problems had a ripple effect. Many men were forced to leave their families and travel to find work. Lack of money led to numerous tax and mortgage foreclosures on homes and property.[2]

Economic Consequences

Shantytowns, such as Little Hollywood, located at the lower end of the Deschutes Estuary in Olympia, increased in size, and vagrants wandered through the area in search of jobs and food.

Times were hard even for professionals. Patients had difficulty covering their medical expenses. They often paid in goods to Dr. Leo Alphonsus Campbell of Bucoda. According to the doctor's daughter, "One day he came home from a call with two Dalmatian puppies. He named them Measles and Mumps."[3] Other patients built a house for the doctor on Offut Lake.

In a way, the Thurston County Fair can be seen as a barometer for the changing economics of the area during the Great Depression. In 1930 both a county fair in Tenino and an Olympia-Lacey Fair Festival in Lacey took place. The year 1931, when the Depression had taken hold, saw no Thurston County Fair. Then a much smaller Harvest Fair was held at various sites from 1932 through 1940. Finally in 1941, with improving economic conditions, the Thurston County Fair reappeared in what is now known as Heritage Hall on the current county fairgrounds near Lacey.

During the Great Depression and for the next 70 years, Thurston County residents and visitors state-wide sought to let their hair down at the Evergreen Ballroom. Erected by Michael Sholund in 1931, the ballroom in Lacey became a favorite entertainment and dining spot. The "Green" welcomed the best big bands of the 1930s and '40s, along with marquee attractions such as Louis Armstrong, Charlie "Bird" Parker, Hank Williams, Nat King Cole, Ray Charles and Little Richard. In the 1960s, it served as an incubator for Northwest rock n' roll musicians such as the Wailers, Kingsmen, and Fonics. After a suspected arson attempt in 1932, the ballroom was rebuilt, but didn't survive a second fire on July 21, 2000. (Courtesy Washington State Archives)

Phases of the Great Depression

The Great Depression in America and Thurston County can be seen as going through several phases. The first phase, lasting from 1930 into early 1933, witnessed a heavy onslaught of problems. Then, during the second phase which extended from late 1933 to 1937, a partial economic recovery occurred due to federal programs initiated by President Franklin D. Roosevelt. Various local industries started to reopen, including Mutual Lumber Company of Bucoda and Olympia Harbor Lumber in 1933. That same year Prohibition ended, and the Olympia Brewing Company soon began operations in a new Tumwater building. A series of national and regional labor strikes broke out in the mid-1930s as people sought better pay and working conditions. They included dock workers, loggers/lumber mill employees, and even auto mechanics.

The last phase of the Great Depression, from 1937 into 1941, was a period of renewed recession that followed cuts in federal spending. Thurston County suffered along with the rest of the nation, and some local businesses closed. For example, the Gruber-Docherty Mill of Yelm ceased operations in 1937. Expanded federal and state spending helped stabilize the economy, but a lasting recovery from the Depression occurred only with the coming of World War II and wartime production.

Various Responses

The residents of Thurston County responded to the Great Depression in various ways. Many became more self-reliant. Historian Julie McDonald Zander noted about Bucoda inhabitants, "Most people grew a garden. Some raised their own meat; many used gaff hooks on round poles to catch fish near the mill's log-pond dam. Most heated their homes with coal or wood, plentiful in the nearby hills."[5]

Others were driven by terrible circumstances to take desperate measures. Marches of the Hungry to Olympia first in January and then in March 1933 brought hundreds of unemployed to the State Capitol in search of government assistance. One hunger marcher explained his situation in January to a newspaper reporter, "We can't sit back and starve. . . I've been out of work three years. . . Of course there have been some small jobs, but no real money. I've tried hard to find work too... I used to earn six dollars a day. Now they pay $3, but there ain't no jobs."⁶

The second Hunger March was met by the "American Vigilantes of Thurston County" who forced the peaceful demonstrators to Olympia's Priest Point Park where they endured a night surrounded by police and local citizens bearing guns and broom handles. The next day the protesters were pushed out of town. Both January and March demonstrations ended with increased frustrations and little political action.

Sometimes people turned to extreme political parties. The Silver Legion of America held a mass meeting at the Eagles Hall in Olympia on August 14, 1936.⁷ This fascist group, commonly known as the Silver Shirts, was led by William Dudley Pelley. The hate-filled organization later collapsed after the United States entered World War II.⁸

At the same time, a number of individuals were moved by compassion to help those in need. This assistance came through personal and family action, as well as through the activities of charity groups such as the American Red Cross and Salvation Army. The Jingle Club in December 1931 distributed 500 Christmas boxes to the poor in Thurston County. These boxes held "large supplies of produce, groceries, Christmas stockings for the kiddies and other Yule-time wares."⁹

Cities and Thurston County government also attempted to mitigate the effects of the Great Depression, but the economic woes were simply too much for private and local governmental efforts. The federal programs of President Roosevelt's New Deal, working with state government, met the difficult economic situation head-on. These programs included the Civil Works Administration, Civilian Conservation Corps, Mothers' Pensions, National Youth Administration, Public Works Administration, and Works Progress Administration.

Certainly the federal government sponsored numerous New Deal activities in Thurston County, but not every proposed project was approved. In one significant case, federal agencies rejected the Columbia River-Grays Harbor-Puget Sound Canal project that would, in part, construct a waterway connecting Budd Inlet with Grays Harbor by way of Black Lake, Black River and Chehalis River. Many county residents in the early 1930s supported the canal concept, an idea dating back well into the nineteenth century. A pro-Canal rally in Olympia on July 29, 1933 featured a parade complete with "an effigy of 'Old Man Depression' riding a

The Civilian Conservation Corps (CCC), a major New Deal program during the Great Depression, enrolled unemployed young men across the nation in conservation and park work. In Thurston County's Millersylvania State Park, the CCC developed facilities such as the still-standing Comfort Station #1 (building 6), shown in this picture. Constructed in 1935. WISAARD Photo ID #44456 (Courtesy of Washington State Department of Archaeology and Historic Preservation)

208   Chapter 16 - A Turbulent Age

sawhorse, drawn by members of the carpenters' union..."[10]

Though the canal proposal was backed by numerous local and state individuals and groups, the idea failed to gain the approval of the federal government which saw other projects – such as the Grand Coulee Dam on the Columbia River – as more important to regional and national economic recovery. From the viewpoint in the twenty-first century, it seems strange that discussions of the canal in the 1930s did not consider the massive environmental damage that the project would have created in Thurston County and elsewhere in southwest Washington.

One of the most important programs of the New Deal nationwide and in Thurston County was the Works Progress Administration or WPA (1935-1943), which consolidated many of the federal jobs and construction assistance activities. WPA projects occurred throughout the county. They included expanding the hangar at the Olympia Airport, constructing a school gymnasium in Bucoda, increasing the capacity of the Yelm Irrigation Canal, and improving roads across the county.

Among their many other activities, the WPA sponsored sewing rooms in Olympia, Rochester, and Tenino where women were paid to create clothing for distribution to people receiving relief.[11] Furthermore, in 1938 WPA cooks prepared "hot soup or something equally nourishing and warm" for student lunches "at South Bay, Tenino grade and Tenino high schools, Hays, Collins, Littlerock, and Rochester districts."[12]

Finally, the WPA partially completed the Long Lake Recreation Hall near Lacey in 1938-1940. This log building served as the home of the Thurston County Fair in 1941, but World War II saw the Fair suspended during the years of conflict. In 1946, the Fair resumed and the WPA structure received finishing touches.[13] Today the building, now known as Heritage Hall, is a focal point for Thurston County Fairgrounds activities.

Another major New Deal program which impacted Thurston County was the Civilian Conservation Corps or CCC (1933-1942). The CCC enrolled unemployed young unmarried men to work on a variety of conservation projects across the nation. Camp Rainier near Rainier in Thurston County saw CCC recruits focus on efforts to prevent and fight wildfires. CCC men from Camp Elma in neighboring Grays Harbor County established a forest nursery close to Cedar Creek in the Black Hills of Thurston County and planted millions of seedlings in Capitol State Forest.

CCC Camp Millersylvania from 1933 to 1939 systematically developed Thurston County's Millersylvania State Park by grading roads, building trails, setting up a swimming area, and constructing buildings in either the National Park Service Rustic or Bungalow/Craftsman styles. The CCC work at Millersylvania was done with simple hand tools and much creativity. It is a remarkable legacy that can be appreciated by State Park visitors even today.[14]

With the coming of World War II and wartime production, the Great Depression faded away in America and Thurston County. The lean years of 1930 to 1941 formed an important era in our history. It deeply affected many people and left shadows that endured for decades.

War Comes

Though many people anticipated increased involvement in the fight against the Axis powers of Germany, Italy, and Japan, the Japanese attack on Pearl Harbor on December 7, 1941, was a terrible shock to Americans. It brought the United States directly into a bloody worldwide conflict that lasted almost four years.

Patriotism and Panic

The immediate response in Thurston County, like elsewhere in the country, was a combination of patriotism and panic. People, fearing an attack by the Japanese on the American mainland, began to blacken windows at nighttime. Civil Defense forces (including aircraft warning observers) and air raid sirens were established in Yelm, Tenino, Olympia, and other communities. The siren in downtown Olympia, nicknamed by some "Moaning Minnie," was placed on top of the Rockway-Leland Building.[15]

Civil Defense workers, including both men and

women, remained vigilant in the county until the war's end, but fortunately no enemy airplanes came to bomb the region. Perhaps the most dramatic incident occurred with the "War Pageant" that took place on August 16, 1943, at Olympia's Stevens Field next to Lincoln School. That evening people saw a massive parade of local civilian defense members followed by a dramatic drill. The *Daily Olympian* described the event:

> Explosions ripped Stevens Field last night, and flames tore at the buildings erected on it, in a vividly-simulated air raid before the dazzled eyes of more than 3,500 spectators... The amazed onlookers were packed into the grandstands and lined up outside the danger zones... [A] model of a section of a typical city erected on the field – styled Smaller Olympia – was crushed beneath one bombing raid after another, while the entire forces of larger Olympia's civilian defense organization worked smoothly and efficiently to cope with the disaster.[16]

Home Front Situation

During World War II the home front situation in Thurston County resembled conditions found across America. Numerous young men (and some women) joined the different branches of the US military. Many people also participated in the Red Cross and other organizations that supported the war effort. Some war-related equipment was made by local businesses. Shipbuilding took place on a limited scale (much less than in World War I) in Olympia, while the Bridge Fabricating Company in Bucoda manufactured temporary bridges for the American military forces. War cargo and Lend-Lease goods were shipped through the Port of Olympia on a regular basis.

Fundraising for war bonds and war savings stamps occurred in every community. Perry Jungmayer recalled that "The Bucoda School started a War Saving Stamp program where we bought ten-cent stamps and pasted them in a book. When the book was full, we cashed it in for a $25 war bond. It was a really a big deal, and we really looked forward to pasting the stamps in the book."[17]

Shortages of consumer goods developed, and rationing was introduced for gasoline, sugar, nylon stockings, and many other items. Citizens collected grease, scrap metal, and other needed items for the war effort. Art Zabel later recounted a time at the Zabel family's Capitol Theater in Olympia when "they had a drive to get in copper or different things that they could melt down, and anybody could come to the movie on a certain day and bring pots or pans and things like that, and they'd get in free, ...we had a huge truck that was filled completely up with things that they could use..."[18]

The presence of the military grew in South Puget Sound. Fort Lewis Army Base and McChord Air Force Base in Pierce County expanded their operations. By 1944 Fort Lewis had purchased property in Thurston County which became known as the Rainier Training Area. Military training took place here and at various other locations in Thurston County, including Henderson Inlet. Olympia Airport became an adjunct training

Olympia's first USO Club was built in 1942 on East Fourth Avenue as a center of hospitality for visiting American military forces. Arson fire burned down the building in December 1943, but a replacement was built on the same site and dedicated in late 1944. After World War II ended, this building was converted into the Olympia Community Center. This center served as the home for many community events until it was closed in 1986. Susan Parish Photograph Collection, 1889-1990. (Courtesy of Washington State Archives)

center for McChord Field. Several military airplanes accidentally crashed in the county while practicing. In one case, a P-38 went down near Bucoda, but the pilot survived. Another P-38 crashed into St. Peter Hospital on the Westside of Olympia, tragically killing the pilot.

Soldiers and sailors sometimes traveled to Olympia. The local Senior and Junior Chambers of Commerce established an Army and Navy Club for the visiting military personnel. This club found a home on the first floor of the Old State Capitol in downtown Olympia. Then an Olympia USO Club was built at 1314 East Fourth Avenue with a grand opening on February 6, 1942. Many members of the military were welcomed at the new facility. An arson fire destroyed the USO Club on December 30, 1943, but no one was hurt.[19] Temporary USO headquarters moved back to the Old State Capitol. A new USO building was constructed on the same Fourth Avenue site. Dedicated on November 26, 1944, the replacement structure served as a hub of hospitality through the rest of the war.

Internment

Numerous people in Thurston County during World War II, like elsewhere in the country, held a fierce hostility toward the enemies of the United States. Tragically, this led to mistreatment of individuals of Italian, German, and especially Japanese descent in America who were seen as potential traitors. President Franklin Roosevelt signed Executive Order 9066 on February 19, 1942, permitting the restriction or removal from

This poster, dated May 23, 1942, proclaims the order by Lieutenant General De Witt directing the evacuation and internment of Japanese Americans in much of Western Washington, including Thurston County. It is a reminder of a tragic episode in American history. (Courtesy of Washington State Historical Society)

designated areas persons who might be thought a danger to the success of the war effort.

On March 1, 1942, *The Sunday Olympian* newspaper reported the circulation of petitions at some of the Olympia and Tumwater grocery stores requesting "that the Governor of the State of Washington act immediately in evacuating ALL Japanese from the coast of Washington [including Thurston County], aliens and American-born alike."[20] The next day, March 2, Lieutenant General John L. DeWitt, commander of military forces on America's West Coast, ordered the internment of people of Japanese ancestry who were living in the western section of the coastal states and southern Arizona.

Eight days later FBI agents and state, county, and local police forces systematically raided the homes of "enemy aliens" in Olympia and nearby areas. They looked for contraband such as guns, dynamite, radios, and cameras. The homes of Germans, Italians, and Japanese were all caught up in the raids. No contraband was found, much to the surprise of the law enforcement officials. The *Daily Olympian*'s account of the event noted, "After searching the premises of one Japanese family for an hour and a half, an Olympia policeman expressed the view that the place was just too clean of contraband to be natural. He deduced that the family had made ready for the anticipated officers' visit."[21] Apparently, the fact that the "enemy aliens" were innocent seemed unthinkable.

Personal innocence or guilt did not seem important as security measures focused on interning all Japanese Americans. Across the West Coast, thousands were sent to internment camps. Lieutenant General DeWitt commanded on May 23, 1942, that a number of counties in western Washington "will be cleared of American-born and alien Japanese during the three-day period of June 1 to noon, June 3."[22] The order told the heads of Japanese families in Thurston, Mason, Clallam, Jefferson, and Grays Harbor counties to register either at the U.S. Employment Office in Olympia or the Masonic Temple in Port Townsend.

One hundred and sixty-one Japanese aliens and citizens were sent from the Olympia and Port Townsend assembly stations in 1942 to Tule Lake, an internment camp in California near the Oregon border. The next few years would be very difficult for the thousands of Japanese Americans at Tule Lake and other camps. When internment generally ended in 1945, returning to their former homes was often not an option due to continuing anti-Japanese hostility. Racism had created bitterness that took years to overcome.

Victory

Meanwhile, World War II continued overseas. After years of tough fighting the United States and its Allies achieved victory in Europe (V-E Day on May 8, 1945) and defeated Japan (V-J Day on September 2, 1945). When news of the Japanese surrender was announced on August 15, 1945, spontaneous expressions of happiness erupted across America. Thurston County communities joined in the celebration. *The Daily Olympian* described the reaction in Olympia:

> Exploding in paeans of joy, Olympia celebrated Japan's surrender yesterday and really gave out in noise as it freed the pentup emotions caused by the last few days of waiting and uncertainty. Automobile horns, cowbells, whistles, catcalls and shouts of hundreds of excited persons added to the ear-splitting din of the city's sirens, air raid, fire and police, when the surrender message was received at two minutes after four o'clock yesterday afternoon. Business establishments and taverns immediately closed their doors and jubilant persons crowded downtown sidewalks and overflowed into streets as the sirens wailed without letup.
>
> In 30 minutes the noise had reached a tremendous crescendo, and one by one the sirens stopped their wailing. But the ear-splitting din was carried on by blasting horns of hundreds of automobiles flying streamers of paper and jamming downtown streets. The afternoon and evening excitement was centered within a few blocks on Fourth Avenue, automobiles creeping along, bumper to bumper, horns braying, for hours.[23]

During World War II, various community groups and schools, as well as private individuals, raised money for the war effort. In this 1940s photograph, the entire student body of Lacey School surrounds an Army field ambulance that they purchased for the government by buying War Bonds and Stamps. For many years the Lacey School, located on the corner of Pacific Avenue and Carpenter Road, was a key community institution. David Cody Collection, 2007-001 (Courtesy of Lacey Museum)

Still, the victory in World War II had an enormous human cost. As part of the extensive worldwide casualties of the conflict, over 400,000 American soldiers and sailors died while many others were wounded. More than a hundred of the dead came from Thurston County. They had made the ultimate sacrifice for their country.

A Time of Many Changes: Thurston County since World War II

Since World War II Thurston County has seen many changes. It has been a period of high population growth and increasing diversity. The demographic explosion can be seen in the county's total number of residents, which soared from a population of 37,285 in 1940 to 252,264 in 2010.[24] During this time all the urban centers of Thurston County experienced growth, some more than others.

Lacey is a notable example of the area's population expansion. For most of Thurston County's existence, what is now Lacey was primarily rural with only a few businesses. After World War II more and more people moved into the area. In 1966 South Sound Center, the county's first modern shopping center, opened in the middle of the Lacey community. On December 5 of the same year, the City of Lacey was incorporated. From a population of 9,696 in 1970, the city grew to have 42,393 inhabitants in 2010. A number of the residents have ties to Joint Base Lewis-McChord, the large military base located nearby in Pierce County.[25]

The post-World War II period has also seen an increased diversity of people in Thurston County. Individuals and families have come to the area from many different places. Some initially arrived as refugees fleeing political persecution. For example, when the Baltic States (Estonia, Latvia, and Lithuania) in northeast Europe fell under Communist rule in the 1940s, thousands fled to other countries, including the United States. Part of this group moved to Thurston County.

Later refugees from Southeast Asia fled their homelands in the face of totalitarian rule. Every year during the decade after 1975, 100,000 Southeast

Thurston County - Water, Woods & Prairies 213

Asians came to America. Eventually, about 45,000 settled in Washington State,[26] including a sizable number in Thurston County. The immigrants included Vietnamese, Cambodians, Laotians, Cham, and Ethnic Chinese. It was a difficult transition for the immigrants. As one historian noted, "Once in this country, the refugees and their families overcame great obstacles to learn English, educate their children, and achieve a degree of economic success."[27] This process was greatly aided by community groups formed by the Southeast Asian Americans.

In addition, the recent decades have seen Thurston County's economy change from one that included numerous industries to a system more dependent on government employment and retail sales. Industry after industry has closed, ranging from Bucoda's Mutual Lumber Company in 1946 to Tumwater's Olympia Brewery Company (then owned by SABMiller) in 2003. In their places have popped up more retail businesses to serve the growing population. The Port of Olympia continues its operations as an important seaport and transportation center but now includes on its property such service-oriented operations as the Olympia Farmers Market and Swantown Marina. Many of the new entrepreneurs in the county are graduates of the three local schools of higher education: The Evergreen State College, Saint Martin's University, and South Puget Sound Community College.

The construction of Interstate 5 through Thurston County transformed transportation in the area and changed the landscape. In this 1958 aerial photograph of Tumwater and Olympia, Old Highway 99 runs from the lower left corner to a midpoint on the right side. To the left of Highway 99 the almost completed freeway extends north and then northeast over the Deschutes waterway into the Olympia area. (Courtesy of Olympia Tumwater Foundation)

Modern Era

The modern era has witnessed the triumph of automobiles in transportation across America (including Thurston County). There has been a massive improvement in county and state roads during this time. In addition, the federal freeway, Interstate 5 (I-5), made its way through the area in construction phases lasting from the 1950s well into the 1960s. A key moment was "Freeway Day" on December 12, 1958, when the part of the freeway passing through Tumwater and Olympia was officially dedicated.[28] Certainly, I-5 has increased the efficiency and safety of transportation but not without losses. Much of Tumwater fell before the bulldozers, but the historic Crosby House was saved. Also Olympia's Moss Lake, a traditional swimming hole well loved by generations of young people, perished during the new roadway's construction.

In Thurston County, like elsewhere in America, the years after 1945 have seen the expansion of government at all levels: city, county, and state. This change reflects the increase of governmental responsibilities for a rapidly growing population. Governmental expansion can be physically seen in the Thurston County Courthouse that was completed in 1977 on the Westside of Olympia. The new three-building complex was considerably bigger than the previous 1930 courthouse on Capitol Way. Still, by the beginning of the twenty-first century, the Westside complex is becoming insufficient for Thurston County activities. The need for even larger courthouse facilities is increasingly being discussed.

Another physical sign of governmental growth is the enlargement of the Washington State Capitol Campus in Olympia. For a time in the early 1950s, many state agencies shifted their headquarters out of the Capital City to other localities. A court case successfully challenged the legality of these moves in 1953. It resulted in the transfer (over time) of the various headquarters back to Olympia, and the expansion of the State Capitol Campus to accommodate the increasing number of workers. Indeed, due to the continued growth of state employment and a ruling by the State Attorney General in the 1980s allowing the practice, State offices began to be built in Lacey and Tumwater. They are considered to be "in the 'vicinity' of the state capitol."[29]

Recent years have also seen a strengthening of ties between the different levels of government. A key step in this direction was the establishment of the Thurston Regional Planning Council in 1967. Now including twenty-one jurisdictions and organizations, the Council "carries out regionally focused plans and studies on topics such as transportation, growth management, and environmental quality,"[30] and sponsors public forums on planning issues. Other regional commissions and boards have increased the web of ties linking governmental entities. They all aim to increase cooperation and decrease competition among cities, county, and state.

Working for a Better Life

The post-World War II era brought some positive changes to Thurston County, but - as is normal with all human societies - problems and issues have continued to trouble the residents of the area. In

In 1966 the first modern shopping center in Thurston County, South Sound Center, opened to the public in the Lacey area. The local community now had enough people and businesses to become a city. Indeed, Lacey incorporated on December 5, 1966. The first mayor of Lacey, Al Homann, was appropriately sworn into office within the new South Sound Center. Homann Collection, 1983-002 (Courtesy of Lacey Museum)

Thurston County - Water, Woods & Prairies   215

MUSIC IN THURSTON COUNTY

by Len Balli

In 1983 Calvin Johnson, Bret Lundsford, and Heather Lewis started the band Beat Happening. With little to no experience playing instruments or performing in front of an audience as a band they immediately recorded and released a self-titled LP on Calvin Johnson's K Records label.

This became the standard blueprint for forming a band. What followed was an artistic explosion Olympia had never seen before! The Tropicana, Smithfield Café, and North Shore Surf Club allowed bands to play to an all-new audience. In August 1991 Calvin Johnson and Candace Pederson, co-owners of K Records, organized the International Pop Underground Convention at the Capitol Theater, a six-day event complete with bands, a peace vigil, and a Planet of the Apes movie marathon. Festivals became the standard, beginning with Yoyo A Go Go, Ladyfest, and Homo a Go Go festivals and the annual Olympia Experimental Music Festival.

Women were included in Olympia's music scene. As artists they demanded to be taken seriously and formed bands, made zines (handmade magazines covering any topic or interest), and challenged the misogyny usually found in the male-dominated punk rock scene. Dubbed Riot Grrrls, their songs tackled serious and personal topics like depression, eating disorders, and rape. These new subjects changed songwriting into a more personal narrative instead of a traditional storytelling device. Leading the charge were Kathleen Hanna and Tobi Vail of the band Bikini Kill; and Allison Wolfe and Molly Neuman of Bratmobile. These feminist bands found support from fellow musician Slim Moon who released albums by Bikini Kill, Gossip and Sleater-Kinney on his record label Kill Rock Stars. Together these women were able to transform culture, challenge societal norms, and empower young girls to find their artistic way in the world.

Calvin Johnson of Beat Happening at Mecca Normal/Beat Happening/Fugazi Show, Chambers Prairie Grange on June 2, 1990. (Courtesy of Lois Maffeo)

Len Balli is an expert on the Northwest Indie music scene of the 1980s and 1990s.

Chapter 16 - A Turbulent Age

From 2010-2018 the Tumwater Historical Association, in cooperation with many other groups, sponsored "Thurston County Through the Decades," a series of semi-annual living history gatherings in the County. Each event portrayed a twenty-five year period of local history. Performances, activities, and displays at these gatherings celebrated Thurston County's heritage. This picture shows Civil War reenactors at an October 2012 event in Tumwater Falls Park. (Courtesy of Tumwater Historical Association)

response, many people and organizations have worked for a better life in the county. It is an ongoing struggle.

Efforts to help the poor and disadvantaged have long occurred in the region. Often religious groups have been involved. A notable example is the work of the Salvation Army, which first came to Olympia in the 1890s. The extent of this organization's activities can be seen in a news article which noted that the Olympia Salvation Army in the previous year "provided 629 desperately needy transient families with groceries, lodging, and in some cases clothing. Meal tickets and beds were given to 166 male transients. More than a thousand individuals in hospitals were given assistance. And . . . the Salvation Army has made thousands of family visits, offering welfare and financial counsel and spiritual assistance."[31] The group's current work includes both seasonal assistance and long-term social services to those in need.

The unique prairies and oak woodlands of Thurston County have faced the challenges of development and invasive plants. In response dedicated volunteers and professionals steadily work to restore and preserve these rare ecosystems. (Courtesy of Center for Natural Lands Management South Sound Prairies Program)

Thurston County - Water, Woods & Prairies

SOUTH PUGET SOUND COMMUNITY COLLEGE

by Kati Sagawa

We've got something to say at SPSCC: Get the skills you need for the life you want! Because anyone can—and we make it possible.

South Puget Sound Community College has a history of fulfilling the unique needs of our Thurston County community. Initially started in 1957 by the Olympia School Board, the institution has had various names, including Olympia Vocational Technical Institute, Olympia Technical Community College, and since 1984, South Puget Sound Community College. SPSCC became its own district after splitting off from Centralia College in 1988. Throughout its history SPSCC has remained agile in order to meet the changing educational needs of the district's residents. The community college has proudly maintained an affordable and quality environment for local students to learn and prepare for life's next steps—whether a student plans to transfer to a four-year institution, move immediately into a career, or develop skills for personal enrichment.

SPSCC supports student success and builds prosperity by collaborating with leaders across all types of organizations in our community. We employ devoted people who mirror the diversity of our community and contribute to an inclusive, welcoming environment. By investing in the creativity of our staff and faculty, we construct clear and compelling pathways that lead our students to successful outcomes on their educational journeys.

We are fiscally strong and our mindful use of technology embedded in purposeful instruction helps students persist and achieve their academic goals.

The Center of Student Success (opened in 2014) ensures that South Puget Sound Community College students have a single location to address all of their needs. (Courtesy of South Puget Sound Community College)

Our graduating class is a reflection of the community we serve and our students successfully transition from higher learning into the leaders and innovators of tomorrow.

SPSCC's Core Themes include:
1. Expand Student Retention and Completion
2. Inspire Teaching and Learning Excellence
3. Advance Equity and Embrace Diversity
4. Champion Innovation
5. Build Community

Kati Sagawa holds the position of Communications Consultant 3 in the Public Relations Office of South Puget Sound Community College.

Hunger has remained a hardship for some inhabitants of Thurston County. Various groups have worked to change the situation so that everyone has enough to eat. For example, the Thurston County Food Bank was established in 1972. Its mission is simply "to eliminate hunger within our community."[32] To do this, the organization runs a network of services which includes a central location in Olympia, fifteen satellite food banks, nine mobile food banks at low-income neighborhoods, and partnerships with four school districts. Furthermore, the Thurston County Food Bank collaborates with rural food banks in Rochester, Tenino, and Yelm.

Homelessness has become more of an issue in Thurston County in recent decades. A number of organizations, such as Sidewalk and Quixote Village, have striven in different ways to get people off the streets and into housing. South Puget Sound Habitat for Humanity has worked in Thurston County since 1989 to develop and build affordable housing communities. A local affiliate of Habitat for Humanity International, it "serves the very-low income families whose dream is to shed the shackles of poverty, own their own homes and self-determine their own futures."[33] With donations of money, materials, and labor the nonprofit has constructed homes throughout the county.

Increasing population and urbanization of Thurston County have put heavy pressure on the region's natural environment. In response, numerous people and organizations have struggled to fight pollution and preserve habitat for plants and animals. One outstanding individual in local environmental efforts was Margaret McKenny, a notable naturalist and author. She led efforts in the 1950s and 1960s to save Sylvester Park and create Watershed Park in Olympia. Also, she helped with the efforts of Flo Brodie and the Nisqually Delta Association to save the Nisqually Delta from industrial development. These efforts proved successful, and the Nisqually National Wildlife Refuge (now renamed Billy Frank Jr. Nisqually National Wildlife Refuge) was created in 1974.

In recent decades the fight for the environment has taken many forms. Starting in 1990, for example, the Stream Team has worked "to protect and enhance the water resources, associated habitats, and wildlife of Thurston County through citizen education and action."[34] The Capitol Land Trust (incorporated in 1987) protects and cares for natural areas and working lands in Southwest Washington, while the Nisqually Land Trust (formed in 1989) focuses its attention on acquiring and managing environmentally critical land in the Nisqually River Watershed. Furthermore, the local Native American Tribes – Squaxin, Nisqually, and Chehalis – have actively participated in efforts to preserve and restore the natural environment.

One area of particular environmental concern in Thurston County has been the preservation and restoration of its unique prairies and oak woodlands. Numerous groups, both nonprofit and government, have striven over the years to protect these rare ecosystems from development, and the onslaught of Scotch broom, Douglas fir and other invasive plants. It is an ongoing task, but the patient work of professionals and volunteers can be seen each spring at the annual Prairies Appreciation Day. Visitors enjoy guided walks and activities while they view the blue camas and other plants in bloom at the County's Mima Mounds Natural Area Preserve and Glacial Heritage Preserve.

Arts and culture have long played a role in the improvement of Thurston County life. The area has provided a home over the years for many talented

Many volunteers have helped in the ongoing struggle against hunger in Thurston County. Airmen from the 627th Air Base Group in this photo are packaging food at the Thurston County Food Bank during the Thurston County Day of Sharing. (Courtesy of Thurston County Food Bank)

THE EVERGREEN STATE COLLEGE

by Todd Sprague

In 1967, the State of Washington enacted legislation to create a new four-year college in southwestern Washington—from the ground up. In describing what would become The Evergreen State College (TESC), then-Governor Daniel J. Evans declared the need for a "flexible and sophisticated educational instrument," as opposed to the "vast and immobile establishment," and expressed the need to "unshackle our educational thinking from traditional patterns."

With that mandate for innovation, the college opened its doors in 1971 and continues to be a leader in higher education today. Evergreen students experience the depth and rigor of a liberal arts education in distinctive, full-time coordinated studies programs, incorporating a range of disciplines around a central theme and often taught by multiple faculty members. A coordinated schedule gives students greater opportunities to participate in labs, field studies, service learning, site visits and study abroad, with an emphasis on hands-on experience and putting theory into practice. Thinking beyond the limitations of letter grades, the faculty provide students with narrative evaluations of their work and progress. This allows students to work together and concentrate on learning rather than competing for grades.

Evergreen's 1,000-acre campus includes half a mile of beach on Puget Sound and serves as a living laboratory for creative and scientific inspiration and research.

TESC is frequently recognized as one of the nation's best colleges by *Princeton Review*, *Fiske Guide*, *US News & World Report* and *Colleges That Change Lives*.

The Evergreen State College's campus in west Olympia includes modern classrooms, science laboratories, arts studios, computer centers, video production facilities, residence halls, student apartments, performance spaces, art galleries, an organic farm, a Native American longhouse, recreational facilities and an extensive library. (Courtesy of The Evergreen State College)

Today Evergreen serves more than 4,000 students in its Olympia, Tacoma and reservation-based programs, and offers three graduate degrees: Master in Teaching, Master of Public Administration and Master of Environmental Studies.

The college now has more than 40,000 alumni. About 15 percent of all bachelor's degree holders in Thurston County earned their degree at Evergreen.

Todd Sprague is the Executive Director of Marketing, Communications and College Relations at The Evergreen State College.

artists. Art organizations, like the Olympia Art League and Olympia Film Society, support these artistic endeavors. Performance venues range from the small Triad Theater in Yelm to the (relatively) large Washington Center for Performing Arts in Olympia. Community arts events, including Olympia's Arts Walk and the Procession of the Species, help bring culture directly to people on a regular basis. Some musical groups from Thurston County, like the Fleetwoods and a number of bands originating in the 1980s/1990s, have achieved national fame.

Value of History

Finally, many individuals have worked hard to preserve and interpret the history of Thurston County, a fragile resource too often subject to neglect and loss. Since 1984, the Thurston County Historic Commission, an advisory committee of Thurston County government, has striven to promote and conduct "public information, education and interpretive programs pertaining to county history and county cultural resources."[35] Other historic preservation commissions exist in Lacey, Olympia, Tumwater, and Yelm.

In addition, dedicated people have come together across the county to form various historical societies and museums. Their exhibits and educational programs bring history alive to those who will take the time to look and listen. Thurston County heritage is important. As the writer G. K. Chesterton once said, "The disadvantage of men [and women] not knowing the past is that they do not know the present. History is a hill or high point of vantage, from which alone men [and women] see the town in which they live or the age in which they are living."[36] Indeed, history can help us to understand our present and perhaps motivate us to work for a better future.

Since 1995 the Procession of the Species Celebration in Olympia has worked to create cultural connections between communities and the natural world. This picture of the 2017 Procession parade shows some of the creative imagination displayed by participants. (Courtesy of ThurstonTalk.com)

MAPS OF THURSTON COUNTY

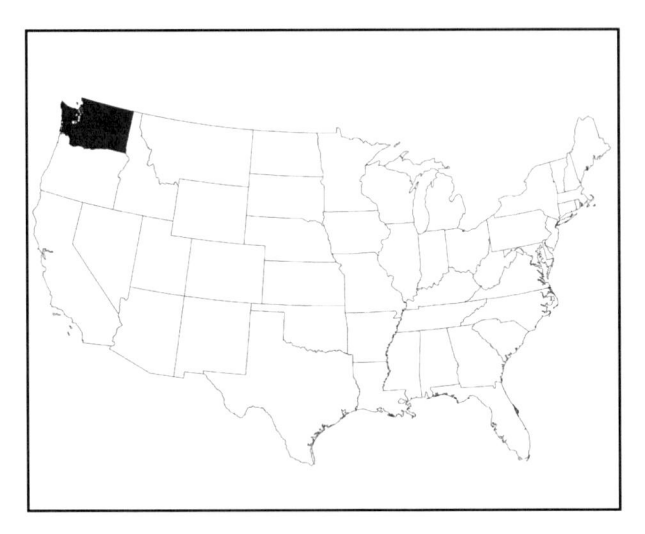

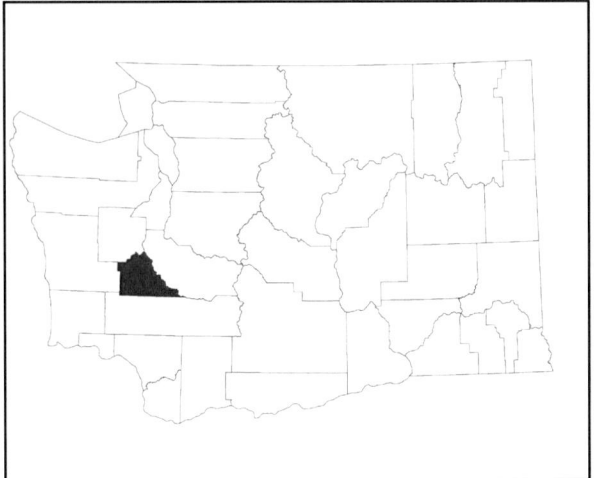

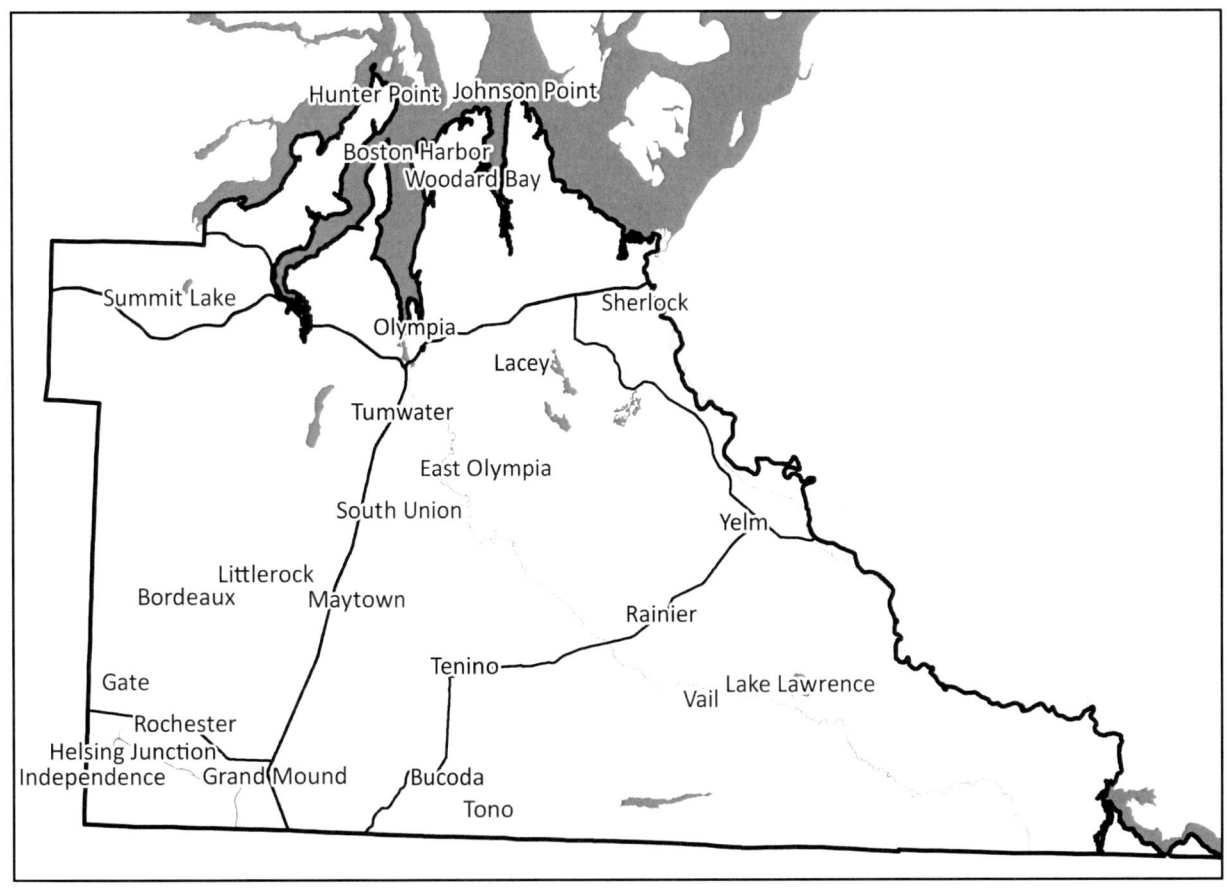

The top maps show the location of the State of Washington within the continental US and Thurston County within the state. Below, a map of Thurston County shows current and historic locations discussed in this publication, 2018. (Courtesy of Thurston GeoData Center)

Excerpt, Washington State Tribal Land Map, Thurston County vicinity, 2018. (Courtesy of Washington State Department of Transportation)

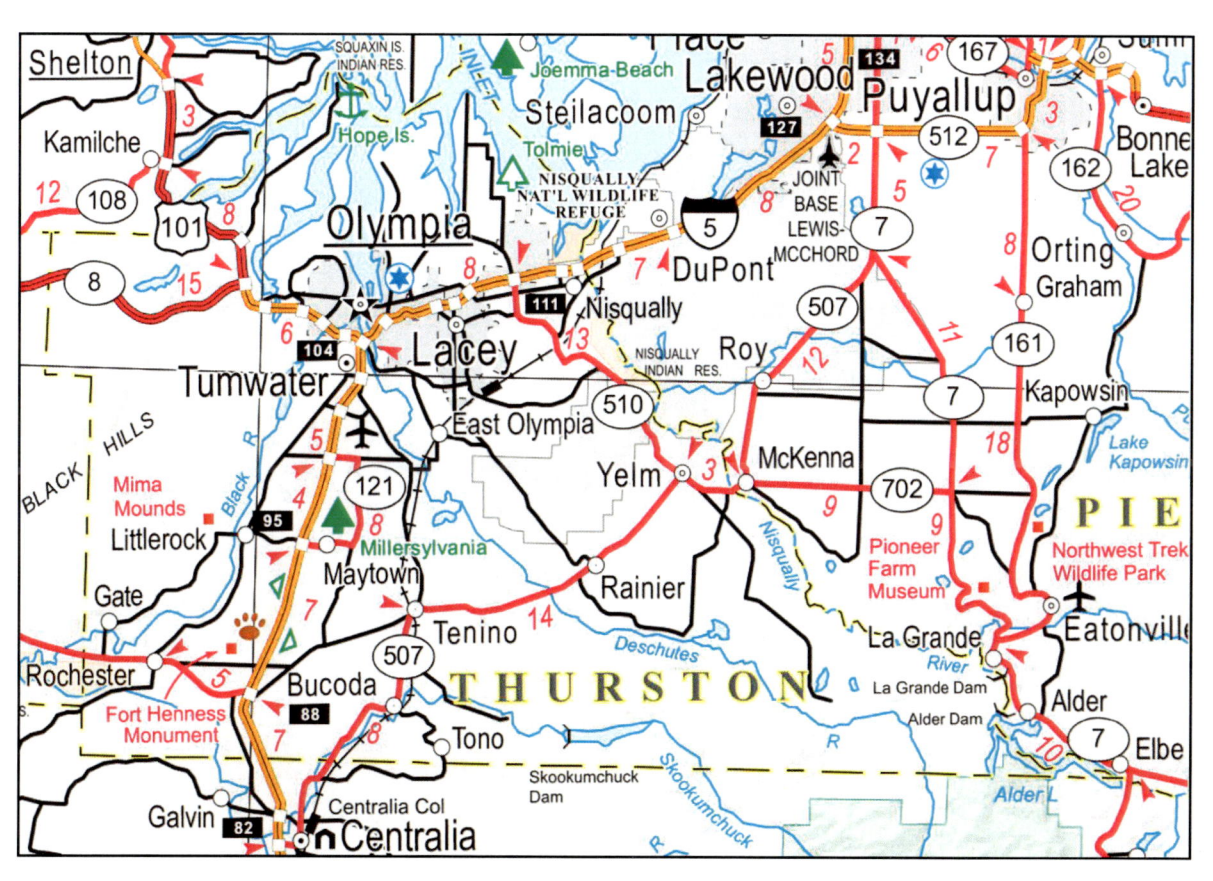

Excerpt of Washington State Highway Map, Thurston County vicinity, 2014. (Courtesy of Washington State Department of Transportation)

Thurston County - Water, Woods & Prairies   223

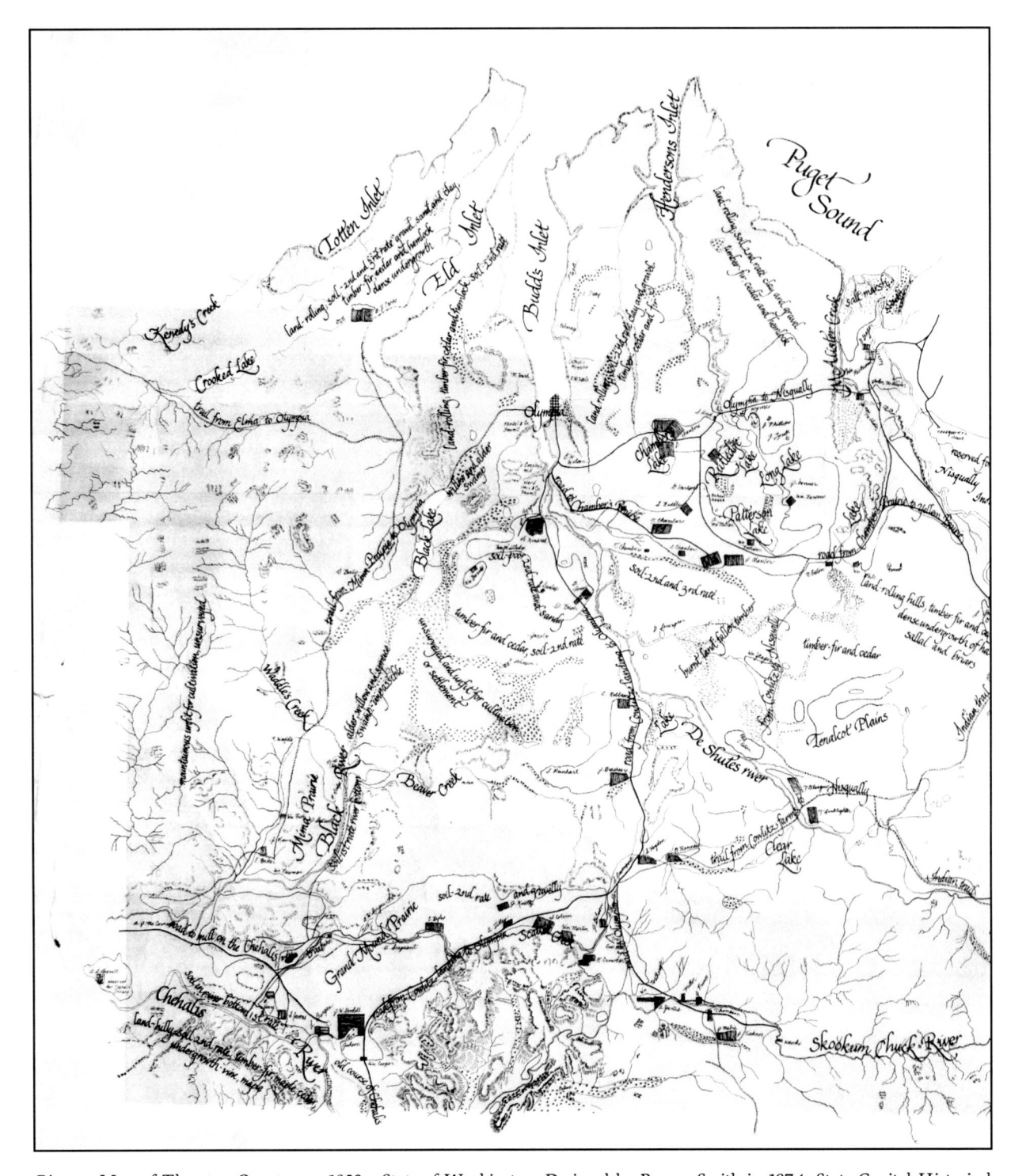

Pioneer Map of Thurston County, ca. 1850s, State of Washington. Designed by Barney Smith in 1974. State Capitol Historical Association. (Courtesy of Thurston County)

Pioneer Map of Thurston County

This map is based on a composite of thirty-six General Land Office Township Plats, drawn from the reconnaissance of federal land surveyors in the 1850's. These marks, ▨ denote cultivated land and not the full extent of a donation land claim. This map is the re-creation of a frontier landscape and society as the surveyors reported it; any oversights or deletions are theirs.

Published by the State Capitol Historical Association © 1974
Research by David Nicandri
Designed by Barney Smith

Acknowledgments: Walt Savage of the Bureau of Surveys and Maps of the Washington State Dept of Natural Resources
Calligraphy - Karen Porter

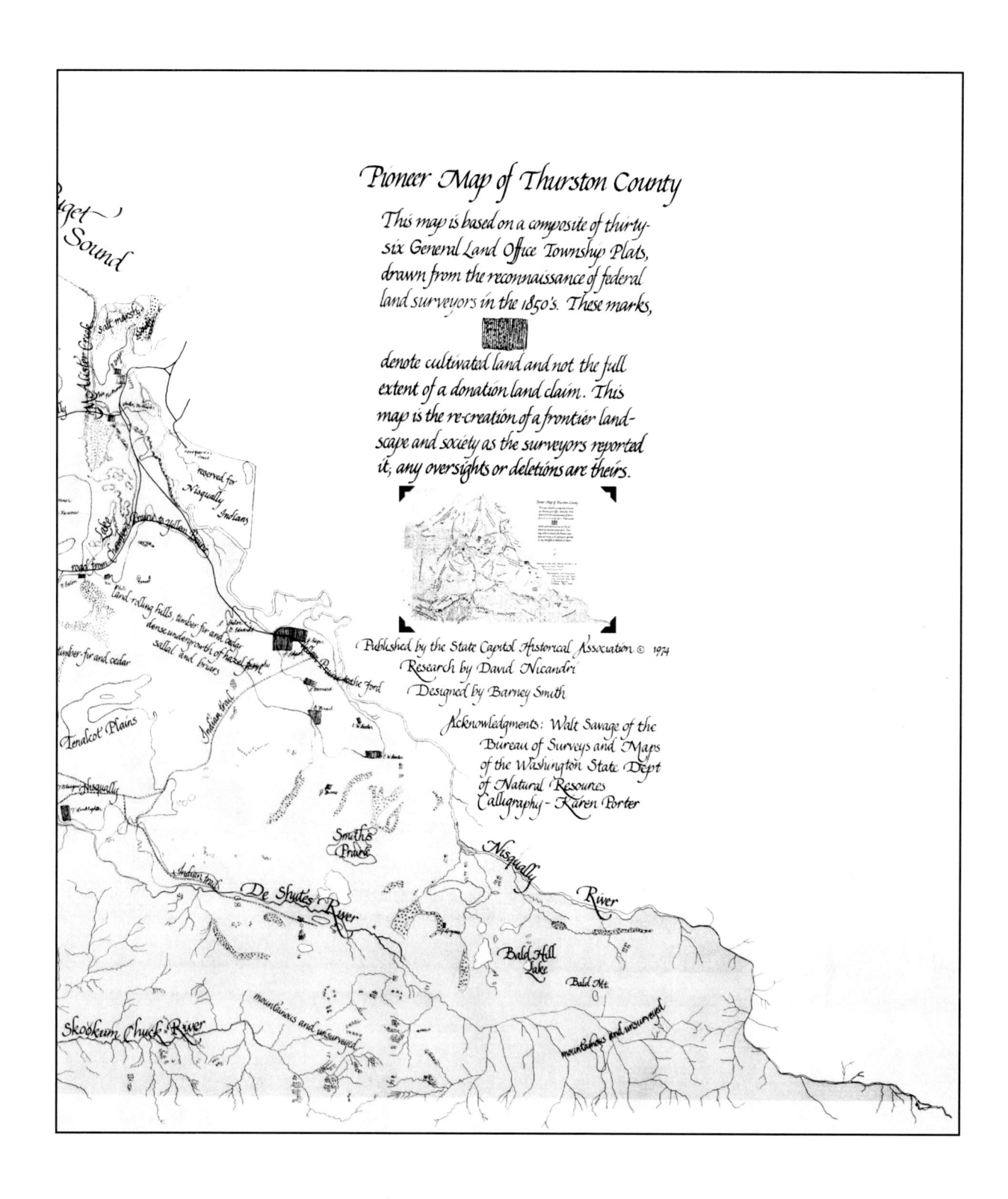

MEET THE AUTHORS

Sandra A. Crowell

Editor Sandra A. Crowell found her passion for local history and a sense of place to her childhood on a historic homestead in the Colorado Rockies. She is the co-author of *Up the Swiftwater* about the Upper Saint Joe River in North Idaho, the author of *The Land Called Lewis, A History of Lewis County, Washington*, and numerous publications. Professionally Sandra has worked with both the Nisqually and Chehalis Tribes in southwest Washington, seeking to promote an understanding of their unique place in Northwest history through technical writing and presentations. She holds a B.A. in English and speech and an MBA. As a member of the Thurston County Historic Commission, she initiated and organized the production of *Thurston County: Water, Woods, & Prairies* and co-edited it with Shirley Stirling.

Les Eldridge

Les Eldridge is the author of five novels of the American Civil War at sea, a book of verse, and co-author of two maritime histories. He is president of the South Sound Maritime Heritage Association, executive secretary of the Washington State Friends of the Cruiser USS *Olympia*, chaired the Maritime Committee of the Washington State Centennial Commission, and serves on the Thurston County Historic Commission. Les retired from careers in university administration, elected office, and administrative law, and held appointments from six Washington State governors and the state's Supreme Court Chief Justice.

Don Trosper

Don Trosper is the Public History Manager for the Heritage Builders local history program of the Olympia Tumwater Foundation, based in the historic Schmidt House. A descendant of the pioneer Trosper family for whom the road is named, he was inspired to make the transition from his radio broadcasting career to local history writing, speaking and promotion of the rich legacy of the Tumwater area, the Schmidt family and the Olympia Brewing Company. He has written several books. Don's focus now includes increasing visibility of Tumwater through organizing local history talks, tours, videos, and articles, educating the public and attracting tourism.

Shanna Stevenson

Shanna Stevenson earned a Bachelor of Arts in history and education from Gonzaga University and a Master's Degree in Public Administration from The Evergreen State College. She served as the Historic Preservation Officer for Olympia, Thurston County, and Tumwater for nearly 20 years. She has also served as the Coordinator of the Women's History Consortium project for the Washington State Historical Society. She has written several local history publications including *Olympia, Lacey, and Tumwater: A Pictorial History* and was a contributor to *The River Remembers A History of Tumwater, 1845-1995*. Recently she worked as an independent historian and historic preservation consultant. Shanna promotes local heritage through her work with the Washington State Governor's Mansion Foundation and the Olympia Historical Society and Bigelow House Museum.

Gerry L. Alexander

Gerry L. Alexander is a retired Chief Justice of the Washington Supreme Court with the distinction of being the longest-serving chief justice in the state's history. A Western Washington native, he graduated with a BA in History from the University of Washington and a JD from the UW Law School. Aside from his private law practice and public service in the courts, Gerry has served the local community in various capacities in charitable, religious, historical, and civic organizations, including presiding over the Bigelow House Preservation Association. His efforts led to the preservation of the 1930s-era Thurston County Courthouse and in the development of the *Thurston County Historical Journal*.

James S. Hannum, M.D.

James S. Hannum M.D. continued a life-long interest in railroad history after moving to Western Washington in the 1970s. He has published several books covering that topic in Thurston County and the immediately surrounding area. They include *Gone But Not Forgotten-Abandoned Railroads of Thurston County, Washington*; *South Puget Sound Railroad Mania*; and *Delusions of Grandeur-The Olympia & Tenino Railroad*. Now retired from the surgical specialty of Ear, Nose, and Throat, he is often involved with groups devoted to the preservation of local history.

Karen L. Johnson

Karen L. Johnson has volunteered and worked in the museum field since 2001. Her interests in early transportation and the pioneer era have led to organizing two stagecoach runs between Olympia and Longview, writing many articles on local and regional history and co-authoring with Dennis Larsen, two books about a Washington pioneer: *A Yankee on Puget Sound: Pioneer Dispatches of Edward Jay Allen, 1852-1855* and *Our Faces Are Westward: The 1852 Oregon Trail Journey of Edward Jay Allen*. She currently works as curator for the Olympia Tumwater Foundation and serves as editor of the *Thurston County Historical Journal*.

Jennifer Crooks

Jennifer Crooks, daughter of Drew Crooks, grew up in Olympia. She has followed her father's footsteps into a career in history. She graduated from Saint Martin's University in 2014 with a B.A. in History. Her senior thesis received the award as the top senior thesis in history and political science. In 2017 she earned a Master's Degree in History at Central Washington University. She has also written for ThurstonTalk.com, *Columbia*, *Thurston County Historical Journal*, and the DuPont Historical Society.

Drew Crooks

Drew Crooks has lived in Olympia since he was two years old. He received a Bachelor's degree in history and anthropology and a Master's degree in museum studies from the University of Washington. For over 30 years Drew has worked with various museums in South Puget Sound and written many articles and four books on the region's heritage. He has also given talks about history to many community groups and school classes ranging from second grade to college.

Temporary bridge on Nisqually River near Olympia, Washington. Postcard. #10899 (Courtesy of a private collection)

Editors and Layout

Chris Colton

Chris Colton has lived in Thurston County for the past 25 years. She has a BA in English literature from the University of California, Santa Cruz, and a Masters in Education from Claremont Graduate University. She taught English and history, mainly Pacific Northwest history, at Maple Lane School for 18 years. She has served on the Tumwater Timberland Library Advisory Council, the Thurston County Parks and Recreation Commission, and currently is a member of the Thurston County Historical Commission.

Shirley A. Stirling

Shirley is a past Thurston County Historic Commissioner and current Historian of the Washington State Society Daughters of the American Revolution (DAR). In 2016 she co-authored a book documenting the contributions of the DAR in establishing and maintaining historical monuments throughout the State of Washington, between 1894-2016. Shirley is originally from Eastern Washington and retired from state government with 30 years service, mainly in the Department of Social and Health Services, working in social services and administration and with a Master of Social Work degree. She is an artist, and displays locally at the Splash Gallery in Percival Landing, Olympia.

PHOTO CREDITS

Albert Farrow Collection
Art Dwelley Collection
Bancroft Library, UC Berkeley
Bill Holland
Cami Petersen
Carole Rambo Holt
Center for Natural Lands Management South Prairies Program
Chehalis Tribe
Chris Colton
City of Rainier
David James Family Collection
Debbie Santelli
Dick Erickson
Experience Olympia & Beyond
Gale Johnson Photography Studio
Gene Weaver
Gordon R. Newell, ed. H.W. McCurdy Marine
Henderson House Museum, City of Tumwater
Jack Curtwright
James Hannum
Jennifer Crooks
Kurt and Kit Anderson
Lacey Museum
Leonard Docherty Collection
Lewis County Museum
Library of Congress
Lois Maffeo
Lola Ritter Bowen Stancil
Mary Eldridge
National Portrait Gallery, Creative Commons
History of the Pacific Northwest
Nisqually Indian Tribe
Northwest Indian Fisheries Commission
Olympia Historical Society and Bigelow House Museum
Olympia Tumwater Foundation
Oregon Historical Society Research Library
Oregon State Archives
Patricia Rambo McBride, In Memory of
Paul Knight
Private Collection - name on file.

Providence Archives, Seattle
Riley McLaughlin
Rob Kirkwood
Robert McIntosh Collection, Henderson House Museum
Roger Easton Collection
Royal Ontario Museum, Toronto
Rutledge Family
Saeger Family
Saint Martin's University
Sharon Mathews
Shirley A. Stirling
Sisters of Providence
South Puget Sound Community College
Squaxin Island Tribe
Swedish-Finn Historical Society
The Evergreen State College
Thurston County Food Bank
Thurston County GeoData Center
ThurstonTalk.com
Tumwater Historical Association
University of Washington Digital Archives
University of Washington Library
University of Washington Special Collections
Velma Rogers
Washington State Archives & Washington State Digital Archives
Washington State Department of Archaeology and Historic Preservation
Washington State Department of Transportation
Washington State Historical Society
Washington State Library
Washington State Library, Washington Rural Heritage project
Wikimedia/Wikipedia
Yale University's Beinecke Rare Book and Manuscript Library
Yelm Prairie Historical Society

SPECIAL THANKS

Northern Pacific's Sherlock station was located south of the Nisqually River. The settlement of Sherlock appears on maps in the early decades of the 20th century. Sherlock Station, later known as Nisqually, became a post office in the early 1900s. No date, Fleetwood Collection. (Courtesy of the Lacey Museum)

Water, Woods & Prairies is almost entirely the work of volunteers. We extend deep gratitude to the many people who donated their time and talents to create this book, particularly the authors of each chapter and sidebars who graciously shared their expertise. In the words of Drew and Jennifer Crooks, "Many individuals, both living and deceased, provided information for our chapters of the book directly and through their writings." Those whose contributions must be acknowledged are Cami Petersen, Thurston County Community Planning & Economic Development (CPED), for her patience in seeing this project to completion; Shirley Stirling, layout designer, co-editor, copy editor, proofreader, photo researcher, and fact-checker who took on this immense project as a volunteer and conquered Adobe InDesign to lay it out; Chris Colton, volunteer copy editor, photo researcher, fact-checker, and proofreader, whose attention to detail in the end notes and bibliography is profound; Karen Johnson and Drew Crooks, who applied their historical knowledge to fact-checking, proofreading, and overall consultation; Sharon Mathews, writing, consultation, proofreading; Charlie Roe, writing, proofreading, and support; Sara Ivey, consultation; Sue Walston proofreading; Bill Lindstrom, proofreading; Thurston County Historic Commission and Board of County Commissioners; staff of Washington State Library and Washington State Archives, especially Benjamin Helle.

Acknowledgments from Authors:

Sandra Crowell:
Cathy Wolfe, former Thurston County Commissioner, and Dave Shipley, former chair Thurston County Historic Commission for their vision in this project; Charlene Krise, Squaxin Island Tribe; Dan Penn and the late Richard Bellon, Confederated Tribes of the Chehalis Reservation; Annette "Nettsie" Bullchild and Jackie Wall, Nisqually Tribe; Dr. Dale Croes; Julie McDonald Zander, author, colleague, and friend; and the late George Nikula, history buff.

Special Thanks

Les Eldridge:
Historian Drew Crooks; The Evergreen State College Librarian Randy Stilson; Olympia Tumwater Foundation's Karen Johnson; my wife Mary Eldridge; and my dear friend and colleague, the late John W. Hough.

Don Trosper:
Olympia Tumwater Foundation, City of Tumwater, Tumwater Historical Association, the Washington State Library, and past and present members of the local history community. Drew Crooks, Karen Johnson, and Sharon Mathews for proofreading and fact-checking.

Shanna Stevenson:
Kelly McAllister; Ed Echtle; Mary Elizabeth Rutledge Miller; Phil Rutledge; Dick Erickson; Erin Quinn Valcho; Rene Corcoran; Dex McCullough; Lila Sjodin; Carole Rambo Holt; Sue Lean; Rita Robison; Velma Rogers; Deb Ross; Mary Evans; Fred Colvin; Kay and Ron Nelson; Nicolette Bromberg; David Hilpert; Lynn Erickson; Laura Johnson; Jewell Dunn; Ben Helle; Sandra Saeger; James S. Hannum, M. D; John T. Marshall; Ferol Max.

Jennifer Crooks and Drew Crooks:
We would especially like to acknowledge Ken Balsley, Ed Bergh, Daeg Aerlic Byrne, Rebecca Christie, Benjamin Helle, Karen Johnson, Gordon Newell, Tracy Rebstock, Dale Sadler, Ann Shipley, Shanna Stevenson, and Julie McDonald Zander; and the assistance of the knowledgeable staff at the Washington State Library and Washington State Archives. In addition, Len Balli, Todd Sprague, Genevieve C. Chan, and Kati Sagawa contributed sidebars that focus on specific topics. Karen Crooks supported us on this multi-year project. Our sincere thanks to them all. Furthermore we thank Karen Johnson for reviewing our chapters (and other parts of the book); Sandra A. Crowell, Shirley A. Stirling, and Chris Colton for editing the publication.

END NOTES

Olympia looking east with the Percival House, built in the 1870s, in the foreground. (Courtesy of a private collection)

Chapter 1 - The Original Residents

    1. "Nisqually Chief Leschi is Hanged on February 19, 1858," http://www.historylink.org/File/5145 (accessed September 15, 2018).
    2. Stevens, Isaac, Letters, 1854-56. From Washington State Archives. *Governor Isaac Stevens' Letters*, 1854-56.
    3. Lisa Blee, *Framing Chief Leschi: Narratives and Politics of Historical Justice* (Chapel Hill, NC: University of North Carolina, 2014), 3-5.
    4. Richard Kluger, T*he Bitter Waters of Medicine Creek: A Tragic Clash Between White and Native America* (New York: Alfred A. Knopf, 2011), preface.
    5. Peter Callaghan, "The site of Chief Leschi hanging," *Olympian*, October 15, 2013, http://www.theolympian.com/news/local/article25321789.html#storylink=cpy (accessed September 15, 2018).
    6. Kluger, *Bitter Waters*, 281.
    7. *Seattle Times*, December 10, 2004, 3-4.
    8. Wayne Suttles, ed., *Handbook of North American Indians, Vol 7: Northwest Coast* (Washington DC: Smithsonian Institute, 1990).
    9. Personal Interview, Yelm, Washington, 2016.
    10. Cecelia S. Carpenter, *Where the Waters Begin: The Traditional Nisqually History of Mount Rainier* (Seattle: Northwest Interpretive Association, July 2001), 2.
    11. "The Chehalis People," Confederated Tribes of the Chehalis Reservation, 2000 update.
    12. Website, Squaxin Island Tribe, 1972.
    13. Indian Claims Commission, Squaxin Indians, 1972.
    14. Murray C. Morgan, *Puget's Sound, A Narrative of Early Tacoma and the Southern Sound* (Seattle: University of Washington Press, 1979), 13-14.
    15. Charlene Krise, Personal Interview, Shelton, Washington, 2016.
    16. Dan Penn, Personal Interview, Oakville, Washington, 2016.
    17. Carpenter, *Where the Waters*, 19.
    18. Penn.
    19. "The Chehalis People."
    20. Krise.

21. Cecelia Svinth Carpenter, *They Walked Before: The Indians of Washington State* (Tacoma, WA: Washington State American Revolution Bicentennial Commission, 1977).

22. Dale Croes, Personal Interview.
23. Penn.
24. Vine Deloria Jr., *Indians of the Pacific Northwest: From the Coming of the White Man to the Present Day* (Golden, CO: Doubleday & Company, 2011).
25. "Chehalis People."
26. Suttles, *Handbook*.
27. Penn.
28. Kluger, *Bitter Waters*, 70.
29. Deloria, *Indians of the Pacific Northwest*, 40-51.
30. Krise.
31. "Treaty of Medicine Creek," http://www.historylink.org/File/5253 (accessed September 19, 2018).
32. James Gilchrist Swan, *The Northwest Coast: Or, Three Years' Residence in Washington Territory* (Seattle: University of Washington Press, 1992), 345-346.
33. Ibid., 357.
34. Carpenter, *They Walked*, 31.
35. "The Dawes Act, 1887," National Archives, https://www.ourdocuments.gov/doc.php?flash=true&doc=50 (accessed September 13, 2018).
36. "Indian Claims Commission Cases Through September 1978," https://www.narf.org/nill/documents/icc_final_report.pdf. See Chehalis, Upper, Dkt 237 4 301 Findings 6/25/56 $754,380.00 Opinion 6125/56 for land p. 31; Nisqually, Dkt 197 Dismissed $80,013.07 p. 61; Squaxin, kt 206 21 295 Opinion - Title 6/30/69 $7,661.82 301 Findings 6/30/69 for land p. 100 (accessed September 19, 2018).
37. Sandra Crowell, unpublished document (2015-16).
38. "Indian Gaming Regulatory Act," National Indian Gaming Commission, https://www.nigc.gov/general-counsel/indian-gaming-regulatory-act (accessed September 13, 2018).

Chapter 2 - Early Encounters

1. Cecelia Svinth Carpenter, *Fort Nisqually: A Documented History of Indian and British Interactions* (Seattle: Tahoma Research Publication, 1986).
2. D. A. Horr, F. Drucker & E. Gunther, *American Indian Ethnohistory, Indians of the Northwest* (New York: Garland Publishing, 1974).
3. Ibid.
4. Ibid.
5. Frances B. Barkan, *The Wilkes Expedition: Puget Sound and the Oregon Country* (Olympia: Washington State Capital Museum, 1987).
6. Horr, *American Indian*.
7. Robert C. Wing with Gordon Newell, *Peter Puget: Lieutenant on the Vancouver Expedition, fighting British naval officer, the man for whom Puget Sound was named* (Ashland, OH: Graybeard Publishing, 1979).
8. Ibid.
9. Ibid.
10. Warren L. Cook, *Flood Tide of Empire: Spain and the Pacific Northwest* (New Haven, CT: Yale University Press, 1973)
11. John Kendrick, *The Men with Wooden Feet: The Spanish Exploration of the Pacific Northwest* (Toronto, ON: NC Press Limited, 1986).
12. Derek Pethick, *First Approaches to the Northwest Coast* (Vancouver, Canada: Douglas & McIntyre, Ltd., 1976).
13. Donald C. Cutter, *Malaspina and Galiano: Spanish Voyages to the Northwest Coast 1791 and 1792* (Seattle: University of Washington Press, 1991).
14. Beth Hill and Cathy Converse, *The Remarkable World of Frances Barkley: 1765-1845* (Canada: Touchwood Editions, 2008).
15. J. Richard Nokes, *Columbia's River: The Voyages of Robert Gray, 1787-1793* (Tacoma, WA: Washington State Historical Society, 1991).

16. Herbert C. Taylor, "John Work on the Chehalis Indians" in *Coast Salish and Western Washington Indians III*, ed. D. A. Horr (New York: Garland Publishing, 1974.)

17. Barkan, *The Wilkes Expedition*.

18. Drew Crooks, *Past Reflections: Essays on the Hudson's Bay Company in the Southern Puget Sound Region* (Tacoma, WA: Fort Nisqually Foundation, 2001).

19. T. C. Elliot ed., "Journal of John Work" (*Washington Historical Quarterly*, 1955).

20. Carpenter, *Fort Nisqually*.

21. Nathaniel Philbrick, *Sea of Glory: America's Voyage of Discovery: The U.S. Exploring Expedition, 1838-1842* (New York: Penguin Books, 2004).

22. Edmond S. Meany, "Diary of Wilkes in the Northwest," *Washington Historical Quarterly* 16 (1925): 49-61, 137-145, 207-223, 291-301; 17 (1926): 43-65, 129-144, 223-229

23. William A. Hagelund, *The Dowager Queen: The Hudson's Bay Company SS Beaver* (Canada Hancock House, 2001).

24. David B. Tyler, *The Wilkes Expedition: The First United States Exploring Expedition, (1838-1842)* (Philadelphia: American Philosophical Society, 1968).

25. Herman Joseph Viola and Carolyn Margolis, ed., *Magnificent Voyagers: The U.S. Exploring Expedition, 1838-1842* (Washington DC: The Smithsonian Institution, 1985).

26. Murray C. Morgan, *Puget's Sound: A Narrative of Early Tacoma and the Southern Sound* (Seattle: University of Washington Press, 1980).

27. Barkan, *The Wilkes Expedition*.

28. Patrick Haskett, *The Wilkes Expedition in Puget Sound, 1841* (Olympia, WA: Washington State Capital Museum, 1974).

29. William Reynolds, *Voyage to the Southern Ocean, the Letters of Lieutenant William Reynolds from the U.S. Exploring Expedition, 1838-1842*, ed. Anne Hoffman Cleaver and E. Jeffrey Stann (Annapolis, MD: Naval Institute Press, 1988).

30. Philbrick, *Sea of Glory*.

31. Wing, *Peter Puget*.

32. Jerry Gorsline, *Rainshadow: Archibald Menzies and the Botanical Expedition of the Olympic Peninsula* (Port Townsend, WA: Jefferson County Historical Society, 1992).

33. Jack Nisbet, *The Collector: David Douglas and the Natural History of the Northwest* (Seattle: Sasquatch Books, 2010).

34. Crooks, *Past Reflections*.

Chapter 3 - Settlers, Steamers, and Statehood

1. Drew Crooks, *Past Reflections: Essays on the Hudson's Bay Company in the Southern Puget Sound Region* (Tacoma, WA: Fort Nisqually Foundation, 2001).

2. Ibid.

3. Cecelia Svinth Carpenter, *Fort Nisqually: A Documented History of Indian and British Interactions* (Seattle: Tahoma Research Publication, 1986).

4. Crooks, *Past Reflections*.

5. Mike Vouri, *The Pig War, Standoff at Griffin Bay* (Seattle: Discover Your Northwest, 1999).

6. Lesley J. Gordon, *General George E. Pickett in Life and Legend* (Chapel Hill, NC: University of North Carolina Press, 1998).

7. Edward G. Longacre, *Pickett, Leader of the Charge: A Biography of General George E. Pickett*, C.S.A. (Shippensburg, PA: White Man Publishing, 1995).

8. William A. Hagelund, *The Dowager Queen: The Hudson's Bay Company SS Beaver* (Canada: Hancock House, 2003).

9. Gordon Newell, *Ships of the Inland Sea: The Story of the Puget Sound Steamboats* (Hillsboro, OR: Binfords & Mort, 1960).

10. Ibid.

11. Newell, *Ships*.

12. Jean Cammon Findlay and Robin Paterson, *The Mosquito Fleet of South Puget Sound* (Charleston, SC: Arcadia, 2008).

13. Chuck Fowler and the Puget Sound Maritime Historical Society, *Tall Ships on Puget Sound* (Charleston, SC: Arcadia, 2007).

14. Thurston County Historical Commission, "Short History of Budd Inlet" (1992).

15. Findlay, *Mosquito Fleet*.
16. Newell, *Ships*.
17. M. S. Kline, *Steamboat Virginia V* (Seattle: University of Washington Press, 1986).
18. Steve Lundin, *The Closest Governments to the People* (Pullman, WA: Washington State University, 2007).
19. J. C. Rathbun, *History of Thurston County, Washington from 1845 to 1895* (Seattle: Shorey Bookstore, 1972).
20. Division of Naval Militia Affairs, Register of the Naval Militia of the United States (2016).
21. Chuck Fowler and Capt. Mark Freeman, *Tugboats on Puget Sound* (Charleston, SC: Arcadia, 2009).

Chapter 4 - Early Days in Tumwater

1. T. C. Shaw, *Reminiscences of 1844*, http://www.oregonpioneers.com/tcshaw.htm.
2. Darrell Millner, "George Bush of Tumwater: Founder of the First American Colony on Puget Sound," *Columbia*, Winter 1994-95.
3. Ibid.
4. "Michael T. and Elizabeth Simmons," Masonic Memorial Park, Tumwater, WA. http://www.masonicmemorialpark.com/index.php/notable-locations/michael-t-elizabeth-simmons (accessed September 20, 2018).
5. Don Trosper, *The Founding of Tumwater* (Tumwater, WA: Tumwater Historical Association, 1985).
6. Millner, "George Bush."
7. Library of Congress, "Nathaniel Crosby II House, Tumwater, Thurston County, Washington," https://www.loc.gov/item/wa0181/ (accessed September 20, 2018).
8. Don Trosper with Janet Haag, *New Market* (Tumwater, WA: Tumwater Historical Association, 1987).
9. *Electric Journal*, Vol 1-7: 187, https://books.google.com/books?id=sS4yAQAAMAAJ&pg=PA187&lpg=PA187&dq=electric+generating+plant+tumwater+falls&source=bl&ots=ZG6RrxCxK_&sig=Dv7IeZ1C3q6YrA9VFjFnQSd3X6A&hl=en&sa=X&ved=0ahUKEwjzm6vsytbZAhUl6YMKHYtWBOcQ6AEIeDAL#v=onepage&q=electric%20generating%20plant%20tumwater%20falls&f=false (accessed January 19, 2019).
10. Don Trosper, *The Train Stops Here* (Tumwater, WA: Tumwater Historical Association, 1995).

Chapter 5 - Call of the Prairies

1. John C. Rathbun, *History of Thurston County, Washington from 1845 to 1895* (Seattle: Shorey Book Store, 1972), 22.
2. Georgiana Blankenship, *Early History of Thurston County, Washington, Together with Biographies and Reminiscences of Those Identified with Pioneer Days* (Olympia, WA:1914), 94.
3. Andrew Jackson Chambers, *Recollections* (Fairfield, WA: Ye Galleon Press, Reprint 1975), 5, 11.
4. Ibid., 24.
5. Gayle Palmer and Shannon Stevenson, eds., *Thurston County Place Names: A Heritage Guide* (Olympia, WA: Thurston County Historic Commission, 1992), 15.
6. Elizabeth Harrison Chambers, *Incidents in the Life of Elizabeth Harrison Chambers: Collected from Memory's Pages and Compiled November 23rd, 1910, after the hand on the dial-plate of time had measured me off 82 years* (Washington State Library: unpublished typewritten manuscript #4032).
7. Dean Hooper and Roberta Longmire, "James Longmire's Story," *Yelm Pioneers and Followers: 1850-1950* (Yelm, WA: Yelm Prairie Historical Society, 1995), 3-9.
8. Ibid., 9.
9. Ed Bergh, "Yelm and the New Deal" (Yelm, WA: Yelm History Project, 2010).
10. Drew W. Crooks, *Essays on the Hudson's Bay Company in the Southern Puget Sound Region* (Tacoma, WA: Fort Nisqually Foundation, 2001), 25-31, 32-45, 85-87.
11. Ibid., 64.
12. Blankenship, *Early History*, 355-359.
13. Ibid., 128.
14. Shanna Stevenson, "Freedom," *Sunday Olympian, Totem Tidings*, October 19, 1980, 4-5.
15. Ibid.; Edna Irene Kelsey, *The History of the Freedom Community*, 1934 (unpublished manuscript); *Pioneer Days in Freedom Community* (unpublished manuscript); William J. Betts, "Old Fort Eaton, Ghost of the Blockhouse Era: It Shielded Settlers From Indian Attack," *Tacoma News Tribune, Magazine Section*, December 11, 1960, 6; "Freedom Homemaker's Club Long Established in Thurston County," *Daily Olympian*, April 12, 1970, 22; Mrs. H. R. Kagy, "Pioneer Schools in the Freedom Community," *Told by the Pioneers: Tales of Frontier Life as Told by Those Who Remember the Days of Territory and Early Statehood of Washington, Vol 3* (Works Progress Administration, 1937-38), 193-194.
16. Blankenship, *Early History*, 69.

17. Zelma Bernd, "All My Children: A Lacey Pioneer Story," 1994, https://www.sos.wa.gov/_assets/legacy/pioneers-story.pdf (accessed September 15, 2018).

18. Blankenship, *Early History*, 225.

19. John Rogers James, "Autobiography of John Rogers James," *Told by the Pioneers: Tales of Frontier Life by Those Who Remember the Days of the Territory and Early Statehood of Washington, Vol 2* (Olympia, WA: Works Projects Administration, 1937-38), 81.

20. Julie McDonald Zander, *Bucoda: The Little Town with a Million Memories* (Centralia, WA: Bucoda Community Foundation, 2010), 16; "Pioneer Resident of 80 Years Recounts History," *Tenino Independent*, March 1, 1935.

21. Blankenship, *Early History*, 193.

22. Arthur G. Dwelley, *Prairies & Quarries: Pioneer Days Around Tenino, 1830-1900* (Tenino, WA: Independent Publishing Company, 1989), 8-10; see also Pioneer Map of Thurston County (Olympia, WA: State Capitol Historical Association, 1974).

23. "Alexander Yantis," in Blankenship, *Early History*, 189-194; "B.F. Yantis," Ibid., 272-274.

24. "Thurston County Pioneers Before 1870, Henry Harrison Tilley," http://content.statelib.wa.gov/cdm/singleitem/collection/pioneers/id/198/rec/1 (accessed September 13, 2018).

25. "John Rogers James," *Told by the Pioneers*, 81.

26. David A. James, *From Grand Mound to Scatter Creek: The Homes of Jamestown* (Olympia, WA: State Capitol Historical Association of Washington, 1981), 60.

27. Ibid., 27.

28. Palmer and Stevenson, *Place Names*, 93.

29. Judith Upton with Karyl Groenveld, *Glimpses of Gate: A Pictorial History of Gate, WA: 1880-1920* (Rochester, WA: Printed by Gorham Printing, 2003,) 17.

30. Palmer and Stevenson, *Place Names*, 52, 53.

31. Lizzie McAllister Hawk, "The McAllister Family," *Tacoma Ledger*, July 10, 1892.

32. *Told by the Pioneers: Tales of Frontier Life by Those Who Remember the Days of the Territory and Early Statehood of Washington*, (Olympia, WA: Work Projects Administration, 1937-38, Vol 1), 168.

33. Del McBride, "McAllister & Wells - The Nisqually Sawmill Company," *Occurrences* XVII, No. 3 (Summer 2000), 15-18.

34. "Letter from John McAllister to James McAllister, September 19, 1852," from private collection.

35. Pioneer Map of Thurston County.

36. Rathbun, *History*, 75.

Chapter 6 - A New County and a New Territory

1. Edmond Meany, *History of the State of Washington* (New York: The Macmillan Company, 1941), 87-90.

2. Ibid., 141-149.

3. Newton Carl Abbot and Fred Carver, *The Evolution of Washington Counties*, compiled by J. W. Helm (Goldendale, WA: Yakima Valley Genealogical Society and Klickitat County Historical Society, 1978), 1-20.

4. Hubert Howe Bancroft, *The History of Washington, Idaho and Montana, 1845-1889* (San Francisco: The History Company, 1890), 44.

5. Meany, *History*, 135-136.

6. Ibid., 40.

7. *Oregon Spectator*, Public Meeting, July 29, 1851, 1. Despite the lack of a newspaper north of the Columbia River, the proceedings of all these meetings are recounted in the *Oregon Spectator*, though somewhat belatedly.

8. Edmond Meany, "The Cowlitz Convention: Inception of Washington Territory," *Washington Historical Quarterly*, XIII, no. 1 (January 1922), 3-19. Meany explained that it was this petition rather than the Monticello Convention a year later that precipitated Joseph Lane's first political action before Congress for the establishment of Washington Territory on December 6, 1852. See also: Thomas Prosch, "The Political Beginnings of Washington Territory," *Oregon Historical Quarterly*, 6: 147-158.

9. Bancroft, *History*, 51.

10. *Journal of House of Representatives*, Oregon Territorial Legislature, December 17, 1851, 32-33.

11. Meany, *History*, 155-156.

12. Bancroft, *History*, 53.

13. Oregon State Archives, Calendar #4638.

14. Elwood Evans, "Address of the Town Clerk," *Washington Standard*, July 6, 1861, 1 detailing the controversy; results of the election held July 6, 1861 at State Archives.

15. John M. McClelland, Jr., "Washington Had Its Beginning Here on Cowlitz 100 Years Ago," *Longview Daily News - Monticello Centennial Edition*, November 25, 1952, 5.

16. Bancroft, *History*, 61.

17. *Washington Standard*, "Original Story of Arrival Here of Governor Stevens", November 29, 1912, 1, 3.

18. Hazard Stevens, *Life of General Isaac I. Stevens by His Son Hazard Stevens with Maps and Illustrations in Two Volumes* (Boston: Houghton, Mifflin and Company, 1900), vol. 1, 441-442. This includes a vivid account of the Olympia area when the family arrived in December, 1854.

19. David Nicandri and Derek Valley, *Olympia Wins: Washington's Capital Controversies* (Olympia, WA: Washington State Capitol Museum, 1980).

20. Biographical Directory of the United States Congress, http://bioguide.congress.gov/scripts/biodisplay.pl?index=T000258 (accessed September 20, 2018).

Chapter 7 - From Settlements to Cities

1. Thomas Talbot Waterman, 1885-1936, *Puget Sound Geography* (Washington, DC: The Smithsonian Institution, 1920), 392; (microfilm of manuscript at Smithsonian Institution, filmed 1968, for the University of Washington Libraries).

2. Account of Lurana Percival in Georgiana (Mitchell) Blankenship, *Early History of Thurston County, Washington: Together with Biographies and Reminiscenses of Those Identified with Pioneer Days* (Olympia, WA: 1914) (Binder's title: *Tillicum Tales of Thurston County*), 336; Hazard Stevens, T*he Life of Isaac Ingalls Stevens by his son, Hazard Stevens with Maps and Illustrations in Two Volumes* (Boston: Houghton, Mifflin and Company, 1900), vol 1, 442.

3. James Robert Tanis, ed., "The Journal of Levi Lathrop Smith, 1847-1848," *Pacific Northwest Quarterly* (October, 1952), 277-301.

4. Ibid., 281.

5. John Swan, "Olympia, the Pioneer Town of Washington, Its Socialization, Origin, and Early History from a Pioneer's Retrospection," manuscript at the University of Washington, Allen Library, Special Collections; Murray C. Morgan, *The Meares Expeditions*, http://cdm17061.contentdm.oclc.org/cdm/singleitem/collection/p17061coll6/id/88/rec/42 (accessed September 16, 2018).

6. Susan B. Anthony Papers, Library of Congress, *Daybook and Diaries 1856-1906*, Box 2 Reel 1-2, October 18, 1871.

7. Guy Reed Ramsey, *Postmarked Washington: Thurston County*, ed. by Susan Goff et al. (Thurston County, WA: Thurston County Historical Commission, 1988), 9-30.

8. Phoebe Judson, *A Pioneer's Search for an Ideal Home: a book of personal memoirs* (Lincoln, NE: University of Nebraska Press, 1984), 96.

9. Harvey Steele, "Customs Service Herald Arrival of United States," Special Supplement, *Daily Shipping News* (January 11, 1991), 2.

10. David Nicandri, *Olympia's Forgotten Pioneers: the Oblates of Mary Immaculate* (Olympia, WA: State Capitol Historical Association, 1976).

11. Ibid., 69.

12. John C. Rathbun, *History of Thurston County, Washington from 1845 to 1895* (Seattle: Shorey Book Store, 1972), 17.

13. Blankenship, *Early History*, 132-133.

14. "Mrs. Rebecca H. Howard, 1862-1883," unpublished manuscript compiled 1999, http://www.blackpast.org/aaw/howard-rebecca-groundage-1827-1881 (accessed September 21, 2018).

15. Shanna Stevenson, *St. Peter Hospital: A Century of Caring. A Commitment to Quality* (Olympia, WA: St. Peter Hospital, 1987); see also http://stmikesolympia.org/#/about-us/history (accessed September 21, 2018); http://washington.providence.org/about/history/ (accessed September 21, 2018); "St. Michael's School: 100 Years 1882-1982," Mike Contris, ed. (1982) https://stmikesolympia.org/about/history/ (accessed September 19, 2018).

16. Judson, *Pioneer's Search*, 93.

17. Blankenship, *Early History*, 336.

18. Ibid.

19. Ibid, 118.

20. Ibid.

21. Rathbun, *History*, 38.

22. "Bridge Across Budd's Inlet," *Pioneer and Democrat*, October 15, 1854, col 3, says the contract had been let and the bridge was to be completed in December; the 1856 U.S. Coast Survey, "Reconnaissance of Olympia Harbor," map shows the bridge; Rathbun, *History*, 51, says the Marshville drawbridge was completed in May, 1859.

23. "Casco Company Erects Many Buildings," *Daily Olympian*, April 26, 1928, 2.

24. Gordon R. Newell, *Rogues, Buffoons & Statesmen* (Seattle: Hangman Press, 1975), 132-33.

25. David Nicandri and Derek Valley, *Olympia Wins: Washington's Capital Controversies* (Olympia, WA: Washington State Capitol Museum, 1980); "Supreme Court Had Many Homes Before Big Temple of Justice," *Daily Olympian*, April 15, 1941, 15.

26. Ibid., 26; WISAARD National Registration nomination for the Old Capitol https://fortress.wa.gov/dahp/wisaardp3/api/api/resultgroup/1163/Document/185889 (accessed September 22, 2018).

27. Shanna Stevenson, *Superior Shipping Service - A History of the Port of Olympia* (Olympia, WA: Port of Olympia, 1982).

28. "Action Filed Against Property Owners of Resorts Below the Line," *Olympia Daily Recorder*, November 10, 1910, 1.

29. "Canning Company Does $200,000 Business Yearly," *Morning Olympian*, March 15, 1916.

30. The bridge was named "The Olympia-Yashiro Friendship Bridge;" http://olympiawa-gov/community/about-olympia/history-of-olympia-washington (accessed September 19, 2018).

31. "Plywood in Retrospect, Olympia Veneer," Plywood Pioneers Association (1969) https://www.apawood.org/data/Sites/1/documents/monographs/7-olympia-veneer-co.pdf; "Plywood in Retrospect, Washington Veneer," Plywood Pioneers Association (1971) (accessed September 13, 2018). https://www.apawood.org/data/Sites/1/documents/monographs/11-washington-veneer-co.pdf (accessed September 13, 2018).

32. Shanna Stevenson, *The Port of Olympia: A 75 Year History, 1922-1997*, with updates by Chuck Fowler (Olympia, WA: Port of Olympia, 1997); http://www.portolympia.com/105/History (accessed September 21, 2018).

33. Newell, *Rogues*, 336, 338. The legislature marched up the hill to the new chambers in March, 1927, but the executive offices were not occupied until February, 1928.

34. Rebecca Christie, *Workingman's Hill: A History of an Olympia Neighborhood* (Olympia, WA: Bigelow House Preservation Association/Bigelow Highlands Neighborhood Association, 2001), 153-155.

35. Washington Department of General Administration, "Capitol Lake: A Vision for the Next Ten Years, 2003-2013" (October, 2002).

36. Shanna Stevenson, "A Freeway Runs Through it," in Gayle Palmer, ed., *The River Remembers: A History of Tumwater, 1845-1995* (Tumwater, WA: City of Tumwater, 1996).

37. Olympia Heritage Commission, "Mid-Twentieth Century Olympia: A Context Statement on Local History and Modern Architecture, 1945-1975," April 2008, olympiawa.gov/~/media/Files/…/MAContextStatementAPRIL2008reformatted.ashx (accessed September 13, 2018).

38. Olympia population in 1960 was 18,273 and in 1970, 23,296. Thurston Regional Planning Council, "The Profile 2013", Table II-1, ii-9.

39. "The Tradition Continues - Celebrating 10 Years of Outstanding Performance, The Washington Center for the Performing Arts, 1985-1995," brochure (1995); Shanna Stevenson, *Lacey, Olympia, and Tumwater: A Pictorial History* (Norfolk, VA: The Donning Company, 1985), 222.

40. See https://des.wa.gov/services/facilities-leasing/capitol-campus/parks-and-attractions/heritage-park (accessed September 21, 2018).

41. For general Lacey history see: Lanny Weaver, "The Story of Lacey: From Community to City, Part I: 1848-1891," and "Part II, 1892-1948." http://thurstontalk.com/2016/04/04/lacey-histry-2/ (accessed September 21, 2018); http://www.thurstontalk.com/2016/07/04/city-lacey-histry-2/ (accessed September 21, 2018).

42. Barbara Lane, *Political and Economic Aspects of Indian-White Culture Contact in Western Washington in the Mid-19th Century*, Manuscript (May 10, 1973), 7, referencing George Gibbs.

43. For information about Nisqually food gathering and preparation, see Cecelia Svinth Carpenter, *The Nisqually - My People* (Seattle: Tacoma Research Service, 2002), 39-59.

44. Drew Crooks, "The Mystery of Tyrell's Lake Farm" (Lacey, WA: Lacey Historic Commission, January, 1995) available at Lacey Museum.

45. "Early Settlers of Lacey" (Lacey, WA: Lacey Historic Commission, May, 1993) available at Lacey Museum; *Transactions of the 53rd Annual Reunion of the Oregon Pioneer Association, July 1, 1925* (Portland: F. W. Baltes and Company, 1928).

46. Lanny Weaver, "The Story of Lacey;" Drew Crooks, "Lacey: An Interesting History and Unusual Place Name," http://www.thurstontalk.com/2013/08/18/lacey-history/ (accessed September 19, 2018).

47. "Old Lacey Historic Area" (Lacey, WA: Lacey Historic Commission, June, 1994) available at Lacey Museum.

48. Lanny Weaver, "The Hunt for O. C. Lacey" (Lacey, WA: Lacey Historic Commission, 1995) available at Lacey Museum.

49. Ibid.

50. Ibid.

51. Lanny Weaver, "The True Story of Lacey's Racetrack," *Lacey Museum Musings*, Fall, 2015.

52. Father John C. Scott, O. S. B., *This Place Called Saint Martin's: 1895-1995* (Virginia Beach, VA: The Donning Company, 1996), 28.

53. "Union Mills Lumber Company" (Lacey, WA: Lacey Historic Commission, March, 2004) available at Lacey Museum.

54. "The Foy Store" (Lacey, WA: Lacey Historic Commission, 1995) available at Lacey Museum.

55. Ken Balsley, "Pioneers to Panorama - The 'City Within a City' has Roots in Lacey's Pioneers," http://www.thurstontalk.com/2016/03/05/panorama-lacey-history (accessed September 19, 2018).

56. "A Rich History," Lacey Historic Museum, http:// http://www.ci.lacey.wa.us/living-in-lacey/a-rich-history (accessed September 13, 2018).

57. "Lacey Women's Club" (Lacey, WA: Lacey Historic Commission, January, 1994) available at Lacey Museum.

58. Scott, *Saint Martin's*, 85, 101; *Between the Years: 1895-1945* (Lacey, WA: Saint Martin's College), https://www.stmartin.edu/about/history (accessed September 22, 2018).

59. "Commercial Development Key to City's Past - and Future," *Daily Olympian*, February 6, 1983, B1.

60. Scott, *Saint Martin's*, 194.

61. Lacey Historic Register Files; Crooks, "Lacey: An Interesting History."

62. Arthur G. Dwelley, *Prairies & Quarries, Pioneer Days Around Tenino, 1830-1900* (Tenino, WA: Independent Publishing Co, 1989), 1-5.

63. Ibid., 6-20.

64. Guy Reed Ramsey, *Postmarked Washington: Thurston County* (Thurston County, WA: Thurston County Historic Commission, 1988), 44.

65. Jim Hannum, personal correspondence, 2016; Arthur G. Dwelley, "The Tie That Binds: The Northern Pacific Railroad in Cowlitz County," *Columbia Magazine* 3, no. 4 (1989-90): 38-43.

66. Arthur G. Dwelley, "A Brief History of Tenino," https://tb2cdn.schoolwebmasters.com/accnt_187599/site_187600/Documents/BriefHistory_Tenino.pdf (accessed September 14, 2018).

67. Dwelley, *Prairies*, 36.

68. Ibid. 31.

69. Arthur G. Dwelley, "Sandstone quarries gave Tenino a boost from village to town," *Tenino Independent*, 60th anniversary edition, June 16, 1982, 26.

70. "Opening of First Tenino Quarry Told by S. W. Fenton," *Thurston County Independent*, June 7, 1935, 1, 3.

71. Ibid., 1; "Tenino sandstone quarries were founded 100 years ago," *Tenino Independent*, January 4, 1989; Dwelley, "Sandstone quarries."

72. Dwelley, *Prairies*, 54.

73. Don Major, "The Story of Tenino Wooden Money," *Thurston County Independent*, February 19, 1965.

74. Dwelley, *Prairies*, 54.

75. *Thurston County Independent*, "Incorporation of Tenino Told by H. J. Keithahn," June 14, 1935.

76. Shanna Stevenson, *Pictorial History*, 188.

77. Gayle Palmer and Shanna Stevenson, eds., *Thurston County Place Names: A Heritage Guide* (Olympia, WA: Thurston County Historic Commission, 1992), 96.

78. Drew Crooks, *Past Reflection: Essays on the Hudson's Bay Company in the Southern Puget Sound Region* (Tacoma, WA: Fort Nisqually Foundation, 2001), 32-33, 84.

79. Ibid., 35.

80. Richard and Floss Loutzenhiser, *The Story of Yelm: The Little Town With the Big History, 1848-1948*, (Yelm, WA: Yelm Prairie Historical Society, 1999), 63.

81. "Magnificent Views and Vistas: Mountaineers Climbs 1912-1916," Tacoma Public Library, http://mtn.tpl.lib.wa.us/climbs/climbing/people/fuller.asp (accessed September 13, 2018).
82. Ibid.
83. Dean Hooper and Roberta B. Longmire, *Yelm Pioneers and Followers, 1850-1950* (Yelm, WA: Yelm Prairie Historical Society, 1999), 63.
84. City of Yelm. http://www.ci.yelm.wa.us/ (accessed September 19, 2018).
85. Hooper and Longmire, *Yelm Pioneers*, 66.
86. Ibid., 114.
87. Neil B. Corcoran, *Bucoda: A Heritage of Sawdust and Leg Irons* (Bucoda, WA: published as a Bicentennial project by the Bucoda Improvement Club, 1976), 17-18.
88. National registry nomination for Seatco Prison Site, https://npgallery.nps.gov/NRHP/GetAsset/95ce0b7e-5d85-4fa0-887d-6d017dd5a14f/?branding=NRHP (accessed September 21,2018).
89. Ibid., 26.
90. Ibid., 22-31.
91. Ibid., 35.
92. Ibid., 41-44.
93. Julie McDonald Zander, *Chapters of Life in Bucoda* (Centralia, WA: Chapters of Life, 2010), 139, 147, 163-168.
94. City of Rainier, http://cityofrainierwa.org (accessed September 19, 2018); "Rainier Endures Despite Family Scraps," *Olympian*, February 13, 1983.
95. WISAARD file for Rainier School and Zion Evangelical Lutheran Church, https://fortress.wa.gov/dahp/wisaardp3/api/api/resultgroup/1163/Document/185912 (accessed September 22,2018).

Chapter 8 - The Three R's

1. Frederick Bolton and Thomas Bibb, *History of Education in Washington*, Bulletin 1934 No. 9 (Washington, DC: U.S. Government Printing Office, 1934), 45-46.
2. Angie Burt Bowden, *Early Schools of Washington Territory* (Seattle: Lowman and Hanford Company, 1935), 148.
3. Marie Rowe Dunbar, "Indians Haunted Pioneer of Olympia," *Tacoma Sunday Ledger Magazine Section*, November 19, 1923, 5.
4. Bowden, *Early Schools*, 148.
5. Ibid., 136.
6. Bolton and Bibb, *Education*, 91.
7. Ibid., 423.
8. Ibid., 75.
9. Ibid., 80.
10. Bernadine Dafoe, *History of Maytown* (Maytown, WA: B. Dafoe, South Thurston County Historical Society Distributor, 1985), 9.
11. *10th Biennial Report of the Superintendent of Public Instruction*, 12, 16.
12. *22nd Biennial Report of the Superintendent of Public Instruction*, 69, 81.
13. Dorothy Hammerschmith (Brown) in Dean Hooper & Robert B. Longmire, *Yelm Pioneers and Followers, 1850-1950* (Yelm, WA: Yelm Prairie Historical Society, 1999), 72.
14. *29th Biennial Report of the Superintendent of Public Instruction*, 160, 165, 178.
15. Hale is listed as Pamelia Towe in the "Quincentennial Catalogue of Officers and Students of Mount Holyoke, 1837-1895" (South Hadley, MA: Mount Holyoke, 1895). The list noted she had married Calvin Hale.
16. Georgiana Blankenship, *Early History of Thurston County Washington, Together with Biographies and Reminiscences of Those Identified with Pioneer Days* (Olympia, WA: 1914), 52.
17. Esther Knox, *Diary of the Olympia School District, 1852-1976*, n.d., 7.
18. Hale was appointed to the Territorial Board of Education by then Governor Newell, *Washington Standard*, April 8, 1881, 4.
19. John C. Rathbun, *History of Thurston County, Washington from 1845 to 1895* (Seattle: Shorey Book Store, 1972), 78.
20. Allene H. Kearns, "The Woman's Club of Olympia," *Olympian, Totem Tidings*, March 6, 1883, 4-5.
21. "The Ladies Relief Society," *Washington Standard*, December 14, 1888, 3.
22. Rathbun, *Thurston County*, 63. Pamela Hale was Secretary of the Woman Suffrage

Association at Olympia.

    23. Subscriptions for the Hotel Olympia, *Washington Standard*, May 10, 1889, 1; information about Olympia Gas Works from Rathbun, *Thurston County*, 87-88.

    24. The Hale Block (built in 1891) is shown at 4th and Jefferson on the 1896 Fire Insurance Map of Olympia.

    25. Death Notice for Pamela Hale, *Washington Standard*, September 21, 1917, 8.

Chapter 9 - Battle for the Capital

    1. Don Brazier, *History of the Washington State Legislature 1854-1963* (Olympia, WA: Washington State Senate, 2000), 1-12.

    2. David Nicandri and Derek Valley, *Olympia Wins: Washington's Capital Controversies* (Olympia, WA: Washington State Capitol Museum, 1980), 33-34.

    3. Arthur S. Beardsley, "Early Efforts to Locate the Capital of Washington Territory," *Pacific Northwest Quarterly 32*, no. 3 (July 1941): 239-241.

    4. Brazier, *History*, 3.

    5. Beardsley, *Early Efforts*, 243-244.

    6. Ibid., 249-251.

    7. Brazier, *History*, 10-12.

    8. "Brief History of the Washington State Supreme Court," Washington Courts, https://www.courts.wa.gov/education/?fa=education.supreme (accessed September 13, 2018).

    9. Charles H. Sheldon and Michael Stohr-Gillmore, "In the Beginning: The Washington Supreme Court a Century Ago," *University of Puget Sound Law Review* 12:247, 251.

    10. Beardsley, "Early Efforts", 283-285.

    11. Washington Territory, Supreme Court, Opinions of the Supreme court of the territory of Washington, in cases argued and determined in said court, from its organization (1854) to the term ending January 29, 1864. Published by authority (Olympia, WA, 1854), 139-144.

    12. Ibid., 144-153.

    13. Gordon R. Newell, *Rogues, Buffoons, and Statesmen* (Seattle: Hangman Press, 1975).

    14. Brazier, *History*, 41.

    15. Ibid., 65.

    16. Ibid., 69.

    17. WISAARD National Register nomination for General Administration Building, https://fortress.wa.gov/dahp/wisaardp3/api/api/resultgroup/186701/doc/1462211166089 (accessed September 22, 2018).

    18. "Washington's Attorneys General - Past and Present," Washington State Office of the Attorney General, https://www.atg.wa.gov/washingtons-attorneys-general-past-and-present (accessed September 13, 2018).

    19. "Ralph M. Davis," *Seattle Times Obituaries*, http://www.legacy.com/obituaries/seattletimes/obituary.aspx?n=ralph-m-davis&pid=124443808 (accessed September 13, 2018).

    20. "Perspectives on the Bench and Bar of Thurston County Since Statehood," November 14, 2014, http://thurstoncountybar.com/wp-content/uploads/2014/11/WA125WrittenMaterials.pdf (accessed September 13, 2018).

    21. "State Ex Rel. Lemon v. Langlie," Justia US Law, https://law.justia.com/cases/washington/supreme-court/1954/32910-1.html (accessed September 13, 2018).

Chapter 10 - Farms and Fields

    1. Marian Smith, *The Puyallup-Nisqually* (New York: Columbia University Press, 1940), 273; Estella Leopold, "An Ecological History of Old Prairie Areas in Southwestern Washington," *Indians, Fire, and the Land in the Pacific Northwest*, Robert Boyd, ed. (Corvallis, OR: Oregon State University Press, 1999), 153.

    2. James Gibson, *Farming the Frontier: The Agricultural Opening of the Oregon Country, 1786-1846* (Seattle: University of Washington Press, 1985), 96.

    3. Drew Crooks, "From the Orkney Islands to Tenalquot Prairie: The Life of Thomas Linklater," *Occurrences X*, no. 111 (Fall 1991), 10-12.

    4. *Washington's Centennial Farms: Yesterday and Today* (Olympia, WA: Washington State Department of Agriculture, 1989), 13-21.

    5. Clinton Snowden, *History of Washington: Rise and Progress of the American State, Volume 3*

(New York: Century History, 1909-1911), 37-38.

6. "Autobiography of John Rogers James," *Told By the Pioneers: Tales of Frontier Life as Told By Those Who Remember the Days of Territory and Early Statehood of Washington*, Volume 2 (Olympia, WA: Works Progress Administration, 1937-38), 79.

7. Darrell Millner, *The River Remembers: A History of Tumwater, 1845-1995*, ed. Gayle L. Palmer (Tumwater, WA: City of Tumwater, 1996), 41-50.

8. Ibid.; "John Rogers James," 85.

9. David Nicandri, *Olympia's Forgotten Pioneers* (Olympia, WA: Washington State Capitol Historical Association, 1976), 8.

10. *The Columbian* (September 11, 1852), 2.

11. *Told By the Pioneers*, Volume 1, 168.

12. Judith Upton with Karyl Groenevelt, *Glimpses of Gate: A Pictorial Journal of Gate, WA: 1880-1920* (Rochester, WA: printed by Gorham Printing, 2003), 183.

13. "John Rogers James," 80.

14. Georgiana Blankenship, *Early History of Thurston County Washington, Together with Biographies and Reminiscences of Those Identified with Pioneer Days* (Olympia, WA: 1914), 93.

15. *Centennial Farms*, 42; see also WISAARD file for Rutledge House and Barn, https://fortress.wa.gov/dahp/wisaardp3/api/api/resultgroup/1163/Document/186419 (accessed September 22, 2018).

16. Ibid., 43.

17. *Washington's Centennial Farms: Yesterday and Today Update* (Olympia, WA: Washington State Department of Agriculture, 2014), https://agr.wa.gov/FP/Pubs/docs/469-O-WACentennialFarms-s25YrsLater-Overview.pdf (accessed September 17, 2018).

18. *Centennial Farms*, 43.

19. *Centennial Farms Update*.

20. *Centennial Farms*, A-8; *Centennial Farms Update*.

21. "Thurston County Agriculture," *Agricultural Data Series 1956, Washington Crop and Livestock Reporting Service Bulletin*, 3.

22. "The Farm in Its Relation to Olympia and Thurston County, Wash., Bulletin No. 3" (Olympia, WA: Olympia Chamber of Commerce, 1913).

23. Agricultural Census Data for Thurston County.

24. Olov. G. Gardebring, "The Swedes of the Independence Valley (Rochester), Washington Area", *The Swedish-American Historical Quarterly* XLIX, no. 1 (January 1998), 5-42.

25. Ibid.

26. Anna Ditch and Hilma Englund, *A Little History of Independence Valley, Washington* (Olympia, WA: Washington State Capitol Museum, 1976).

27. Ibid., 32.

28. *The South Bay: Its History and Its People, 1840-1940* (Olympia, WA: South Bay Historical Association, 1986), 115.

29. Dean Hooper and Roberta Longmire, *Yelm Pioneers and Followers, 1850-1950* (Yelm, WA: Yelm Historical Society, 1999), 109-121.

30. Charles Rough in Lynn L. Larson, and Jerry V. Jermann, "A Cultural Resources Assessment of the Nisqually Wildlife Refuge," Office of Public Archaeology, Institute for Environmental Studies, University of Washington, Reconnaissance Report (Seattle, June 1978); Mark Nielsen, "The Brown Farm on the Nisqually Delta, 1904-1919. A Photographic Essay," *Pacific Northwest Quarterly* 71, no. 4 (October 1980): 162-171.

31. Shanna Stevenson, *Olympiana* (Olympia, WA: Washington State Capitol Museum, 1982), 56-59.

32. William H. Cochran, *Washington's State Institutions* (1915); Excerpts from the Biennial Reports of the Board on Control for the State of Washington; Gordon Newell, "The State's Got Us Now," *Perspective* 13, no. 2 (Fall 1969); Papers of Governor Ernest Lister, Washington State Archives.

33. Ed Shinck, personal interview, His father was farm superintendent; Merton Hill, personal interview, employee of the ranch and cannery; Theresa Conner, "Haying fever hits old ranch balers," *Olympian*, July, 17, 1985.

34. Robert W. McKay, "Abundance of Water in County Accounts for Many Fine Crops", *Daily Olympian*, May 27, 1953, 7A.

35. Jeffrey R. Risher, "Farmland Preservation in Thurston County" (MES Thesis, The Evergreen State College, June 2009), 7, 9.

36. Washington State University, "Agriculture in Thurston County," http://extension.wsu.edu/thurston/agriculture (accessed September 13, 2018).; Washington State University, "Agriculture: A

Cornerstone of Thurston County's Economy," http://extension.wsu.edu/thurston/wp-content/uploads/sites/12/2014/01/Agriculture-A-Cornerstone-of-Thurston-Countys-Economy.pdf (accessed September 13, 2018).

37. Jerre Redecker, "Bountiful Byway: Thurston County Trail leads to farms, hikes - and attention," *Olympian*, April 16, 2016.

Chapter 11 - Inlets of Harvest and Home

1. Thanks to Edward Echtle for his review of this section. See: http://olympiawa.gov/city-services/parks/percival-landing/olympia-oyster (accessed September 22, 2018).

2. Georgiana Blankenship, *Early History of Thurston County Washington, Together with Biographies and Reminiscences of Those Identified with Pioneer Days* (Olympia, WA: 1914), 197.

3. "Thurston County Oyster Industry," *The Coast* (Seattle: Coast Publishing Co.,1909, reprinted 1976), 153.

4. Ibid.

5. E. N. Steele, *The Rise and Decline of the Olympia Oyster* (Elma, WA: Olympia Oyster Growers Association, 1957), 14. See also E. N. Steele, *The Immigrant Oyster (Osterea Gigas) Now Known as the Pacific Oyster* (Olympia, WA: Pacific Oyster Growers, 1964).

6. Ibid., 15

7. Ibid., 16.

8. *The Coast*, 155.

9. Ibid., 154.

10. Larry Smith's Eighth Grade English Class, *How the West Was Once* (Olympia, WA: 1974), 23.

11. Steele, *Rise and Decline*, 120-126.

12. Northwest Indian Fisheries Commission, "Commercial Shellfish Growers Settlement," http://nwifc.org/about-us/shellfish/commercial-shellfish-growers-settlement (accessed September 13, 2018).

13. Gayle Palmer and Shanna Stevenson, eds., *Thurston County Place Names: a Heritage Guide* (Olympia, WA: Thurston County Historic Commission, 1992), 9, 21.

14. "Thurston County Pioneers Before 1870," http://content.statelib.wa.gov/cdm/landingpage/collection/pioneers (accessed September 13, 2018).

15. "Tells of Their Big Plans," *Morning Olympian*, April 7, 1907; "Tells All About the New Townsite," *Morning Olympian*, May 18, 1904.

16. "Boston Harbor New City's Name," *Morning Olympian*, September 18, 1907; "Crowd of 2,000 People Join Rush for Lots," *Morning Olympian*, October 14, 1907.

17. Edrie Shaw, *Memories of the Heart: Nellie, Edrie, and Lillian*, unpublished manuscript.

18. "One Hundred Families Will Settle on Land at or Near Boston Harbor," *Olympia News*, August 10, 1928.

19. "Boston Harbor Site Chosen for Gigantic Rural Relief Center," *Daily Olympian*, January 19, 1935.

20. John T. Marshall, *A History of Boston Harbor and Gull Harbor Area*, n.p., 2013.

21. Ibid.

22. National Register of Historic Places, US Department of the Interior, National Park Service, https://npgallery.nps.gov/NRHP/GetAsset/NRHP/93001339_text (accessed September 23,2018).

23. Carole Rambo Holt, *Poncin Estate Johnson Point: The Camp Set in Clover*, monograph, privately printed, 1989.

24. Ibid., 31-54.

25. Ibid., 59-63.

26. Ibid., 66-83.

27. Palmer and Stevenson, *Place Names*, 37.

28. Lancaster Pollard and Lloyd Spencer, "The Hunter Family" in *History of Washington* (New York: Historical Society, 1937), 548.

29. Shanna Stevenson "Hunter Point was the site of early resort," *Olympian, Totem Tidings*, March 25, 1984, 5.

30. Ibid.

31. Richard and Floss Loutzenhiser, *The Story of Yelm 1848-1948* (Yelm, WA: Yelm Prairie Historical Society, 2004), 35.

32. WISAARD File for Lake Lawrence Pavilion, https://fortress.wa.gov/dahp/wisaard/3/ (accessed September 22, 2018).

Chapter 12 - The Ebb and Flow of Communities

1. David James, *From Grand Mound to Scatter Creek* (Olympia, WA: State Capitol Historical Association, 1980), 93.

2. Gayle Palmer and Shanna Stevenson, eds. *Thurston County Place Names: A Heritage Guide* (Olympia, WA: Thurston County Historic Commission, 1992), 31; see also WISAARD file for Grand Mound, https://fortress-wa-gov/dahp/wisaardp3 (accessed September 22, 2018) and James, *From Grand Mound*.

3. Noel V. Burasaw, "The Goodell Family of Vermillion, Ohio, and Early Settlers of Washington Territory - Part One." *Skagit River Journal* (2005), http://www.skagitriverjournal.com/WA/Southwest/Pioneer/Goodell/Goodell02-Family1.html (accessed September 15, 2018).

4. Elizabeth Cady Stanton, Susan B. Anthony, Matilda Joslyn Gage, and Ida Hused Harper, eds., *History of Woman Suffrage* (Rochester, NY: J.J. Little & Co.: 1881-1922) vol 3, 784-785; "Results of Election," *Olympia Transcript*, June 11, 1870, 2.

5. Palmer and Stevenson, *Place Names*, 2; Larry Smith's Eight Grade English Classes, Jefferson Junior High School, *How the West Was Once: A History of West Olympia*, (1974), 27-34.

6. Guy Reed Ramsey, *Postmarked Washington: Thurston County* (Olympia, WA: Thurston County Historic Commission, 1988), 59-60; Dale Rutledge, "Early History of Littlerock, WA," Good Old Days for Littlerock (privately published monograph).

7. Palmer and Stevenson, *Place Names*, 71.

8. Ibid., 70; Robert Hitchman, *Place Names of Washington* (Tacoma, WA: Washington State Historical Society, 1985), 253.

9. "Pioneer Brothers Raised on Site of Rochester," *Thurston County Independent*, May 31, 1935; "Pioneer Life of Mound Prairie is Described," *Thurston County Independent*, March 29, 1935.

10. Daughter Ruby Cogwell Bishop is a noted jazz pianist. See http://www.blackpast.org/aaw/bishop-ruby-1919 (accessed September 13, 2018).

11. Palmer and Stevenson, *Place Names*, 29.

12. Judith Upton with Karyl Groeneveld, *Glimpses of Gate: A Pictorial Journal of Gate, WA: 1880-1920* (Rochester, WA: printed by Gorham Printing, 2003), 65.

13. Dan Wheat, "Gate? Yes, But Memories of Old Logging Town are Fading Fast," *Olympian*, April 9, 1978.

14. Upton and Groeneveld, *Gate*, 54.

15. Ibid., 99.

16. Ibid., 74.

17. See WISAARD File at the Department of Archaeology and Historic Preservation, https://fortress.wa.gov/dahp/wisaardp3/ (accessed September 22, 2018).

18. Dick Erickson, *Immigrants of the Independence Valley, Centralia* (Seattle: Swedish Finn Historical Society, 2016), 20.

19. Ibid., 36.

20. Anna Ditch and Hilma Englund, *A Little History of Independence Valley, Washington State* (Olympia, WA: State Capitol Museum, 1976), 18.

21. Ibid., 22.

22. Hubert Howe Bancroft, *History of Washington, Idaho, and Montana, 1845-1889* (San Francisco: The History Company, 1890); Neil Corcoran, *Bucoda, A Heritage of Sawdust and Leg Irons* (Bucoda, WA: Bucoda Improvement Club, 1976); Neil Corcoran, "Local Mining History," series in *Tenino Independent*, February 10, 17, 24, 1982; Rod Cardwell, "Welcome to the Land of the Cyclops," *Tacoma News Tribune & Sunday Ledger*, November 21, 1965, B2; "Tenino Expedition Visits Depths of Tono Coal Mine," *Tenino Independent*, March 16, 1934, 1.

23. Emmett O'Connell, "Tono - Ghost Town with a Ghost Landscape," ThurstonTalk, http://www.thurstontalk.com/2013/10/29/tono-ghost-town-ghost-landscape/(accessed September 16, 2018). This article also includes alternate naming history.

24. Palmer and Stevenson, *Place Names*, 92.

25. Hal Hogan, "When Logs Were King," *Daily Olympian*, October 3, 1969, 25; E. A. Batwell, "Building a Town is a Trick," *Puget Sound Electric Journal*, April 1928, 3; "Introduction to Vail-McDonald Farms," *Weyerhaeuser Timber*, October 7, 1949, Weyerhaeuser Archives; "Shareholders Visit Vail-McDonald Operation," n.d., Weyerhaeuser Archives; see also WISAARD file for Vail, https://fortress.wa.gov/dahp/wisaardp3/ (accessed September 22, 2018).

26. Andrew Poultridge, *Boomtime: A History of the Woodard Bay National Resources*

Conservation Area, (Olympia, WA: Washington State Department of Natural Resources, 1991), 19.

27. Ibid., 21-27.

28. Ibid., 29, 32.

29. Margaret Elley Felt, *Capitol Forest: The Forest That Came Back* (Olympia, WA: Washington State Department of Natural Resources, 1975); "Logged His Way to Leadership," *American Lumberman*, February 26, 1927; "Nearing the Last Turn," *The Timberman*, October 1941, 14; "It's Swan Song for Lumber Town," *Daily Olympian*, September 26, 1941.

30. "$100,000 Loss When Blaze Destroys Mill and Homes," *Morning Olympian*, July 29, 1925, 1.

31. Information from Maytown History manuscript by Bernadine Dafoe, original at the Tenino Depot Museum, completed in the 1980s and Lila Davis Sjodin in the *Olympia Genealogical Quarterly*, July 2012.

32. Sue Japhet and Brenda Moorefield, "History of Summit Lake," typewritten manuscript, n.d, n.p.; "The Rededication of Pioneer Rock Also Known as Calder Rock, September 12, 1990" (Olympia, WA: Thurston County Historic Commission); both from Thurston Regional Planning files.

Chapter 13 - Big Trees Big Business

1. "The Lumber Trade," *Washington Standard*, June 12, 1885.
2. *Lumberman's Directory* (Chicago and New York: Rand, McNally & Company, 1891), 587-595.
3. *The Coast* (Seattle: Coast Publishing Company, March 1909).
4. Ibid.

Chapter 14 - Rails and Timber

1. Gordon R. Newell, *So Fair a Dwelling Place: A History of Olympia and Thurston County, Washington* (Olympia, WA: The Olympia News Publishing Company, 1950), 27.

2. James S. Hannum, *Delusions of Grandeur. The Olympia & Tenino Railroad* (Olympia, WA: Hannum House Publications, 2009).

3. Washington State Railroad Historical Society, http://www.wsrhs.org/date1880s.htm (accessed September 23, 2018).

4. Donald B. Robertson, *Encyclopedia of Western Railroad History - Volume III* (Caldwell, ID: Caxton Printers, 1995); Jeff Asay, *Union Pacific Northwest* (Edmonds, WA: Pacific Fast Mail Publications, 1991); Brian Ferris, *History of the Northern Pacific Prairie Line*, https://www.tacoma.uw.edu/sites/default/files/global/documents/facilities/prairielineterminalsectiondocumentation_i-20.pdf (accessed September 23, 2018).

5. "Weyerhaueser Chehalis Western, Vail logging line, Curtis, Milburn & Eastern." http://www.trainweb.us/cwwr/#sthash.QcmTlAFx.dpbs (accessed September 13, 2018).

6. St. Paul & Tacoma Lumber Company Records, 1879-1958, Archives West, http://archiveswest.orbiscascade.org/ark:/80444/xv60895/op=fstyle.aspx?t=k&q=st.+paul+and+tacoma+lumber (accessed September 16, 2018).

7. Washington State Archives, Frontier Justice Record Series, Thurston County, Case Number THR-2738, 1889.

8. James S. Hannum, *Gone But Not Forgotten: Abandoned Railroads of Thurston County, Washington* (Olympia, WA: Hannum House Publications, 2012).

9. John Caldick, "The Railroads of Jefferson and Clallam Counties," http://www.historylink.org/File/11096 (accessed September 15, 2018).

10. "Puget Sound & Pacific Railroad PSAP #640," Union Pacific: Building America, https://www.up.com/customers/shortline/profiles_l-p/psap/index.htm (accessed September 13, 2018).

11. "Puget Sound and Willapa Harbor Ry," *Poor's Manual of Railroads*, vol 50, https://books.google.com/books?id=vGJJAAAAMAAJ&printsec=frontcover&source=gbs_ge_summary_rcad=0#v=oneage&q&f=false (accessed September 16, 2018)

12. "Olympia Light & Power Co. Records, 1891-1912," Archives West, http://archiveswest.orbiscascade.org/ark:/80444/xv69332 (accessed September 23, 2018).

13. "Puget Sound Power & Light Co. Records, 1868-1897," Archives West, http://archiveswest.orbiscascade.org/ark:/80444/xv05960 (accessed September 23, 2018).

14. "Gruber and Docherty Lumber Company," Yelm History Project, http://www.yelmhistoryproject.com/?p=2047 (accessed September 13, 2018) and http://www.yelmhistoryproject.com/?p=763 (accessed September 13, 2018).

15. "Washington to sell timber on school lands - shingle mills organizing," *The Timberman*, April 1910, 36.

16. Frank W. Telewski & Frank Barrett, *Logging Railroads of Weyerhaeuser's Vail and McDonald Operation* (Hamilton, MT: Oso Publishing, 2004).

17. "S.1946 - Staggers Rail Act of 1980," https://www.congress.gov/bill/96th-congress/senate-bill/1946 (accessed September 13, 2018).

Chapter 15 - It's the Water

1. "A Baker's Plight," *It's the Water News*, November, 1962 (Tumwater, WA: Olympia Brewing Company, November, 1962), 14, located at Schmidt House Archives, Olympia Tumwater Foundation.

2. Leopold F. Schmidt, "How and Why the Olympia Brewery was located in Thurston County. The Treatment It Has Received" (circa 1904), located at Schmidt House Archives, Olympia Tumwater Foundation.

3. Ibid.

4. Peter G. Schmidt, speech to Daughters of Pioneers of Washington, Tumwater, WA (October 5, 1948), located at Schmidt House Archives, Olympia Tumwater Foundation.

5. Leopold F. Schmidt letter to Wahl and Henius, November 9, 1895, in *Leopold F. Schmidt Letter Book, 1895-1899*, 6 (accession 100.01.258), located at Schmidt House Archives, Olympia Tumwater Foundation.

6. Leopold F. Schmidt letter to "Friend Gehrmann," June 16, 1896, in *Leopold F. Schmidt Letter Book, 1895-1899*, 378 (accession 100.01.258), located at Schmidt House Archives, Olympia Tumwater Foundation.

7. Capital Brewing Company, *Records of Meetings of the Stockholders of the Capital Brewing Company of Olympia, Washington, 1896 -*, located at Schmidt House Archives, Olympia Tumwater Foundation.

8. Leopold F. Schmidt letter to the Vilter Manufacturing Company, October 10, 1896, in *Leopold F. Schmidt Letter Book, 1895-1899*, 484-485 (accession 100.01.258), located at Schmidt House Archives, Olympia Tumwater Foundation.

9. Frank Kenney, "Birth of a Slogan," *It's the Water News* (Tumwater, WA: Olympia Brewing Company), August 1951, 3, 6, located at Schmidt House Archives, Olympia Tumwater Foundation.

10. Capital Brewing Company, *Amended Articles of Incorporation changing name to Olympia Brewing Company* (Olympia, WA: 1902), located at Schmidt House Archives, Olympia Tumwater Foundation.

11. *1976 Annual Report* (Tumwater, WA: Olympia Brewing Company, 1976), 16, located at Schmidt House Archives, Olympia Tumwater Foundation.

12. Ibid., 17-18.

13. "Our 1,000,000th Visitor," *It's the Water News* (Tumwater, WA: Olympia Brewing Company) September, 1962, 7, located at Schmidt House Archives, Olympia Tumwater Foundation.

14. Olympia Brewing Company, *1976 Annual Report*, 19, located at Schmidt House Archives, Olympia Tumwater Foundation.

15. Ibid.

16. Robert A. Schmidt letter to Olympia Brewing Company shareholders, June 11, 1982, courtesy of Paul Knight.

17. Jill Tokarczyk, "End comes to Olympia Brewing," *Olympian*, March 19, 1983.

Chapter 16 - A Turbulent Age

1. Department of Commerce, Bureau of the Census. "Statistics of Population of Washington: Table 2.—Population of Minor Civil Divisions: 1910, 1900 and 1890," in *State of Washington Department of State Bureau of Statistics and Immigration Population Statistic of the State of Washington Compiled from United States Census Reports and Published by The State Bureau of Statistics and Immigration. I. M. Howell, Secretary of State, ex-officio Commissioner, Harry F. Giles*

Deputy Commissioner (Olympia: Bureau of Statistics and Immigration, 1911), 23.

2. Gordon Newell, *Rogues, Buffoons and Statesmen* (Seattle: Hangman Press, 1975), 137-138.

3. "Huge Crowd Sees Matinee Races at Carlyon's Park," *Morning Olympian*, July 5, 1901, 1.

4. Drew Crooks, "Was the People's University a Precursor to The Evergreen State College?" ThurstonTalk.com, August 30, 2015, http://www.thurstontalk.com/2015/08/30/evergreen-olympia-history/ (accessed September 19, 2018).

5. Pacific Shellfish Institute, "Final Project Report - Shellfish at Work - Reducing Nutrient Pollution in Budd Inlet Watershed," National Estuary Program (NEP) Toxics and Nutrients, Award No. 61300036, Prepared for the Washington Department of Ecology, December, 2014, 3.

6. Rebecca Christie, *Workingman's Hill: A History of an Olympia Neighborhood* (Olympia, WA: Bigelow House Preservation Association/Bigelow Highlands Neighborhood Association, 2001,), 124.

7. "Trade Council Formed," *Morning Olympian*, April 19, 1902, 3.

8. Fred Hudson, "Central Council is Representative of Labor," *Olympia Trades Council, Labor's Year Book and Buyers' Guide* (Olympia, WA: Olympia Trades Council, ca. 1917), 12.

9. George G. Cody, "Printers, True Pioneers in Olympia," *Official Yearbook 1929* (Olympia, WA: Olympia Building Trades Council, 1929), 58.

10. "Mysterious Trio Believed I.W.W. Scouts," *Olympia Daily Recorder*, April 3, 1912, 1.

11. "I.W.W. Agitator Sends Defy to City," *Olympia Daily Recorder*, April 5, 1912. But J. F. Hurd, secretary of the I.W.W. Local 354 of Aberdeen, sent a letter dated April 4th to the city which stated: "Dear Sir - As being a I.W.W. agitator, I was in town today and read in your paper what you had to say about "Mysterious Trio Believed I.W.W. Scouts," and I want to let you know that any time we want to speak on the streets of Olympia we will do so, whether the chief of police likes it or not. You can put this in your pipe and smoke it."

12. "Agitators to Storm Little Rock Rumored," *Morning Olympian*, April 30, 1912, 4.

13. "Epidemic of Typhoid at Logging Camps," *Olympia Daily Recorder*, August 27, 1913, 1.

14. "Dr. Strickland Dies of Cancer in Seattle," *Olympia Daily Recorder*, September 23, 1911, 1.

15. "Salvage Tots from Illness Without Cost Twenty Children Examined First Day of Red Cross Clinic," *Morning Olympian*, July 25, 1922, 1.

16. "Slogan is Great Hit," *Morning Olympian*, April 30, 1910, 1.

17. "Rogers Resigns as Police Chief," *Morning Olympian*, November 20, 1909, 1.

18. "Local Organizations Join to Perfect an Associated Charities," *Morning Olympian*, December 8, 1914, 1.

19. "Society," *Morning Olympian*, January 30, 1921, 3. The organization was planning on meeting at Jesse T. Mills' funeral parlor on 414 Franklin Street, Olympia.

20. "Society for Prevention of Tramps and Aiding Unfortunates is Planned," *Morning Olympian*, December 17, 1911, 1.

21. "There is No Wood to be Cut but Plenty of Snow to Shovel," *Olympia Daily Recorder*, January 3, 1916, 1.

22. H. C. Peterson and Gilbert C. Fite, *Opponents of War, 1917-1918* (Seattle: University of Washington Press, 1968); numerous books and articles also take up this theme.

23. "Mayor Tells of Flu Here," *Olympia Daily Recorder*, October 31, 1918, 1; "Council to Meet, May Remove Flu Ban," *Olympia Daily Recorder*, January 21, 1919, 1.

24. "Crew of Piledriver to Demand Increase," *Morning Olympian*, October 21, 1919, 1.

25. "Work Abandoned on 4th St. Bridge," *Olympia Daily Recorder*, October 26, 1919, 1.

26. "Bridge Workers Back at Same Pay," *Morning Olympian*, November 20, 1919, 1. They were members of a union of structural iron workers and had asked for an immediate modest wage increase from around $7.50- $8.00 to $8.00-$9.00 per day. In addition, they demanded a second raise by the first of the year to $9.00-$12.00. They lost the strike and were forced to return to work in an "open shop" with no pay raise. Their power had been significantly diminished.

27. "Thurston County will Teach Americanism in Public School Course," *Morning Olympian*, December 16, 1919, 1.

28. "Fake Defiance Drew Posses to Bordeaux While Hanson Escaped," *Morning Olympian*, November 25, 1919, 1.

29. "Posse of 65 Men Comb Bordeaux Camps; Shot Fired in Olympia Search," *Morning Olympian*, November 23, 1919, 1.

30. "Anti-Syndical and Sabotage Acts Approved," *Morning Olympian*, March 20, 1919, 1.

31. "Thurston County Cleaning House," *Morning Olympian*, December 6, 1919, 1. Although

they were tried together, there are no indications that the men even knew each other beforehand. The two men could not afford any lawyers for their defense and refused to enter a plea when brought to Judge John M. Wilson (who also presided at the Centralia trials).

32. "I.W.W. Agitator Convicted under Syndicalism Law by Thurston County Jury," *Olympia Daily Recorder*, January 15, 1920, 1; "I.W.W. Guilty of Felony," *Morning Olympian*, January 15, 1920, 1. Both stories are identical. The prosecution read I.W.W. literature at the trial and had Tacoma police officers testify to their experience with I.W.W. in general. Hastings was identified as a Wobbly organizer from the Tacoma Headquarters while Matson seemed to be a more rank-and-file member employed at Bordeaux's Camp 4. A. C. Durham, representing the two men, made little argument except to say if there was an anti-government uprising, soldiers and veterans would put it down. Durham was a veteran of the Spanish-American War and World War I and was an American Legion member, which likely indicated that he was against the I.W.W. He had four character witnesses testify for the defendants. Judge Wright denied the motion and declared the two guilty. He delayed sentencing and an appeal to the State Supreme Court was expected. The newspaper was quick to emphasize that the jury consisted of farmers and union members. Matson and Hastings, whose name is spelled Hestings in Supreme Court records, lost an appeal to the Washington State Supreme Court in March 1921 in State v. Hestings et al. Arthur Remington, *Washington Reports Vol. 115 Cases Determined in the Supreme Court of Washington March 8, 1921-May 23, 1921* (Seattle: Bancroft-Whitney Company, 1922), 19. 33. "Strike Order Not Causing Great Alarm," *Morning Olympian*, April 27, 1923, 1, 4.

34. "Hundreds of Strikers Pass Through City," *Morning Olympian*, April 26, 1923, 1.

35. "Sugoff is Freed by Jury," *Morning Olympian*, December 8, 1920, 1, 4; "Verdict of Not Guilty for Sugoff," *Olympia Daily Recorder*, December 8, 1920, 1.

36. "Tono," *Morning Olympian*, April 7, 1927, 1.

37. Newell, *Rogues*, 318-319.

38. Christie, *Workingman's Hill*, 142.

39. Nathan Miller, *New World Coming: The 1920s and the Making of Modern America* (New York: Scribner, 2003), 290-293.

40. Norman H. Clark, *The Dry Years: Prohibition and Social Change in Washington* (Seattle: University of Washington Press, 1988), 34, 45. The author interpreted this as a change in the social makeup of the Prohibition Movement. In addition, Murphy was well-known for his drinking.

41. "Drys Make Good Fight But City Favors License," *Morning Olympian*, November 6, 1912, 1.

42. "Initiative and Referendum Measures and Constitutional Amendment," *Morning Olympian*, November 5, 1914, 1.

43. "Complete Figures From 38 Precincts," *Morning Olympian*, November 7, 1918, 1.

44. Tom Streissguth, *An Eyewitness History: The Roaring Twenties* (New York: Facts on File, Inc., 2001), 27-35.

45. Dean Hooper and Roberta B. Longmire, *Yelm Pioneers & Followers: 1850-1950* (Yelm, WA: Yelm Prairie Historical Society, 1999), 103.

46. Christie, *Workingman's Hill*, 48.

47. Anna Pitch and Hilma Englund, *A Little History of Independence Valley, Washington* (Olympia, WA: State Capitol Museum, 1970), 29-30.

48. "Society: 'Hard Times Frolic' at Club Successful," *Sunday Olympian-Recorder*, September 19, 1926, 2.

Chapter 17 - Facing the Future

1. Ed Bergh, "Yelm and the New Deal," Yelm History Project, August 2, 2010, www.yelmhistoryproject.com (accessed August 11, 2015).

2. Legal notices for tax foreclosures in local newspapers make for chilling reading today. See, for example, "Notice and Summons in General Tax Foreclosure for Thurston County, 1931," *Daily Olympian*, December 31, 1931, 2, 3.

3. Julie McDonald Zander, *Bucoda: the Little Town with a Million Memories* (Toledo, Washington: Chapters of Life, 2010), 172.

4. Ann Shipley, *Memories: The History of the Thurston County Fair* (Rochester, WA: printed by the author, 2006), 226.

5. Julie McDonald Zander, *Chapters of Life in Bucoda* (Toledo, WA: Chapters of Life, 2010), 103.

6. James F. Rowe, "Hunger Marchers Wishes," *Daily Olympian*, January 18, 1933, 6.

7. "Silver Shirts Will Have Rally Here," *Olympia News*, August 13, 1936, 6.

8. For more information on the Silver Shirts, see Eckard V. Toy, Jr., "Silver Shirts in the Northwest: Politics, Prophecies, and Personalities in the 1930s," *Pacific Northwest Quarterly* 80, no. 4: 139-146.

9. "Mainly About People," *Daily Olympian*, December 18, 1931, 1. Ninety of the boxes were built by Otto Jacobson of Washington Veneer.

10. "Canal Support is Pledged at Rally," *Sunday Olympian*, July 30, 1933, 6. One dedicated supporter of the canal, Betty Bowlsby, wrote a 1933 poem that concluded in the following way: "What's the matter? Where's the jam? All's O.K. with Uncle Sam - Come on! Let's go Washington! Dig the canal! It can be done!" (Betty Bowlsby, "It Can Be Done," 1933 newspaper clipping, Washington State Library's collection of the scrapbook of clippings on the Olympia Grays Harbor canal, 1933-1943, MS 0167, Washington State Library).

11. "WPA Projects for County Approved," *Daily Olympian,* December 11, 1937, 1. This article indicated that "The women work 30 hours a week and receive $44 a month." In other words, they made approximately $0.35 per hour.

12. "Mainly About People," *Daily Olympian,* February 8, 1938, 6; "Rochester," *Daily Olympian,* October 7, 1940, 6. In 1940, food from a garden in Oakville was used by WPA cooks as part of a complete meal for grade and high school students in Rochester. A newspaper article noted that "In order to defray expenses, a charge of five cents per serving will be made. This may be paid in commodities. Pupils will also be given the chance to work out all or part of their lunch expenses. Each child will be asked to donate to the P.T.A. a complete table service in unbreakable dishes as far as possible. W. E. Kearns, high school principal, stated that about 360 children will be served."

13. Shipley, *Memories*, 70-73, 81.

14. Jennifer Crooks, "Thrifty Thurston Looks Back at the History of the Civilian Conservation Corps at Millersylvania State Park," http://www.thurstontalk.com/2017/03/30/millersylvania-state-park-history/ (accessed September 23, 2018).

15. "Moaning Minnie Sounds Off," *Daily Olympian,* January 14, 1942, 1.

16. Alice Adams Watts, "More Than 3,500 See Spectacular War Pageant," *Daily Olympian*, August 17, 1943, 1. "Only one real casualty occurred during this event, when a woman tripped on the baseball dugout steps and fell backwards. She was safely taken to the local St. Peter's Hospital for treatment. It was quite a contrast with the carnage then occurring overseas in the war."

17. Zander, *Bucoda: the Little Town*, 223.

18. Rebecca Christie, *Workingman's Hill: A History of an Olympia Neighborhood* (Olympia, WA: Bigelow House Preservation Association/Bigelow Highlands Neighborhood Association, 2001), 154.

19. "Fire Destroys USO Clubhouse, *Daily Olympian*, December 30, 1943, 1.

20. "Petitions Urge Jap Evacuation," *Sunday Olympian*, March 1, 1942, 1.

21. "Olympia Aliens' Homes Searched," *Daily Olympian*, March 10, 1942, 1.

22. "Army Sets Dates for Japanese Evacuation," *Sunday Olympian*, May 24, 1942, 1.

23. "Olympia Celebrates Surrender," *Daily Olympian*, August 15, 1945, 1, 2.

24. James R. Fox, ed. *Washington State Almanac* 2014 (Sammamish, WA: Electronic Handbook Publishers, 2013), 142.

25. Ken Balsley, "Most Significant Events in the County's History," *Ken's Corner and Real News*, 28, no. 8 (May 2015), 2

26. David A. Takami, *Shared Dreams: A History of Asians and Pacific Americans in Washington State* (Seattle: Washington Centennial Commission, 1989), 11.

27. David A. Takami, "Southeast Asian Americans," Essay #894, February 17, 1999, HistoryLink.org/index.cfm?DisplayPage=output.cfm&file_id=894 (accessed February 4, 2016).

28. "Freeway Era Starts in Olympia Area," *Daily Olympian*, December 12, 1958, 1.

29. Balsely, *Most Significant Events*, 1.

30. "About Us," Thurston County Regional Planning, trpc.org/27/About-Us (accessed March 17, 2016).

31. "The Community Chest," *Daily Olympian*, September 6, 1951, 17.

32. "Mission Statement," Thurston County Food Bank, thurstoncountyfoodbank.org/about_us (accessed March 17, 2016).

33. "About Us," South Puget Sound Habitat for Humanity, spshabitat.org/about-us (accessed March 18, 2016).

34. "About Stream Team," Stream Team, streamteam.info/about (accessed March 18, 2016).

35. "Thurston County Historic Commission," Thurston County, WA, https://www.co.thurston.wa.us/permitting/historic/historic-home.html (accessed March 19, 2016).

36. G. K. Chesterton, "On St. George Revivified," in *All I Survey: A Book of Essays*, 1933 (Freeport, NY: Books for Libraries Press, Reprint 1967), 126.

SELECTED BIBLIOGRAPHY

10th Biennial Report of the Superintendent of Public Instruction.
22nd Biennial Report of the Superintendent of Public Instruction.
29th Biennial Report of the Superintendent of Public Instruction.
Abbott, Newton Carl and Fred Carver. *The Evolution of Washington Counties.* Compiled by J. W. Helm. Goldendale, WA: Yakima Valley Genealogical Society and Klickitat County Historical Society, 1978.
Agricultural Census Data for Thurston County.
American Historical Quarterly. 1998. XLIX, no. 1, January 1998.
American Lumberman. 1927. "Logged His Way to Leadership." February 26, 1927.
Archives West. "Olympia Light & Power Co. Records, 1891-1912." http://archiveswest.orbiscascade.org/ark:/80444/xv69332 (accessed September 23, 2018).
_____. "Puget Sound Power & Light Co. Records, 1868-1897." http://archiveswest.orbiscascade.org/ark:/80444/xv05960 (accessed September 23, 2018).
Asay, Jeff. *Union Pacific Northwest.* Edmonds, WA: Pacific Fast Mail Publications, 1991.
Balsley, Ken. "Pioneers to Panorama - The 'City Within a City' has Roots in Lacey's Pioneers." http://www.thurstontalk.com/2016/03/05/panorama-lacey-history (accessed September 19, 2018).
_____. "Most Significant Events in the County's History." *Ken's Corner & The Real News,* 28, No. 8, May 2015.
Bancroft, Hubert Howe. *History of Oregon.* San Francisco: History Co., 1886-88.
_____. *History of Washington, Idaho and Montana, 1845-1889.* San Francisco: History Co., 1890.
Barkan, Frances B. *Peter Puget: Lieutenant on the Vancouver Expedition, fighting British naval officer, the man for whom Puget Sound is named.* Ashland, OH: Graybeard Publishing, 1979.
_____. *The Wilkes Expedition: Puget Sound and the Oregon Country.* Olympia, WA: Washington State Capitol Museum, 1987.
Batwell, E. A. "Building a Town is a Trick." *Puget Sound Electric Journal,* April 1928.
Beardsley, Arthur S. "Early Efforts to Locate the Capital of Washington Territory." *Pacific Northwest Quarterly* 32, no. 3 (July 1941): 239-287.
Bergh, Ed. "Yelm and the New Deal." Yelm, WA: Yelm History Project, August 2, 2010.
Bernd, Zelma. "All My Children: A Lacey Pioneer Story." Last modified 1994. https://www.sos.wa.gov/_assets/legacy/pioneers-story.pdf (accessed September 15, 2018).
Betts, William J. "Old Fort Eaton, Ghost of the Blockhouse Era: It Shielded Settlers from Indian Attack." *Tacoma News Tribune, Magazine Section.* December 11, 1960.
Biennial Reports of the Board on Control for the State of Washington.
Biographical Directory of the United States Congress. "Samuel Royal Thurston." Bioguide.congress.gov. http://bioguide.congress.gov/scripts/biodisplay.pl?index=T000258 (accessed September 20, 2018).
Blankenship, Georgiana. *Early History of Thurston County, Washington, Together with Biographies and Reminiscences of Those Identified with Pioneer Days.* Olympia, WA, 1914.
Blee, Lisa. *Framing Chief Leschi: Narratives and Politics of Historical Justice.* Chapel Hill, NC: University of North Carolina, 2014.
Bolton, Frederick and Thomas Bibb. *History of Education in Washington, Bulletin 1934 No. 9.* Washington DC: US Government Printing Office, 1934.
Bourasaw, Noel V. "The Goodell Family of Vermillion, Ohio, and Early Settlers of Washington Territory - Part One." *Skagit River Journal,* 2005. http://www.skagitriverjournal.com/WA/Southwest/Pioneer/Goodell/Goodell02-Family1.html (accessed September 15, 2018).
Bowden, Angie Burt. *Early Schools of Washington Territory.* Seattle: Lowman and Hanford Company, 1935.
Bowlsby, Betty. "It Can Be Done." Scrapbook clippings on Olympia-Grays Harbor canal, 1933-1943, held

at Washington State Library.

Boyd, Robert, ed. *Indians, Fire, and the Land in the Pacific Northwest.* Corvallis, OR: Oregon State University Press, 1999.

Brazier, Don. *History of the Washington State Senate.* Olympia, WA: Washington State Senate, 2000.

Caldick, John. "The Railroads of Jefferson and Clallam Counties." http://www.historylink.org/File/11096 (accessed September 15, 2018).

Callaghan, Peter. "The Site of Chief Leschi hanging." *The Olympian*, October 15, 2013. http://www.theolympian.com/news/local/article25321789.html#storylink=cpy (accessed September 15, 2018).

Capital Brewing Company. *Records of Meetings of the Stockholders of the Capital Brewing Company, Washington. Olympia: 1896 -.* Tumwater, WA: Capital Brewing Company.

_____. *Amended Articles of Incorporation, Capital Brewing Company of Olympia changing name to Olympia Brewing Company, Olympia: 1902.* Tumwater, WA: Olympia Brewing Company.

Cardwell, Rod. "Welcome to the Land of the Cyclops." *Tacoma News Tribune and Sunday Ledger*, November 21, 1965.

Carpenter, Cecelia S. *Fort Nisqually, Indian and British Interaction.* Seattle: Tahoma Research Publication, 1986.

_____. *The Nisqually - My People.* Seattle: Tahoma Research Service, 2002.

_____. *They Walked Before: The Indians of Washington State.* Tacoma, WA: Washington State American Revolution Bicentennial Commission, 1977.

_____. *Where the Waters Begin: The Traditional Nisqually History of Mount Rainier.* Seattle: Northwest Interpretive Association. First American Edition, July, 2001.

Chambers, Andrew Jackson. *Recollections.* Fairfield, WA: Ye Galleon Press, 1975 (reprint).

Chambers, Elizabeth Harrison. *Incidents in the Life of Elizabeth Harrison Chambers: Collected from Memory's Pages and Compiled November 23rd, 1910, after the hand on the dial-plate of time had measured me off 82 years.* Unpublished typewritten manuscript #4032, at Washington State Library.

Chesterton, G. K. "On St. George Revivified." in *All I survey: A Book of Essays, 1933.* Reprint, Freeport, NY: Books for Libraries Press, 1967.

Christie, Rebecca. *Workingman's Hill: A History of an Olympia Neighborhood.* Olympia, WA: Bigelow House Preservation Association/Bigelow Highlands Neighborhood Association, 2001.

City of Lacey. "A Rich History." http://www.ci.lacey.wa.us/living-in-lacey/a-rich-history (accessed September 13, 2018).

City of Olympia. "Mid-Twentieth Century Olympia: A Context Statement on Local History and Modern Architecture, 1945-1975." Olympia Heritage Commission. April 2008. olympiawa.gov/~/media/Files/.../MAContextStatementAPRIL2008reformatted.ashx (accessed September 13, 2018).

_____. "The Olympia-Yashiro Friendship Bridge." Olympiawa.gov. http://olympiawa.gov/community/about-olympia/history-of-olympia-washington (accessed September 19, 2018).

City of Rainier. http://cityofrainierwa.org (accessed September 19, 2018).

City of Yelm. http://www.ci.yelm.wa.us (accessed September 19, 2018).

Clark, Norman H. *The Dry Years: Prohibition and Social Change in Washington.* Seattle: University of Washington Press, 1988.

Coast, March 1909.

_____. 1909 (reprinted 1976). "Thurston County Oyster Industry."

Cochran, William H. *Washington's State Institutions.* s.n., 1915.

Cody, George G. "Printers, True Pioneers in Olympia." *Olympia Building Trades Office Year Book 1929.* Olympia, WA: Olympia Building Trades Council, 1929.

Columbian, September 11, 1852.

Confederated Tribes of the Chehalis Reservation. *The Chehalis People.* 2000 update.

CONGRESS.GOV. "S.1946 - Staggers Rail Act of 1980." Congress.gov. https://www.congress.gov/bill/96th-congress/senate-bill/1946 (accessed September 13, 2018).

Conner, Theresa. "Haying fever hits old ranch balers." *The Olympian*, July 17, 1985.
Contris, Mike, ed. "St. Michael's School 100 Years 1882-1982." https://stmikesolympia.org/about/history/ (accessed September 19, 2018).
Cook, Warren L. *Flood Tide of Empire: Spain and the Pacific Northwest*. New Haven, CT: Yale University Press, 1973.
Corcoran, Neil B. *Bucoda: A Heritage of Sawdust and Leg Irons*. Bucoda, WA: Bucoda Improvement Club, 1976.
_____. "Local Mining History." series in *Tenino Independent*, February 10, 17, 24, 1982.
Crooks, Drew W. "From the Orkney Islands to Tenalquot Prairie: The Life of Tom Linklater." *Occurrences* X, no. III (Fall 1991): 10-12.
_____. "Lacey: An Interesting History and Unusual Place Name." http://www.thurstontalk.com/2013/08/18/lacey-history/ (accessed September 19, 2018).
_____. *Past Reflections: Essays on the Hudson's Bay Company in the Southern Puget Sound Region*. Tacoma, WA: Fort Nisqually Foundation, 2001.
_____. "The Mystery of Tyrell's Lake Farm." Lacey, WA: Lacey Historic Commission, January 1995.
_____. "Was the People's University a Precursor to The Evergreen State College?" http://www.thurstontalk.com/2015/08/30/evergreen-olympia-history/ (accessed September 19, 2018).
Crooks, Jennifer. "Legacy: The Civilian Conservation Corps at Millersylvania State Park." Unpublished article written for ThurstonTalk, 2015.
_____. "Thrifty Thurston Looks Back at the History of the Civilian Conservation Corps at Millersylvania State Park." http://www.thurstontalk.com/2017/03/30/millersylvania-state-park-history/ (accessed September 23, 2018).
Crowell, Sandra. Unpublished document. 2015-2016.
Cutter, Donald C. *Malaspina and Galiano: Spanish Voyages to the Northwest Coast 1791 and 1792*. Seattle: University of Washington Press, 1991.
Dafoe, Bernadine. *History of Maytown*. Maytown, WA: B. Dafoe, South Thurston County Historical Society Distributor, 1985.
_____. *Maytown History*. Manuscript at Tenino Depot Museum, 1980.
Daily Olympian. 1928. "Casco Company Erects Many Buildings." April 26, 1928.
_____. 1931. "Mainly About People." December 18, 1931.
_____. 1931. "Notice and Summons in General Tax Foreclosure for Thurston County, 1931." December 31, 1931.
_____. 1935. "Boston Harbor Site Chosen for Gigantic Rural Relief Center." January 19, 1935.
_____. 1937. "WPA Projects for County Approved." December 11, 1937.
_____. 1938. "Mainly About People." February 8, 1938.
_____. 1940. "Rochester." October 7, 1940.
_____. 1941. "It's Swan Song for Lumber Town." September 26, 1941.
_____. 1941. "Supreme Court Had Many Homes Before Big Temple of Justice." April 15, 1941.
_____. 1942. "Fire Destroys USO Clubhouse." March 1, 1942.
_____. 1942. "Moaning Minnie Sounds Off." January 14, 1942.
_____. 1942. "Olympia Aliens' Homes Searched." March 10, 1942.
_____. 1945. "Olympia Celebrates Surrender." August 15, 1945.
_____. 1951. "The Community Chest." September 6, 1951.
_____. 1958. "Freeway Era Starts in Olympia Area." December 12, 1958.
_____. 1970. "Freedom Homemaker's Club Long Established in Thurston County." April 12, 1970.
Deloria, Vine Jr. *Indians of the Pacific Northwest: From the Coming of the White Man to the Present Day*. Golden, CO: Doubleday & Company, 2011.

Department of Commerce, Bureau of the Census. "Statistics of Population in Washington: Table 1. - Population of Minor Civil Divisions, 1910, 1900 and 1890." https://www2.census.gov/library/publications/decennial/1910/volume-3/volume-3-p1.pdf (accessed September 19, 2018).

Ditch, Anna and Hilma Englund. *A Little History of Independence Valley, Washington.* Olympia, WA: Washington State Capitol Museum, 1976.

Dunbar, Marie Rowe. "Indians Haunted Pioneer of Olympia." *The Tacoma Sunday Ledger Magazine Section,* November 18, 1923.

Dwelley, Arthur G. "A Brief History of Tenino." https://tb2cdn.schoolwebmasters.com/accnt_187599/ite_187600/Documents/BriefHistory_Tenino.pdf (accessed September 14, 2018).

_____. *Prairies & Quarries: Pioneer Days Around Tenino, 1830-1900.* Tenino, WA: Independent Publishing Company, 1989.

_____. "Sandstone quarries gave Tenino a boost from village to town." Tenino, WA: *The Tenino Independent*, 60th Anniversary Edition, June 16, 1982.

_____. "The Tie That Binds: The Northern Pacific Railroad in Cowlitz County." *Columbia Magazine* 3, no. 4 (1989-90): 38-43.

Echtle, Ed. "The Cultural History of the Olympia Oyster." http://olympiawa.gov/city-services/parks/percival-landing/olympia-oyster (accessed September 22, 2018).

Electric Journal, vol 1-7: 187, https://books.google.com/books?id=sS4yAQAAMAAJ&pg=PA187&lpg=PA187&dq=electric+generating+plant+tumwater+falls&source=bl&ots=ZG6RrxCxK_&sig=Dv7IeZ1C3q6YrA9VFjFnQSd3X6A&hl=en&sa=X&ved=0ahUKEwjzm6vsytZAhUl6YMKHYtWBOcQ6AEIeDAL#v=onepage&q=electric%20generating%20plant%20tumwater%20falls&f=false (accessed September 20, 2018).

Elliott, T. C. ed. "Journal of John Work." *Washington Historical Quarterly,* 1955.

Erickson, Dick. *Immigrants of the Independence Valley, Centralia.* Seattle: Swedish Finn Historical Society, 2016.

Evans, Elwood. "Address of the Town Clerk." *Washington Standard,* July 6, 1861.

Felt, Margaret Elley. *Capitol Forest: The Forest That Came Back.* Olympia, WA: Washington State Department of Natural Resources. 1975.

Ferris, Brian. *History of the Northern Pacific Prairie Line.* https://www.tacoma.uw.edu/sites/default/files/global/documents/facilities/prairielineterminalsectiondocumentation_i-20.pdf (accessed September 23, 2018).

Findlay, Jean Cammon and Robin Paterson. *The Mosquito Fleet of South Puget Sound.* Charleston, SC: Arcadia, 2008.

Fisher, Jeffrey R. "Farmland Preservation in Thurston County." MES Thesis, The Evergreen State College, 2009.

Fowler, Chuck and Capt. Mark Freeman. *Tugboats on Puget Sound.* Charleston, SC: Arcadia, 2009.

Fowler, Chuck and the Puget Sound Maritime Historical Society. *Tall Ships on Puget Sound.* Charleston, SC: Arcadia, 2007.

Fox, James R. ed. *Washington State Almanac 2014.* Sammamish, WA: Electronic Handbook Publishers, 2013.

The Foy Store. Lacey, WA: Lacey Historical Commission Publication, 1995.

Gardebring, Olov G. "The Swedes and Swede-Finns of the Independence Valley (Rochester), Washington Area." *The Swedish-American Historical Quarterly* XLIX, No. 1 (January 1998): 5-42.

Gibson, James. *Farming the Frontier: The Agricultural Opening of the Oregon Country, 1786-1846.* Seattle: University of Washington Press, 1985.

Gordon, Lesley J. *General George E. Pickett in Life and Legend.* Chapel Hill, NC: University of North Carolina Press, 1998.

Gorsline, Jerry. *Rainshadow: Archibald Menzies and the Botanical Expedition of the Olympic Peninsula.* Port Townsend, WA: Jefferson County Historical Society, 1992.

Hagelund, William A. *The Dowager Queen: The Hudson's Bay Company SS Beaver.* Canada: Hancock House, 2001.

Hannum, James S., MD. *Gone but Not Forgotten: Abandoned Railroads of Thurston County, Washington.* Olympia, WA: Hannum House Publications, 2012.

———. *Delusions of Grandeur. The Olympia and Tenino Railroad.* Olympia, WA: Hannum House Publications, 2009.

Hanson, Marianne. "Bishop, Ruby (1919-)." BlackPast.org. www.blackpast.org/aaw/bishop-ruby-1919 (accessed September 13, 2018).

Haskett, Patrick. *The Wilkes Expedition in Puget Sound, 1841.* Olympia, WA: Washington State Capitol Museum, 1974.

Hawk, Lizzie McAllister. "The McAllister Family." *Tacoma Ledger,* July 10, 1892.

Hill, Beth and Cathy Converse. *The Remarkable World of Frances Barkley: 1765-1845.* Surrey, BC, Canada: Touchwood Editions, 2008.

HistoryLink.org. "Nisqually Chief Leschi is Hanged on February 19, 1858." http://www.historylink.org/File/5145 (accessed September 15, 2018).

Hitchman, Robert. *Place Names of Washington.* Tacoma, WA: Washington State Historical Society, 1985.

Hogan, Hal. "When Logs Were King." *Daily Olympian*, October 3, 1969.

Holt, Carole Rambo. *Poncin Estate Johnson Point: The Camp Set in Clover.* Monograph, privately printed, 1989.

Hooper, Dean and Roberta B. Longmire. *Yelm Pioneers and Followers, 1850-1950.* Yelm, WA: Yelm Prairie Historical Society, 1999.

Horr, D. A., F. Drucker, and E. Gunther. *American Indian Ethnohistory, Indians of the Northwest.* New York: Garland Publishing, 1974.

How the West Was Once: A History of West Olympia. Larry Smith's Eighth Grade English Classes. Olympia, WA: 1974.

Hudson, Fred. "Central Council is Representative of Labor." *Olympia Trades Council, Labor's Year Book and Buyers' Guide.* Olympia, WA: Trades Council, ca. 1917.

Indian Claims Commission. Squaxin Tribe. 2016.

It's the Water News. 1962. "A Baker's Plight." Tumwater, WA: Olympia Brewing Company, November 1962.

James, David A. *From Grand Mound to Scatter Creek: The Homes of Jamestown.* Olympia, WA: State Capitol Historical Association of Washington, 1980.

James, John Rogers. "Autobiography of John Rogers James." *Told by the Pioneers: Tales of Frontier Life as Told by Those Who Remember the Days of the Territory and Early Statehood in Washington.* Olympia, WA: Works Projects Administration, vol 2, 1937-38.

Japhet, Sue and Brenda Moorefield. "History of Summit Lake." Typewritten manuscript, n.d.

Justia US Law. "State Ex Rel. Lemon v. Langlie." Law.justia.com. https://law.justia.com/cases/washington/supremecourt/1954/32910-1.html (accessed September 13, 2018).

Judson, Phoebe. *A Pioneer's Search for an Ideal Home: a book of personal memoirs.* Lincoln, NE: University of Nebraska Press, 1984.

Kagy, Mrs. H. R. *Told by the Pioneers: Tales of Frontier Life as Told by Those Who Remember the Days of the Territory and Early Statehood in Washington.* Olympia, WA: Works Progress Administration, vol 3, 1937-39.

Kearns, Allene H. "The Woman's Club of Olympia." *The Olympian, Totem Tidings,* March 6, 1993.

Kelsey, Edna Irene. *The History of the Freedom Community, 1934.* Unpublished manuscript.

Kendrick, John. *The Men with Wooden Feet: The Spanish Exploration of the Pacific Northwest.* Toronto, ON: NC Press Limited, 1986.

Kenney, Frank. "Birth of a Slogan." *It's the Water News.* Tumwater, WA: Olympia Brewing Company, August 1951.

Kline, M. S. *Steamboat Virginia V.* Seattle: University of Washington Press, 1986.

Kluger, Richard. *The Bitter Waters of Medicine Creek, A Tragic Clash Between White and Native America.* New York: Alfred A. Knopf, 2011.

Knox, Esther. *Diary of the Olympia School District, 1852-1876.* s.n., n.d.
Lacey Historic Commission. 1993. "Early Settlers of Lacey." May 1993.
_____. 1994. "Lacey Women's Club." January 1994.
_____. 1994. "Old Lacey Historic Area." June 1994.
_____. 2004. "Union Mills Lumber Company." Lacey, WA: Lacey Historical Commission Publication, March 2004.
Lane, Barbara. *Political and Economic Aspects of Indian-White Cultural Contact in Western Washington in the Mid-19th Century.* Manuscript, May 10, 1973.
Leopold, Estella. "An Ecological History of Old Prairie Areas in Southwestern Washington." *Indians, Fire, and the Land in the Pacific Northwest.* Edited by Robert Boyd, 153. Corvallis, OR: Oregon State University Press, 1999.
Library of Congress. "Nathaniel Crosby II House, Tumwater, Thurston County, Washington." https://www.loc.gov/item/wa0181/ (accessed September 20, 2018).
Lister, Ernest. *Papers of Ernest Lister.* Washington State Archives.
Longacre, Edward G. *Pickett, Leader of the Charge: A Biography of General George E. Pickett, C.S.A.* Shippensburg, PA: White Mane Publishing, 1995.
Longmire, James. "James Longmire's Story." *Dean Hooper & Roberta B. Longmire, Yelm Pioneers and Followers: 1850-1950.* Yelm, WA: Yelm Prairie Historical Society, 1995.
Loutzenhiser, Richard and Floss. *The Story of Yelm: The Little Town with the Big History, 1848-1948.* Yelm, WA: Yelm Prairie Historical Society, 2004.
Lumberman's Directory. Rand McNally & Company, 1891.
Lundin, Steve. *The Closest Governments to the People.* Pullman, WA: Washington State University, 2007.
Major, Don. "The Story of Tenino Wooden Money." *Thurston County Independent,* February 19, 1965.
Map: "Reconnaissance of Olympia Harbor." U.S. Coast Survey, 1856.
Marshall, John T. *A History of Boston Harbor and Gull Harbor Area.* s.n., 2013.
Masonic Memorial Park, Tumwater, WA. "Michael T and Elizabeth Simmons." http://www.masonicmemorialpark.com/index.php/notable-locations/michael-t-elizabeth-simmons (accessed September 20, 2018).
McBride, Del. "McAllister & Wells - the Nisqually Sawmill Company." *Occurrences* XVII, no. 3 (Summer 2000): 15-18.
McClelland Jr., John M. "Washington Had Its Beginning Here on Cowlitz 100 Years Ago." *Longview Daily News - Monticello Centennial Edition,* November 25, 1952.
McConaghy, Lorraine. *Warship Under Sail: The USS Decatur in the Pacific Northwest.* University of Washington Press, 2009.
McKay, Robert W. "Abundance of Water in County Accounts for Many Fine Crops." *The Daily Olympian,* May 27, 1953.
Meany, Edmond S. "Diary of Wilkes in the Northwest." *Washington Historical Quarterly* 16 (1925): 49-61, 137-145, 207-223, 291-301; 17 (1926): 43-65, 129-144, 223-229.
_____. *History of the State of Washington.* New York: The Macmillan Company, 1941.
_____. "The Cowlitz Convention: Inception of Washington Territory." *Washington Historical Quarterly* XII, no. 1 (January 1922): 3-19.
Miller, Nathan. *New World Coming: the 1920s and the Making of Modern America.* New York: Scribner, 2003.
Milner, Darrell. In *The River Remembers: A History of Tumwater, 1845-1995,* ed. Gayle Palmer, 41-50. Tumwater, WA: City of Tumwater, 1996.
Morgan, Murray C. *The Meares Expedition.* http://cdm17061.contentdm.oclc.org/cdm/singleitem/collection/p17061coll6/id/88/rec/42 (accessed September 16, 2018).
_____. *Puget's Sound: A Narrative of Early Tacoma and the Southern Sound.* Seattle: University of Washington Press, 1979.

Morning Olympian. 1902. "Trade Council Formed." April 19, 1902.
_____. 1904. "Tells All About the New Townsite." May 18, 1904.
_____. 1907. "Boston Harbor New City's Name." September 18, 1907.
_____. 1907. "Crowd of 2,000 People Join Rush for Lots." October 14, 1907.
_____. 1907. "Tells of Their Big Plans." May 7, 1907.
_____. 1909. "Rogers Resigns as Police Chief." November 20, 1909.
_____. 1910. "Huge Crowd Sees Matinee Races at Carlyon's Park." July 5, 1910.
_____. 1910. "Slogan is Great Hit." April 30, 1910.
_____. 1911. "Society for Prevention of Tramps and Aiding of Unfortunates is Planned." December 17, 1911.
_____. 1912. "Agitators to Storm Little Rock Rumored." April 30, 1912.
_____. 1912. "Drys Make Good Fight But City Favors License." November 6, 1912.
_____. 1914. "Initiative and Referendum Measures and Constitutional Amendment." November 5, 1914.
_____. 1914. "Local Organizations Join to Perfect an Associated Charities." December 8, 1914.
_____. 1916. "Canning Company Does $200,000 Business Yearly." March 15, 1916.
_____. 1918. "Complete Figures From 38 Precincts." November 7, 1918.
_____. 1919. "Anti-Syndical and Sabotage Acts Approved." March 20, 1919.
_____. 1919. "Bridge Workers Back at Same Pay." November 20, 1919.
_____. 1919. "Crew of Piledriver to Demand Increase." October 21, 1919.
_____. 1919. "Fake Defiance Drew Posses to Bordeaux Camps While Hanson Escaped." November 25, 1919.
_____. 1919. "Posse of 65 Men Comb Bordeaux Camps; Shot Fired in Olympia Search." November 23, 1919.
_____. 1919. "Thurston County Cleaning House." December 6, 1919.
_____. 1919. "Thurston County Will Teach Americanism in Public School Course." December 16, 1919.
_____. 1919. "Work Abandoned on 4th St. Bridge." October 26, 1919.
_____. 1920. "I.W.W. Guilty of Felony." January 15, 1920.
_____. 1921. "Society." January 30, 1921.
_____. 1922. "Salvage Tots from Illness without Cost Twenty Children Examined First Day of Red Cross Clinic." July 25, 1922.
_____. 1923. "Hundreds of Strikers Pass Through City." April 26, 1923.
_____. 1927. "Tono." April 7, 1927.
_____. 1925. "$100,000 Loss When Blaze Destroys Mill and Homes." July 29, 1925.

Mount Holyoke. 1895. "Quincentennial Catalogue of Officers and Students of Mount Holyoke, 1837-1895." South Hadley, MA.

National Archives. "The Dawes Act, 1887." Ourdocuments.gov. https://www.ourdocuments.gov/doc.php?flash=true&doc=50 (accessed September 13, 2018).

National Indian Gaming Commission. "Indian Gaming Regulatory Act." Nigc.gov. http://www.nigc.gov/general-counsel/Indian-gaming-regulatory-act (accessed September 13, 2018).

Newell, Gordon R. *Rogues, Buffoons & Statesmen*. Seattle: Hangman Press, 1975.
_____. *Ships of the Inland Sea: The Story of the Puget Sound Steamboats*. Hillsboro, OR: Binfords & Mort, 1960.
_____. *So Fair a Dwelling Place: A History of Olympia, and Thurston County, Washington*. Olympia, WA: The Olympia News Publishing Company, 1950.
_____. "The State's Got Us Now." *Perspective*, 13, no. 2 (Fall 1969).

Nicandri, David. *Olympia's Forgotten Pioneers*. Olympia, WA: Washington State Capitol Historical Association, 1976.

Nicandri, David and Derek Valley. *Olympia Wins: Washington's Capital Controversies*. Olympia, WA: Washington State Capitol Museum, 1980.

Nielsen, Mark. "The Brown Farm on the Nisqually Delta, 1904-1919, A Photographic Essay." *Pacific

Northwest Quarterly 71, no. 4. (October 1980): 162-171.

Nisbet, Jack. *The Collector: David Douglas and the Natural History of the Northwest.* Seattle: Sasquatch Books, 2010.

Nokes, J. Richard. *Columbia's River: The Voyages of Robert Gray, 1787-1793.* Tacoma, WA: Washington State Historical Society, 1991.

Northwest Indian Fisheries Commission. "Commercial Shellfish Growers Settlement." Nwfic.org. https://nwifc.org/about-us/shellfish/commercial-shellfish-growers-settlement/ (accessed September 13, 2018).

O'Connell, Emmett. "Bordeaux, Washington-Last Remnants of a Thurston County Ghost Town." http://www.thurstontalk.com/2013/10/09/bordeaux-wa-last-remnants-thurston-county-ghost-town/ (accessed September 16, 2018).

_____. "Tono - Ghost Town with a Ghost Landscape." http://www.thurstontalk.com/2013/10/29/tono-ghost-town-ghost-landscape/.

Olympia Brewing Company. "Our 1,000,000th Visitor." *It's the Water News*, September 1962. Tumwater, WA: Olympia Brewing Company.

_____. *Annual Report, 1976.* Tumwater, WA: Olympia Brewing Company.

Olympia Chamber of Commerce, 1913. "The Farm in Its Relation to Olympia and Thurston County, Wash., Bulletin No. 3."

Olympia Daily Recorder. 1910. "Action Filed Against Property Owners of Resorts Below the Line." November 10, 1910.

_____. 1911. "Dr. Strickland Dies of Cancer in Seattle." September 23, 1911.

_____. 1912. "I.W.W. Agitator Sends Defy To City." April 5, 1912.

_____. 1912. "Mysterious Trio Believed I.W.W. Scouts." April 3, 1912.

_____. 1913. "Epidemic of Typhoid at Logging Camps." August 27, 1913.

_____. 1916. "There is No Wood to be Cut But Plenty of Snow to Shovel." January 3, 1916.

_____. 1918. "Mayor Tells of Flu Here." October 31, 1918.

_____. 1919. "Council to Meet; May Remove Flu Ban." January 21, 1919.

_____. 1920. "I.W.W. Members Convicted Under Syndicalism Law by Thurston County Jury." January 15, 1920.

_____. 1920. "Verdict of Not Guilty for Sugoff." December 8, 1920.

Olympia News. 1928. "One Hundred Families Will Settle on Land at or Near Boston Harbor." August 10, 1928.

_____. 1936. "Silver Shirts Will Have Rally Here." August 13, 1936.

Oregon Spectator, July 29, 1851.

Oregon State Archives. Calendar #4638.

Oregon Territorial Legislature. *Journal of House of Representatives.* December 17, 1851.

Olympia Transcript. 1870. "Results of Election." June 11, 1870.

Pacific Shellfish Institute. "Final Project Report - Shellfish at Work - Reducing Nutrient Pollution in Budd Inlet Watershed." National Estuary Program (NEP) Toxics and Nutrients, Award No. 61300036, Prepared for the Washington Department of Ecology, December, 2014.

Palmer, Gayle and Shanna Stevenson, eds. *Thurston County Place Names: A Heritage Guide.* Olympia, WA: Thurston County Historic Commission, 1992.

Perry, James R., Richard H. Chused, and Mary DeLano. "The Spousal Letters of Samuel R. Thurston, Oregon's First Territorial Delegate to Congress." *Oregon Historical Quarterly*, 96, no. 1 (Spring 1995): 5-79.

Peterson, H. C. and Gilbert C. Fite. *Opponents of War, 1917-1918.* University of Washington Press, 1968.

Pethick, Derek. *First Approaches to the Northwest Coast.* Vancouver, Canada: Douglas & McIntyre, 1976.

Philbrick, Nathaniel. *Sea of Glory: America's Voyage of Discovery: The U.S. Exploring Expedition, 1838-1842.* New York: Penguin Books, 2004.

Pioneer and Democrat. 1854. "Bridge Across Budd's Inlet." October 15, 1854.

Pioneer Days in Freedom Community. Unpublished manuscript.

Pioneer Map of Thurston County. State Capitol Historical Association, 1974.

Plywood Pioneers Association. "Plywood in Retrospect, Olympia Veneer." Apawood.org. 1969. https://www.apawood.org/data/Sites/1/documents/monographs/7-olympia-veneer-co.pdf (accessed September 13, 2018).

Plywood Pioneers Association. "Plywood in Retrospect, Olympia Veneer." Apawood.org. 1971. https://www.apawood.org/data/Sites/1/documents/monographs/11-olympia-veneer-co.pdf (accessed September 13, 2018).

Pollard, Lancaster and Lloyd Spencer. "The Hunter Family". *History of Washington.* New York: Historical Society, 1984.

Poor's Manual of Railroads, Volume 50. https://books.google.com/books?id=vGJJAAAAMAAJ&printsec=frontcover&source=gbs_ge_summary_r&cad=0#v=onepage&q&f=false (accessed September 16, 2018).

Port of Olympia. http://www.portolympia.com/105/History (accessed September 21, 2018).

Poultridge, Andrew. *Boomtime: A History of the Woodard Bay National Resources Conservation Area.* Olympia, WA: Department of Natural Resources, 1991.

Prosch, Thomas. "The Political Beginning of Washington Territory." *Oregon Historical Quarterly,* 6: 147-158.

Providence Health Services Washington. http://washington.providence.org/about/history/ (accessed September 21, 2018).

Ramsey, Guy Reed. *Postmarked Washington: Thurston County.* Olympia, WA: Thurston County Historic Commission, 1988.

Rathbun, John C. *History of Thurston County, Washington from 1845 to 1895.* Seattle: Shorey Book Store, 1972.

Records of "Mrs. Rebecca H. Howard, 1862-1883." Unpublished manuscript compiled 1999. Olympia, WA: Southwest Regional Archives and Olympia Timberland Library.

Redecker, Jerre. "Bountiful Byway: Thurston County trail leads to farms, hikes - and attention." *Olympian*, April 16, 2016.

Register of the Naval Militia of the United States. Division of Naval Militia Affairs, 2016.

Reynolds, William. *Voyage to the Southern Ocean, The Letters of Lt. William Reynolds from the U.S. Exploring Expedition, 1838-1842,* edited by Anne H. Cleaver and E. Jeffrey Stanns. Annapolis, MD: Naval Institute Press, 1988.

Risher, Jeffrey R. "Farmland Preservation in Thurston County." MES Thesis, The Evergreen State College, June 2009.

Robertson, Donald B. *Encyclopedia of Western Railroad History - Volume III.* Caldwell, ID: Caxton Printers, 1995.

Rough, Charles, in "A Cultural Resources Assessment of the Nisqually National Wildlife Refuge" by Lynn L. Larson and Jerry V. Jermann. Office of Public Archaeology, Institute for Environmental Studies, University of Washington, Reconnaissance Report No. 21, June 1978.

Rowe, James F. "Hunger Marcher Wishes." *Daily Olympian*, January 18, 1933.

Rutledge, Dale. "Early History of Littlerock, WA." *Good Old Days for Littlerock.* Privately published monograph.

Saint Martin's University. *Between the Years: 1895-1945.* https://www.stmartin.edu/about/history (accessed September 22, 2018).

St. Michael Parish, http://stmikesolympia.org/#/about-us/history (accessed September 21, 2018).

St. Paul & Tacoma Lumber Company Records, 1879-1958. http://archiveswest.orbiscascade.org/ark:/80444/xv60895/op=fstyle.aspx?t=k&q=st.+paul+and+tacoma+lumber (accessed September 16, 2018).

Schmidt, Leopold F. "How and Why the Olympia Brewery was located in Thurston County. The Treatment It has Received." s.n. (circa 1904).

_____. Letter to "Friend Gehrmann," June 16, 1896. *Leopold F. Schmidt Letter Book, 1895-1899.* Olympia Tumwater Foundation, Tumwater, WA.

_____. Letter to the Vilter Manufacturing Company, October 10, 1896. *Leopold F. Schmidt Letter Book, 1895-1899.* Olympia Tumwater Foundation, Tumwater, WA.

_____. Letter to Wahl & Henius, November 9, 1895. *Leopold F. Schmidt Letter Book, 1895-1899.* Olympia Tumwater Foundation, Tumwater, WA.

Schmidt, Peter G. Speech to Daughters of Pioneers of Washington, Tumwater, WA, October 5, 1948. Olympia Tumwater Foundation, Tumwater, WA.

Schmidt, Robert A. Letter to Olympia Brewing Company shareholders, June 11, 1982. Olympia Tumwater Foundation, Tumwater, WA.

Scott, Father John C., O.S.B. *This Place Called Saint Martin's: 1895-1995.* Virginia Beach, VA: The Donning Company, 1996.

Seattle Times. December 10, 2004.

_____. "Ralph M. Davis." *Seattle Times* Obituaries. http://www.legacy.com/obituaries/seattletimes/obituary.aspx?n=ralph-m-davis&pid=124443808 (accessed September 13, 2018).

Shaw, Edrie. *Memories of the Heart: Nellie, Edrie, and Lillian.* Unpublished manuscript.

Shaw, T. C. *Reminiscences of 1844.* http://www.oregonpioneers.com/tcshaw.htm (accessed September 20, 2018).

Sheldon. Charles H. and Michael Stohr-Gillmore. "In the Beginning: The Washington Supreme Court a Century Ago." *University of Puget Sound Law Review* 12:247, 251.

Shipley, Ann. *Memories: the History of the Thurston County Fair.* Rochester, WA: printed by the author, 2006.

Silverstone, Paul. *Civil War Navies, 1855-1883.* Naval Institute Press, 2001.

Sjodin, Lila Davis. *Olympia Genealogical Quarterly,* July 2012.

Smith, Marian. *The Puyallup-Nisqually.* New York: Columbia University Press, 1940.

Snowden, Clinton. *History of Washington: Rise and Progress of the American State, Volume 3.* New York: Century History, 1909-1911.

The South Bay: Its History and Its People, 1840-1940. Olympia, WA: South Bay Historical Association, 1986.

South Puget Sound Habitat for Humanity. "About Us." spshabitat.org/about-us (accessed March 18, 2016).

Squaxin Tribe. 2016. squaxinisland.org (accessed September 23, 2018).

Stanton, Elizabeth Cady, Susan B. Anthony, Matilda Joslyn Gage, and Ida Husted Harper. *History of Woman Suffrage.* Rochester, NY: J. J. Little & Co, 1881-1922.

State Capitol Historical Association of Washington. 1974. "Pioneer Map of Thurston County." Olympia, WA.

Steele, E. N. *The Immigrant Oyster (Osterea Gigas) Now Known as the Pacific Oyster.* Olympia, WA: Pacific Oyster Growers, 1964.

_____. *The Rise and Decline of the Olympia Oyster.* Elma, WA: Olympia Oyster Growers Association, 1957.

Steele, Harvey. "Customs Service Herald Arrival of United States." Special Supplement, *Daily Shipping News,* January 11, 1991.

Stevens, Governor Isaac. Letters, 1854-56. Washington State Archives.

Stevens, Hazard. *The Life of Isaac Ingalls Stevens by his son, Hazard Stevens with Maps and Illustrations in Two Volumes.* Boston: Houghton, Mifflin and Company, 1900.

Stevenson, Shanna. "A Freeway Runs Through It," in *The River Remembers: A History of Tumwater, 1845-1995,* edited by Gayle Palmer. Tumwater, WA: City of Tumwater, 1996.

_____. "Freedom." *Sunday Olympian, Totem Tidings,* October 19, 1980, 4-5.

_____. "Hunter Point was Site of Early Resort." *The Olympian, Totem Tidings,* March 25, 1984.

_____. *Olympia, Tumwater and Lacey: A Pictorial History.* Norfolk, VA: The Donning Company, 1985.

_____. *Olympiana.* Olympia, WA: Washington State Capitol Museum, 1982.

_____. *St. Peter Hospital: A Century of Caring. A Commitment to Quality.* Olympia, WA: St. Peter Hospital, 1987.

_____. *Superior Shipping Service - A History of the Port of Olympia.* Olympia, WA: Port of Olympia, 1982.

_____. *The Port of Olympia: A 75 Year History, 1922-1997*. Olympia, WA: Port of Olympia, 1997. with updates by Chuck Fowler.
Stream Team. "About Stream Team." streamteam.info/about (accessed March 18, 2016).
Streissguth, Tom. *An Eyewitness History: The Roaring Twenties*. New York: Facts on File Inc., 2001.
Sunday Olympian-Recorder. "Society: 'Hard Times Frolic' at Club Successful," September 19, 1926, 2.
Sunday Olympian. 1933. "Canal Support is Pledged at Rally." July 30, 1933.
_____. 1942. "Army Sets Dates for Japanese Evacuation." May 24, 1942.
_____. 1942. "Petitions Urge Jap Evacuation." March 1, 1942.
_____. 1983. "Commercial Development Key to City's Past - and Future." February 6, 1983.
Susan B. Anthony Papers: Daybook and Diaries 1856-1906. Library of Congress. Box 2 Reel 12, October 18, 1871.
Suttles, Wayne, ed. *Handbook of North American Indians, Volume 7: Northwest Coast*. Washington DC: Smithsonian Institution, 1990.
Swan, James Gilchrist. *The Northwest Coast: Or, Three Year's Residence in Washington Territory*. Seattle, WA: University of Washington Press, 1992.
Swan, John. "Olympia, the Pioneer Town of Washington, Its Socialization, Origin and Early History from a Pioneer's Retrospection." Manuscript at the University of Washington, Allen Library, Special Collections.
Tacoma Public Library. "Magnificent Views and Vistas: Mountaineers Climbs 1912-1916." Tpl.lib.wa.us. http://mtn.tpl.lib.wa.us/climbs/climbing/people/fuller.asp (accessed September 13, 2018).
Takami, David A. *Shared Dreams: A History of Asians and Pacific Americans in Washington State*. Seattle, WA: Washington Centennial Commission, 1989.
_____. "Southeast Asian Americans." Essay #894, February 17, 1999. http://www.historylink.org/File/894.
Tanis, James Robert, ed. "The Journal of Levi Lathrop Smith, 1847-1848." *Pacific Northwest Quarterly*, October 1952.
Taylor, Herbert C. "John Work on the Chehalis Indians" in *Coast Salish and Western Washington Indians III*, edited by D. A. Horr. New York: Garland Publishing, 1974.
Telewski, Frank W. and Scott Barrett. *Logging Railroads of Weyerhaeuser's Vail and McDonald Operation*. Hamilton, MT: Oso Publishing, 2004.
Tenino Independent. 1989. "Tenino sandstone quarries were founded 100 years ago." January 4, 1989.
Thurston County Bar. "Perspectives on the Bench and Bar of Thurston County Since Statehood." November 14, 2014. Thurstoncountybar.com. http://thurstoncountybar.com/wp-content/uploads/2014/11/WA125WrittenMaterials.pdf (accessed September 13, 2018).
Thurston County Food Bank. "Mission Statement." Thurstoncounty foodbank.org. http://thurstoncountyfoodbank.org/?page_id=50 (accessed September 13, 2018).
Thurston County Historic Commission. https://www.co.thurston.wa.us/permitting/historic/historic-home.html (March 19, 2016.).
_____. 1990. "Rededication of Pioneer Rock Also Known as Calder Rock, September 12, 1990."
_____. *Short History of Budd Inlet*. 1992.
Thurston County Independent. 1934. "Tenino Expedition Visits Depths of Tono Coal Mine." March 16, 1934.
_____. 1935. "Opening of First Tenino Quarry Told by S. W. Fenton." June 7, 1935.
_____. 1935. "Pioneer Brothers Raised on Site of Rochester." May 31, 1935.
_____. 1935. "Pioneer Life of Mound Prairie is Described." March 29, 1935.
_____. 1935. "Pioneer Resident of 80 Years Recounts History." March 1, 1935.
_____. 1935. "Incorporation of Tenino Told by H. J. Keithan." June 14, 1935.
Thurston County Regional Planning. "About Us." trpc.org. https://www.trpc.org/404.aspx?aspxerrorpath=/27/About-Us (accessed September 13, 2018).
Thurston, Samuel Royal. "Diary of Samuel Royal Thurston." *Oregon Historical Quarterly* 15, no. 3 (September 1914): 153-204.
Timberman. 1910. "Washington to sell timber on school lands - shingle mills organizing." April 1910.
_____. 1941. "Nearing the Last Turn." October 1941.

Tokarczyk, Jill. "End comes to Olympia Brewing." *The Olympian*, March 19, 1983.

Told by the Pioneers: Tales of Frontier Life as Told by Those Who Remember the Days of the Territory and Early Statehood in Washington. Olympia, WA: Works Projects Administration, Vol 1, 1937-38.

Toy, Eckard, V. Jr. "Silver Shirts in the Northwest: Politics, Prophecies, and Personalities in the 1930s." *Pacific Northwest Quarterly*, 80, No. 4.

Trainweb.US. "Weyerhaueser Chehalis Western, Vail logging line, Curtis, Milburn & Eastern." Trainweb.com. http://www.trainweb.us/cwwr/#sthash.QcmTlAFx.dpbs (accessed September 13, 2018).

Transactions of the 53rd Annual Reunion of the Oregon Pioneer Association, July 1, 1925. Portland: F. W. Baltes and Company, 1928.

Treaty of Medicine Creek, http://www.historylink.org/File/5253 (accessed September 19, 2018).

Trosper, Don. *The History of Tumwater, Volume 1: The Founding of Tumwater.* Tumwater, WA: Tumwater Historical Association, 1985.

_____. *The History of Tumwater, Volume 2: New Market.* Tumwater, WA: Tumwater Historical Association, 1987.

_____. *The History of Tumwater, Volume 3: Fortress Tumwater.* Tumwater, WA: Tumwater Historical Association, 1992.

Tyler, David B. *The Wilkes Expedition: The First United States Exploring Expedition (1838-1842).* Philadelphia: American Philosophical Society, 1968.

Union Pacific: Building America. "Puget Sound & Pacific Railroad PSAP #640." Union Pacific: Building America. UP.com. https://www.up.com/customers/shortline/profiles_l-p/psap/index.htm (accessed September 13, 2018).

United States Indian Claims Commission. *Final Report.* https://www.narf.org/nill/documents/icc_final_report.pdf (accessed September 19, 2018).

United States Department of the Interior, Dofflemeyer Point Lighthouse, National Register Nomination. https://npgallery.nps.gov/NRHP/GetAsset/NRHP/93001339_text (accessed September 23, 2018).

_____. Seatco Prison Site, National Register Nomination. http://npgallery.nps.gov/nrhp/GetAsset?assetID=1629c3aa-8326-46c8-b781-1f2477e3b496 (accessed September 21, 2018).

Upton, Judith with Karyl Groeneveld. *Glimpses of Gate: A Pictorial Journal of Gate, WA: 1880-1920.* Rochester, WA: Gorham Printing, 2003.

Viola, Herman J. and Carolyn Margolis., eds. *Magnificent Voyagers: The U.S. Exploring Expedition, 1838-1842.* Washington, DC: Smithsonian Institution, 1985.

Vouri, Mike. *The Pig War, Standoff at Griffin Bay.* Seattle: Discover Your Northwest, 1999.

Washington's Centennial Farms: Yesterday and Today. Olympia, WA: Washington State Department of Agriculture, 1989.

Washington's Centennial Farms: Yesterday and Today. Olympia, WA: Washington State Department of Agriculture, updated 2014. https://agr.wa.gov/FP/Pubs/docs/469-O-WACentennialFarms25YrsLater-Overview.pdf (accessed September 17, 2018).

The Washington Center for the Performing Arts. 1995. "The Tradition Continues - Celebrating 10 Years of Outstanding Performance."

Washington Courts. "Brief History of the Washington State Supreme Court." courts.wa.gov. https://www.courts.wa.gov/education/?fa=education.supreme (accessed September 13, 2018).

Washington Standard. April 8, 1881.

_____. June 12, 1885.

_____. 1888. "The Ladies Relief Society." December 14, 1888.

_____. 1889. "Subscriptions for the Hotel Olympia." May 10, 1889.

_____. 1912. "Original Story of Arrival Here of Governor Stevens." November 29, 1912.

Washington State Archives. Frontier Justice Record Series. Thurston County, Case Number THR-2738, 1889.

_____. Papers of Governor Ernest Lister.

Washington State Department of Enterprise Services. https://des.wa.gov/services/facilities-leasing/

capitol-campus/parks-and-attractions/heritage-park (accessed September 21, 2018).

Washington State Department of General Administration. "Capitol Lake: A Vision for the Next Ten Years, 2003-2013." October 2002.

Washington State Department of Agriculture. "Thurston County Agriculture." *County Agricultural Data Series, 1956.* Washington Crop and Livestock Reporting Service Bulletin.

Washington State Department of Archaeology and History. WISAARD National Register nomination for General Administration Building. https://fortress.wa.gov/dahp/wisaardp3/api/api/resultgroup/186701/doc/1462211166089 (accessed September 22, 2018).

_____. WISAARD National Register nomination for Old Capitol. https://fortress.wa.gov/dahp/wisaardp3/api/api/resultgroup/1163/Document/185889 (accessed September 22, 2018).

_____. WISAARD National Register nomination for Rutledge House and Barn. https://fortress.wa.gov/dahp/wisaardp3/api/api/resultgroup/1163/Document/186419 (accessed September 22, 2018).

_____. WISAARD file for Grand Mound. https://fortress.wa.gov/dahp/wisaardp3/ (accessed September 22, 2018).

_____. WISAARD file for Lake Lawrence Pavilion. https://fortress.wa.gov/dahp/wisaardp3/ (accessed September 22, 2018).

_____. WISAARD file for Gate. https://fortress.wa.gov/dahp/wisaardp3/ (accessed September 22, 2018).

_____. WISAARD file for Vail. https://fortress.wa.gov/dahp/wisaardp3/ (accessed September 22, 2018).

_____. WISAARD file for Rainier School and Zion Evangelical Lutheran Church, https://fortress.wa.gov/dahp/wisaardp3/api/api/resultgroup/1163/Document/185912 (accessed September 22, 2018).

Washington State Library. "Thurston County Pioneers Before 1870, Henry Harrison Tilley." Statelib.wa.gov. http://content.statelib.wa.gov/cdm/singleitem/collection/pioneers/id/198/rec/1 (accessed September 13, 2018).

_____. "Thurston County Pioneers Before 1870." Statelib.wa.gov. http://content.statelib.wa.gov/cdm/landingpage/collection/pioneers.

Washington State Office of the Attorney General. "Washington's Attorneys General-Past and Present." ATG.wa.gov https://www.atg.wa.gov/washingtons-attorneys-general-past-and-present (accessed October 10, 2018).

Washington State Railroad Historical Society. http://www.wsrhs.org/date1880s.htm.

Washington State University. "Agriculture in Thurston County." Extension.wsu.edu. https://extension.wsu.edu/thurston/agriculture/ (accessed September 13, 2018).

_____. "Agriculture: A Cornerstone of Thurston County's Economy." Extension.wsu.edu. http://extension.wsu.edu/thurston/wp-content/uploads/sites/12/2014/01/Agriculture-A-Cornerstone-of-Thurston-Countys-Economy.pdf (accessed September 13, 2018).

Washington Territory, Supreme Court. *Opinions of the Supreme Court of the territory of Washington, in cases argued and determined in said court, from its organization (1854) to the term ending January 29, 1864. Published by authority.* Olympia, WA, 1854.

Waterman, Thomas Talbot. *Puget Sound Geography.* Washington, DC: The Smithsonian Institution, 1920.

Watts, Alice Adams. "More Than 3,500 See Spectacular War Pageant." *Daily Olympian.* August 17, 1943.

Weaver, Lanny. "The Hunt for O. C. Lacey." Lacey, WA: Lacey Historical Museum, 1995.

_____. "The Story of Lacey: From Community to City, Part I: 1848-1891." http://www.thurstontalk.com/2016/04/04/lacey-history-2/ (accessed September 21, 2018).

_____. "The Story of Lacey: From Community to City, Part II: 1892-1948." http://www.thurstontalk.com/2016/07/04/lacey-history-2/ (accessed September 21, 2018).

_____. "The True Story of Lacey's Racetrack." *Lacey Museum Musings*, Fall, 2015.

Weyerhaeuser Timber. 1949. "Introduction to Vail-McDonald Farms." October 7, 1949.

Weyerhaeuser Timber Archives. "Weyerhaeuser Timber Company. Shareholders Visit Vail-McDonald Operation." Weyerhaeuser Timber Archives.

Wheat, Dan. "Gate? Yes, But Memories of Old Logging Town are Fading Fast." *The Olympian*, April 9, 1978.

_____. "Rainier Endures Despite Family Scraps." *The Olympian*, Feb. 13, 1983.

Wing, Robert with Gordon Newell. *Peter Puget*. Gray Beard Publishing, 1979.

Yelm History Project. "Gruber and Docherty Lumber Company." Yelmhistoryproject.com. http://www.yelmhistoryproject.com/?p=2047. See also http://www.yelmhistoryproject.com/?p=763 (accessed September 13, 2018).

Zander, Julie McDonald. *Bucoda: The Little Town with a Million Memories*. Centralia, WA: Bucoda Community Foundation, 2010.

_____. *Chapters of Life in Bucoda*. Centralia, WA: Chapters of Life, 2010.

Capitol Historical Association dinner at State Capitol Museum, 1962. Photographer Vibert Jeffers. Susan Parish Photograph Collection, 1889-1990. AR-25501080-ph003412, #8681 (Courtesy of Washington State Archives)

INDEX

Page numbers with an *f* refer to a figure or a caption; *t* refers to a table; *n* refers to an endnote.

A

Active, USS, 35f, 42–43
Adams, Hank, 24, 27
Admiralty Inlet, chart of, 35f
Agate, Alfred, 39
Agate Grange, 48, 48f
agriculture
    declining prices, 203
    farming organizations, 128–33
    farms
        centennial, 125–26
        late nineteenth century, 127
        mid-twentieth century, 131
        Native American, 121
        other, 127–28
        pioneer, 121–25
        scientific "modern," 191
        size reductions, 131
    Hudson's Bay Company and, 19, 121
    as pillar, 190
    in south county prairies, 64
agritourism, 131
air raid sirens, 209
Alaska Natives, raids on Washington settlers, 43
Alaskan marble, in courthouse, 78f
alcohol
    abstinence, 198f
    prohibition of, 180f, 181, 201–2
Alden, James, 35f, 42
Alexander, Gerry, 12
Alida, 44
Alien Land Law (1921), 188
Allen & Son Mill Company, laborers, 192f
ambulance, students' purchase of, 213f
American Red Cross, 208
American settlers, hostilities of, 41
American Vigilantes of Thurston County, 208
animal husbandry, by Native Americans, 17
animal rights, 198f
Annamour, Francis N., 32

Antarctic land mass, discovery of, 33, 36f, 37
anti-Japanese hostility, 212
aquaculture, 134–41
archeology, at Mud Bay, 25
arms depository, Congressional funding for, 41
Army and Navy Club, 211
Art Moderne architecture, 78f
Associated Charities, 198
Astoria. *See* George, Fort
Athapascan family, Pacific Group of, 21f
automobiles
    ca. 1910, 148f, 149f
    ca. 1920s, 202, 202f
    highways for. *See* highways
    as steamer replacement, 47
Avanti High School, 109
Axtell, Mr. and Mrs., 125
Ayers' Hill, 61

B

Bailey Gatzert, 46, 46f
Baker, Joseph, 30, 31f
Balch, Lafayette, 41, 44
Bald Hills quarry, 95
Balli, Len, 216
Bank of Bucoda, 100f
Banker, Lloyd, 174f
bankruptcy
    of Brown Farm, 129
    of Yelm Irrigation District, 128
    See also economic cycles
Barbers' Union, 194–95
Barkley, Charles William, 30
Barnes, George and Mary Ann, 84
Barnes, Nelson, 58
baskets
    of Parsons, 68f, 69
    of Squaxin Island tribe, 12f
Bates, Kate Stevens, 130
beach, Indian huts/canoes on, 87

Beacon Beach Resort, 138
Bean, E. L., 200
Beat Happening (band), 216
Beatty, David, 61
Beatty, Mary Thompson, 61, 125
Beaver, SS, 34f, 43–44
Beer Bottlers' Union, 194–95
Beer Drivers' and Helpers Union, 194–95
Bellingham, Olympia brewery at, 180
berry industry, 128, 131, 205
Berry Pickers' Ball, 98, 128
Bettman, Amalia Koblenzer, 84
Bettman, Louis, 83f, 84
Bettman Store, 83f, 84
bicycle toll trail, 98
Bigelow, Ann Elizabeth White, 62, 82, 82f, 105, 132
Bigelow, Daniel Richardson
　about, 82, 83
　as county superintendent, 106
　as Grange member, 132
　photo of, 82f
　as pioneer lawyer/politician, 71f
　as Washington Territory advocate, 73
Bigelow House Museum, 82, 82f
Bikini Kill (band), 216
Biles, Fannie, 179
Biles family, 62
Billings, William, 101
Billy Frank Jr. Nisqually National Wildlife Refuge, 27, 129, 219
Bison, Percy, 174f
Black Bear Mine, 95
black exclusion laws, 54, 56
Black Hills & Northwestern Railway, 164, 173, 175
Black Hills, logging of, 148, 153
Black Hills Tree Farm, 164, 166
Black Lake & Sherman Valley Railroad, 170
Black Lake corridor, as transportation route, 6
Black Lake, ferry service for, 64
Black Lake Mill Company, 160f
Black Lake Portage, 126
Black River (community). *See* Littlerock
Black River (river)
　Chehalis settlement on, 14
　fertile land along, 65, 125, 126
　logging railroad along, 172
　mounds near, 36
　as Native migration route, 148

black walnut tree, 74f
Blakely Mill Company, 170
Blankenship, Georgiana, 84, 87
Bloomingdale Lumber and Logging, 151
Blumauer Lumber Company, logging railroad, 95
Blume, Bob, 93
Bob White, lumber mill, 102
Bodega y Quadra, Juan Francisco de la, 30
Bolander, J. D., 100
Boldt Decision (1974), 20, 24, 27
boosterism, 191
Bordeaux, 153, 154f, 171f, 199
Bordeaux, Joseph, 153
Bordeaux, Thomas and Margaret, 153
Bordeaux Brothers Logging Company, 153
Bordeaux Logging Camp, food suppliers for, 66
Boston Harbor, 137, 137f
Boston Street Bridge, 58f
Boy Scout Camp Thunderbird, 154
Brackenridge, William, 34f, 36, 38, 39
"bragging rights," for steamboat speed, 46f
Brail family, 66
Brando, Marlon, 27
Bratmobile (band), 216
Brenner, John Joseph, 136f
Brewer, Reese and Eliza, 65
breweries
　Hamm's and Lone Star as acquisitions, 184
　Olympia brewery. *See* Olympia brewery
Brewery Workers, 194–95
Bricklayers' and Masons' Union, 194–95
Bridge Fabricating Company, 210
bridges
　Custer Way/Boston Street, 58
　4th Avenue, 89
　over Budd Inlet, 87
　for wagons, 57f
Brighton Park Grange, 132f
Brodie, Flo, 219
Brooks, Quincy, 83
brothels, Olympia brewery refusal to serve, 182
Brown, Alson L. and Emma, 128, 191
Brown, B. F., 46
Brown, Benjamin, 87
Brown, James B., 137
Brown, Mary Olney, 87, 145, 145f
Brown, Oscar, 87
Brown Farm, 128–29, 129f, 191
Brown's Point, 137

Buckley, William, 100
Bucoda
    about, 100, 102
    Seatco Prison, 101, 101f
    view of, 100f
Bucoda Lumber Company, 100
Bucoda Shingle Company, 100f
Budd, Thomas, 37
Budd Inlet
    bridge across, 87, 237n22
    Dana Passage and, 39
    docks on, 46
    mothballed ships in, 49
    naming of, 37
    pollution of, 192
    shipyards at, 45–46
Bureau of Indian Affairs, liability of, 24
Burlington Northern Santa Fe Railway, 175f
Burmeister, Mary, 84
Burt, James, 42–43
buses, 172–73, 202
Bush, George
    about, 121
    drawing of, 53f
    journey to Tumwater, 53–55
    land claims of, 56
    land grant by act of Congress, 123
Bush, Henry Sanford, 123
Bush, Isabella James, 121
Bush, January Jackson, 123
Bush, Joseph Tolbert, 123
Bush, Lewis Nesqually, 123
Bush, Mandana Smith Kimsey, 123
Bush, Rial Bailey, 123
Bush, William Owen, 123
Bush Act (1895), 135–36
Bush family, 123f
Bush Prairie, 55f
Bush Prairie School, 107f
Butler, John, 42–43, 44

C

Calder Rock, 154
California, Olympia beer brewed in, 185
California gold rush, 64, 81, 123
callousness in 1920s, 203
Callow Act, 136
camas root, 16–17, 90
Camp Jolly, 91f

Camp Lewis. *See* Joint Base Lewis-McChord
canneries, crops for, 130–31
Cannery Ranch, 130–31
Cannon, William, 31, 32
Canoe Journey
    about, 25
    art commissioned for, 25f
    paddlers and canoes, 26f
canoes, 14
Capital Brewing Company, 177f, 179, 179f
    See also Olympia brewery
Capital City, 46, 46f
capitalism, opposition to, 191f, 195
Capitol buildings
    construction of, 89–90, 115f, 190
    details of, 116f
Capitol Historical Association dinner, 263f
Capitol Lake, 90, 119f
Capitol Land Trust, 219
Capitol State Forest, 164, 166
Capitol Theater, 216
Capitol Way, 90
captain's wife overboard, 45
Carlyon, P. H., 88
Carlyon Fill
    dredging/filling of, 88
    as industrial area, 89
    promotion of, 189f
    seismic susceptibility of, 190–91
Carpenter, Cecilia Svinth
    on Native coexistence with nature, 16
    on reservations, 23
    They Walked Before: The Indians of Washington State, 17
    Where the Waters Begin: The Traditional Nisqually History of Mount Rainier, 13
Carr, Charles R., 199
Carroll, P. P., 137
Carter tannery site, 179
Case, Jim, 98
Casey, Silas, 43
casinos, tribal income from, 24–25
Castle Brothers, 98
Catholic missionaries
    Indian boys school established by, 83, 105, 105f
    as vegetable farmers, 124
    See also Oblates of Mary Immaculate
Caton, A. S., 198
Cayuse War, 63f

CCC (Civilian Conservation Corps), 166, 208, 208f, 209
cedar, as sacred, 14
cemeteries, uprooting of, 23
census. *See* population
Centennial Brewing Company (Butte, MT), 178
centennial farms, 125–26
Central School, Olympia, 109f
Centralia, railroad connections, 148, 151
Centralia College, SPSCC split from, 218
Centralia Land Company, 146
Centralia Massacre, 199
Chadwick, H.A.
    Men Behind the Seattle Spirit—Argus Cartoons, 181f
chain stores, 203
Chalcraft, Edwin L., 22f
Chambers, A. H., 86, 90–91
Chambers, Andrew, 61–62, 124f
Chambers, David and Elizabeth Harris, 61f, 62
Chambers, Thomas M. and Lestina, 61–62
Chambers family, crops, 124f
Chambers Prairie, 61–62, 81, 90
Chambers Prairie Grange, 216f
Chan, Genevieve C. 193
Chaplin, John, 191–92
Chapman, J. B., 71
Chapman, John, 47
charitable giving, tribal, 25
charitable groups, 208
charity care, 196–97
Charles, Pierre, 32
Chatham, HMS, 29
Chehalis Indian School, 22f
Chehalis tribe
    about, 29
    enterprises of, 24–25, 144
    environmentalism of, 219
    Grand Mound as ancestral site, 143
    Hale's studies of, 38f
    Holloweena tribe as belonging to, 36
    Kwalhioqua Tribe, 21f
    land claims payment to, 23
    as original inhabitants, 8, 12
    precontact lifestyle of, 13–14
    reservation of
        about, 22
        business center for, 148
        Heck at, 20f

Chehalis Tribe *(continued)*
    location of, 21f, 146, 223f
    scholars at, 18f
    at treaty negotiations, 20, 22
    Youckton family, 21f
Chehalis Western public hiking trail, 167
Chehalis Western Railroad, 164, 169, 173f, 175
Chelm. *See* Yelm
Chesterton, G. K., 221
Chicago, Milwaukee, Saint Paul & Pacific Railroad. *See* Milwaukee Railroad
Chinook Jargon, 14, 20, 52
Chinook tribe, 20, 22
Chong Lee Laundry, 200f
Christensen, Nels, 44f
Christmas Eve serenade, 167
Church at South Union, 155f
churches, as schools, 106
circuit-riding preachers, 57
cities
    Bucoda, 100–102
    Lacey, 90–93
    Olympia, 80–90
    Rainier, 102–3
    Tenino, 93–98
    Yelm, 98–100
Citizens Bank of Tenino, closure of, 95, 205
City of Aberdeen, 44
City of Shelton, 48f
city woodpile, 198
Civil Defense workers, 209–10
Civil War, Wilkes' impact on, 37
Civil Works Administration, 208
Civilian Conservation Corps (CCC), 166, 208, 208f, 209
Clackamas district, 71
Clara Brown, 45
Clark County, formation of, 71
Cleveland, Jesse, 149f
Clinton, C. D., 129
Cloverfields dairy farm, 129–30, 191
Coal Bank, 94
coal mining, 95, 152
Coates family, 98
Cobell v. Salazar (2009), 24
Cock, William and Sarah, 84
Cogwell, James Edward, 147
Cogwell, Margaret Ann Carter, 147, 147f
Cogwell, Ruby Carol, 147

Thurston County - Water, Woods & Prairies   267

Collegiate Institute, 191–92
Collins, Catherine and William, 43
Columbia River
    to Fraser River, exploration, 32
    naming/exploration of, 30f
Columbia River-Grays Harbor-Puget Sound Canal, rejection of, 208–9, 248n10
The Columbian, 83
Colvin, Ignatius, 65, 126
Colvin Ranch, 125, 126
Colvocoresses, George, 34, 34f, 36
commercial farming. *See* agriculture
communities
    about, 192
    Bordeaux, 153
    Gate, 148
    Grand Mound, 143–45
    Independence, 151
    Littlerock, 148–49
    Maytown, 154
    Rochester, 146
    Summit Lake, 154
    Tono, 152
    Vail, 152
    Woodard Bay, 152
community pride, 191
community-supported agriculture, 131
Concomly, Chief, 36, 39
Conine, Frank and Jennie, 139
Conner family, 62
Constitution (state), 113f, 117
Constitution, USS (Old Ironsides), 47f, 50, 95f
constitutional convention, delegates to, 113f
Constitutionally guaranteed free speech, 199
controlled burning, as Native American practice, 17, 121, 126
Cook, James, 30
cooking vessels, baskets as, 69
Cooperative Extension Service, 4-H in, 128
Cooper's Point, as The Evergreen State College site, 192
Corcoran, Neil B., 101
corruption
    in Prohibition enforcement, 202
    in vice districts, 197–98
Corwin, Thomas, 41
Cosgrove, Samuel, 117
Cosmopolis, treaty negotiations at, 20, 22
Cottick, Lou, 149f

Coulter, Samuel, 100
county commissioners, women as, 79
Cowichan River. *See* Fraser River
Cowlitz Convention, 71, 73, 236n8
Cowlitz Landing, reservation of, 23
Cowlitz Trail, 2, 55
    See also Oregon Trail
Cowlitz tribe
    about, 29
    Hale's studies of, 38f
    trail closure by, 31
    at treaty negotiations, 20, 22
criminal syndicalism act (1919), 199
Croes, Dale, 17
Crooked Lake. *See* Summit Lake
crops
    bounty of, 123–25
    for cannery, 130–31
    in Grand Mound/Rochester, 146, 147
Crosby, Bing, 56f
Crosby, Clanrick, 57
Crosby, Nathaniel, 57
Crosby Family House, 56f, 59, 215
Crowder family, 65
Crowley Marine, 48
culling houses, 136
Cummins, Earl, 149f
Cushman, Elizabeth, 138
Cushman Point. *See* Hunter Point
Custer Way Bridge, 58f
customs offices, 72, 83
cutover farms, 127–28

D

Daily Olympian, 75f
dairy cooperatives, 128
dairy farms, 131, 146
Damariscove, 41
Dana, James Dwight, 37, 39
Dana Passage, 37, 39
dances, 138, 140
Daughters of Charity. *See* Sisters of Providence
Daughters of the American Revolution, 74f
David, J. B., 100
Davidson, Al, 202
Davis, "John Doe," 199
Davis, Mr., 149f
Davis, Ralph, 118
Davis & Sons Store, 149f

Dawes Act (1887), land ownership snarl from, 23
Day, Fred and Iva (Ivy) Whitney, 197f
Decatur, USS, 42, 42f, 43
deepwater port, 190
Deer Lodge brewery, 178
defense councils, 198–99
Delphi Community Association, 109
Denny, A. A., 73
Depression, effects of, 108
Deschutes, lumber mill, 102
Deschutes Falls generator, 140
Deschutes River
    damming of, 90
    hydroelectric power from, 58
    photo of, 54f
    power generating plant on, 58f
    Tumwater Falls on, 52
    Upper Tumwater Falls on, 3
Deschutes River Boom Company, 164
Deutsch, Herman, 6
DeWitt, John L., 211f, 212
Dickenson, Thomas, 37
Dickenson Point, 37
Discovery, HMS, 29, 30, 31f
discrimination
    against African Americans, 53, 54
    against Chinese/Japanese, 95, 187f, 211–12
diseases, decimation by, 18
dissent, hostility toward, 199
District of Vancouver (1845), 71
diversity, 213–14
Djie'kc1L. *See* Hunter Point
Doane, Elizabeth, 84
Docherty, Benjamin, 169f
docks/wharves, 46
Dodge, Ada, 67f
Dodge, Robert Bruce, 65–66, 67f
Dodge family, 65
Dodge Prairie, 66
Dofflemyer, Cyrus, 137
Dofflemyer, Isaac and Susan Allen, 137
Dofflemyer Point, 137
Dofflemyer Point Lighthouse, 137, 137f
dog barks, as navigation tool, 45
dog hair, for blankets/clothing, 17
Donation Land Claim Act (1850), 60, 72, 122
donkey engines, 162f
Donworth, Charles, 118
Dooley's Store, 149f

Douglas, David
    drawing of, 37f
    Menzies as mentor to, 38
    as scientist, 37–38
    Work as aid to, 32, 32f
    work of, 39
Douglas, James, 43, 143
Douglas fir, 37f, 38
Doyle, Peter, 199
Draham, George, 118, 119
Drayton, Joseph, 39
drying kilns, 153
DuPont, Wilkes expedition at, 33f
Durgin, Leonard D., 65, 125, 143
Durgin, Lucetta, 65
Durham, A. C., 247n32
Duwamish tribe, 29

E
earthquakes
    in 1949, 75f, 88f
    Nisqually, 89
Eaton, Charles, 63f
Eaton, Fort, 62, 63f
Eaton, Nathan, 62, 63f
Eaton family, 62
Eaton house, 63f
Eaton Prairie, 63f
Ebey, Isaac, beheading of, 41
economic cycles
    about, 190–92
    Great Depression. *See* Great Depression
    Panic of 1893, 94, 148, 171, 190
ecosystems preservation, 217f, 219
Edgar, John and Betsy, 62
education
    about, 105–11
    charities and, 198
    in Clark County, 106
    colleges/universities
        The Evergreen State College, 192, 220, 220f
        Saint Martin's University. *See* Saint Martin's University
        South Puget Sound Community College, 218
        Washington State University, 124
    governance of, 106
    high schools. *See* high schools

education *(continued)*
    Indian schools. *See* Indian schools
    patriotic instruction/loyalty teaching, 199
    teacher salary reductions, 206
    of tribal members, 25
    in Walla Walla, 106
    See also teachers; *specific schools*
Eighteenth Amendment, 202
eighth-grade education, 108
eight-hour day, 201
Eklund, George, 118, 119
Eld, Henry, 34, 34f, 36
Eld Inlet (Mud Bay)
    archaeological excavation at, 25
    features of, 36–37
    log dump at, 173
    naming of, 34
    oyster harvesting at, 135, 136
    Squaxin villages on, 29
electric power generation, 58–59, 58f
Eliza Anderson, 44, 45f
Ellis, Ike, 170
Ellis, Isaac, 92
Elma, 63f
employment
    of Chinese/Japanese, 92, 95, 187f, 188
    in government, 59, 214, 215
    at Olympia Brewing Company, 59, 183, 184
    at Providence St. Peter Hospital, 86
    in retail sales, 214
    from tribal enterprises, 24
    at Union Mills, 92
    at veneer mills, 89
enacting clause, as legal requirement, 115
"enemy aliens," raids on, 212
England, as cannery market, 130
Enterprise, 44
environmentalism, 219
epidemics, 196
Erickson, Jonas and Maria Lovisa, 127f
Erickson Home, 151f
Eureka Quarry, 96
European immigrants, 188
Evans, Daniel J., 133f, 220
Evans, Elwood, 83
Everett Massacre, 45
The Evergreen State College, 192, 220, 220f
Evergreen Valley, 63f
Executive Order 9066, 211–12, 211f

Executive Order of January 20, 1857, 22
explorers
    Grand Mound as landmark for, 143
    Hudson's Bay Company affiliated scientists, 39
    McMillan, James, 31–32
    Menzies, Archibald, 38–39
    Native Americans as, 29
    scientist-adventurers as, 37–38
    Vancouver, George, 29–30
    Wilkes, Charles, 33–34, 36–37
    Wilkes expedition "scientifics," 39
extreme political parties, 208

F
Fairy, 44
farmers' markets, 131, 214
farms. *See* agriculture
federal regulation, of tidelands, 135–36
federal spending, during Great Depression, 207
Federal Union, 194–95
feminist bands, 216
Fenton, S. W., 96
Ferndale Lumber, 148
Ferry, Elisha, 87f
ferry service, for Black Lake, 64
festivals, 216
Fidalgo, Salvador, 30
fill land, for industrial sites, 88
Finnish Lutheran Church, 151
Fir Tree, lumber mill, 102
fire department changes, 197
fires
    in Bucoda, 92, 100, 102
    courthouse gutted by, 75f
    in Gate, 148
    by the KKK, 201
    in Maytown, 154
    in Rainier, 102
    at Seatco Prison, 101
    at South Union, 155f
    in Tenino, 94
    USO Club arson, 210f, 211
    in Yelm, 98
First Peoples. *See* Native Americans
First Salmon celebrations, 17
first-growth timber, depletion of, 108, 146
fish die-offs, from pollution, 192
Fish Wars (1960s), 24, 27

fishing equipment, of Native Americans, 16f, 17
fishing rights
    fight for, 24
    as specified in treaties, 20, 22
    See also Billy Frank Jr. Nisqually National Wildlife Refuge
Fleetwood, 46, 46f
Fleetwood family, 62
Fleetwoods, 221
Fleming, Julia C., 146
flour mills, 57, 58, 65
flu epidemic (1918), 199
Flying Fish, USS, 39
Follensby, Professor, 109f
food banks, 219, 219f
food sources
    geoduck harvesting, 14f
    of Native Americans, 13–14, 16–17, 20f, 90
Ford, S. S., 73
Ford, Sidney and Nancy, 64
forestry, sustained yield, 164
Fort Lewis Army Base, 210
Foss Marine, 48
Foster, George, 47, 169–70
4-H, 128
4L (Loyal Legion of Loggers and Lumbermen), 195, 200
Fourth Avenue bridge, 194, 199, 202
Fowler, Henry, 62
Foy Store, 92
Frank, Billy, Jr.
    fishing rights fight led by, 24, 27
    photo of, 27f
    Presidential Medal of Freedom, 27
Fraser River, 31–32, 32, 32f
Frazier, Catherine and Andrew, 62
free speech restrictions, 199
Freedom, 62
Freedom Hall, 63f
Freedom Homemaker's Club, 63f
Freeman, Minnie, 109f
French, Charlotte Emily Olney, 87, 145, 145f
French, John, 46, 87
French, Washington, 87
Fuller, Fay, 99, 99f
fur trading posts, 18–19, 71

G

Gale, J. A., 135
Gardner, Booth, 50
Garfield School, Olympia, 110f
Garland, Jerome, 100
Gaston, George, 196
Gate, 148, 148f
Gate City Lumber Company, 148
Gate School, 148
Gehrke, Albert and Maria, 102
Gelbach Flour Mill, 58
Gel-lop-it-ith. *See* Gate
gender equality, in music, 216
geoduck harvesting, 14f
George, Fort, 31, 39
George S. Allen & Son Logging Co., 172f
Georgia, Strait of, 30f, 40
Georgiana, 41
Gephart, Magdalena, 126
Germans, as "enemy aliens," 211–12
Gholson, Richard Dickerson, 43
Gibbs, George, 19
Gibson family, 65
Giddings, Edward, 46
Gitskan, slave raids by, 29
Glacial Heritage Preserve, 219
Glasgow, Thomas and Julia, 62
Goldman & Rosenblatt store, 84
Goodell family, 65
government, expansion of, 215
Grand Coulee Dam, 209
Grand Mound
    about, 143–44, 143f
    along NP railroad corridor, 127
    Chehalis settlement at, 14, 18, 32
    reservation at, 23
    settlers at, 62, 65
    women's suffrage at, 145
Grange Insurance Association, 133
Grange Movement, 128, 132–33, 132f, 147
    See also *specific granges*
Grange Week, 133f
Grant, Ulysses S., 87
grave robbery, 23
Graves, Michael, 193
Gray, Robert, 50
Grays Harbor
    landmarks en route, 154
    routes to, 126, 148

Grays Harbor County, Thurston County inclusion of, 61
Great Britain, United States joint occupancy treaty with, 31, 33, 33f
Great Depression
    about, 205–7
    irrigation system impact from, 128
    phases of/responses to, 207–9
    poor farm closure of, 194
Great Northern Railway, 171
Great Wolf Lodge, 25, 144
Greyhound, 46, 46f
gristmills, 2, 56, 161
Gruber-Docherty Mill, 98, 102, 169f, 207
Güemes Padilla Horcasitas y Aguayo, Juan Vicente de, 30
guilty verdicts, 200
Gull Harbor, crops from, 130–31

H
Habitat for Humanity, 219
Haida Gwaii, shipwreck in, 41
Haidas, 41
Hale, Calvin, 111
Hale, Horatio, 38, 38f, 39
Hale, Pamela Tower Case, 111, 111f
Hale Passage, 38f
Hammersley Inlet, 36–37
Hands On Children's Museum, 90
Hanna, Kathleen, 216
Hanson, Charles, 169–70
Hanson, Ole, 199
Hard Times Frolic, 203
Harm & Brown Lumber Company, logging railroad, 95
Haro Strait, as international boundary, 35f
"Harriman City," 137
Harstad Lumber Company, 98
Hartman, Sarah McAllister, 66
Hartsock, India Ann, 64
Hartsuck, Charles A., 24f
Hastings, Frank, 199–200, 247nn31–32
hate groups, 208
Hawaiians (Kanaka), in Thurston County, 31
Hawk, John W., 62, 90–91
Hawks Prairie, 62, 92
health issues. *See* mortality
Hearne, Samuel, 29
Heck, Lena, 20f

Helping Hand, 198
Helser, David, 135
Helsing Junction, 151, 170f
hemlock mill, 153
Henderson, James, 37
Henderson House, 59
Henderson Inlet
    Dana Passage and, 39
    naming of, 37
    oyster harvesting at, 136
Henness, Benjamin Lee, 143–44
Henness, Fort, 143–44, 144f
Henry, Hewitt A., 117
Henry McCleary Timber Company, 154
herbal medicine, by Native Americans, 17
Hercules Quarry, 96
Hercules Sandstone Company, 95
Heritage Hall, 206, 209
Hewitt, C. C., 117
Hezeta, Bruno de, 30
Hicks, Urban East and Eliza Jane, 64
Hicks family, 62
Hicks Lake, 64, 91, 93
high schools
    Avanti High School, 109
    earliest of, 108
    Olympia High School, 110f, 130
    William Winlock Miller High School, 110f
highways
    Highway 99, 214f
    Highway 101, 59
    impact of, 215
    Interstate 5, 59, 59f, 90, 93, 214f
    Littlerock to Tumwater road, 125
    Olympic, 89, 202
    Pacific, 89, 92, 94, 202
    water travel replaced by, 47, 202
Hill, Bennett, 41
Hill, Mathew, 118
Hillman, C. D., 137
Hilpert, David A., 126
Hilpert Farm, 125, 126
Himes, George, 62
Himes, Lestitia Z., 62, 63f
Himes, Tyrus and Emeline, 62
Himes family, 62, 90–91
historic preservation, 221
Hobo Point, 194

Hodgdon, Stephen and Deborah, 94
Hodgdon's Station, 94
Hogum Bay, 92
Holloweena tribe, 29, 32, 36
Homann, Al, 215f
home front, 194f, 198–99, 210–11
homelessness, 194, 219
homes, as schools, 106
Homestead Act (1862), 122
Homo a Go Go (festival), 216
Hopkins, Ebenezer, 55f
hop-picking, 126f
Hoquiam, railroad connections, 151
Horr, Samuel, 46
horse racing, 91f, 92
horses, Native Americans' ownership of, 13
hostilities, Puget Sound tribes vs. settlers, 23
Hotel Olympia, 111
Hotel Rochester, 146f
housing, of Native Americans, 17–18
Howard, Alexander and Rebecca Groundage, 84, 85
Howe, Samuel D., 41
Hudson, Captain, 39
Hudson's Bay Company
    Fort Nisqually established by, 90
    fur trading/agriculture by, 18–19
    and Native Americans balance with, 41
    Northwest Company absorption by, 31
    outposts proximity to Thurston County, 71
    rights purchased by U.S., 19
    settler opposition to, 71
    Simmons/Bush employment for, 55
    Thurston as foe of, 72
    Tumwater Falls as transfer point, 52
    U.S. government purchase of, 19, 39
    Wilkes guided by, 33
    in Yelm, 98
Huggins, George, 92
Humane Society, 198
hunger, 219, 219f
Hunter, Alfred and Sara Emma Daniels, 138
Hunter, George, 138
Hunter Point, 138
Hunter-ONeil-Boyd General Merchandise Store, 146f
Huntington, H. D., 74f
Hurd, J. F., 247n11

I

Ich-tals. *See* Rochester
immigrants, 188, 213–14
Independence, 151
Independence Day celebrations, 191
Independence Ladies Aid, 151f
Independence Logging Company, 162f
Indian Agents, Simmons as, 56
Indian Claims Commission, 23
Indian Gaming Regulatory Act (1988), 24
Indian girls and canoe, Puget Sound, 9f
Indian schools
    about, 23
        Indian Boys' School at Priest Point, 83, 105, 105f
        Wa He Lut Indian School, 25
Indian Shaker Church, 15
Indian Summer Golf & Country Club, 124f
Indian War (1855 - 1856), 35f
Indians. *See* Native Americans
Indigenous Peoples. *See* Native Americans
industrial pollution
    Carlyon Fill and, 190–91
    fish die-offs from, 192
    oyster decimation from, 136
    view of, 195f
Industrial Workers of the World (IWW; Wobblies)
    about, 191f
    Everett Massacre, 45
    during the Red Scare, 199–201
    in South Puget Sound, 194, 195
    on street speaking, 247n11
infant mortality, 196
Influenza Pandemic (1918), 199
Inside Passage, exploration of, 30f
insurance, for farmers, 133
intermarriage
    among tribes, 17
    fur trappers and Native women, 19
    interracial, 54
international boundary. *See* United States-Canadian border
International Pop Underground Convention, 216
internment of Japanese, 211–12
Interstate 5 freeway, 59, 59f, 90, 93, 214f
Iola, 45
Iroquois, in Thurston County, 31
Italians, as "enemy aliens," 211–12
"It's the Water," 176

IWW. *See* Industrial Workers of the World
Iyall, Cynthia, 12

J
J. J. Brenner Oyster Company, 136, 136f
J. M. Adams Acre Tracts, 91
Jack, Kanaka and Kiki, 138
Jackson, Charles, 200
James, Anna Maria, 66f
James, Arthur, 66f
James, Clara Minnie Hell, 66f
James, Cornellia Saccoon, 66f
James, David, 66f
James, Eliza, 66f
James, Elizabeth, 66f
James, John Rogers, 64, 123
James, Jon Rogers, 66f
James, Mary Ann Frances, 66f
James, Richard Oregon, 66f
James, Samuel, 66f, 144
James, Samuel and Anna Maria, 65
James, Thomas, 66f
James, Toone Ah and Nettie Chiang, 187f
James, William, 66f
James family, 65
James McIntosh Tram Road, 160f
Japanese, internment of, 211–12
Japanese oyster drill (boring worm), 136
Jim Case lumber mill, 98
Jingle Club, 208
Johnson, Calvin, 216, 216f
Johnson, J. R., 138
Johnson Point, 138
Joint Base Lewis-McChord, 93, 100, 193, 213
joint occupation treaty (1818 - 1827), 31, 33, 33f, 71
Jonas Spar & Lumber Company, 95
Jones, Elizabeth, 22f
Juan de Fuca, Strait of, 30f, 40
judicial bias, 200
Judson, Phoebe Goodell, 83, 84, 87
Jungmayer, Perry, 210
Junior Grange, 133

K
K Records label, 216
Kalama, Joe, 13
Kelly, Pete, 181f
Kelly, Walt, 181f

Kendall Company store, 87
Kenney, Frank M., 180f
Kladys family, 62
Kl-ko-minn. *See* Chambers Prairie
Knight, J. Z., 98, 100
Koepkey, Fred, 190f
Kopiah, 152
Krise, Charlene
    on cedar, 14
    on disease decimation, 18
    on longhouse construction, 17
    on Squaxin Island tribal misery, 23
Ku Klux Klan (KKK) revival, 201
Kuntz, J. E., 200
Kwalhioqua Tribe, 21f

L
L. N. Rice and Company, 128
labor
    mobility of, 192
    strikes, 199, 200, 247n22
    unions, 45, 191f, 194–95, 199–201
        See also Industrial Workers of the
        World; *specific unions*
Labor Day parade, 93f
labor projects, as meal ticket, 198
Lacey
    history of, 90–93
    incorporation of, 93, 213, 215
    population growth in, 213
    settlers at, 62
    state offices in, 215
Lacey, O. C., 91
Lacey Women's Club, 93
Ladenburg, John, 12
Ladies' First Aid, 201
Ladies' Relief Society, 198
Lady Washington, 50, 50f
Ladyfest (festival), 216
Lake Superior and Puget Sound Land Company, 94
land allotments, for qualified Indians, 23
Lane, Joseph, 74, 236n8
Lange, Edward, 61f, 160f, 177f, 188f
Langley, Fort, 32
Langlie, Arthur B., 51, 118
Langlie, Jimmie, 117f
lavender, as statewide leader in, 131
Lawrence, Asa, 73

Lawrence, Lake, 139–40
Lawrence, Lindley and Sam, 139
Lea Lumber Company. *See* Tumwater Lumber Company
Legislative Building
    architects for, 190
    building of, 90
    details of, 116f
    view of, 117f, 119f
legislators' lodging, at St. Peter Hospital, 86
Lemon, Gerry, 118, 119
Leschi, Territory of Washington vs., 11f
Leschi of the Nisqually
    conviction/sentencing/execution of, 10, 11f, 23
    exoneration of, 12
    portrait of, 10f
    quote attributed to, 25
    Tolmie as friend of, 19, 38f
    at treaty negotiations, 9, 20
Lewis, Fort, Nisqually land condemned for, 23
    See also Joint Base Lewis-McChord
Lewis, Heather, 216
Lewis County
    formation of, 71
    Hudson's Bay farming in, 19
    Simmons' move to, 56
    Thurston County created from, 73
"Liberty Ships," 49
Liichaat, 13
Lincoln, Abraham, 22, 117
Lincoln Flour Mill, 57
Lindstrom and Hanford, lumber mill, 102
Linklater, Thomas and Mary, 62
Little Hollywood
    about, 194
    elimination by Capitol Lake, 90
    government demolition/burning of, 205f
Littlejohn, A. J., 47
Littlerock
    about, 148
    agriculture at, 125
    along NP railroad corridor, 127
    downtown, 149f
    Rutledge Farm at, 125, 125f
    to Tumwater, 125
    United Methodist Church, 148f
    women's suffrage at, 145
Littlerock Hotel, 149f

livestock, 19, 124, 131
locomotives
    Baldwin, 173f
    Heisler, 173, 174f
    homemade, 172f
    Shay, 169f, 173
logging
    about, 159–66
    companies
        listing of, 161t
        Bordeaux Brothers Logging Company, 153
        Independence Logging Company, 162f
        Mason County Logging Company, 154f, 164
        Mumby Shingle and Lumber Company, 153
        Mutual Lumber Company, 162f
        Weyerhaeuser Timber Company, 152, 164, 166f, 167
    as non-sustainable, 192
    railroads used for. *See* railroads
    trucks for, 164, 173
Long Lake, 62, 92, 93
Long Term Agricultural designation, 131
longhouses, 17–18
Longmire, James and Virinda, 62, 67f, 98
Louisson & Company store, 84
Lower Chehalis people. *See* Chehalis tribe
Loyal League of Washington, 199
Loyal Legion of Loggers and Lumbermen (4L), 195, 200
lumber mills
    listing of, 165t
    exports from, 202
    on Lake Lawrence, 139
    mobility of, 192
    peak production from, 164
    processing, 88, 89
    Puget Sound Agricultural Company supplied by, 66
Lummi tribe, 29
Lundsford, Bret, 216
Lushootseed, 12–13, 20

M
Mabie, Jeremiah, 65
Magnolia, 46
mail fraud conviction, 137

Main Street. *See* Capitol Way
mall construction, 90
Manifest Destiny, 53, 60
Maple Lane School, 130, 144
Marches of the Hungry, 206f, 207–8
Marcus Pavilion, 93
Marcy, Ada, 66
maritime industries, contemporary, 49
markets
    for beer, 179, 184
    for canned foods, 130
    for farm products, 127
    for lumber, 159, 173
    for Tenino sandstone, 96
Marsh, Edwin, 83
Marshville, 83, 87
Martin, Clarence, 137
Martin, J. B., 139
Martin, William, 65
Mason County Logging Company
    about, 164
    at Bordeaux, 154f
    railway as subsidiary of, 173
    strike at, 200
    view of, 171f
Mason County, Thurston County inclusion of, 61
Masonic Temple, 190f
Massachusetts, USS, 41, 43
maternal mortality, 196
Mathews, Sharon, 48, 120, 115, 132
Matson, Elias, 199–200, 247n31
Maytown, 154
Maytown School, 154f
McAllister, Charlotte Smith, 66
McAllister, James, 66
McAllister, John Wesley and Mary Jane Thomas, 66–67
McAllister family, crops, 124–25
McArthur, W. M., 96
McChord Air Force Base, 210
McDonald, "Bagpipe Bill," 167
McDonald, R. A., 167
McElroy, William, 100
McIntosh, James, 163
McIvor, George, 174f
McKay, Thomas, 32
McKenny, Margaret, 219
McKenzie family, 98
McKinley, William, assassination of, 196f

McLoughlin, John, 54, 55, 72
McMicken, Helen Parker, 105f
McMillan, James, 31–32
McMillan family, 62
McNeill, William, 41
Mead, Albert, 117
meal tickets, work in exchange for, 198
Mecca Normal/ Beat Happening/Fugazi Show, 216f
medical care
    cost of, 196–97
    as paid in goods, 206
    prepaid, 86
Medicine Creek treaty negotiations
    about, 9, 13f
    fishing rights assured by, 27
    goals of, 19–20
    tree marking location of, 18f
Men Behind the Seattle Spirit—Argus Cartoons (Chadwick), 181f
Mendota, 152
Mentzer Brothers, logging railroad, 95
Menzies, Archibald, 29, 37–39, 37f
mercantile stores, 84
Mercy (animal rights), 198
Messegee, Cassandra, 199
Messenger, 45
Methodist denomination camp meetings, 148, 150f
migrant laborers, 192, 194
Miles, Luella, 125
military
    Washington Territorial Volunteers, 143–44
    during World War I/II. *See* World War I; World War II
military training, 210–11
Miller, William Winlock, 83
Miller family, 65
Millersylvania State Park, 208f, 209
Milwaukee Railroad, 151, 170f, 171
Mima Mounds Natural Area Preserve, 219
Mima Prairie/Mima Mounds, 33–34, 36, 65–66, 148
mining
    for coal, 95, 152, 152f
    as non-sustainable, 192
    railroad use for, 95
Ministerial Association, 198
Minute Women, 198–99
Mission of St. Josephs, 124

Mitchell I and *II, United States v.*, 24
Mizpah, 46, 46f
"Moaning Minnie" (air raid siren), 209
Monticello Convention, 74f, 236n8
Moon, Slim, 216
moonshine production, 202
Morning Mist (Haida wife), 43
The Morning Olympian, 91, 154
Morris, Bob, 149f
Morris, Clarence, 149f
Morris, Mark, 149f
mortality
 epidemics, 18
 infant/maternal, 196
 in 1918 flu epidemic, 199
 in World War II, 213
mosaic plant disease devastation, 205
Moses, A. B., 9
Moses, A. J., 84
Moses, Lizzie, 83
Moses, Simpson P., 41, 83
Mosman family, 98
Mosquito Fleet, 43–48
Moss Lake, 215
Mother Joseph, 86
Mothers' Pensions, 208
motorcycle police officer, 190f
Mottman, James Frederick "Fritz," 118, 119
Mottman Industrial Park, 59
Mountain View Golf Course, 92–93
mountaineering newspaper column, 99
Mounts, Catherine McLeod, 69
Mounts basket collection, 69
Muckleshoot tribe
 reservation of, 20
 at treaty negotiations, 9, 18f
Mud Bay log dump, 174–75f
Mud Bay Logging Company, 173, 174f, 175, 200
Mud Bay (Totten Inlet), 136
Multnomah, 48f
Mumby Shingle and Lumber Company, 153
Munro, Ralph, 50
Murphy, John Miller
 Washington Standard, 201
mushrooms, as statewide leader in, 131
music, 216
Mutual Aid Fair. *See* Thurston County Fair
Mutual Lumber Company
 about, 102

Mutual Lumber Company *(continued)*
 closing of, 205, 214
 Great Depression impact on, 205
 locomotive owned by, 162f
 railroad owned by, 164
 reopening of, 207

N

naming landforms, by explorers, 30f, 33, 36–37
narrow-gauge railroads, 169, 173
National Canning Company, 130
National Oceanographic and Atmospheric Agency (NOAA), 35f
National Register of Historic Places
 Colvin Ranch, 126
 Dofflemyer Point Lighthouse, 137f
 Erickson farmstead, 127f
 Gate School, 148
 Monticello Convention site, 74f
 Seatco Prison, 101
National Youth Administration, 208
Native American longhouse, 220f
Native Americans
 Alaska Native slave raids, 41
 camas root/crops of, 120, 121
 compensation for BIA mismanagement, 24
 fishing at Tumwater Falls, 52
 history of
  Leschi trial/execution, 9–12
  lifestyle before European arrival, 12–14, 16–18
  post-European arrival, 18–20, 22–23
  snarl of land ownership, 23
  tribal enterprises/successes, 24–25
 as hop-pickers, 126f
 and Hudson's Bay Company balance with, 41
 land claims, efforts to extinguish, 72
 as Naval Militia enlistees, 47
 personalities
  Frank, Billy, Jr. *See* Frank, Billy, Jr.
  Parsons, Nancy Jim, 68
  Slocum, John, 15
 shellfish harvesting, 135
 at Tumwater Falls, 2
 in western Washington, 21f
Natural Resources Conservation Area, 152
Naval Militia, 47
navigation by sound, 44–45
navigation lights, ships guided by, 137, 138

Nelson, Andrew and Gustave, 126
New Deal programs, 108, 208–9, 208f
New York Stock Exchange, crash (October 1929), 205
Newell, Gordon
    Rogues, Buffoons & Statesmen, 117
Ninemire-Morgan Mill, 151
1918 flu epidemic, 199
Nippon Maru, 50
Niscloten. *See* Skookumchuck Valley
Nisqually, 66
Nisqually, Fort
    building of, 18
    establishment of, 90
    Tolmie at, 19
    view of, 121f
    as Wilkes' headquarters, 33
    wintering over at, 55
Nisqually Delta Association, 219
Nisqually Land Trust, 219
Nisqually River
    irrigation water from, 128
    temporary bridge on, 228f
    See also Billy Frank Jr. Nisqually National Wildlife Refuge
Nisqually tribe
    about, 29
    enterprises of, 24–25
    environmentalism of, 219
    fishing rights fight, 24
    Hale's studies of, 38f
    land claims payment to, 23
    as original inhabitants, 8, 12, 90
    photo of, 10f
    precontact lifestyle of, 13
    reservation of
        about, 20, 22, 223f
        condemnation for Camp Lewis, 23
    at treaty negotiations, 9, 18f
    Wa He Lut Indian School, 25
Nisqually Valley, farmland preservation in, 131
NOAA (National Oceanographic and Atmospheric Agency), 35f
Noe, Isom J., 154
non-Indian land ownership on reservations, 23
non-treaty tribes, 22
Nooksack tribe, 29
Norpia Stock Company, 137
North Shore Surf Club, 216

Northcraft family, 65
Northern Light, 48f
Northern Pacific Railway
    agreement on Point Defiance Line, 171
    in Bucoda, 100
    to Grays Harbor, 148
    in Independence, 151
    in Lacey, 91
    level grades for, 95
    in Rochester, 146
    Sherlock Station (Nisqually), 230f
    small towns along, 127
    in Tenino, 94, 95, 169
    in Yelm, 98
The Northwest Coast: Or, Three Years' Residence in Washington Territory (Swan), 22
Northwest Company, Hudson's Bay Company absorption of, 31
Northwest Indian Fisheries Commission, 27
Northwest Passage, exploration for, 28, 29
Núñez Gaona, 30

O

oak woodlands, 217f, 219
Oakland Bay pulp mills, sulfite poisoning from, 136
Obama, Barack, 27
Oblates of Mary Immaculate, 83, 105
Odd Fellows Hall, 102
Offut Lake, 91f
Old Homestead Inn, 138, 139f
Old Ironsides (*Constitution*, USS), 47f, 50, 95
Old State Capitol, 190
Olden, Robert, 129
Oliphant, Ethelbert, 117
Olympia
    as All-America City, 90
    centennial of, 89f
    Chinatown in, 187f, 188
    as county seat, 73–74
    downtown expansion, 190
    founding of, 58
    government of, 90
    incorporation of, 87
    Old Ironsides in, 47f
    Percival House and, 232f
    precinct at, 73
    settlers at, 62
    as state capital, challenges to, 113–19, 236n7

Olympia *(continued)*
   street scenes in, 84f, 88f
   view of, 81f, 188f
   wooden money of, 95, 95f
   1845 - 1889, 80–87
   1889 - present, 87–90
   1889 - 1929
      about, 187–88
      economic cycles, 190–92
      issues of the era, 192, 194
      population growth, 188
      Prohibition, 201–2
      reform, 194–98
      unrest, 199–201
      World War I, 198–99
Olympia & Chehalis Valley Railroad, 161, 169, 171, 172f
Olympia & Mt. Rainier Railroad, 170
Olympia & Tenino Railroad, 95, 169
Olympia Airport
   Bush homestead proximity to, 55f, 56
   industrial areas around, 59
Olympia Art League, 221
Olympia brewery
   artesian water for, 179
   in cartoons, 180–81f
   history of
      years preceding, 177–79
      founding/operation of, 179–81, 183–84
      name change, 179f, 180
      Prohibition/repeal of, 180f, 181, 183–84, 207
      demise of, 185, 185f, 214
   I-5 route influenced by, 59
   illustrations of, 177f, 180f, 183–85f
   "It's the Water," 176, 177, 180, 180f
   transportation to, 172
Olympia Cannery, 190
Olympia Canning Company, 89, 130
Olympia Experimental Music Festival, 216
Olympia Film Society, 221
Olympia Gas Works, 111
Olympia Golf and Country Club, 203
Olympia Harbor Lumber, 207
Olympia High School, 110f, 130
Olympia Knitting Mill, 189f
Olympia Ladies Relief Society, 111
Olympia Light and Power Company, 58f, 129–30, 140, 172
Olympia National Bank, 205

Olympia Oyster Company, 135, 136
Olympia oyster (*Ostrea lurida*), 135
Olympia Shipbuilding Company, 45–46
Olympia Terminal Railway Company, 172
Olympia Trades Council, 194
Olympia Transit Company, 172–73
Olympia Treaty (1856), 22
Olympia Tumwater Foundation, 182
Olympia Veneer, 89
Olympic Auto Camp, 57f
Olympic University, 191
Olympus, MV, 51, 51f
one-room schools, contemporary use of, 109
one-school districts, 106
open primary, Grange role in, 132
oral history, 18
Order of Saint Benedict, land purchase by, 92
Oregon Country Provisional Government, 71
Oregon Spectator, 236n7
Oregon Territory (1848), 71, 73f
Oregon Trail
   about, 2
   Bigelow (D.R.) on, 82
   Bush-Simmons party on, 53
   deaths on, 65
   markers for, 144
   Rutledge on, 125
   See also Cowlitz Trail
Organic Act, 115
Ostrea lurida (Olympia oyster), 135
Owillapsh tribe, extinction of, 21f
oxen hauling logs, 159f
Oxford Bar, 149f
ox-hobbles, 48f
Oyster Bay. *See* Eld Inlet
oysters
   beds preparation, 141f
   harvesting of, 134–36, 135f, 141f

P
Pabst Brewing Company, Olympia brewery purchase by, 185
Pacific, charting of, 37
Pacific House Hotel, 84, 85
Pacific Power and Light, 152
Packwood family, 62, 66
Page, Emma, 198f, 201
Page, Mary, 201
Panic of 1893, 94, 148, 171, 190

Panorama City retirement community, 93
Pariseau, Esther. *See* Mother Joseph
Parker Colter & Co., 84
Parsons, John, 69
Parsons, Nancy Jim, 68f
Parsons family, 62
patriotism, 198–99
Patrons of Husbandry. *See* Grange Movement
Pattison, Jane, 62
Pattison family, 62
Pattison Lake, 62, 92, 92f, 93
Pavtin, Pierre, 32
Peacock, USS, 38f, 39
Peale, Titian, 38, 39
Pearl, Orpha and Della, 126
Pearl Harbor, Japanese attack on, 209
Pederson, Candace, 216
Penn, Dan, 16
People's University, 191–92
Percival, Sam, 46
Percival, Samuel and Lurana, 87
Percival House, Olympia, 232f
Percival Landing, murals surrounding, 25f
Perez, Juan, 30
Pettit and White, lumber mill, 98, 102
Phillips family, 62
photography studio, 62
Pickering, Charles, 39
Pickett, George Edward, 43, 43f
Pickett, Jimmie, 43
Pierce, Franklin, 19, 113
Pig War (1859), 35f, 43
Pike, Charlie, 167
"Pine Tree" Washington Hotel, 84, 84f
Pioneer Rock, 154
Plumb, William, 126
Point Defiance Line, 95, 171, 175
Point Moody. *See* Johnson Point
pole lamps, ships guided by, 137
police
　police chief resignation, 197
　Progressive reforms impact of, 197
　raids on "enemy aliens," 212
　salary reductions, 206
　shantytowns burned by, 194
　technology adoption by, 190f
political prisoners, at Leavenworth penitentiary, 200
Poncin, Gamma and Eliza, 138, 138f, 140f

poor houses/farms, 194
population
　in 1853, 61
　in 1880, 67
　in 1960s/1970s, 90
　after statehood, 188
　environmental impact of, 219
　growth of, 213
　in Tenino, 94, 98
　in Yelm, 100
Porpoise, USS, 34, 39
Port Gamble, battle of, 41
Port of Olympia
　as deepwater port, 88
　formation of, 49
　role of, 89
　services offered by, 214
　voter approval of, 202
Port Townsend, Olympia brewery at, 180
Port Townsend Southern Railroad, 95, 169, 171
Portland & Puget Sound Railroad, 171
postal service
　about, 83
　at Coal Bank, 94
　Grange role in, 133
　at Littlerock, 148
　at Sherlock Station, 228f
　Thurston's role in, 72
poultry, 131, 146
poverty
　chronic, 194
　labor projects and, 198
　See also economic cycles
Powell, John Wesley, 21f
prairies
　vs. forested land, 61
　preservation of, 217f, 219
Prairies Appreciation Day, 219
Prater, Lois, 194
Pray, James B., 154
Prays Lake. *See* Summit Lake
Preemption Act (1841), 122
Presidential Medal of Freedom, Frank as recipient of, 27
price wars, among steamers, 44
Priest Point Park, 83, 83f, 191
Prince family, 65
"Princess Charlotte," 36

280　Index

Printers' Local, 194–95
prison labor, 101
Procession of the Species Celebration, 221f
"Progressive Era" (1890-1920), 196
Prohibition, 180f, 181, 201–2
prostitution, 197–98
Providence Academy, 108f
Providence Saint Amable boarding school, 86
Providence St. Peter Hospital, 86
prudent harvesting, by Native Americans, 16
public health problems. *See* mortality
public places, creation of, 191
Public Works Administration, 208
Puget, Peter, 29, 31f, 37f
Puget Sound
    chart of, 35f
    exploration of, 29–30, 30f
    to Grays Harbor, migration route, 126, 148
    landmarks en route, 154
    pollution of, 192
    in Salish Sea, 40
    as transportation corridor, 44
Puget Sound Agricultural Company, 19, 121
Puget Sound Indian War (1855-56)
    about, 22–23
    Leschi and, 9–10
    naval role in, 42–43
    school during, 106
    settler deaths during, 62, 66
    stockade at Grand Mound Prairie, 143–44
    stockade construction during, 62
Puget Sound Power & Light, as streetcar operator, 172
Purchase of Development Rights, 131
Puyallup tribe
    about, 29
    fishing rights fight, 24
    reservation of, 20, 223f
    at treaty negotiations, 9, 18f

Q
Queen Charlotte Islands. *See* Haida Gwaii, shipwreck in
Quiemuth of the Nisqually, 9–10, 20, 23
Quileute tribe, 20, 22
Quinault tribe, 20, 22
Quixote Village, 219

R
Rabbeson, Antonio, 10
racism
    Japanese internment as, 211–12
    in Missouri, 53
    in Oregon City, 54
radicals, arrest of, 199
railroad land grants, 122
railroad spur, 89
railroads
    about, 169–75
    map of, 157f
    companies
        Burlington Northern Santa Fe Railway, 175f
        Great Northern Railway, 171
        Milwaukee Railroad, 151, 170f, 171
        Northern Pacific. *See* Northern Pacific Railway
        Olympia & Tenino Railroad, 95, 169
        Olympia Terminal Railway Company, 172
        Port Townsend Southern Railroad, 95, 169, 171
        Portland & Puget Sound Railroad, 171
        Tacoma, Olympia & Grays Harbor Railroad, 171
        Union Pacific Railroad, 151, 152, 170f, 171–72, 175f
        Westside Railway Company, 172
    for logging
        listing of, 161t
        Black Hills & Northwestern Railway, 164, 173
        Black Lake & Sherman Valley Railroad, 170
        Bordeaux, 153
        Chehalis Western Railroad, 164, 169, 173f, 175
        Mentzer Brothers, 95
        Mutual Lumber Company, 164
        Olympia & Chehalis Valley Railroad, 161, 169, 171, 172f
        Olympia & Mt. Rainier Railroad, 170
        Skookum Railway & Logging Company, 95
        Skookumchuck Railroad, 164, 175
        in Tenino, 95
        Thurston County Railway, 173, 174–75f

railroads *(continued)*
    in Vail, 152f
    Weyerhaeuser Timber Company, 164, 166f
    logging precursors for
        oxen/horses, 159f, 163, 170
        skid roads, 159f, 163, 164, 169
        standard steel rails, 163
        tram roads, 159f, 163, 170
    population growth from, 188
    trucks as replacement for, 164, 175
Rainier, 102, 102–3f
Rainier, Mount
    ascent of, 99
    naming of, 13
    views of, 102
Rainier Training Area, 210
Ramtha's School of Enlightenment, 98, 100
Rand McNally & Company's Lumberman's Directory, 163–64
ransom payment, 41
rate bill schools, 106
rationing of consumer goods, 210
real estate prices, Yelm Irrigation System and, 128
Reavis, Judge, 109f
Rector, Emma Peck, 126
Red Cross, 197, 198
Red Scare, 195, 199
Redding, Thomas, 45
reforestation, 164, 166
refugees, 213–14
Reichel, H. L., 167
religions, of Native Americans, 15
reservations
    location of, 223f
    maps of, 223f
    negotiations for, 19–20, 22–23
    See also *specific reservations*
Retail Clerks' Union, 194–95
Rhoads, T. M. and Mary, 146
Ricard, Pascal, Fr., 83, 124
Rice family, 98
Rich, William, 39
Richardsonian Romanesque architecture, 75f, 88
Ricker, Cordelia, 126
Riot Grrrls, 216
rising sea levels, likely impact of, 190
Robinson family, 137

Rochester
    about, 146
    along NP railroad corridor, 127
    crops from, 130–31
    street scene in, 146f
Rochester Grange, 147
Rocky Prairie, agriculture at, 125
Rodgers, John, 196f
Rogers, Edmund, 197
Rogues, Buffoons & Statesmen (Newell), 117
Roosevelt, Franklin D., 207, 208, 211–12
Roosevelt, Teddy, 201f
Roosevelt federal programs, 207, 208
Rosenthal, Kate, 84
Rotch, Francis, 100
Royal Society, plant specimens for, 29
Ruddell, Stephen Duley, 62
Ruddell, Winiford Kelly Hicks Croghan, 62, 64
Ruddell family, 90–91
Ruddle, S. T., 132
rural free delivery, Grange role in, 133
Russell, Donald G., 96
Russell House, 93
Russian Alaska colony, Hudson's Bay as suppliers for, 19
Rutledge, Bert Vincent and Cecil, 149f
Rutledge, Bob, 149f
Rutledge, Clarence, 149f
Rutledge, George Washington, 65
Rutledge, Louisa, 149f
Rutledge, Mark, 149f
Rutledge, Thomas, 65, 125–26, 149f
Rutledge, William and Zella, 149f
Rutledge family, crops, 125
Rutledge Farm, 125–26, 125f
Rutledge Lake. *See* Hicks Lake

S

S & P Company, Pabst purchase by, 185
S'~mamish tribe, at treaty negotiations, 18f, 20
SABMiller, Olympia brewery closure by, 185
Saegar, Calvin and Mary, 48f
Sagawa, Kati, 218
Sa-heh-wamish tribe, at treaty negotiations, 18f, 20
sailing ships, economics of, 47–48
Saint Clair, Lake, 63f, 93
Saint Clair Station (Northern Pacific Railroad), 171
Saint Joseph Olympia mission, 105f

Saint Joseph's of New Market (mission), 83
Saint Martin's University
   about, 192
   evolution of, 193
   expansion of, 93
   land purchased for, 92
   Old Main at, 193f
   view of, 93f
Saint Michael's School, 86
salary reductions, Great Depression and, 206
Salem, OR, Olympia brewery at, 180
Salish people
   dialects of, 12–13, 20
   Hale's studies of, 38f, 39
   in Lacey, 93
   in Olympia, 81
   social/political organization of, 29
   as victims of slave raids, 41
   See also *specific Salish tribes*
Salish Sea, 29–30, 40
Salish welcome figure, 25f
salmon, Native American outlook on, 17
Salvation Army, 208, 217
San Francisco, CA, Olympia brewery at, 180
Sand Man, 48, 49f
Sargent, Asher and Matilda, 62
Sarjent, E. Nelson and Rebecca, 62
Satellite, HMS, 35f
Sat-sulth. *See* Dodge Prairie
sawmills
   listing of, 163t
   about, 202
   as electric powered, 92
   in Gate, 148
   hydroelectric power for, 58
   local, 163–64
   in Tumwater, 161
   in Yelm, 98
Scalopine, John, 14, 17–18
Scatter Creek, 62, 64, 65, 126
Scheel, H. P., 96
Schelm. *See* Yelm
Schilter family farm, 131f
Schmidt, Adolph, Jr., 183
Schmidt, Clara (daughter), 182f
Schmidt, Clara Muench (mother), 182, 182f
Schmidt, Fritz and Georgia Hunter, 138, 139f
Schmidt, Leopold
   about, 177–81

Schmidt, Leopold *(continued)*
   cartoons of, 180–81f
   ethics of, 182
   photo of, 178f
   Swiss chalet donated by, 191
Schmidt, Louis, 179
Schmidt, Margaret, 182f
Schmidt, Marie, 182f
Schmidt, Peter G., Sr.
   at Olympia brewery, 179, 181, 183
   photos of, 178f, 182f
Schmidt, Peter, Jr., 182
Schmidt, Robert, 183
Schmidt, Trueman, 183
Schmidt family, 59
Schmidt House, 59, 182
school buses, Olympia, 110f
school districts, 106, 108
school lands, 122
school lunch program (WPA), 209, 249n12
schoolhouses
   construction of, 106
   high schools. *See* high schools
   one-room, 57–58
Schuyler, A. E., 138
Scouler, John, 37–38, 39
seasonal cycles, of Native Americans, 17
Seatco Manufacturing Company, 100
Seatco Prison, 101, 101f
Seattle, state agencies relocation to, 118
Seattle Post-Intelligencer, exposé by, 51
Selden's Home Furnishings, 75f
self-reliance, during Great Depression, 207
Sequalitchew Creek, 34, 36f
Servants of the Poor. *See* Sisters of Providence
settlements
   Euro-American
     early, 53–59
     on the prairies, 61–64
     south county, 64–68
   Native American
     Chehalis, 14
     Nisqually, 13
     Squaxin Island, 14
Seymour, Joe, 25f
Shannon, George, 128
shantytowns, demolition/burning of, 90, 205f, 206
Shaser, Mary, 66
Shaser Donation Land Claim, 128

Shaser family, 66
Shaw, B. F., 19
Shaw, Edrie, 137
Shaw, Frank, 20
She Nah Nam Creek, 66
Shead, Oliver, 100, 101
Shelley, Joseph and Sarah Gunstone, 154
shellfish industry regulation, 135–36
Shelton, David, 73
Sherlock Station (Northern Pacific Railroad), 171, 228f
shingle mills
    listing of, 165t
    Bucoda Shingle Company, 100
    Mumby Lumber and Shingle Company, 153, 153f
    peak production of, 164
    workers at, 45, 92f
Shingle Weavers' Union, 194–95
shipbuilding, during World War I, 45–46
ship's whistle, as navigation tool, 45
shipwrecks, in Haida Gwaii, 41
shipyards, 45–46
Shore and O'Dell Mill, 98
Shotwell, Bernard, 149f
Shotwell, John, 125
Shotwell, Louisa, 125–26
Shotwell, Walter, 149f
Shotwell family, 65
shrimp processing plant, 137
Shroll, "Hell-roarin' Jack," 44
Sidewalk, 219
Silver Legion of America (Silver Shirts), 208
Simmons, Christopher Columbus and Asenath Kennedy, 203f
Simmons, Christopher Columbus, family of, 54f
Simmons, Elizabeth, 54f, 55, 203f
Simmons, Michael T.
    as Indian Agent, 23
    journey to Tumwater, 53–55
    land claims of, 56
    as merchant, 84
    photo of, 53f
    as postmaster, 83
    Simmons, Christopher as son of, 54f, 203f
    as Tumwater founder, 52
Simmons Oyster Company, 136
Simpson, George, 31, 154
Simpson Logging Company, strike at, 200
Simpson Timber, 154

Sisters of Providence
    about, 86
    photo of, 86f
    Providence Academy and, 108f
Skagit tribe, 29
skid roads, 159f, 163, 164, 169
skippers, personality of, 44
S'Klallam tribe, 29
Skog, Henry, 131
Skokomish tribe, 29, 38f
Skookum Creek Tobacco Company, 25
Skookum Railway & Logging Company, 95
Skookumchuck Railroad, 164, 175
Skookumchuck River, 126, 152
Skookumchuck Valley, 64–65, 64f, 125
Sloan Shipyard, 45–46
Slocum, John, 15, 15f
Smith, A. J., 135
Smith, Charles, 84
Smith, Jeremiah K., 101
Smith, Levi Lathrop, 81, 124
Smithfield Café, 216
Smith-Miller Mill, 192
Smithsonian Institution
    Bush family acclaim from, 124
    specimens for, 33, 37
Snowden, Clinton, 123
social gatherings, of Native Americans, 17
soil fertility, 124–25
Sol G. Simpson, 46, 46f
South Bay, 62
South Bay Grange, 109
South Puget Sound Community College (SPSCC), 93, 218
South Sound Shopping Center, 93, 213, 215f
South Union Grange, 155f
Southwick Lake, 93
Spiller, John, 118, 119
Spirlock, James Dillard, 126
Spirlock-Nelson Farm, 125, 126
Spoon, Diana, 107f
Sprague, Todd, 220
SPSCC (South Puget Sound Community College), 93, 218
Spurgeon Creek Grange, 63f
Squaquid Creek, 66
Squa-tsucks. *See* Johnson Point
Squawksin tribe, at treaty negotiations, 18f, 20
Squaxin Island Museum Library and Research Center, 25

Squaxin Island tribe
- about, 29
- baskets of, 12f
- enterprises of, 24–25
- environmentalism of, 219
- Hale's studies of, 38f
- Jones, Elizabeth, 22f
- land claims payment to, 23
- lifestyle of, 13f
- as original inhabitants, 8, 12
- reservation of, 13f, 20, 23, 223f
- at treaty negotiations, 9, 18f, 20

Squi-Aitl tribe, at treaty negotiations, 18f, 20
St. Peter Hospital, 86
stagecoach service, 143, 148f
Staggers Rail Act (1980), 175
State Capitol Campus
- architects for, 190
- enlargement of, 215
- St. Peter Hospital site as, 86
- street name changes and, 90
- Tivoli Fountain on, 182
- view of, 119f

State Capitol Museum, 263f
State School for Girls. *See* Maple Lane School
steamships
- cars/buses as replacement for, 202
- *Georgiana* incident, 41
- Mosquito Fleet, 43–48
- navy in Puget Sound Indian War, 42–43
- routes of, 46

Steh-chass tribe, at treaty negotiations, 18f, 20
Steilacoom, Fort, 41, 43, 43f, 44
Steilacoom, precinct at, 73
Steilacoom tribe, at treaty negotiations, 18f, 20
Steiner, Johanna, 178
Stephens, Sarah, 62
Stevens, Hazard, 129–30, 191
Stevens, Isaac
- arrival of, 74, 84, 87
- career of, 35f
- designation of Olympia as provisional capital, 113
- as governor, 19–20
- during Pig War, 43
- treaty failures of, 42
- at treaty negotiations, 9, 18f
- tribal organization as convenience for, 29
- on Tsus-sy-uch's murder, 43

Stocking, Fred and George, 144
stone quarries, railroad use by, 95
    See also Tenino sandstone
strawberry plant stock, as statewide leader in, 131
street speaking, 247n11
streetcars
- electricity for, 172
- Olympia - Tumwater line, 58, 58f, 87–88
- as steamship replacement, 202

Strickland, Henry S., 197
Stumer, Henry and Irene, 138
stump land, farms established on, 127–28
Subordinate Grange, 133
subscription schools, 106
suffrage movement, 133, 145, 196
Sugoff, Alex, 200
Summit Lake, 154
Summit Lake Community Club, 154
Summit Lake logging camp, 155f
Sunnybay Plantation, 131
Superintendent of Indian Affairs, 72
Superintendent of Public Instruction, 75f, 190
Supreme Court
- decisions in favor of Olympia, 115, 117, 118
- makeup of, 113

Suquamish tribe, 29
Surveyor General for Oregon, 72
sustained yield forestry, 164
Swan, James G.
    The Northwest Coast: Or, Three Years' Residence in Washington Territory, 22

Swan, John, 81, 83, 125
Swantown, 83, 87, 89
Swantown Marina, 214
swastika, in Squaxin Island baskets, 12f
Swede Days (Rochester), 151
Swedish Lutheran Church, 151f
swimming pool, stone quarry as, 96
Swiss chalet (Priest Point Park), 83f, 191
Sylvester, Edmund, 81, 114, 201f
Sylvester Park, 87, 201f, 219
syndicalism law, 199, 247n32

T

T. J. Potter, 46
Tacoma
- as proposed alternative capital site, 117
- shipyards at, 45

Tacoma, Olympia & Grays Harbor Railroad, 148, 171

Thurston County - Water, Woods & Prairies   285

Tacoma Mill Company, 163, 169–70
Taft, William, 201f
Ta-Ko-Bet (mountain), 62
Taylor Lumber and Shingle Company, 154
teachers
    salaries/housing, 108, 206
    selection/training of, 106
    White Bigelow as, 105
temperance activism, 201
Temple of Justice, 90, 118, 190
Tenalquot, 62
Tenderloin districts, 89, 182, 197–98
Tenino
    about, 93–95, 98
    agriculture at, 125
    incorporation of, 94
    Labor Day parade in, 93f
    Northern Pacific Railway in, 169
    Olympia & Chehalis Valley Railroad in, 172f
    sandstone. *See* Tenino sandstone
    street scene in, 94f
    wooden money of, 95, 95f
Tenino Depot Museum, 95
Tenino sandstone
    about, 96
    in courthouse structure, 78f
    quarry cutting area, 96f
    Tenino as showplace for, 94
Tenino Stone Company, 94, 96
Territorial Board of Education, 111
Territorial Capitol building
    delegates to, 113f
    governor's inauguration at, 87f
    replica of, 114f
territorial education, 106
Territory of Washington vs. Leschi, 11f
Tha-mux-I, 39
They Walked Before: The Indians of Washington State (Carpenter), 17
Thompson, D. A., 198
Thompson, W. O. "Black Lake," 64, 64f
Thurston, Samuel Royal
    county named after, 73
    photo of, 72f
    as territorial delegate, 72, 83
Thurston Bountiful Byway, 131f
Thurston County
    1792 - 1855, 70–74

Thurston County *(continued)*
    1930 - present
        Great Depression. *See* Great Depression
        modern era, 215–21
        World War II, 209–13
        since World War II, 213–15
    courthouses
        as a Capitol building, 190
        enlargement of, 215
        photos of, 75f, 78f, 207f
    employment. *See* employment
    explorers. *See* explorers
    industries. *See* agriculture; logging; Olympia
    under joint occupancy treaty, 31
    maps of, 7f, 156f, 222–25f
    music, 216
    Native Americans. *See* Native Americans
    Oregon Territorial designation of, 61
    original inhabitants of, 8, 12
    petition to form, 75–77f
    railroad map, 157f
    schools/student population of, 106, 108–9
    Superintendent of Education, 111
    transportation. *See* highways; railroads; steamships
    Tualatin/Clackamas district division in, 71
    value of history, 221
Thurston County Fair, 123–24, 206
Thurston County Historic Commission, 221
Thurston County Railway, 173, 174–75f
Thurston County Register of Historic Places, 126
"Thurston County Through the Decades," 217f
Ticknor, Joe T. and Elizabeth Ford, 64–65, 64f
Ticknor house, 64f
tidelands, title to/regulation of, 135–36
tides, life regulated by, 48f
Tilley, Abram and Sarah, 65
Tilley Hotel, 65
Timber Culture Act (1873), 122
Tinneh family, 21f
Tivoli Fountain (State Capitol Campus), 182
Tlingits
    avenging Tsus-sy-uch's murder, 42–43
    slave raids by, 29, 41
Tolmie, William Fraser
    as Fort Nisqually Chief Trader, 39, 55, 71

Tolmie, William Fraser *(continued)*
    as Leschi friend, 19
    marriage of, 32f
    photo of, 38f
    in Thurston County, 37–38
Tolmie State Park, 19
Tono, 152, 152f
Top Two Primary, Grange role in, 133
Totten Inlet (Mud Bay), 36–37, 135–36
towing enterprises, 48
T'Peeksin tribe, at treaty negotiations, 18f, 20
Trades Council, 198
trading
    by Hudson's Bay Company, 32
    trails for, 14
    with Yakamas, 13
tram roads, 159f, 163, 170
tramps, 194
Transalta, 152
transportation. *See* highways; railroads; steamships
treaties
    boundary with Canada. *See* United States-Canadian border
    failures of, 42
    Medicine Creek negotiations. *See* Medicine Creek treaty negotiations
    museum exhibition of, 12
Triad Theater, 221
tribal enterprises, income from, 24–25
The Tropicana, 216
Trosper, Nate and Belle, 57f
Troy, Preston, 118
Troy, Smith, 118, 119
Truax, P. B., 129
truck logging, 164
Truman, Harry S., 51
Tsamosan, 12–13
Tsi-at-co, 100
Tsimshians, slave raids by, 29, 41
Tsus-sy-uch, murder of, 42
Tualatin district, 71
tugboats, 47–48
Tule Lake (internment camp), 214
Tumwater
    artesian water, 179
    Biles family in, 62
    early settlers, 53–59

Tumwater *(continued)*
    illustration of, on back cover
    incorporation, 58
    Interstate 5 impact, 215
    James McIntosh Tram Road, 160f
    as oldest Euro-American settlement on Puget Sound, 2
    state offices in, 215
Tumwater canyon, 2
Tumwater Falls
    history of, 52
    photos of, 2, 54f, on front cover
Tumwater Falls Park, 58f, 59, 182, 184
Tumwater Historical Association, 217f
Tumwater Historical Park, 59
Tumwater Lumber Company, 164, 164f
Tumwater Methodist Church, 55f, 57
Tumwater School, 106f, 109f
Tumwater Valley Golf Course, 184
"Turkey Shoot" festival, 147
Turner, Benjamin Buckman (B. B.), 170
Turner, Oretta J., 170
"Twin Barns," 129
Tyrell, Freeman, 62
Tyrell, Rebecca Davis Prince, 62
Tyrell's Lake. *See* Long Lake
Tyrell's Prairie. *See* Hawks Prairie

U
Union Bridge Company, 199
Union Mills, 92, 92f, 188
Union Pacific Railroad, 151, 152, 170f, 171–72, 175f
United Methodist Church, 148f
United Mine Workers, 200–201
United States
    v. Mitchell I and *II*, 24
    v. Washington, 24, 27
United States, Great Britain joint occupancy treaty with, 31, 33, 33f
United States-Canadian border (1843; 1846)
    about, 31
    49th parallel as, 39, 43, 71
    59th parallel as, 71
    Haro Strait as, 35f
Upper Chehalis people. *See* Chehalis tribe
Upper Tumwater Falls, 3
U.S. Congress, Bush petition for land ownership, 56

US Department of Agriculture, farming easement, 126
USO Club, 210f, 211

V
Vail, 152, 166f, 167, 175
Vail, Tobi, 216
Van Tine, George N., 96
Van Trump, Philemon Beecher, 99
Vancouver, as proposed alternative capital site, 114–15
Vancouver, Fort, 54
Vancouver, George, 29–30, 30f
Vancouver Island, exploration of, 30f
Vanderhoef, John, 45
Vashon, 44, 45
veneer mills, 89
Verona, Everett Massacre and, 45
vice districts, 89, 182, 197–98
victory in Europe (V-E Day), 212
victory over Japan (V-J Day), 212
Vincennes, USS, 34, 36f, 39
Vincent, Grover, 149f
Vincent, J. K., 149f
Vincent, Si (Plunker), 149f
violence, Fish Wars and, 27
violence, unionism and, 191f
Viora. *See* Littlerock
Virginia (I - IV), 44f, 46
Virginia V, on National Registry of Historic Sites, 44f, 47
Volstead Act, 202
Volunteer Park, 102
von Briesen, Fritz, 99

W
Wa He Lut Indian School, 25
Waddell, Robert and Susan, 65
wagon bridge, 57f
Wahl, John, 167
Walker, Mary Richardson, 74f
Wallgren, Monrad "Mon," scandal of, 51
war bonds/savings stamps, 210, 213f
War of 1812, diplomacy after, 71
Ward's Shipyard, 45–46
Warner family, 154
Warre, Henry J., 121f
Washington, United States v., 24, 27
Washington Center for the Performing Arts, 90, 221
Washington coast, exploration of, 29–30
Washington Fire Relief Association, 133
Washington Hotel, 84, 84f
Washington School (Old Washington), 109
Washington Standard, 161, 201
Washington State, exploration of, 33–34
Washington State ferries, operation by tides, 48f
Washington State Growth Management Act, farmland preservation and, 131
Washington State University, founding of, 124
Washington statehood, 88
Washington Territory (1853)
    creation of, 41, 61, 74
    map of, 73f
    petition to form, 73, 236n8
    sign commemorating, 74f
    women voting in, 144, 145
Washington Union Coal Company, 152
Washington Veneer, 89
water containers, baskets as, 69
water quality
    in tidal waters, 49
    at Tumwater, 2
Watershed Park, 219
WCTU (Woman's Christian Temperance Union), 198, 198f, 201
Webster, Aaron, 100
Weiks, Carl, 167
Wells, William P., 66
West Coast Grocery, 130
Western Washington Industrial Association, 124
Westside Railway Company, 172
Weyerhaeuser, George, 167
Weyerhaeuser, Phil, 167
Weyerhaeuser Timber Company
    about, 164
    Chehalis-Western Railroad, 173f
    founding of, 169
    Skookumchuck Railroad, 175
    at Vail, 152, 152f, 166f, 167
wharves, 87
Where the Waters Began: The Traditional Nisqually History of Mount Rainier (Carpenter), 13
Whidbey, Joseph, 29, 31f, 37f
White, Ann Elizabeth. *See* Bigelow, Ann Elizabeth White
White, Harry, 89–90, 190
White, Margaret Stewart, 62

White, William, 62
White family, 62
Wilder, Walter, 89–90, 190
Wilkes, Charles, 33–34, 33f, 36–37
Wilkes Observatory Site, 34
Willey family, 48f
William Winlock Miller High School, 110f
Willie, 46
Wilson, Ivy Gilmore, 93f
Wilson, John M., 195–96, 200, 247nn31–32
Wilson Brothers, 151
Wiman, S. P., 47
Wiseman, Fred (Birdman), 189f, 190
Wobblies. *See* Industrial Workers of the World
Wohleb, Joseph, 180f, 207f
Woman's Christian Temperance Union (WCTU), 198, 198f, 201
Woman's Club of Olympia, 111
women's suffrage
   in 1910, 196
     at Grand Mound/Littlerock, 145
     Grange role in, 133
Wood Family, 154
Woodard Bay, 152
Woodland. *See* Lacey
Woodland Driving Park, 91f, 92
Woodland Hotel, 91f
Woodmen of the World, 200f
Woodruff, Sam, 148
Wood's Lake. *See* Hicks Lake
Work, Jane, 32f
Work, John, 32, 32f, 36, 37–38, 41
worker co-op, lumber mill as, 154
working conditions
   as difficult and dangerous, 192f
   IWW/union concern for, 191f, 194, 195–96
Works Progress Administration (WPA; 1935–1943)
   about, 208–9
   public school upgrading by, 108
   school lunch program, 249n12
   women's wages, 249n11
World Fairs, Bush family acclaim from, 124
World War I
   financial reversals during, 129
   4-H role in, 128
   home front organizations for, 194f
   IWW and, 195
   patriotism, 198–99
   shipbuilding during, 45–46

World War II
   about, 209–13
   farm decline after, 127
   role in, 90, 102
   shipbuilding during, 49
   shipping restrictions during, 182f
   victory gardens, 182
WPA. *See* Works Progress Administration
wreck masters, 47
Wright, Charles T., 118, 119, 248n32
Wright, D. F., 118
Wyche, James, 117
Wyman, Chauncey "Chance," as dog-bark navigator, 45
Wyman, Gertrude, as first woman licensed skipper, 45

Y
Yakama Indians, 9, 13
Yantis, Alexander N. and Sarah Green, 65, 65f
Yantis, Benjamin and Ann Hall, 65
Yantis, Sarah, 100
Yelm
   about, 98, 100
   crops from, 130
   dairy products from, 131
   Home Guard, 194f
   incorporation of, 98
   moonshine production in, 202
   settlers at, 62
   street scene in, 98f
Yelm Irrigation System ("Yelm Ditch"), 98, 128, 128f
Yelm Jim, fishing equipment of, 16f
Yelm Prairie, reservation at, 23
Yelm Women's Civic Club, 98
Youckton family, 21f
Young family, 65
Young Men's Christian Association (YMCA), 198
Yoyo A Go Go (festival), 216
Yung, Marj Pierson, 79, 79f
Yung, Vance, 79

Z
Zabel, Art, 210
Zanaton, 192
Zander, Julie McDonald, 207
Zillman, A. J., 177
Zion Evangelical Lutheran Church, 102, 103f